Management Information Systems
Text and Cases

Management
Information Systems

Text and Cases

by

John Dearden
Professor of Business Administration

and

F. Warren McFarlan
Assistant Professor of Business Administration

both of the
Graduate School of Business Administration
Harvard University

1966
RICHARD D. IRWIN, INC.
HOMEWOOD, ILLINOIS

First Printing, April, 1966
Second Printing, January, 1967
Third Printing, November, 1967

*Case material of the Harvard Graduate School of Business Ad-
ministration is made possible by the cooperation of business firms
who may wish to remain anonymous by having names, quantities
and other identifying details disguised while maintaining basic relationships. Cases are prepared as the basis for class discussion
rather than to illustrate either effective or ineffective handling of
administrative situations.*

Library of Congress Catalog Card No. 66-24600
PRINTED IN THE UNITED STATES OF AMERICA

To
Dr. Ronald L. McFarlan

Preface

This book is intended to provide students of business management with an understanding of how the computer may be used as a management information tool and the problems associated with its use therein. It assumes that the student has a prior knowledge of the technical aspects of data processing, and it concentrates on developing his ability to make effective use of it as a manager. The book is intended for use in a semester course in data processing whose students have had a previous course in computer programming. It may also be used as part of a full year course on data processing where other material is used to introduce the students to the more technical aspects of EDP.

In selecting material for this book we were guided by the following three criteria:

1. Only material relevant to the manager or student of management would be included.

2. Only those areas of business that have been affected by the computer would be discussed. For example, such subjects as mathematical decision-making techniques, not dependent on the computer, were excluded.

3. Only management problems related to the computer are discussed.

The book is divided into three sections. Section I is concerned with the management problems created by the computer. This section is written primarily from the viewpoint of the manager. As such, it contains no coverage of systems analysis techniques because, we believe, these are not the province of the manager. This function can and should be delegated to systems specialists. Section II considers mathematical programming. Here the management viewpoint has also been taken exclusively. Our purpose is to emphasize what these techniques can do rather than how they do it.

Section III contains a series of cases. These cases have been selected because of their interest and educational value as a basis for class discussion. They provide a basis for class discussion and decision making on the material presented in the text. They are not intended to present illustrations of either ineffective or effective handling of administrative problems. Except where specifically indicated all cases in this book were developed for use in courses at the Harvard Graduate School of Business Administration and are copyrighted by the President and Fellows of Harvard College. Over three quarters of the cases are "field" cases—that is based on actual field research within the companies involved. Only those companies who have permitted their cases to appear in undisguised form can be publicly thanked here. These are the International Harvester Company, The William Carter Company, State Consumer Reporting Bureau, and New England Gas and Electric Association. We are, however, very grateful for the cooperation of those firms which prefer to remain anonymous.

The material in this book is the outgrowth of experience in developing and teaching a course entitled "Management Information Systems" at Harvard Business School. Consequently, we are indebted to Dean George Baker and Associate Dean George Lombard for providing us the time and opportunity to develop the course. Professor Walter Frese and Dr. Ronald L. McFarlan provided many valuable suggestions and encouragement during the development of the material. Michael Scott-Morton, research associate at the Harvard Graduate School of Business Administration, also provided much valuable assistance.

In addition to material prepared by the authors, case material written by Michael Scott-Morton, William Abernathy, and Robert Collings, as staff members at the Harvard Business School, is included here. Professors E. Raymond Corey, Alva F. Kendall, Ralph Sultan, and Harry R. Tosdal have also contributed to the book. Two cases have come from members of other institutions: Professor Chauncey Beagle of the University of Colorado and Dean Glenn D. Overman of Arizona State University. Each has permitted us to use a case developed by him.

We are deeply indebted to many of our colleagues here at the Harvard Graduate School of Business Administration for the encouragement and advice that they provided during the writing of the book. Finally, we would like to express our appreciation to Miss Marion Sears for the fine job she did on editing some of the manuscript and to Mrs. Jill Lee and Miss Mary O'Leary for typing it.

JOHN DEARDEN
F. WARREN McFARLAN

March, 1966

Table of Contents

SECTION III. CASE STUDIES

Section I

MANAGEMENT PROBLEMS OF COMPUTER INFORMATION SYSTEMS

The purpose of this section of the book is to acquaint the reader with the management problems that have been created by developments in the computer and related information technology. The section is divided into three chapters, as follows:

Chapter 1 is concerned with business information. Specifically, it considers the nature and characteristics of business information, the types of information systems, and the adaptability of business information to automation.

Chapter 2 is concerned with the management problems that occur *before* a computer is acquired.

Chapter 3 is concerned with the management problems that occur *after* a computer is acquired.

Chapter 1

Information Systems
and Automation

THIS CHAPTER introduces some basic concepts concerning business information and its systemization and automation. The chapter is divided into four parts. The first part discusses the nature and characteristics of business information. The second part is concerned with the way this information is organized into information systems. The third part describes how these systems may be affected by computer technology. The final part of the chapter considers the problem of *when* management should consider automating its information system.

BUSINESS INFORMATION

Webster gives the following definition of information: "knowledge communicated by others or obtained by study and investigation."

Pattern of Information in the Typical Business

Using this definition, what are the sources of information received by the typical business? One important channel of information is the mail. Each day hundreds or even thousands of items of information come into a business via the United States Post Office. Much of this information is routine—such as orders for products, invoices for material purchased, confirmation of goods shipped, bills of lading, or checks in payment of accounts. Some of the information entering a business through the mails is less routine—for example, letters of complaint, requests for job interviews, or requests for information about former employees.

Information also enters a business through other channels of com-

3

munication such as the telephone, telegraph, and teletype. On a less formal basis, businesses are visited every day by people from outside of the firm, who frequently bring written or oral information with them. Or conversely, executives and employees visit other companies and pick up pieces of information. Other sources of information are printed documents, papers, magazines, and books.

Within the company, information is generated and transmitted. Letters, telegrams, and telephone calls from the field inform executives about the status of the sales efforts or the amount of goods shipped to customers. Information on production, inventory levels, and costs are transmitted from the factory to interested parties. The accounting department distributes financial statements, budget reports, and standard cost variance reports. Executives develop plans and policies and transmit these to the affected parties.

Just as information is received daily, all companies transmit information daily. For example, they place orders, hire personnel, pay bills, or answer customer complaints. In short, a great deal of time is spent in all businesses either receiving or transmitting information. Most of management's time is directly or indirectly involved with information.

If a business is to operate effectively, it must develop some means for handling all of this information efficiently. Yet, since the information received, generated, transmitted, and published throughout an organization can have very different characteristics, there must be different systems for handling the different kinds of information.

Classification of Business Information

Business information is not homogeneous. Different kinds of information must be treated differently. Consequently, we have found it useful to divide information into several different classifications. These classifications have been helpful in understanding many of the aspects of information systems.

Action v. Nonaction Information

One dichotomy of information is action and nonaction information. Action information requires that the recipient take some action; for example, orders received from customers. The initial recipient of this information must transmit it through the system until the order is filled.

Action information can be of several kinds, depending upon the urgency of the need for action. One kind of information is that which will always require immediate action, such as the receipt of an order. Another type of information always requires future action, for example, a bill to be paid in ten days. Handling this type of information requires a filing system that will assure that action is initiated at the proper time. Another kind of action information requires possible but not definite action; for example, when a manufacturing manager receives an overhead budget report, he may decide either to take action immediately or to wait for another month and then take action if cost performance has not improved. He also may decide that no action is necessary at all.

Nonaction information also can be divided into several kinds. Perhaps the most important type is that which indicates some action has already taken place; notification that a bill has been paid, a shipment made, or a payroll met are examples. Another common type of nonaction information is that which will eventually become part of an action report. Most accounting information in the process of being accumulated falls into this category. A third kind of nonaction information includes that received from periodicals and books.

Recurring v. Nonrecurring Information

Another dichotomy of information is recurring and nonrecurring. Most information may recur occasionally over a long enough period of time. For purposes of this classification, however, recurring information is that which is generated at regular intervals at least once a year. Recurring information includes almost all accounting, production, inventory, and sales reports. The most important kind of nonrecurring information is that included in studies made to assist management in strategic planning, such as the building of a plant or expansion of a product line.

Documentary v. Nondocumentary Information

A third dichotomy of information is documentary and nondocumentary, or oral information. Documentary information is that which is expressed in writing or which has been converted into some kind of permanent form, e.g., punched cards, punched paper tapes, or magnetic tapes. Nondocumentary information is information that is transmitted through word of mouth or that has been received from personal observation and that is not preserved in some written form.

Internal v. External Information

A fourth dichotomy is information generated internally and that generated from external sources. Accounting statements, budget reports, production schedules, and payrolls are examples of internally generated information. External information can also be of several types. One kind concerns the status of an order placed with an outside firm. Another kind is data assembled by an industrial service group and sent to participating members. A third kind is the product plans of a competitor. Clearly, internal information usually is much easier to obtain than external. Also, much desirable external information is never available.

Historical Information v. Future Projection

A fifth dichotomy is historical information and future projections. Most forward management decisions are based on projections, and historical information is useful principally as a basis for these projections.

The most important difference among future projections is their degree of reliability. For example, a study of expected cost savings from the acquisition of a new machine is likely to have significantly more reliability than profit projections from the introduction of a new product line. These differences in reliability are practically never stated explicitly, and consequently it is up to the user of the information to decide upon its reliability.

Analysis of Business Information

To summarize, we have five important dichotomies of business information:

1. Action and nonaction
2. Recurring and nonrecurring
3. Documentary and nondocumentary
4. Internal and external
5. Historical and future

It is possible with this classification to divide all business information into 32 categories which can be useful in analysis of the information requirements of a business. For example, they may be used in the following generalizations about business information:

1. Action, recurring, documentary, internal, historical information is the prime candidate for automation. In fact, this classification of

information will form the "data base" for most automated information systems.

2. The timing and accuracy of action information is usually important.
3. Precise timing usually is not a factor in the reporting of nonaction information.
4. Nonaction information is a prime candidate for elimination.
5. Nondocumentary information is just about impossible to control.
6. Nonrecurring information usually is not subject to automation.
7. The higher the management decisions, the more important become external information and future projections.

BUSINESS INFORMATION SYSTEMS

In order to handle effectively the information that is entering, circulating, being generated and leaving a business, it is necessary to organize logical systems for handling data. The purpose of this part of the chapter is to describe the information systems that have been designed to handle business information. There are three major information systems in a typical company, and a varying and indefinite number of minor systems. A major system is one that affects the entire structure of an organization. A minor system is one that is confined to a single functional part of an organization. (This is not to imply that it has *minor* importance; it is minor only in the sense that it applies only to a limited part of the company.) Let us look at the major systems first.

Major Information Systems

Financial Information

Every company has a financial information system of some kind. The basis of this system is the flow of dollars through the organization. The financial system is largely concerned with recurring, documentary, internal and historical monetary information, although in budgeting or capital investment analysis, the system does provide future projections.

Personnel Information

The personnel information system is concerned with the flow of information about people working in an organization. Almost every company maintains records of its personnel. In smaller companies these records may be quite sketchy. In larger companies they can be very elaborate and, in some instances, maintained on random-access equipment.

The data in a personnel information system are exclusively concerned with people. The information also is largely recurring, documentary, internal and historical, although some information is obtained from outside sources.

Logistics Information

The logistics system is concerned with information about the physical flow of goods through an organization. It covers procurement, production and distribution. It includes such activities as inventory control, production planning and control, scheduling, and transportation.

There can be several separate logistics systems in any one company. Where separate product lines are manufactured in separate facilities, each product line could have a more or less independent logistics information system.

A logistics system, like the other two major systems, is principally concerned with recurring, documentary, internal and historical information.

Other Information Systems

The financial, personnel, and logistics information systems have several characteristics in common: they exist in nearly all companies; they affect almost all parts of the business; they usually involve handling large amounts of data; and they are principally concerned with recurring, documentary, internal and historical data.

There are many other information systems in any company besides these major ones. Some of these are as follows:

Marketing Information

One of the most important systems in many businesses is that which provides marketing information. The characteristics of this kind of system will differ widely among companies. For example, some systems maintain a great deal of data about such things as competitive actions, customer profiles, and advertising effectiveness; other systems maintain only information about sales records. A marketing information system tends to be handled completely within the marketing function.

Research and Development

Many companies have systems for exchanging information on the results of research findings. Other companies set up systems to examine and store the literature on relevant research.

Strategic Planning

The three main information systems in our classification are largely concerned with historical, internal data. The two minor ones just described are largely concerned with historical, external data. A strategic planning system deals with still another aspect: future projections. Although a strategic planning system will use information developed for other systems, it will tend to use it in a different manner, i.e., as a basis for projecting the future. Also, because of the confidential nature of much strategic planning, this group tends to be separated organizationally, and the information developed is carefully guarded.

Executive Observation

Much important management information comes from the personal observations of company executives or discussions with outside people at clubs and meetings. These sources comprise a system (if it can be called a system) which is concerned with nondocumentary information; yet it can be of primary importance to top management. In fact, some companies would miss this information more than they would miss the monthly financial statements!

THE AUTOMATION OF BUSINESS INFORMATION

The next question to be considered is how the computer can be used to improve the effectiveness of each of the information systems described in the preceding part of the chapter. The purpose of this part of the chapter is to answer this question. It is divided into two sections: the first section describes the characteristics of information that make it adaptable to automation; the second section then analyzes the characteristics of each of the information systems to determine the extent to which the computer can be effective in improving it.

Information Characteristics and Automation

A computer can be used to best advantage in processing information with the following general characteristics:

1. *A Number of Interacting Variables*
   One of the computer's most important features is its ability to perform arithmetic and logic operations at tremendous speed. This feature is required for solving problems with a number of interacting variables. In fact, until the development of the computer, mathematical models with even a relatively small number of variables could not be solved by hand calculation in time to provide any help to management.

2. *Reasonably Accurate Values*
   It must be possible to place reasonably accurate values on the coefficients of the equations. Also, the equations themselves should express accurately the relationships among the variables. This requirement is important because the results of any calculations are no more accurate than the assumptions upon which these calculations are based. If it is not possible to develop a mathematical model that has a high degree of reliability, there is considerable question as to whether it is worthwhile to develop a model at all. General approximations, taking into account only the principal variable, may be just as satisfactory and much cheaper to calculate.

3. *Speed an Important Factor*
   The value of a computer in an information system will tend to vary directly with the necessity for speed of processing data. Before the development of the computer, management could not use much information, because it could not be provided in time to help make decisions. As a result of the speed of the modern digital computer, it is now possible to provide this information to management *before* it must make the decision. To this extent, the computer will add to the information available to management.

4. *Repetitive Operations*
   The computer can more profitably be applied to repetitive operations. There are two reasons for this:
   (a) The cost of developing an information system or mathematical model is likely to be substantial. If it is to be used only occasionally, it may be of questionable economic value.
   (b) A repetitive operation is generally required to develop a reliable mathematical model. This is particularly true if the mathematical model contains probabilistic elements.

5. *Accuracy Required*
   In general, the greater the degree of accuracy that is required in the output, the more likely it is that a computer will be helpful. A digital computer can be programmed to obtain results with nearly any degree of accuracy—assuming, of course, that the information

provided to the computer has that degree of accuracy. If great accuracy is not required, it may be cheaper to use general approximations than to develop and use a more exact computer system.

6. *Large Amounts of Information*
   As previously stated, computers are able to handle large amounts of data quickly; it is logical, therefore, that the larger the amounts of information that must be processed, the more likely it is that a computer can be profitably employed.

Although computers can best be used to handle information having the characteristics listed above, the information does not have to have *all* these characteristics to be highly adaptable to automation. Also, note that all these characteristics can exist in wide differences of degree.

Information Systems and Computer Adaptability

Each of the information systems described in the second part of this chapter may consist of a number of subsystems. For example, the logistics system could consist of a procurement information system, a raw material inventory control system, a production scheduling and control system, a finished goods inventory control system, and a distribution system. The financial system may consist of a general accounting system, a standard cost accounting system, an expense budget system (which in turn may consist of several subsystems), and a profit budget system. In general these subsystems differ somewhat in information characteristics. Consequently, any generalization made regarding the entire system may not be correct when applied to a particular subsystem. This fact should be kept in mind in the following discussion.

Logistics Information Systems

The logistics systems of a manufacturing company will generally be the most adaptable to automation of all of management information systems. The reason for this is that the computer can help significantly in the solution of the critical logistics problems. The timing of information and the necessity of handling large quantities of data quickly and accurately are critical to the effective functioning of a logistics system. Prior to the development of the computer, these problems resulted in considerable inefficiencies in the typical logistics system. Further, no really effective solution was found to these problems before the development of the computer.

To illustrate this point, perhaps one of the best examples of a logistics subsystem is production scheduling and control in a manufacturing plant. A typical production scheduling and control system has all the characteristics that make effective automation likely. There are many interacting variables; yet, because of the physical nature of the system, reasonable values usually can be placed on many of these variables. Speed of information is also very important. In fact, instantaneous information is frequently desirable, because an unanticipated change in one part of the system generally affects other parts of the system. For example, the breakdown of a machine producing a given part could affect the entire scheduling system. The schedule must be adjusted to take into account the change in the availability of the part; otherwise, a line may be shut down at some point. Production scheduling and control is a repetitive operation. Not only does it go on each day, but schedules are constantly being revised for changes in sales plans or production capability. Production scheduling and control systems require accuracy; that is, rough approximations are rarely satisfactory. Finally, these systems usually involve handling large amounts of data. In summary, therefore, the typical production scheduling and control system has all the characteristics of an information system that make it adaptable to automation.

Not all logistics subsystems, of course, can be so successfully automated as the system described above. Still, all logistics systems are repetitive; most require speed and accuracy; many involve complex physical systems for which it is possible to determine the value of the variables with a reasonable degree of accuracy. We believe, therefore, that the logistics system of a company offers the best opportunity for improving management information systems and this is the area that probably should be studied first. It is important to note also that the computer is only one of the devices that is at present available for accumulating and transmitting logistics data. Professor James Bright named twenty such devices (e.g., closed circuit television and two-way radio) in a paper presented at the International Conference of the American Institute of Industrial Engineers in September 1963.

Financial Information Systems

Most financial systems are adaptable to automation because of the large amounts of historical, recurring data that are handled. Automation of financial systems helps to reduce the cost of data processing. There is, however, considerably less opportunity to improve the quality of the information system by using a computer than in the case of the logistics system. The reason is that the computer will not solve any of the critical problems of the financial information system. In general, it will help to do better what is already done fairly well; but it is of little help in the areas where improvement is most needed. To illustrate, let us look at a typical financial subsystem—a manufacturing expense budget and reporting system.

Annually, a budget covering direct labor and manufacturing overhead costs is prepared by the plant controller, approved by the plant manager, and submitted to top management for approval. Expenses have been divided between fixed and variable so that they may be adjusted monthly to reflect the actual volume of production. The budget has been developed by departments so that each department manager can be held responsible for his portion of it.

After approval, the budget becomes the basis for a monthly report. Each month the budgeted costs are adjusted to the actual level of production. The budget figures are then compared by expense series (e.g., indirect labor, supplies, utilities) to the actual costs and the resulting variances explained

The budget becomes the basis by which top management exercises control over factory cost. This control is exercised in the following ways:

(a) Top management can tell whether costs are in line with plan. If they become significantly out of line, management can take action.

(b) Top management can evaluate the factory manager on the basis of his performance. If the performance is not satisfactory, top management may take such action as replacing the manager or strengthening his staff.

(c) Top management can tell whether corrective action has been taken effectively. For example, assume that the cost of scrapped parts in January is out of line with budget. If the plant manager assures top management that this condition has been corrected, it is possible to determine from the February report whether, in fact, it has.

Two of the hard-to-solve problems in a budgetary control system are establishing equitable budgets and deciding when a budget report requires action by management. The computer will not help significantly with either of these problems. It is quite possible to put the budget reporting system on a computer with some savings in data handling cost. It is unlikely, however, that the automation of the budgetary control system will improve significantly the quality of the information available to management. First, there are not many complex, interacting variables. The principal concern is actual cost and budgeted cost. The use of a computer will not, in itself, provide any improvement over the manual handling of this information. To be sure, it is possible to use more complex formulae for adjusting the budgeted expense to the actual level of production. In general, however, a linear approximation will be satisfactory, and the improvement provided by a more complex exponential curve will be small. Also, it is not possible in most cases to determine exactly what the level of expense should be. There is little advantage in running approximate levels of expense through complex mathematical equations; the results will still be approximate. Another characteristic of budgetary control systems is that speed is not a critical factor in the same way that it is in a logistics system. The budget shows the summation of what has happened throughout the month. It is not, therefore, an instrument for taking direct actions. (For example, you do not wait for the budget report to fix a broken steam pipe.) Even if the budget report came out the first day after the end of the month, something could have happened thirty days ago about which management would not have been informed. Consequently, whether a budget report is issued five days after the end of the month or eight days is of little consequence. If top management wants to know immediately when certain things happen in a plant, it must rely on another communication system than the budget. (Instructions that the plant manager telephone top management when certain conditions arise may be all that is required to cover such contingencies.)

It *is* true that the budget report is repetitive and may involve handling large amounts of data. To this extent, therefore, it might be economical to use a computer in budget reporting. Note, however, that it may not in any way improve the quality of the information system for management; it will only make it cheaper to handle this information. An exception to this generalization is the use of the so-called "What if" game. This is used principally in profit budgeting and requires a computer simulation model of the budget and its key variables. At the budget meeting, management can obtain quickly the answers to a number of alternatives by asking "*What if* the volume of Product A is $\frac{1}{3}$ of that projected?" or "*What if* the cost of Product B is 10 percent higher than projected?" and so forth. This has the advantage of allowing management to consider many more alternatives than would be possible without the simulation model.

Not all financial subsystems are like the budgetary control system described. Yet many involve assigning responsibility to an individual to carry out part of the company's plan, and then measuring how effectively the assignment is being carried out. In most instances, therefore, there is neither a large number of interacting variables nor a precise determination of performance levels. In a few cases speed of information is of vital importance. We may conclude from this that financial systems are much less adaptable to improvement from automation than are logistics systems.

Personnel Information Systems

As might be expected, the personnel information system, of all of the major systems, generally is the least adaptable to successful automation. The main problem with handling personnel information is the efficient storing and retrieval of this information. Consequently, the adaptability to automation is directly related to the amount of information that is maintained on each person, the number of persons on which information is maintained, and the speed with which any information is required. Another consideration is the amount of information that is duplicated by other systems. For example, the financial information system has certain data on personnel. In some instances, it might be advantageous to include personnel data in a common computer data base, even though it would not be economical to automate the personnel information as a separate system. In general, personnel information systems will be less improved both in cost and quality by automation than the previous two systems.

Other Systems

Because other information systems can differ widely, it is impossible to generalize about their adaptability for automation. The factors listed earlier in the chapter can be used as a general guide to whether automation might be successful in a particular case. Also, as in personnel information systems, the availability of information already being used by some other system might make automation practicable because use could be made of a common data base.

Some of the uses of computers in minor information systems are as follows:

Marketing—The computer is used to analyze marketing data.

Research—The computer is used to store and retrieve the results of research studies.

Strategic Planning—The computer is used to test alternative plans by simulating the business.

Routine Data Processing

Actually a routine data processing system is a subsystem of one of the major management information systems. Because this subsystem provides little or no management information, the responsibility for developing it is usually delegated to a data processing group. Because routine data processing subsystems can, in effect, be "pulled" out of a management information system, they are treated separately in many companies. For example, it is typical to put the payroll system on a computer as a first step in information systems automation.

The extent to which routine data processing can be economically automated will depend on the volume of transactions and the amount of processing (e.g., calculating and classifying) that must be done with each transaction. Also, the extent to which these routine data processing systems use a common data base will be an important consideration in whether or not to automate.

Clearly, the main benefit that comes from automating routine data processing is in the savings in the processing cost. In some instances, however, the automation can improve the service: e.g., filling customers' orders.

Summary and Conclusion

1.   Logistics information systems are the best adapted to automation. The payoff from an automated logistic system comes from better performance (e.g., smaller inventories) as well as reduced costs of data handling.

2.   Financial information systems are usually adaptable to automation because of the large amount of data that is handled. The payoff from automating the financial control system is largely from cost reductions in processing the data.

3.   Personnel information systems usually are the least adaptable to automation and, consequently, the payoff tends to be the smallest.

4.   Routine data processing systems are subsystems of larger management information systems that may be isolated because they provide no specific management information. These systems are prime candidates for automation, but the payoff is almost exclusively in the cost savings of handling the data.

WHEN SHOULD MANAGEMENT CONSIDER AUTOMATION?

In many companies, management is concerned with the extent to which computers should be used to automate their information systems. A more important concern, however, is the *adequacy* of the management information system. Consequently, it appears to us that it is vital to examine the quality of the management information system *first* and to consider automating it *second*. Not all management information can be improved by the use of a computer. Nor does all information generated by a computer qualify as management information.

The most important consideration for the business manager is to have an effective management information system. To the extent that computers help in this, he should use them. He should not make the mistake, however, of thinking that extensive computer use guarantees a good management information system. For example, take the case of a very large multidivisional company with which we are familiar. This company has extensive computer applications in the areas of production control and accounting. In production control, this company successfully uses computer information systems to schedule and control an extremely intricate, multiplant production process. In the accounting field, it has a well integrated computer system for payroll, general accounting, billing, payment of payables, and cost accounting. In short, it has made good use of computers and, in fact, has been cited by at least one authority as a model for others to follow in adopting computer systems. Yet this company has *no* formal (and practically no informal) system for long-range planning; it has no budgets of any kind; its cost accounting system is archaic and, consequently, seriously inaccurate. In other words, this company is being run by the "seat-of-the-pants" in spite of extensive computer installations. It has a totally inadequate management information system. And, incidentally, its profit performance reflects this situation. This company is exceptional only because of its size. Most companies of even a quarter of the size of this one have much better management information systems. In many medium-sized companies, however, it has been our experience that management is not using one tenth of the information that could be made available *without a computer*. At the same time, the management of these companies seems to be deeply concerned that, unless they acquire additional computer capacity, they will be left behind competitively.

On the other hand, poor utilization of a computer does not mean that the company has an ineffective management information system. In another company, the computer is used only for routine data processing. The production control and inventory control systems are handled by a combination of tabulating equipment and manual processing; budgets and costs are prepared on tabulating equipment. In spite of this, management has an adequate control system.

The important consideration for management, therefore, is the effectiveness of the information system and not whether to acquire computer capability. For companies with computers, it is important that the computers be used effectively; but using computers effectively is not so important as having an effective management information system. It is important to understand that these two factors (the effectiveness of the computer installation and the effectiveness of the management information system) are not necessarily the same. The optimum situation is, of course, to have *both* good computer systems and good management information systems, and this is the ideal toward which a company should work.

In this part of the chapter, the characteristics for potential automation are described. The purpose is to provide the manager with some insight into whether or not he should be considering initiating or expanding the automation of the information systems in his business.

Routine Data Processing

Although hard and fast rules cannot be laid down as to the kind of company that should automate its routine data processing systems, two characteristics can be used as a general guide in specific situations. Each of these characteristics is discussed below.

Size

Much has been written in the past few years concerning the entrance of the small business into the computer field. The increase in the availability of service centers, the possibility of "time sharing", and the development of small computers has brought computer capability to the small company. Do not be misled by this trend into thinking that size is no longer important in determining potential computer use. We believe that it is still an important factor. Although the amount of data processing is a major factor in determining the size (and, therefore, the cost) of the hardware, the amount of data processing may have little to do with the cost of the systems and programming work. For example, it might cost nearly as much to develop a billing system for a company with $1,000,000 in sales as for a company with $50,000,000 in sales. To management, this means that where the level of activity is high computer applications may pay off handsomely even though the initial cost of systems development and programming is high. If the activity is low, however, the computer must be restricted to those systems having relatively low development and programming costs. Size, therefore, continues to be an important consideration. The larger the company, the more likely it is that a computer can be used economically for the routine processing of data.

Proportion of Total Cost in Data Processing

Somewhat related to size is the proportion of total company expense devoted to routine processing of data. This is important for two reasons: (1) the larger the proportion of total cost that is in data processing, the larger will be the absolute cost and, consequently, the more probable will be the number of profitable computer applications; and (2) the greater the proportion of data processing cost, the more vulnerable the company is to competitive action.

The first of these points is clear. The second, however, deserves a little further explanation. If a significant portion of a company's costs is incurred in routine data processing, the failure to take advantage of new developments in this area could be very serious, if competition were to take advantage of these developments. This could be true of a small company as well as a large one, although new developments are most likely to apply to the large company. This means that the managements of companies incurring a substantial proportion of their costs in data processing must spend more time and money keeping up to date on new developments than other companies. For example, it is more important for managers of banks and insurance companies to be aware of the latest developments in data processing equipment and systems than for managers of the typical manufacturing enterprise.

Logistics Systems

Although the potential use of a computer in routine data processing is influenced significantly by the size of a company, this conclusion is not necessarily true of logistics systems. The key indication of potential computer use in the logistics area is in the existence of a complex logistics problem, for example, a warehouse operation with a large number of different parts or a production operation with a complex scheduling problem. Since the payoff in this type of computer application results from improved performance, the amount of the data handling is not the key factor. From a management point of view, therefore, the existence of a complex logistics system makes it reasonable to consider seriously the possibility of automation.

Financial Systems

A computer will not significantly improve the quality of a financial control system, although it may reduce the costs of operating the system.

For example, we believe that the management of companies like Du Pont, General Motors, Ford, or General Electric, to name a few, will not be able to make better decisions in the management control area as a result of having their financial systems on a computer. This statement does not mean, however, that the development of the computer will not have an effect on financial control. We believe that the opposite will be true for two reasons:

1. The developments in high-speed data processing are having the effect of making management examine its information systems. It would be the height of folly simply to automate an old, out-of-date and inadequate information system. As a consequence, many financial systems are being greatly improved. (Note, however, that usually the same objectives could be accomplished with a manual system).
2. As a result of the lowered cost of handling data, some companies have adopted more sophisticated financial control systems than they believed were economically justified before automation. Where the information systems have been properly integrated, the marginal cost of an improved financial control system is frequently relatively small.

This development has particular significance for the manager of the medium-sized company. (The small company does not generally need extensive formal control systems, while the large companies already have adequate control systems.) The implication to the manager of the medium-sized business is this: the increased automation of information systems has indirectly resulted in upgrading the financial control systems of many medium-sized businesses. This development could have significant competitive consequences for those companies that do not improve their control systems.

Chapter 2

Management Problems of Data Processing

Part I—The Feasibility Study

THE GROWTH in the capability of modern data processing and transmission equipment has created new and complex problems for management. One of the most important of these new problems is to decide whether to acquire a new computer, or if one or more have already been acquired, whether to increase computer capability. Any study designed to help management make this decision is commonly called a "feasibility" study. The purpose of this chapter is to describe the management problems of the feasibility study.

COMPUTER ACQUISITION AS A CAPITAL INVESTMENT DECISION

The decision to acquire a computer is really just another type of capital investment decision. Consequently, capital investment techniques are appropriate in making this decision. Several features of computer acquisition, however, make this decision different from the decision to acquire a traditional piece of capital equipment. These differences are:

1. In deciding whether or not to acquire a computer and, if so, which one, the typical company is faced with a degree of uncertainty not usually experienced in a capital investment decision because:
   a. It is often *difficult* to *estimate savings:*
      (1) an information system is not subject to the same precise measurements as a physical system;
      (2) the success of the system will be largely dependent upon

the competency of the people who will be responsible for operating it. This is, at best, only a partially known factor.

    b. The entire field of equipment and systems is undergoing significant changes. It becomes much more difficult, therefore, to anticipate new developments beyond the next two or three years (and sometimes even for that long).

2. A computer system produces (or is supposed to produce) many intangible benefits that are difficult to express in monetary terms. Some of these intangible benefits are:

    a. Information is available sooner

    b. More information is available

    c. Computer capability and experience is valuable so that the benefits of future developments can be a⁻ailable more quickly.

3. A computer system usually will have a much greater impact on the organization than the acquisition of traditional capital equipment. Not only may it affect a larger number of people, but it can have a significant impact on the organization structure. In some instances, even management's ability to make decisions may be affected.

4. Because the acquisition of a new computer involves extensive systems study, a feasibility study may involve a much greater degree of effort than a typical capital investment analysis.

5. There appears to be a definite emotional element in many computer acquisition decisions, not usually found in other capital investment decisions. This emotional element can run the gamut from fear that the computer will replace management to a belief that it is a necessary status symbol in a modern business.

ACTIVITIES IN ACQUIRING A NEW COMPUTER

A company will generally undertake two fairly distinct activities in deciding whether to acquire a new computer. The first is a study to determine whether the company has the type of information problems that might warrant the acquisition of a computer. The second is a study to determine *which* information to automate and which computer to acquire. Each of these activities is discussed below.

Information Problems

The study of information problems will vary widely among companies. Many of the differences in these studies result from differences in the size and nature of the business. In some companies, it is so obvious that a computer can be effectively used that this question takes little or no time to answer. In other companies, the decision may not be evident until a detailed systems study has been completed.

There are no hard and fast rules for conducting a study of this type. As discussed in Chapter 1, the amount of paper work handled by an organization will be a definite indication of possible computer applications. The existence of an inventory control problem, particularly if there are a large number of parts involved, is another indication of possible successful computer applications. All that is looked for in this kind of study is a "yes" or "no" answer as to whether to go further. The real purpose of this study, therefore, is to decide whether there is sufficient likelihood that a computer system will be economically feasible to warrant the cost of a complete study.

At this point, a word of caution must be interjected. Management should recognize that the recommendation of the feasibility study will almost certainly be to acquire a computer and that it will be difficult, at that time, to override this recommendation. In fact, in many instances, the only decision management really makes is to authorize an initial study. From the moment of authorization, the project develops momentum that is just about impossible to stop. Consequently, if management has serious reservations about the desirability of acquiring a computer, it should be very cautious about initiating a feasibility study; if one is made, it must be made by someone whose objectivity can be depended on.

Deciding on a Computer and a System

If it is decided that a computer system appears to be economically justified, the next step is to consider the details of the specific system to be installed and the type of equipment to acquire. (Note, however, that at this point the decision might be to acquire no computer; a detailed study of possible applications may indicate that the expected savings will not warrant the costs.)

The study to decide on a computer and a system will have three parts:

(1)   The information systems to be automated
(2)   The equipment to be acquired
(3)   The cost savings to be realized.

The Systems to Be Automated

In many respects, the decision as to which information to automate is crucial to the success of the computer installation. A decision to undertake simple applications that have little payoff may delay more economic applications indefinitely. On the other hand, too ambitious projects may result in management dissatisfaction because of the length of time needed to make the information system operative. Even more likely, they may fail because the people involved did not have the ability to handle such complex projects.

The basic decision is whether to concentrate on operational control problems (e.g., production scheduling or inventory control) or whether to settle for routine data processing applications. In some companies, the decision is easy. In banks, insurance companies, and brokerage firms, for example, routine data processing is so important an activity that the savings from automation are substantial. In some other companies the impetus to acquire a computer will come from problems experienced in operational control systems. Consequently, the decision as to the applications on which to concentrate has already been made. In most companies, however, the decision is not so clear-cut. These companies have potential applications in both areas. The problem as to which type of applications to undertake boils down to this: the systems which are relatively easy to install generally have a low potential payoff; the systems with a high payoff are generally difficult to install.

Although no hard and fast rules can be established to solve this problem, the following generalizations might apply in specific cases:

(1) The attitude of management and the availability of people should have a strong influence on the decision. Both management understanding and support and good people are needed to develop operational systems. Without them it is dangerous to start. Routine data processing applications, however, can be successfully developed without the same degree of management support and able personnel.

(2) One reason for undertaking routine data processing applications is to gain computer experience on relatively simple tasks. This is a perfectly valid reason; but be sure the cost is known. A year's delay in installing a production scheduling system, because time has been devoted to routine data processing, might result in a substantial opportunity cost from the loss of higher potential savings.

(3) There appears to be some evidence that the companies that concentrate on operational systems have the most successful computer installations.[1]

(4) The decision may be dependent upon the nature of the company. Some companies have little need for automated operational systems. In other companies, automating operational systems is not practical. In these cases, only the routine data processing can be automated.

---

[1]See John T. Garrity, "Top Management and Computer Profits," *Harvard Business Review*, July-August, 1963.

The Equipment to Be Acquired

The decision as to the equipment to be acquired is usually less crucial than the decision as to the systems to automate. It is important, however, to obtain the type of equipment that best serves the needs of the company. Once the computer applications have been decided upon, the general size and type of equipment should be evident. At this point the company must decide which make of equipment to acquire. Some different approaches to this problem are as follows:

(1) Limit the study immediately to one or two makes. This has the advantage of reducing the time required for the study. Also, more help can usually be obtained from the manufacturer when he knows that he has a good chance of obtaining the business. This approach has the obvious disadvantage of possibly eliminating from consideration the make that is best suited to the company's needs.

(2) Make a detailed study of all makes. This action is the opposite of number (1) and, consequently, the advantages and disadvantages stated above will be reversed.

(3) Make an overall survey and then limit the choice to one or two makes. This is a compromise between (1) and (2). To the extent that this survey allows the elimination of those makes not suited to the company's needs, it is the best approach.

(4) Rely on the advice of a consultant. The advisability of this method depends on the ability of the consultant. Frequently, the depths of experience that many consultants have allows them to determine quickly the best make for a particular company.

There is, of course, no simple best approach to deciding which make of computer to acquire. In addition to the cost of the hardware, consideration must, of course, be given to the available software and the quality of the service. Also, a look at only the immediate applications is insufficient. It is necessary to consider the problems that will exist over the next few years and to decide which manufacturer can best help with them. In this regard, an important factor to consider in acquiring a computer is "upward" compatibility. This means the ability to acquire larger and more powerful equipment without having to rewrite programs.

Preparing Cost Estimates

The principles for calculating costs and savings for a proposed investment in a computer system are the same as those for any proposed capital investment, although, as explained earlier, the computer system usually presents more difficult problems. In the case of a feasibility study, two specific techniques should be considered:

1. A form of present-value analysis should be used.
2. A cash-flow format that does not require a distinction between investment and savings is usually most applicable.

These two techniques are discussed below.

Present Value

The field of capital investment analysis is outside the scope of this book. Essentially, present-value techniques take into account the differences in the timing of the cash flow. For those unfamiliar with the theory and technique of present-value analysis, we recommend Chapter 19 of R. N. Anthony's *Management Accounting.*[2]

In many capital investment proposals, it is possible to make correct decisions without using sophisticated present-value techniques. We believe, however, that in the case of the feasibility study, the present-value techniques should always be used because:

1. The cash flow for different alternatives tends to be quite different. There could be alternative investments that would both yield the same total dollars but with different patterns of cash flow. Discounting this cash flow is the only way to determine the best investment.
2. The farther into the future the savings are projected, the less reliable will be the estimate. (This is much more so in a feasibility study than on the typical capital investment study.) Using present-value techniques, the effects of estimated cash flows have progressively less impact on the decision, the farther they go into the future.

In other words, present-value techniques are correct for all capital investment analyses. In the case of the feasibility study, however, they are *necessary* because less sophisticated techniques will frequently give incorrect answers.

Cash Flow Analysis

Some types of capital investment analyses require that an "investment" and a series of "savings" be calculated. This is frequently difficult to do with cost comparisons of computer systems and, because it adds nothing the reliability of the study, it can easily be avoided. Consequently, we recommend the use of an analytical format that does not require a distinction between savings and investment. Such a format is demonstrated in the example that follows.

---

[2]R. N. Anthony, *Management Accounting: Text and Cases* (3rd ed.; Homewood, Ill.: Richard D. Irwin, Inc., 1964).

Example of Analytical Technique

The Evans Manufacturing Company decided to investigate the feasibility of acquiring a computer and installing an automated information system. The preliminary study indicated that there was a good likelihood that a computer would pay off. The information systems to be automated were selected and a detailed study was begun. The choices were quickly reduced to two computers: Equipment A and Equipment B. The after-tax cash flow for the next five years was estimated as follows:

Year	Equipment A v. Present System	Equipment B v. Present System
1	−100,000	− 50,000
2	− 50,000	− 50,000
3	+ 25,000	− 25,000
4	+150,000	+ 70,000
5	+100,000	+150,000

It was decided not to go beyond five years because significant new developments were expected by that time. It was not known whether the systems would have any residual value or not at the end of the five years. For comparative purposes, however, it was believed that either system would have about the same value.

These cash flows can be analyzed in two ways. The first is to decide how much the company wishes to earn on its investment and discount these cash flows at that rate. If the sum of the discounted cash flows of either is a plus value, this means that the investment satisfies the required rate of return. If both are plus values, the one with the highest amount is the most desirable. The second way is to estimate the discounted rate of return. This is done by discounting the cash flows at various rates of interest until a rate is found that results in the sum of the discounted cash flows being approximately zero. Figure 2–1 demonstrates the first technique.

Method 1—Required Return 15%

FIGURE 2–1

Equipment A

Year	Cash Flow	Discount Factors*	Discounted Cash Flow
1	−100,000	.870	−87,000
2	− 50,000	.756	−37,800
3	+ 25,000	.658	+16,450
4	+150,000	.572	+85,800
5	+100,000	.497	+49,700
Net			+27,150

FIGURE 2–1—*Continued*

Equipment B

Year	Cash Flow	Discount Factors*	Discounted Cash Flow
1..................	− 50,000	.870	−43,500
2..................	− 50,000	.756	−37,800
3..................	− 25,000	.658	−16,450
4..................	+ 70,000	.572	+40,040
5..................	+150,000	.497	+74,550
Net..................................			+16,840

*This is the present value of $1 received in the year indicated, if money is worth 15 percent. From Table A, R. N. Anthony, *op. cit.*

These analyses show that either alternative will yield better than a 15 percent return but that Equipment A will earn $10,310 more than Equipment B. Other things being equal, therefore, Equipment A would be acquired.

Method 2—Estimated Rate of Return

By trial and error it was found that a discount rate of 24 percent will equate the sum of the discounted cash flows for Equipment A to nearly zero and a discount rate of 20 percent will equate the sum of the discounted cash flows of Equipment B to nearly zero. This is demonstrated as follows:

FIGURE 2–2

Equipment A—Discount Rate

Year	Cash Flow	Discount Factor (24%)	Discount Cash Flow
1..................	−100,000	.806	−80,600
2..................	− 50,000	.650	−32,500
3..................	+ 25,000	.524	+13,100
4..................	+150,000	.423	+63,450
5..................	+100,000	.341	+34,100
Net..................................			− 2,450

Equipment B—Discount Rate

Year	Cash Flow	Discount Factor (20%)	Discount Cash Flow
1..................	− 50,000	.833	−41,650
2..................	− 50,000	.694	−34,700
3..................	− 25,000	.579	−14,475
4..................	+ 70,000	.482	+33,740
5..................	+150,000	.402	+60,300
Net..................................			+ 3,215

The above analysis indicates that Equipment A will earn between 23 and 24 percent, and Equipment B between 20 and 21 percent. This is consistent with the other analysis, which also showed Equipment A to be the more desirable alternative.

Equipment vs. Systems Savings

In preparing cost estimates for a feasibility study, frequently the entire savings from both the new equipment and the improved system are compared to the total investment. In some instances this is necessary because the new equipment and the new system are so interrelated that it is impossible to separate the savings resulting from new equipment from the savings resulting from improved system design. Often, however, it is the improved system rather than the new equipment that accounts for most of the savings. In these cases, it is particularly important to segregate the savings resulting from the system and the savings resulting from the equipment. This is done by subtracting the investment and savings related to the systems design from the total investment and total savings. This will give the cash flow applicable only to the new equipment. The decision then can be broken into two parts:

(1)   Whether to install the new system, and
(2)   Whether to automate it, if it is installed.

In one company, a study was made of the feasibility of installing a computer in an inventory control system. The study indicated that a high rate of return would be earned and, consequently, an order was placed for a computer. When it was learned that delivery could not be made for a year, an investigation was made to see what improvements could be made immediately. It was discovered that *80 percent* of the savings could be realized without the computer. When the costs associated directly with the computer were compared to the 20 percent savings attributed to it, it was discovered that the costs were greater than the savings. Needless to say, the order for the computer was canceled.

Lease vs. Buy

A somewhat unique characteristic of the computer equipment market is the option of either leasing or buying equipment. It is useful to separate this decision from the rest of the feasibility study and make it after the study is largely completed. This decision is purely a financial one, and it usually adds more complexity to an already complex problem if it is not dealt with separately.

The economic calculations involved in deciding whether to lease or buy a computer are similar to those used in any lease or buy analysis. In fact, it has become quite a routine calculation in many instances and some equipment manufacturers have even programmed their computers to make this analysis. If values are provided for the various parameters (e.g., required rate of return and estimated economic life of the equipment), the computer will indicate the most economical action. The real problem, however, is to decide upon the economic life of the equipment. In general, the difference between the purchasing company's estimate of the economic life and the manufacturer's estimate will determine the outcome of a lease-or-buy study. For example, if the company's estimation of life is longer than the manufacturer's, it will probably be economical to buy. If the reverse is true, it will probably be economical to lease. The other factor that will influence the decision is the difference in the value of money to the company and to the manufacturer.

MANAGEMENT CONSIDERATIONS OF FEASIBILITY STUDIES

The evaluation of a feasibility study presents a difficult and unique problem to management. There are many technical aspects of a computer system that management cannot be expected to understand. Yet frequently large amounts of money are involved and, as indicated earlier in the chapter, the typical feasibility study is almost invariably biased in favor of acquiring a computer. Further, the bias always appears to be in favor of acquiring the *largest* computer than can possibly be justified. Management's attitude can, of course play a strong part in creating this bias. If it comes through (directly or indirectly) that management is impressed with the idea that a computer confers "status", it will not be difficult for the study group to justify the acquisition of a computer. Even if management's attitude is completely objective, there may be a strong bias in the study group. One frequent cause for this is that many of the people in the study group, learning about computers for the first time, hear only the favorable things about them. Is it any wonder that many become extremely enthusiastic (to put it mildly) about the potential of the computer? Another influencing factor is that many of the people on the study group will be key people in the new computer installation. If the decision is made not to acquire a computer, they probably will go back to their old jobs. Under these conditions, it is very difficult to take an objective attitude toward the question of computer acquisition.

The real question to which a feasibility study should be directed is: "Should *this* company acquire a computer *now*?" In most companies, it can be ascertained very quickly whether there is enough data processing potential to justify a computer. (Almost all companies above a certain size will have this potential.) Consequently, a feasibility study that shows only that there is sufficient data processing potential is really not very useful to management in making a decision. Most feasibility studies accept as a fact the really critical element in the success or failure of a computer installation—the ability of the people involved. All feasibility studies assume able systems and computer people, acceptance of middle management, and support of top management. Yet, it is the lack of these that most often causes failure. Management, therefore, must insist on having a reasonable and unbiased set of facts concerning the ability of the people who are to work with the proposed system. Although these may be difficult to obtain, a rational decision cannot be made without them.

Evidence of Bias

It is important for management to know whether it is being given an objective study or whether the study is designed to justify a foregone conclusion. The following are some assertions that might indicate a bias on the part of the group preparing a feasibility study.

1. *Our Business Has Grown Too Big and Complex.* A frequent statement is that a computer *must* be acquired because the business has become (or will become) so large and complex that manual or punched card systems cannot handle the work load.

For most companies, this is sheer nonsense. In the early 1950's, General Motors operated one of the best financial control systems and one of the most intricate and complex production scheduling systems without *any* computers and with only a limited amount of punched card equipment. Since few companies today are as large or complex as General Motors was in the 1950's, it hardly seems possible that any company will collapse from sheer paper work if it does not acquire a computer. It is simply a matter of economics, and the feasibility study should show the cost savings from using a computer.

2. *Our Competitors Will Get Ahead of Us.* Another frequent statement is one to the effect that the company will have a competition disadvantage if it does not acquire a computer. This is also sheer nonsense, unless there are also compelling economic reasons for acquisition. If there are no significant savings from the acquisition of a computer, how will competition gain an advantage? (In some

instances, the best thing that could happen to a company is for its competitor to acquire a large, uneconomic computer.) If there are significant economic advantages, the statement about competition is redundant.

3. *No Disadvantages*. When a feasibility study does not describe any major disadvantages, there is some question as to its objectivity. The same is true if the disadvantages are "straw men" that can be quickly disposed of. Since there are always disadvantages, problems, and uncertainities incidental to the acquisition of a computer, these should be explained to management. If they are not, the study is incomplete.

4. *Consideration of Alternatives*. There are always alternatives to the acquisition of a computer. A computer system usually involves processing *all* items in a particular application. Is this necessary? In inventory control systems, often 10 percent of the items account for 90 percent of the volume. Perhaps most of the savings are in the 10 percent of high volume items, and those could be handled without a computer (or with a small one). It is important to consider reasonable alternatives to acquiring a computer; and if none are present in the study, there is some doubt about its objectivity.

Management Responsibility

What should management do to insure that a correct decision is made concerning the acquisition of a computer? As indicated earlier, the success or failure of a computer installation depends largely upon the ability of the people who are to implement it. In this respect, therefore, management is faced with a familiar type of administrative decision. (Except, of course, that management will be evaluating people in an unfamiliar field.) There are, however, enough unfamiliar aspects to a typical computer-acquisition decision to make it different and difficult. Consequently, the following kinds of actions are frequently necessary:

1. Question anything that does not appear to make sense and be sure to insist on getting understandable answers. After all, the value of a computer must be because either it will provide information more cheaply, it will make it possible to do something better, or it will provide better information. The first two are purely matters of economic comparison; the last is really for management to evaluate. Vague statements of abstract advantages (e.g., relationships between variables that were not evident before will provide new insight, etc.,

etc.) should be explained clearly or ignored. If a concept cannot be articulated, there is considerable question as to its validity.

2.   Make sure the personnel problems have been adequately considered. As stated before, this is the most critical area.

3.   Require that a pessimistic estimate be made. Most feasibility studies are based on just about the optimum performance. A pessimistic estimate will probably provide a more correct estimate of the costs and timing of the computer installation. At least it will provide some idea as to the range of likely outcomes.

4.   Insist on a detailed schedule for implementation and be sure to get regular status reports. In this way, if things start to go wrong, action can be taken before it is too late.

CRITERIA OF SUCCESSFUL PERFORMANCE

The basic objective of a feasibility study is to determine whether or not the computer will be successfully utilized. A successful computer installation will be one that increases profits by an amount that represents an adequate return on the investment. Consequently, this is the question that a feasibility study should answer. In the typical company, it can be fairly quickly established whether or not the company has enough potential uses to warrant the acquisition of a computer. We know, however, that different companies will have the same potential for using a computer successfully; yet, one company will have a successful installation and the other will not. What are the differences between these companies that might cause success or lack of success? Computer installations will differ in three major respects:

1.   The type of equipment acquired;
2.   The people involved with the installation of the computer;
3.   The systems to be automated.

The difference between the successful and the unsuccessful computer installation must, therefore, result from these three factors. In most instances, a typical feasibility study will demonstrate only that a company has sufficient data processing potential to acquire a computer. The study assumes that the right equipment will be acquired, that the people involved with the installation will be able and willing to perform as planned, and that the best applications will be undertaken. Management, however, must somehow evaluate these areas if an intelligent decision is to be made. The purpose of this part of the chapter is to indicate some of the things that should be considered in evaluating these three areas.

Equipment

In general, the selection of equipment appears to be the area where fewest mistakes are made. Most computer hardware is quite comparable and prices are related closely to performance features. Assuming that the company can determine approximately what it is going to use the computer for, it is possible to decide upon the configuration of equipment that best suits these needs. This is a technical procedure that management must turn over to the expert. There are, however, two situations that management should look out for. One is where the cost of one make of equipment is significantly less than any other. The other situation is the lack of specific evaluation of the software.

Cost

If one manufacturer's product appears to have a significant cost advantage, management should question this. Since manufacturers tend to charge comparable prices for identical performance characteristics, why should one manufacturer's price be significantly less? One answer could be that a computer is particularly adapted to a specific company's needs. If this is the case, the analysis may be correct. A manager, however, should insist on a reasonable rationale for significant differences in costs among comparable computer models. Significant differences *could* be caused by faulty analysis.

Software

Although hardware tends to be similar among manufacturers, this is not true of the software. Adequate consideration *must* therefore be given to available software. Since the investment in programming may be equal to the cost of the hardware, it is important that a feasibility study include an estimate of the cost effect of these differences. There is a tendency to treat software differences as an "intangible." If, however, these differences are important (and frequently they are) they should be explicitly evaluated in the feasibility study. If estimates of differences in software are not included in the study, management should insist that they be made. We have seen at least two instances where a specific evaluation of the software changed the decision as to the equipment to be acquired.

Personnel

As indicated earlier in the chapter, there are three levels of personnel that can have a significant impact upon the success of a computer installation. At the first level, are the systems and computer personnel. The more ambitious the project, the more capable these people must be. It is, of course, very difficult for management to judge the capabilities of these people, because of the technical nature of their jobs. One thing that can be judged is the level of experience. In general, it is a good idea to be sure that there are some people in the group who have had experience in installing the type of system that is being planned. A key individual is the manager responsible for implementing the data processing and programming. He should have a history of successful accomplishment in this field, in addition to having the usual qualities necessary for a good manager. If there are any serious doubts about the capabilities of a company's people to undertake the installation of the computer systems, it might be well to call in an outside consultant to evaluate the plans and the people and give management an unbiased opinion.

The second level of personnel are the operating people. They will not normally be involved if the computer is going to be used mostly for routine data processing or financial information systems. If, however, the computer is to be used for logistics information systems or marketing information systems, the operating people to be affected by the changes are of vital importance. It is essential that operating people participate actively in any computer system that will affect them directly. Consequently, where the feasibility study includes plans for automating the information systems of operating management, the operating people affected should be receptive to the proposed changes and willing to assign their own people to work on the project.

The third level of personnel is top management. In all instances, top management should exercise careful control over the installation of the new system. This can be done by requiring a complete plan (including a specific timetable for major portions of the plan), and periodically comparing progress with the plan.

In some instances, the automation plans will require some reorganization. When this is the case, top management will have to participate actively in the project, because the data processing people do not have the authority to undertake organization changes. This comment might appear so obvious that it does not need stating;

yet, it is surprising how frequently a feasibility study will include computer applications that may require some organization changes. In evaluating a feasibility study, management should look out for possible organizational implications and, where these exist, plan accordingly.

In general, the more ambitious the plans, the more top management time and attention will be required.

Applications

As indicated in the first part of this chapter, a feasibility study will include a description of the information systems to be automated. The determination of these systems is a key determinant of success. If the computer is to be used merely for routine data processing, the savings will probably be limited. On the other hand, the more comprehensive the proposed applications, the greater the danger of running into serious difficulties.

We believe that a company should be very cautious about attempting to undertake unproven types of applications unless the payoff is large or the cost of failure low. Deciding what is new can be particularly difficult because the literature tends to exaggerate the state of the art. Also, many types of application may be *possible* but the problems of implementation may be so complex as to make success very improbable. In addition, much of the innovation in this field is accomplished by very talented people who are not likely to be available in many organizations.

As a consequence, management should be cautious of approving a project with a new and different type of computer application, particularly if it involves operating activities directly. The probability of success should be carefully compared to the amount of the potential increase in profits. Realizing that to be against innovation is like being against motherhood and country—it must also be realized that one of the major reasons for failures in the data processing field has been trying to undertake too much, too quickly.

DISPLACED PERSONNEL

The installation of a computer for data processing is nearly always accompanied by the elimination of certain jobs. This creates an administrative problem of varying degrees of severity, but one that always exists. The purpose of this part of the chapter is to discuss methods for handling this problem.

Excess Personnel

An excess of personnel is created for the following reasons when a computer is installed:

1. The total number of jobs may be reduced. (How else can the cost of the computer and peripheral equipment be saved?)
2. Although new jobs are created, these jobs usually cannot be filled by the people whose jobs have been eliminated.
3. A computer installation may be accompanied by a geographic centralization of data processing activity. Consequently, job opportunities may be transferred to different cities and this could make the reduction in jobs particularly high in some cities.

Possible Action to Mitigate Effects of Job Dislocation

Several courses of action are open to management to mitigate the effect of job dislocation. These are:

1. Retrain as many people as possible to take over the new jobs that have been created.
2. Where geographic centralization has occurred, move personnel to the city where the jobs are available.
3. Let normal attrition take care of the excess personnel not covered above.

If these three actions result in alternative employment for all displaced personnel, there is no problem. Note, however, that these actions will apply principally to displaced female clerical workers. Only here is there likely to be enough turnover to make attrition an effective means for handling the problem. Also, substantial retraining is often practical only where people are changing from one type of clerical job to another. (Of course, punched card equipment operators are frequently trained to program or operate computers.)

The Problem and Its Solution

If attrition, retraining, and relocation will not take care of all of the people whose jobs have been eliminated, terminating the employment of a certain number of people becomes necessary. The greater this number, the greater will be the problem. From the point of view of the company (the sociological implications are outside the scope of this book), *the problem is how to keep the competent people until the computer system is working effectively.* When people know their jobs are to be terminated, they are likely to start looking for new jobs immediately. Unfortunately, the most competent and experienced people tend to be the ones to obtain new employment soonest.

One solution is to announce that no one's job will be terminated because normal attrition will take care of the problem. This is, of course, highly unethical (although it has been done). Furthermore, it does not work well anyway because the reduction in force usually has to be gradual. As some jobs are terminated, the remaining people will surely be influenced. Another way is to say nothing. This is also unethical and ineffective. Rumors and informal communication will take the place of explicit communication.

The only reliable solution appears to be to provide competent people with an incentive to stay until the job is done. This can be done by paying a certain amount of extra termination pay to those who stay on until their jobs are actually eliminated. The amount of termination pay would normally be varied, depending on the importance of the job and the length of service.

Planning Necessary

The important point is that displacement will nearly always occur and that it will probably cost money. Therefore, this factor must be included in making a decision on the acquisition of a computer. Moreover, once the decision has been made, explicit plans should be made to take care of the problem.

We believe that this problem will become worse in future years. Until now, most data processing applications have been clerical in nature. The people displaced were frequently semiskilled females whose job tenure was likely to be short. As more sophisticated applications are undertaken (e.g., production and inventory control), the problem will be more severe. Retraining will be more difficult and the effect of displacement will impose greater hardships on the employee.

Chapter 3

Management Problems of Data Processing

Part II—Systems Organization and Responsibility

THIS CHAPTER discusses further the management problems that have been created by the computer. Chapter 2 was concerned with the management problems that precede the actual installation of a computer. This chapter is concerned with the management problems that exist after the computer has been installed. These problems are divided into five categories:

1. The Organization of Systems Responsibilities
2. The Problems of Automating Information Systems
3. The Evaluation of Data Processing
4. The Selection and Training of Personnel
5. Accounting for Data Processing

THE ORGANIZATION OF SYSTEMS RESPONSIBILITY

When a company acquires a computer, it usually first automates several independent subsystems. For example, the typical first computer applications are the payroll system, the customer billing system, and the general ledger system. As the number of computer applications grows, however, the need to integrate these systems becomes more urgent. Many companies have found themselves in the position of having computer applications proliferating without any apparent pattern or without any significant coordination. The problem is how to organize to obtain effective integration of these automated information systems and, at the same time, provide operating management with a reasonable amount of control over the information it receives.

39

The organization of the systems and computer activity is probably the most difficult and critical problem with which management is faced. The success of the entire effort may depend upon it; yet there are no hard and fast rules to be used as guides. The principal problem is the degree of centralization. There can be significant benefits from centralization. It is clearly easier to integrate all of the systems if the control is centralized. This can result in substantial cost savings. Also, the systems and computer personnel can often be used more efficiently if the operation is centralized. On the other hand, there can be serious problems associated with a high degree of centralization. First, the operating people may not participate sufficiently in the design of the information system. Second, the greater the degree of integration, the more difficult and costly unanticipated changes become.

The size of the company is an important consideration, because there cannot be much decentralization in a small company. Also, the attitude of operational management people is important. The better their relationships with the staff people, the greater the degree of centralization that will be practicable.

In any event, it seems to us that there are several types of activities included in the systems and computer effort and each of these activities must be considered in deciding on how to organize systems and data processing efforts. In this chapter, we would like to propose a generalized approach to systems and computer organization. Clearly, this approach is not a complete answer to the organization problem. Neither is this approach applicable to all businesses. Many knowledgeable people disagree with this approach quite decidedly. The value of the proposed approach is not that it provides a ready-made organization plan but that it raises questions that should be answered before making organizational decisions.

Our approach to the organization of the systems and data processing effort is to break down these activities both horizontally and vertically. Horizontally, systems activities can be classified by the type of work performed; vertically, systems activities can be classified by the kind of information handled.

Horizontal Classification

The development of an information system is a more or less continuous process from the time that it is first conceived until it is in operation. Each phase tends to blend into the following phase so that there is rarely a clear cutoff point where one phase ends and another phase starts. Consequently, the development of an information system is frequently considered to be a relatively homogeneous operation. The result of this is a tendency to classify certain people as "information systems specialists" and certain organization components as "systems departments," and then to consider these people and departments as specialists in the entire continuum of the development of an information system.

Stage of Development

It appears to us that systems development is not really a homogeneous operation. There are three stages in the development of an automated information system which we believe are distinctly different and which, consequently, should be treated differently—even though the points where one stage stops and another starts will always overlap, since the exact divisions are somewhat arbitrary. These stages are as follows:

Stage 1: Systems Specification. Systems specification includes the design of all of the aspects of a management information system that are important *to the users*. It includes principally the basic decisions as to what information should be provided by the system. In many systems the timing of the information, the output format, and the input format will also be defined at this stage. For example, in a budgetary control system, the format of the budget proposals, the procedure for approval, and the format and timing of the budget performance reports would all be specified because they are important to the users. On the other hand, the specifications for an automated inventory control system might not include the format of the replenishment order to the supplier; as long as the order is intelligible, it makes no difference to the warehouse manager what the order format looks like.

Stage 2: Data Processing Implementation. Data processing implementation is concerned with those things that are important *to the processing of the data*. The purpose in this stage is to design a data processing system that will most efficiently implement the systems specified in Stage 1.

Stage 3: Programming. Programming generally starts with the systems flow charts and ends when the program is running on the computer.

The foregoing stages of systems development are, of course, interrelated. The systems specification must take into account the restraints inherent in the data processing function; the data processing stage must take into account the capability of the equipment available. The important point is that the person responsible for data processing can restrict the systems requirements only as a result of the data processing capabilities; *he is in no way responsible for deciding what kind of information should be generated by the system.* The same is true of the programmer. He develops as efficient a program as possible to provide the specified data processing system.

Distinguishing Characteristics

One of the reasons why these three stages are often confused in business is that different subsystems go through different stages. (A subsystem is a part of one of the general systems described in the next part of the chapter.) Some subsystems will go through only the specification stage. For example, a system for accumulating personnel information on top executives might be handled exclusively in one stage because the data processing, being relatively trivial in nature, can be managed as part of the design of the system.

Other subsystems go through only Stages 2 or 3. There are two major reasons for this:

(1) Many subsystems are well established. Their specifications are already defined when they come up for management decision; the only problem is to automate them. This is often true, for example, when accounting systems are automated.

(2) Many subsystems require no system design at all of the Stage 1 type. The requirements are prescribed by the nature of the task, as for example, in payroll or customer billing.

Systems Specification. From an organization point of view, the most important characteristic of systems specification is that, as a general rule, it should be *decentralized to operating management;* that is, it should be controlled by the people who are to use the information. We conclude this for the following reasons:

1. The operating manager is responsible for the effectiveness of his information system. He cannot delegate this responsibility to a staff group outside of his control. In many areas, developments in new information techniques make it vital that a continuing program of keeping up to date be maintained. It is likely that this process will become more important in these areas. Already, here, the "seat-of-the-pants" operating manager is a thing of the past. The operating manager must now accept the responsibility for adopting new, improved information techniques or be replaced by someone who will. But he cannot be held properly responsible for the adequacy of his information system if the function is performed by an independent staff group.

2.   In general, systems responsibility has proved to be less successful in actual business situations when it has been centralized than
when it has been decentralized. In a study he made of the systems
activities of several companies, Philip H. Thurston observes:

It seems to me that the specialist should *not* dominate and that companies
would do well to give more responsibility to operating managers.[1]

A somewhat similar opinion was reached by John T. Garrity in his
study of computer effectiveness in 27 companies.[2] He concludes that
the factors which marked the difference between those companies
that used computers effectively and those that did not were the involvement of operating management in the selection of computer
projects, the manning of these projects, and the responsibility for the
progress of these projects.

3.   The design of different types of systems requires different
types of skills and knowledge—and frequently there is little overlap.
For example, the skills required to design a manufacturing expense-
budget system are quite different from the skills required to design
a production-scheduling system. In other words, the task of specifying
those things that are important to the user varies from function to
function and company to company.

4.   In designing an information system for management, an intimate knowledge of the particular field is necessary. Often this requires
spending a not inconsiderable amount of time working directly in the
field with the users. For example, it would usually be necessary for
a computer man to work in budgetary control for some time before
he would be qualified to design a budgetary control system. On the
other hand, it would be relatively easier for a budget manager to
gain a knowledge of computers sufficient to enable him to understand
how they could be used to improve his budgetary control system.

5.   Some information systems use new communication devices
other than the computer. For example, Professor James Bright of
the Harvard Business School listed 20 such devices used in production
scheduling and control (e.g., closed-circuit television and two-way
radios) in a paper presented at the International Conference of the
American Institute of Industrial Engineers in September 1963. These
devices tend to be different for different kinds of information systems.

---

[1]"Who Should Control Information Systems?" *Harvard Business Review*,
November-December, 1962, p. 135.

[2]"Top Management and Computer Profits" (Thinking Ahead), *Harvard Business Review*, July-August, 1963, p. 6.

The staff systems specialist will, therefore, usually be less well informed about them than about equipment, like the computer, which is standardized.

In summary, we believe that the systems specification function should be decentralized because management cannot delegate this responsibility to a staff group; because the work does not usually progress well when done by a staff group; and because the knowledge and capabilities required to perform these jobs are not usually found in staff systems specialists.

Data Processing Implementation. As contrasted to systems specification, the data processing activity *can be centralized.* We conclude this for the following reasons:

1. The integration of the data processing activity of a company is usually desirable from an economic point of view. Information once captured (e.g. key punched) and recorded on punched cards, magnetic tape, or disk files may be used in several different systems. Consequently, it is more economical to capture the information once, at the point where it first enters the company. Also, the storing, updating, and processing of the data can frequently be accomplished more efficiently with one integrated system. This integration can be accomplished best where the responsibility for data processing is centralized.

2. Many companies are moving toward developing a company-wide (or, in large, decentralized companies, divisionwide) data base. This consists of storing in one place all the data that will be used in the various automated systems. This not only helps to achieve the economies of integration just mentioned, but frequently makes it possible to provide management with information that otherwise would not be practicable to obtain.

3. The data processing part of an information system can be handled best by staff specialists because knowledge of equipment and data processing techniques is the primary requirement. When information systems development reaches the data processing stage, there is a great deal of similarity among systems. Consequently, data processing implementation tends to be a homogeneous type of activity, not significantly different for different kinds of business information systems.

4. Operating management can delegate the responsibility for implementing the information system to a staff group *once this system*

has been specified and as long as management can be assured of adequate service from the staff group.

In summary, therefore, we believe that the work of implementing a new data processing system should generally be centralized where it provides economies through the integration of information systems.[3]

Programming. As might be expected, of all of the three stages, programming lends itself best to centralization. The reasons are:

(1) Programming is more economically accomplished on a centralized basis.
(2) Writing business programs requires a special knowledge of equipment and programming languages, and there is practically no difference in the skills required to program the different systems.
(3) Management must delegate the task of programming to someone, and it makes little difference whether it is a staff unit or a department reporting directly to the manager.[4]

Vertical Classification

In Chapter 1, information systems were divided into major systems—financial, personnel, and logistics; and minor systems—marketing, research, strategic planning, etc. This is the vertical classification of information systems which we propose. This part of the chapter describes the organizational relationships of these systems.

Financial Information System

The financial system is perhaps the most important single management information system in any company. It is also, probably, the oldest and best developed. The custom has been for management to give the controller the responsibility for administering this system, but management cannot delegate responsibility for the *adequacy* of the system. Top executives have the continuing responsibility for evaluating how well the controller is performing his functions and for replacing him when this performance is not adequate.

---

[3]There may, however, be instances where it might be better to pay some penalty in increased costs to maintain decentralized data processing implementation. This could be true, for example, where an operating manager wants to control his entire production scheduling operation because he feels the central data processing group is not giving him adequate service. The extra cost might well be worthwhile to alleviate the human relations problems that have developed.

[4]Here, again, this depends on the central group providing adequate service to operating management. If they do not provide this service, you can expect the operating manager to hire his own programmers.

Personnel Information System

The responsibility for the personnel information system is usually assigned to the industrial relations officer. Here, also, management is responsible for evaluating the adequacy of the system.

Logistics Information System

The assignment of the responsibility for the logistics information system is not nearly so well developed and thought out in the typical company as the other two systems are. For one thing, being an operating control system, it has not required the degree of top-management involvement which is characteristic of the other two systems. The main concern of top management is that production schedules are being met and that costs are properly controlled. (If they are not, this condition is reflected in the financial information.) A second factor is that the responsibility for coordinating the entire logistics system is almost never assigned to a single executive. As a result, the system in many companies is relatively uncoordinated and far from optimum. In fact, much of the so-called "total systems" development has been designed to overcome problems in the logistics field. Careful examination of the description of a typical "total" system will reveal that it is concerned almost exclusively with the logistics system.

Minor Information Systems

Minor information systems present no organizational problem unless they use the same data base as the major systems. If they do, it is necessary for the data processing activity to coordinate their requirements with those of the major systems to avoid duplicating the capture and storage of data. Where these systems use different data, both the systems specification and the data processing design are generally decentralized.

Proposed Organization

We would now like to propose an organization structure based on the vertical and horizontal classifications just described. This structure is represented diagrammatically in Figure 3–1.

The principal features of this proposed organization are as follows:

1. The systems-specification function (the first stage) is organized by type of system.

2. The responsibility for systems specification is decentralized to the managers who are responsible for using the data.

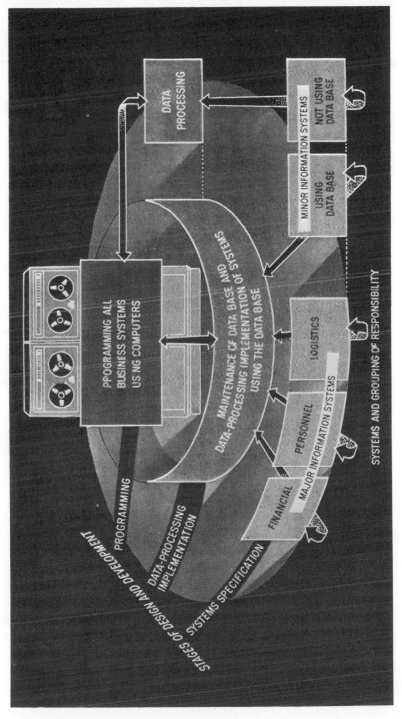

FIGURE 3-1

GENERALIZED ORGANIZATION CHART FOR SYSTEMS AND DATA PROCESSING

3. The data processing function (second stage) is centralized to the extent that it encompasses the responsibility for implementing the data processing of all systems using the same base of facts, figures, and other data.

4. Information systems not using the data base generally control their own data processing implementation (see the right side of Figure 3–1).

5. The programming (third stage) is centralized for reasons stated earlier.

Changes in Management

The effect on the typical company of changing to an organization similar to that proposed in the preceding section may not be so great as might be supposed at first glance. For one thing, most companies have organized their financial information system and their personnel information system in a manner very similar to that proposed. To the extent that this is true, only four major changes are necessary.

1. *A group must be established (probably under the manufacturing vice president) with responsibility for developing and maintaining the logistics information system.* This group would do for the logistics information system what the controllership function does for the financial information system.

The establishment of such a group would be the biggest change that most companies would have to make. Notice, however, that it is frequently the logistics function that has created many of the problems in utilizing computers effectively, and these problems will never be solved until an effective organization to solve them is established.

2. *The data processing function must be removed from the controllership function.* It is not necessary to remove data processing from the supervision of the controller; it should, however, be properly identified as a separate service function for all information systems using the data base.

3. *The systems-specification functions must be removed from the data processing function.* For example, many operations research personnel working in the data processing group would properly be assigned to logistics information specification.

4. *Management must assign the responsibility for developing and maintaining a data base to a central data processing group.* The extent of this group's responsibilities and authority should be precisely and explicitly stated.

Summary

At the present time, many companies tend to mix data processing functions with the task of designing logistics information systems. A symptom of this condition is the development of an inventory control system by a data processing group which reports, say, to the corporate controller. We believe that this condition has led to severe problems in the effective utilization of the computer.

Coordination is necessary among the people responsible for the various stages in the development of an information system. The need to coordinate, however, is no reason to combine unlike activities and differing levels of responsibility into a single group responsible for all information systems. If the data processing group is to be reasonably effective in integrating the data requirements of the various systems using the same main reservoir of data, it will be necessary for it to coordinate carefully with the people responsible for systems specification concerning future plans. This, also, is no reason to combine unlike activities and differing levels of responsibility into a single group responsible for all information systems.

As for the proposed organization plan, it does not preclude the "team" approach to systems development. In fact, this will always be a useful approach, particularly when a company is undertaking a considerable amount of new systems work. The important point is that the responsibility for a team that is developing systems specifications should be with the operating management.

Nor does the proposed organization preclude the use of staff specialists. These specialists, however, should perform an advisory function and, when working directly on a system specification project, report to the operating manager who is to use the system.

In the new scheme of things the data base does not constitute a "total system" by any means. It includes only the information common to the participating systems that can be stored economically and maintained centrally. It will be largely historical, recurring, internal information. There is a great deal more information than this that management will need. In fact, the higher up in the managerial hierarchy we go, the more important becomes external and projected information that may be no part of the data base.

A final word of warning is in order here. The most important thing is to have an effective and efficient management information system. Any organization that can accomplish this goal is satisfactory, regardless of how much it differs from the organization proposed in this chapter. This will be particularly true of the smaller business which cannot afford an extensive systems and data processing organization. Perhaps a single person can perform all systems and data processing effectively. If this is true, it would be folly to change it to comply with some ideal organization scheme. It is likely, also, that no company will fit the proposed scheme exactly. Adjustments will always have to be made to account for local conditions.

PROBLEMS OF AUTOMATING INFORMATION SYSTEMS

The purpose of this part of the chapter is to describe the problems of automating the major information systems.

Routine Data Processing

In considering the problems of automation, it is useful to separate the routine data processing subsystems from each of the major information systems. A routine data processing subsystem has two principal characteristics:

1. It provides little or no information for management decision making. Consequently, management's concern with these subsystems is only that they be performed adequately and efficiently.
2. The output is mostly prescribed by the purpose of the system. Consequently, little or no systems specification is required.

Examples of routine data processing subsystems are payroll, customer billing, much of the routine accounting record keeping, and stockholder record keeping. Some companies, such as banks and insurance companies, have vast amounts of information that comes within this classification; in other businesses, of course, routine data processing is of much less importance.

Routine data processing systems are the easiest to develop of all computer applications, because the output is prescribed and the data are already being processed. Moreover, it must be done in a precise, specified manner because that is the only way that a prescribed output could be assured. Note, also, that complete accuracy of output is usually important. For example, a payroll, a customer's order, or a customer's bill should be completely accurate.

Because this kind of information is the easiest to automate, most automated data processing systems are of this kind. Traditionally, a company acquiring a computer will automate the payroll first. It should be noted, however, that automating this kind of information usually has the lowest payoff. All that has been done is to substitute equipment costs for salary costs—and the equipment does not always cost less. Even when there are cost reductions, these are not likely to be significant, simply because the total cost of handling this kind of information may not be significant in the typical business. The automation of routine data processing systems is most important where the cost of this kind of data processing is most significant as, for example, in banks, insurance companies, and brokerage firms which are largely in the business of handling data with prescribed output.

To summarize:

1. The systems specification is done by the Data Processing Implementation group.
2. These systems are the easiest kind to install.
3. These systems have the lowest payoff.

Logistics Information Systems

Logistics information systems are much more complex than the typical routine data processing system. Most are sufficiently complex that it has been impossible under manual methods of handling data to prescribe complete rules for carrying out the function and, as a consequence, it has been necessary to allow for much human judgment in the system. With the modern computer, under some circumstances, it is now possible to prescribe complete and precise rules to cover all contingencies. That is to say: if the system is sufficiently reliable, it may be possible to replace individual judgment with computer judgment. If this can be done, the system can be completely automated.

The logistics information system has the following characteristics:

1. As stated earlier in the chapter, the systems specification must be the responsibility of the operating manager.

2. It is difficult to automate completely this kind of information, even apart from the technical problems of describing the system mathematically. For one thing, it is necessary to decide exactly what is being done. This can be complicated, because it is likely that a considerable amount of human judgment is being employed in the present system. To automate this system, it is necessary to duplicate this judgment or somehow get around it, and this is often no easy task. In fact, many times even finding out where human judgment is used

is difficult. For example: in a manual production control system, the production control clerk maintained safety stocks of certain parts that, from experience, he found were frequently out of stock if he followed the published procedure. Since he was disobeying rules, he did not let anyone know about these safety stocks. A system developed without these safety stocks, however, ran into serious trouble.

In other instances, people do not even realize that they are using judgment and, consequently, forget to tell the systems analyst about it. In one company it was the custom of a group of ordering clerks (people responsible for ordering parts for inventory) to walk around the warehouse after their lunch. It originally started out as exercise, but soon they were using this opportunity to observe the level of certain critical parts. When stocks appeared low, they reordered immediately without waiting for the paper work to reach them. Because they were doing this almost subconsciously, they failed to inform the systems analyst about it and, as a result, the automated system was not as successful as was anticipated.

Another reason why developing an automated system is difficult is that the present system should probably be changed to take full advantage of the automation. It would be unusual if the best solution were merely to automate the present manual system. Consequently, the automation of a logistics system usually requires a considerable amount of difficult systems specifications analysis.

3. The development and installation of a logistics information system presents greater administrative problems than are usually found in a routine data processing system. First, the replacement of many nonclerical workers can present a serious problem. For example, if a payroll clerk is replaced by a computer, often normal attrition can take care of the problem. This usually cannot be done with, for example, production control personnel. They are usually men, and the turnover is likely to be much less than among young women. Further, their training is more specialized; therefore, there is not a large pool of possible jobs to which to assign them.

Second, this type of application usually affects, in some way, non-clerical workers who must operate the new system. These people frequently have not initiated the automatic system because they do not know enough about modern data processing equipment. Nevertheless, they are the ones best acquainted with the present system. The success of the new system, however, requires that their active cooperation be obtained.

4. The final characteristic of a logistics information system is that the payoff is likely to be significantly greater than from routine data processing systems. This is true because the savings from better performance are potentially much greater than savings resulting from simply reducing clerical costs. For example, an improved inventory control system might nearly eliminate stockouts while reducing significantly the inventory levels. In one case, the savings from better inventory control was greater than the entire cost of operating the data processing system.

To summarize, the characteristics of a logistics information system are:

1. Operating management is responsible for systems specification
2. The system is difficult to develop
3. The administrative problems are important and difficult
4. The payoff is likely to be significant.

Financial Information Systems

Where financial information systems are well developed, the process of automation is usually much easier than with logistic systems. Many financial information systems, however, provide management with only a fraction of the information that could be made available even on a manual basis. Consequently, it is necessary to review the financial information system before automating so that ineffective financial information systems are not incorporated into the automated system. The financial information system has the following characteristics:

1. Systems specification is the responsibility of the controller or chief financial officer.
2. It is generally easy to develop and install because:
   a) Much of the systems specifications will have been previously completed in a good system;
   b) Much of the financial data will already be on punched card equipment.
3. The economic benefits of automating a financial information system are more difficult to estimate. Of course, the cost of a manual system can be compared against an automatic system but this, at best, is only a partial measure. In the first place, there may be new reports that were not considered practicable before automation. What is the value of these reports? What is the value of additional information? More complete information? More timely information? Because of the difficulty of measurement, the benefits from this type of system are usually listed under intangibles.

Personnel Information System

The personnel information tends to be the least complex of the major information systems. The problem is generally one of information storage and retrieval. Specifically, the personnel information system has the following characteristics:

1. The chief industrial relations officer has the responsibility for systems specification.
2. Frequently, it is not necessary to automate this information system. Where it is automated, the system is usually quite easy to install and develop.
3. The economic benefits of a personnel information system are difficult to estimate. For example, what is the value of having more personnel information available sooner?

Summary

	Type of System			
	Routine Data Processing	*Logistics*	*Financial*	*Personnel*
Systems specification	Data processing	Operating Manager	Controller	Industrial Relations Officer
Data Processing Development	Fairly easy	Difficult	Fairly easy	Easy
Economic benefits	Relatively small	Large	Difficult to Measure	Difficult to Measure

EVALUATING DATA PROCESSING

Once having approved the acquisition of a computer and the organization of a data processing activity, management is faced with the problem of evaluating the effectiveness of this activity and exercising control over its operations.

It is difficult for management to evaluate the performance of most staff activities, but data processing presents an even greater problem than that of most other staffs. In the first place, the activity is relatively new and, consequently, management's experience with it is limited. In the second place, much of the activity is technical and, being also relatively new, most managers have only a superficial understanding of the equipment and techniques employed. As a consequence of management's inability to evaluate, and therefore control, this activity, many unfortunate mistakes have occurred.

Although certainly no final answers can be provided for this problem of evaluation, the following guides should serve in specific situations:

1. The ultimate value of any staff activity depends upon what this activity accomplishes. One means of evaluation is simply to determine what has been accomplished to date and what it has cost. There are dangers to this approach, however. First, some types of data processing systems have long gestation periods. No concrete benefits may occur for months or even years, but when they do the results may be well worth the wait. The difficulty is to determine in the middle of such a project the value of what has been done up to that point.

   Second, if it becomes evident that a great deal of weight is being placed on immediate accomplishments, it may result in the data processing groups undertaking only those applications with a fairly quick payoff. Unfortunately, this type of application frequently has a lower total payoff.

2. A second means of evaluating a data processing manager is to see how well he has been meeting his commitments with respect to time and expense. If he meets them reasonably well, it does not necessarily mean that he is doing the most effective job possible. It does mean, however, that management is getting what it agreed to pay for; thus the performance is at least satisfactory. There are, of course, dangers in emphasizing the meeting of time and cost commitments. The principal one is that it may encourage the data processing manager to put enough slack in his proposed projects to handle almost any contingency. This could result in incorrect decisions. Management might reject a project because its cost was estimated at too high a figure; whereas, if the project had been correctly estimated, it would have been accepted.

   Another danger is that, in some instances, the meeting of commitments is a poor basis on which to evaluate performance. The field is relatively new, and many things can happen that could not have been reasonably anticipated. The more difficult the system, the more this is likely to be true. An imaginative manager should not be penalized for using precisely the qualities that will eventually result in the greatest return. Here again, overemphasis on meeting commitments could result in the undertaking of easy systems applications.

3. A third way of evaluating a data processing manager and the general effectiveness of his department is to find out what the operating people think of him. Since his main job is to provide a service to other groups in the company, if they are not satisfied with this service, there may be some question as to its effectiveness. The ability of a data processing manager to accomplish his objectives will depend considerably on his ability to get along with people. Consequently, it is usually a poor sign if the attitude of operating people is unfavorable to the data processing group.

4. A fourth technique for evaluating the data processing manager is to see whether he is making reasonable trade-offs. The development and installation of a data processing system are accomplished through a series of trade-offs—time (and, consequently, money) against an improvement in the system. It would be possible in most complex situations to spend years in developing the perfect system. At some point, however, further improvements are not worth the cost. The ability to determine this point precisely is a major factor in effective systems work. Sometimes, when a project appears to be moving at a slow pace, it is possible to observe the trade-offs being made and decide whether or not they are reasonable.

5. A criterion often used to evaluate the effectiveness of a computer unit is the percentage of time that the equipment is utilized. Poor utilization usually indicates something wrong in either the planning or the execution. The reverse is not true, however. High utilization of equipment does not necessarily mean good performance. We have seen equipment fully utilized, producing more or less useless data. The danger always exists, if equipment utilization is overemphasized, of causing the data processing activity to hurry into relatively uneconomic computer applications.

Although these five criteria of effectiveness have been described in terms of top management evaluation of the data processing manager, they work equally well (and have the same limitations) at lower levels. For example, these criteria could be used by the data processing manager in evaluating his supervisors and by his supervisors, in turn, in evaluating the systems analysts. Clearly, the further down the organization scale one goes, the more intimate will be the knowledge of what is happening and, consequently, the easier it will be to make an accurate evaluation.

The value of an effective data processing manager cannot be overemphasized. It is important to realize that there are *wide ranges of ability* among different individuals. Since the field is so new and relatively technical, many ineffective managers are, as yet, undetected. In fact, the demand for managers is so great that they are frequently promoted before the results of their current work are known. This in no way implies that most people in the information systems field are not effective. The point is that some are not, and it is not easy to determine quickly who the ineffective ones are. At the same time, the entire effectiveness of the system's activity is largely dependent upon the degree of competence of the director. Consequently, management *must* try to evaluate performance even though it often is difficult.

SELECTION AND TRAINING OF PERSONNEL

The selection and training of data processing personnel is, of course, one of the primary responsibilities of the data processing manager. Some familiarity with the problems of selecting and training data processing personnel is useful for the general manager, however, because it helps him to understand what is happening in the data processing area. Many of these problems are the same as those of any other white collar group; many, however, are unique. This part of the chapter describes briefly some of the unique features of selecting and training data processing personnel.

1. A common misconception is that one must be either a mathematician or an engineer to do either programming or data processing implementation work. In most business computer systems, this is not true at all. In fact, a high general intelligence and a good personality are usually more important than a specific technical background. (In the field of scientific programming, however, advanced mathematical training is required.)

2. Most companies find that many of the new programming and data processing jobs can be filled best from within the company. Tests are available that are designed to help determine aptitude. These tests, together with common sense, make it possible to select people with aptitude and interest in computer work. All manufacturers have set up schools to train customers' personnel. In addition, many universities have evening courses in computers and data processing to which selected individuals can be sent.

3. The formal courses given by either a manufacturer or a university are only the start of a person's development; experience also plays an important role. Consequently, there should be a plan for adequate supervision and on-the-job training.

4. Since the field is still relatively new and is in a constant state of change, evaluating people with experience in other companies is difficult. Some of these people have gone through a series of promotions without having their general level of performance evaluated. Some people with an apparently excellent work history are not very competent. The higher the position to be filled, the more difficult it is to evaluate the qualifications of the applicants. For this reason, many companies prefer to take a chance on their own personnel, although it will always be advisable to have some outside, experienced people.

5. A typical data processing group requires people of widely different backgrounds and abilities. A common mistake is to require a college degree for almost all data processing jobs. Many data processing

positions do not require a degree for satisfactory performance. If the company insists on a degree where it is not required, it will end up paying higher salaries than are necessary and, at the same time, creating higher turnover.

ACCOUNTING FOR DATA PROCESSING

Budgeting and accounting for the data processing activity present several unique problems. Because these problems always occur, management should have some understanding of them.

The data processing activity can be divided into three parts for purposes of budgetary control:

1. The administrative organization
2. Data processing implementation
3. Processing.

The first is an administrative activity and can be treated as such in a budgetary and accounting system. That is, a level of expenses can be proposed for this activity by the data processing director. After approval of the proposal (or adjustment thereof), the accounting department can prepare monthly reports that show the actual expenditures compared to the budget.

Activities 2 and 3, however, are not administrative. They provide services for both line and staff operations at the request of these operations. As a result, the level of activity performed by the data processing group is partially outside of its control; it is subject to the demand for its services. This fact presents a number of problems:

(1) The data processing group cannot develop budgets or make forward plans without coordinating these plans with departments likely to use its services.
(2) In approving the budget of the data processing group, the authorization for the work performed for other departments may be obtained from
    (a) The management group that approves the budget, or
    (b) The department that is to use the service.

This brings up the problem of charging the cost of data processing to those that use it. If it is not charged out, method (a) should probably be used. If the cost of service is charged to the using department, method (b) should be used. That is, the Data Processing Department would prepare a budget of its *total* activity but it would obtain its authorization to spend from the user. The user, in turn, would receive budget authority to spend money for data processing from top management.

When possible, it would appear that each operation should pay for the services that are rendered to it. If there is no charge, there is no incentive to keep the demands for service consistent with the value of that service to the user. Several problems occur with this approach, however. Many people believe that charging the operating people with the cost of data processing will slow down the development of new information systems. They believe that it is difficult, at best, to convince operating people of the desirability of improved information systems. If they have to pay for a study, they are likely to be even more resistant.

If the decision is to charge operations for the development work and subsequent processing of the data, how is the amount determined? Should it be a competitive price or a cost allocation? If a cost allocation is used, should it be full costs, including administration? Should it be just the cost of processing? Should it be only out-of-pocket cost?

Clearly, there is no one answer to these questions. The answer will differ with different companies and with the same company at different times. It depends upon what the company is trying to do. If it is trying to extend the use of the computer to educate operating personnel, it probably should not charge them for the service at all. On the other hand, it probably should not continue to provide all data processing services indefinitely without charge. A typical method for handling this problem is as follows:

1. Do not allocate the cost of the administration of the data processing group.
2. Do not charge the cost of data processing implementation projects that are initiated by the data processing group.
3. Charge out-of-pocket costs for the data processing implementation projects that are initiated by operating units.
4. Charge out-of-pocket costs for all processing after the initial test period.

There can, of course, be problems with an arrangement such as described above. For example, delays can be caused when one group tries to get the other group to initiate a particular object.

In summary, then, management should be sensitive to the problems of accounting and budgeting for the data processing activity. An arrangement should be made that will best accomplish the company's immediate objectives in the data processing field. The arrangement should be reviewed and changed as conditions change. We believe that, in the future, there will be an increasing disposition on the part of management to charge the costs of data processing to the users.

Section II

COMPUTER-DEPENDENT MANAGEMENT TECHNIQUES

With the development of the computer, several new management techniques, based essentially on mathematical principles, have come into use. In theory, these techniques can be used without a computer. In practice, however, they can be used only to a limited extent without a computer because of the amount of computation that these techniques require. In this section of the book we describe three of these techniques having the greatest importance to general management. These are: PERT, simulation, and information retrieval.

There are, of course, many other mathematical decision-making techniques that are generally dependent upon the computer; principally, operations research techniques. We have omitted describing operations research techniques for three reasons:

(1) Operations research techniques apply principally to operating management;

(2) The space limitations of this book would allow only a most superficial consideration of them;

(3) They are covered adequately in several other books.

Chapter 4

PERT and the
Critical Path Method

ONE OF THE MOST significant developments in management science in recent years has been the creation and rapid acceptance by government and industry of the PERT (Program Evaluation Review Technique) and CPM (Critical Path Method) techniques. The purpose of this chapter is to describe these techniques and to evaluate their uses as management tools.

CPM and PERT can be defined as the science of using network techniques for the maximum utilization of manpower, machinery, and time in the accomplishment of a project. CPM originated in 1957 through the cooperation of the Remington Rand Division of the Sperry Rand Corporation and E. I. du Pont de Nemours & Company. In 1958 the United States Navy Special Project office implemented the PERT system in connection with the development of the Polaris missile. While the terminology of the two techniques differs somewhat, the fundamental concepts of both are virtually identical. Little attempt, therefore, has been made to distinguish between the two techniques in this chapter.[1] For the purposes of consistency, the terminology of PERT will be used throughout.

The chapter is divided into three parts, as follows: the first part describes network construction and its use in planning project time schedules; the second part describes how costs can be used with time estimates to improve control and to make better decisions; the third part of the chapter is concerned with the management considerations of PERT and CPM.

---

[1]For further discussion of this subject see Moder and Philips, *Project Management with CPM and PERT* (New York: Reinhold Publishing Corp., 1964).

In the chapter, we have tried to stay away from the technical aspects as much as possible. For those who are interested, however, we have included three appendices that describe PERT techniques in more detail.

NETWORK ANALYSIS AND PERT-TIME

The purpose of PERT-TIME analysis is to keep management informed about the time-status of a project. This analysis not only informs management periodically as to the expected completion date but, also, which particular activities are critical to meeting this date. If the project drops behind schedule, the PERT analysis will indicate which activities can be speeded up so that the project can be completed on schedule.

Activities and Events

The first and most important step in preparing a project for PERT analysis is the proper subdivision of the project. The project is divided and subdivided into successively lower levels until the final subdivisions become manageable units for planning and control purposes. Each project is then split into a number of component parts called activities. An *activity* is any definable and time-consuming task, job, or function to be executed in a project. Examples of activities are preparing engineering drawings or installing automatic data processing equipment.

The start and completion of an activity is called an event. An *event* is defined as a specific point in time indicating the beginning or ending of one or more activities. An example of an event would be the completion of the preparation of engineering drawings. In preparing a project for PERT analysis, it has been found most useful to define first the work package's objective (last) event and then to work backward from this point. Experience has indicated that it is often easier to think of all the activities required for an activity to start than to think of all the activities which might be initiated by the completion of an activity.[2] As the activities and events are developed, they are plotted on a piece of paper to create a pictorial description (or network) of the time relationship of the several activities required to complete the project.

---

[2]Fundamentals of Network Analysis, Remington Rand Univac, 1962.

The network developed for each work package can then be combined into a large project network. Figure 4–1 presents a typical example of a network.

FIGURE 4–1

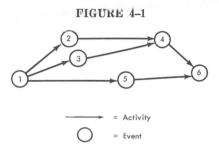

──────▶   = Activity

◯   = Event

The head of an arrow represents the sequence of activities. Thus, in the above diagram Event 3 precedes Event 4 and Event 4 precedes Event 6. It should be noted that the length of an arrow has no relationship to the actual time interval between two events. No activity can start until all the activities leading into the event preceding it have been completed. The following examples indicate the types of relationships most commonly found in a network.

FIGURE 4–2

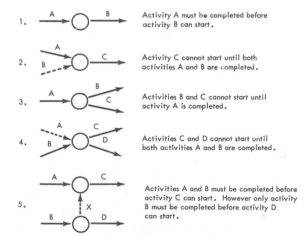

In example 5, X is called a *dummy variable*. It represents a restraint (halting the start of activity C until activity B is completed) which cannot be recognized by the conventional symbols for events and activities. It should be considered as an imaginary activity which can be accomplished in zero time, which is used only to show the proper relationship between activities. Further examples of dummy variables can be seen in Examples 2 and 4. A dummy variable is always represented by a dotted arrow.

A question frequently asked is, How can this network technique represent activities which overlap in time (as demonstrated in Figure 4–3)?

FIGURE 4–3

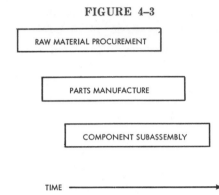

The answer is that there must be something specific which causes the decision to start an activity. The task of the person developing the network is to isolate this decision-causing point and to include it as an event on the network. In the preceding example, the decision to start parts manufacture might be determined by the acquisition of a certain percent of raw material or the arrival of certain specific components.

The following figure shows a sample network for solution of the problem.

FIGURE 4–4

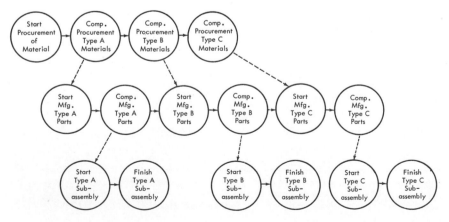

Estimating the Activity Time

When the network is completed, every event is assigned a number. This simplifies reference to specific activities and adapts the network to mathematical and computer analysis. For speed of computer computation, it is customary to have every succeeding event have a larger event number than those of its preceding events.

An estimate must next be made as to how long each particular activity will take. This is accomplished by conferring with the people responsible for the completion of the specific activities. One of two approaches may be used here:

(1) The first is to make one estimate of the most likely time of completion for each activity. (This approach is advocated by adherents of the Critical Path Method.)

(2) The second is to make three time estimates for each activity (this approach is advocated by adherents of the PERT technique): (a) the most likely time for the activity's completion; (b) a pessimistic estimate of the time required to complete the project (this would be realized only if everything went wrong [1 chance in 100] without, however, the occurrence of a major disaster); and (c) an optimistic view of the project's time requirements (this would be realized only if everything proceeded perfectly [1 chance in 100]; its achievement, however, would not involve a major breakthrough). These three estimates are then combined by the following equation:

t_o = optimistic time estimate
t_m = most likely time estimate
t_p = pessimistic time estimate
t_e = expected time (achieved by combining the three previous estimates)[3]
$$t_e = \frac{t_o + 4t_m + t_p}{6}$$

t_e is the value that will be used in all further network calculations.

Proponents of the three-estimate technique point to its increased accuracy and argue that it gives weight to the differing nature of activity risks. For example, they believe that it makes a useful distinction between the following two activities:

---

[3]This formula is based on certain mathematical assumptions that need not be considered here. It is merely one method of calculating the mean (average) time based on the three estimated times. For a technical discussion of the implications of this approach see MacCrimmon and Ryavac, *An Analytical Study of the PERT Assumptions*, (Carnegie Institute of Technology Reprint No. 157, 1964).

1. $t_o = 8$
   $t_m = 9$
   $t_p = 22$ therefore $t_e = 11$
2. $t_o = 2$
   $t_m = 9$
   $t_p = 10$ therefore $t_e = 8$

Using the one-estimate method a t_e of 9 would be used for both activities. (In the one-estimate method, t_e is equivalent to t_m.) Proponents of the one-estimate method believe that the increased complexity of the three-estimate calculation leads to t_e's which are very close to t_m's and, therefore, this extra calculation is wasted effort.

Adherents of the three-estimate method, while acknowledging there is some basis for this remark, believe that it ignores the problem of communicating effectively with the men in charge of activities. There is often a high degree of uncertainty surrounding the preparation of activity times, particularly in the area of engineering. By giving the engineer a chance to express his uncertainty through three estimates, he is less likely to make an optimistic t_m estimate.

The suitability of using the one- or three-estimate method often depends heavily on the nature of the project. Projects that have relatively well-defined tasks on which there has been a considerable amount of past experience (e.g., construction projects) will probably find the one-estimate method to be adequate. Projects where activity duration is quite uncertain (e.g., engineering projects) will probably find the three-estimate method to be more suitable. For purposes of consistency only, the three-time estimate will be used throughout the rest of this chapter.

Developing the Network

After times are estimated for each activity, the next step is to develop the network and to calculate the critical path. This is the easiest part of the job and one that is usually done entirely by the computer.

The network approach has really only one advantage over a simple Gantt Chart (bar chart). This advantage is that a network shows the activities which are critical to meeting the final completion date. Whenever two activities are going on simultaneously, and each of these activities has a different completion time, one (the one with the longer time) will be critical. To demonstrate:

Activity D (Events 4—5) cannot begin until both activity A and

FIGURE 4–5

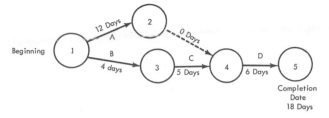

activities B and C are completed. It is estimated that activity A will take 12 days to complete. Activities B and C will take 9 days (4 + 5). Therefore, activity A is critical, because if this activity takes more than 12 days the total project will take more than 18 days. On the other hand, if either B or C is delayed, the effect on the completion date will not be the same, because B and C are scheduled to take only 9 days. If B were delayed 1 day and C 2 days, for example, it still would not affect the completion day. If all other activities were on schedule, it would still take only 18 days. B and C are scheduled to take 3 days less than A (12 − 9) and this is called "slack". The path 1, 3, 4, 5 has 3 days slack; the path 1, 2, 4, 5 has no slack and is, therefore, the critical path. It is important to understand this concept because this is really the entire principle of CPM and PERT-TIME.

The concept, then, is very simple. When activities are scheduled to be performed simultaneously, one series of activities (a path) will be scheduled to take longer than any of the other series. *This is the critical path.* All other paths have slack time equal to the difference between the scheduled time for the critical path and the scheduled time for each of the other paths. (Note that each path will have a different amount of slack.) Although the concept is simple, its application can be very useful for large projects. Imagine, for example, a project with 2,000 events that had as many as 30 different activities going on simultaneously at some point. Of the 30 activities only one is critical and the other 29 have varying degrees of slack. Without a network analysis, it would be impossible to determine where to put your resources to insure prompt completion of the project.

Appendix A describes the technique for developing a PERT-TIME network.

Probability of Completion

Using the three-estimate system, it is possible to make an estimate of the probability of completing the project on time. This probability is used to see whether or not to try to compress (reduce in time) the schedule further. If a project had an estimated completion date of 100 days and project due date of 105 days, one could estimate the probability of completing the project in 105 days. This estimate could then be compared to the cost of being late one day and a decision made as to whether an attempt should be made to compress the project. For example, assume that the probability of completion in 105 days was .9 and the cost of being late was $1,000 a day. By multiplying the probability of being late at least one day (.1) by the cost of being late ($1,000), the expected cost of being late is found to be $100. (This means that there is one chance in 10 of being late and, if this were done a number of times, the average cost would be $100 because the project would be late 1/10th of the time.) If you could compress the schedule 1 day for less than $100, you would do so; if not, you would leave the schedule as it is. By continuing this process until the cost of being late multiplied by the probability is greater than the cost of an additional day's compression, you would optimize the scheduled time.

The method for calculating probability is explained in Appendix B. Note, however, that the probabilities are only "ball park" approximations that have no rigorous mathematical foundations.

Summary

A PERT-TIME system will accomplish the following:

1. Present an organized plan for the project's completion.
2. Provide an estimated time of completion.
3. Identify the critical activities.
4. Identify those activities whose completion can be stretched out, and by how much they can be extended.
5. Provide a means for making an economic trade-off between the cost penalty of being late and the cost penalty for reducing the scheduled time.

PERT-COST

PERT-TIME concerns itself only with the time aspect of a project's completion. Satisfactory completion of a project, however, involves meeting two additional objectives: project costs and project technical quality. To help control the cost aspect of a project, PERT techniques have been adapted to include cost considerations. This part of the chapter describes this technique. (Much of the initial development work on PERT-COST was done by the Department of

Defense [DOD]. Consequently, our description of PERT-COST is heavily influenced by the PERT-COST system developed by DOD.)

The initial steps in applying PERT-COST are similar to those of PERT-TIME. The project is broken down into meaningful work packages and cost estimates are made for each of these packages. The project under consideration is divided and subdivided to successively lower levels until the final subdivisions become manageable units for planning and control purposes. The final subdivisions are then divided into major work packages (e.g., engineering, manufacturing, and testing). The *number* of these work packages will depend on the dollar value of the major work packages and the amount of detail needed by the manager to plan and control his work. Normally, the lowest level work packages will represent a value of no more than $100,000 in cost and no more than three months in elapsed time. They constitute the basic units by which actual costs are collected and compared with estimates for purposes of cost control. (Each work package is generally represented by a number of activities.)

In addition to the cost of each work package, estimates are also made of the cost of compressing the time required to complete each package where compression is possible.

PERT-COST information is used for two purposes:

1. As a planning device before the project is started and as a means of controlling costs during the execution of the project;
2. As a means of determining economic trade-offs where it is necessary to adjust time schedules.

The purpose of this part of the chapter is to discuss these two uses of PERT-COST.

Planning and Control

As a planning tool, PERT-COST is used to evaluate overall project costs before any action is taken. As a control tool, PERT-COST provides bench marks against which actual costs can be compared. This can prove to be very beneficial in controlling project costs. Using traditional control tools, it is often very difficult to tell whether a project is overrun until near the end of the project. Actual dollars spent are, of course, no indication of cost performance. Even when compared to elapsed time, the amount spent does not indicate efficiency. What is needed is to compare the amount spent with the amount accomplished. PERT-COST provides the tool for doing this. Each

FIGURE 4-6

SAMPLE PERT/COST PROGRAM STATUS REPORT

Project—X16-03 Fighter Plane Design

Date: 8/30/65

Beginning Event	Ending Event	Date Completion	Earliest Completion Date	Latest Completion Date	Slack	Actual Cost to Date	Original Estimate	Latest Revised Estimate	Overrun/(underrun)
601	602	8/13/65	8/ 7/65	8/30/65	23	$6,100	$6,100	$6,100	
602	603		9/ 6/65	9/20/65	14		2,300	3,300	$1,000
602	604	8/30/65	8/30/65	9/ 6/65	7	4,200	5,300	4,200	(1,100)
604	607		10/ 1/65	9/11/65	−20		3,600	3,600	
603	605		10/ 8/65	10/ 4/65	−4		3,800	4,000	200

work package is, in effect, a milestone against which the actual cost can be compared. If there is an overrun on the first work package, it will be indicated immediately.

FIGURE 4–7

SCHEDULE OUTLOOK REPORT

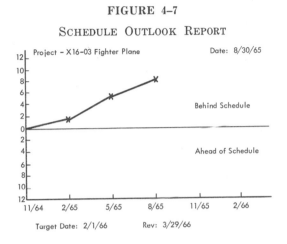

Figures 4–6, 4–7, 4–8, and 4–9 are samples of a typical PERT-COST report. When the manager receives this report, he may take any of the following actions:

1. Adjust the schedule of slack path activities to minimize the need for overtime or additional personnel costs.
2. Reallocate funds to critical areas.
3. Revise the planned resources for work packages by:
   a) Trading off interchangeable resources between critical and slack path activities;
   b) Increasing or reducing the planned resources for activities.
4. Revise the network sequence or content by:
   a) Employing a greater or lesser amount of concurrence in performing activities;
   b) Modifying the specifications or method of performing the work, thereby altering, deleting, or adding activities.

FIGURE 4–8

COST OUTLOOK REPORT

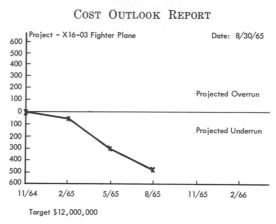

Project – X16–03 Fighter Plane   Date: 8/30/65

Projected Overrun

Projected Underrun

11/64   2/65   5/65   8/65   11/65   2/66

Target $12,000,000

FIGURE 4–9

COST OF WORK REPORT

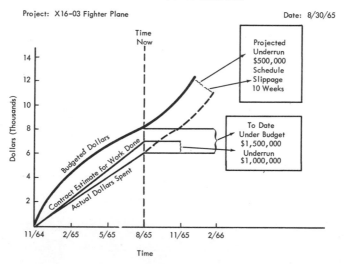

Project: X16–03 Fighter Plane   Date: 8/30/65

Time Now

Projected Underrun $500,000 Schedule Slippage 10 Weeks

To Date Under Budget $1,500,000 Underrun $1,000,000

Budgeted Dollars

Contract Estimate for Work Done

Actual Dollars Spent

Dollars (Thousands)

11/64   2/65   5/65   8/65   11/65   2/66

Time

PERT-COST in Reducing Time Schedules

PERT-COST may also be used to reduce an overlength time schedule to one that will be satisfactory. The problem is to locate the activities that can be shortened most economically. Figure 4–10 demonstrates the typical time-cost relationship for an activity. It indicates that there is a critical point in time beyond which it will become pro-

hibitively expensive to try to shorten the time schedule. It also indicates that lengthening an activity more than a certain amount will
result in negligible cost savings.

FIGURE 4–10

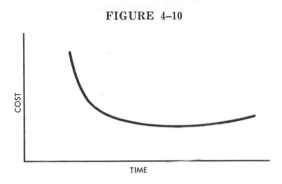

In actual practice PERT-COST considers the cost curve to be
linear. Various estimates are made concerning alternative times and
costs. They can be plotted on a graph similar to Figure 4-11.

FIGURE 4–11

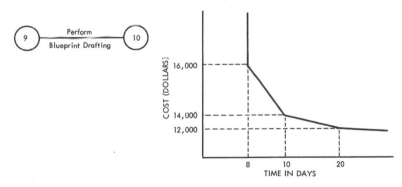

From this curve the added cost per day of shortening the activity
can be computed. For example, the cost per day of shortening from

20 days to 10 days is $\dfrac{\$14,000 - \$12,000}{20 - 10}$ = $200 a day. Shortening

from 10 days to 8 is $\dfrac{\$16,000 - \$14,000}{10 - 8}$ = $1,000 a day. Further

shortening is impossible. This information can be placed on the network as follows:

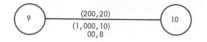

This notation indicates that reducing from 20 days costs $200 a day, reducing from 10 days costs $1,000 a day, and the activity cannot be reduced below 8 days at any cost. The notation also indicates, for example, that the project can be completed in 18 days for an extra cost of $400 ($200/day multiplied by 2 days). For many types of projects, this is a reasonable assumption concerning cost behavior. A continuous reduction in the activity's time can be achieved by diverting a continuously increasing stream of resources to it. The cost functions of some activities, however, do not behave this way. For these activities, time reduction can only be achieved by changing the method of accomplishing the activity. In these cases, for instance, the activity might be accomplished either in 20 days or 10 days. An intermediate value of 15 days is impossible. The cost per day calculation is of great importance in making the decision as to which activity on the critical path should have its time reduced.

The network is prepared as described earlier and the critical path is calculated. Next the costs associated with each activity are attached to its arrow as illustrated above. The critical path length is then compared with the project's target time duration. If the critical path is equal to or shorter than the project's target duration, there is no need to reduce the network. If, however, the critical path is longer than the project's target duration, the following steps should be taken:

1. The ratio of increase in cost to decrease in time for each activity on the critical path is calculated.
2. The activity having the lowest ratio is reduced to the lower time value. (If two or more activities have equal ratios, select the activity that has the least decrease in time.)
3. Using the new time, the network's critical path is recalculated.
4. Steps 2 and 3 are repeated until the critical path is equal to or less than the project target duration.
5. Once the critical path has been reduced to the target duration, review all slack paths. Slack activities should be shifted to longer-time, lower-cost points where this can be done without causing the critical path to exceed the target duration in length.

Appendix C gives an example of how a PERT network can be compressed using PERT-COST data.

MANAGEMENT CONSIDERATIONS OF PERT

Benefits of PERT

The use of PERT on a project offers advantages in both planning the project and controlling its progress. In the planning stages these advantages include the following:

1. Project members are forced to consider the sequencing and implementation of various phases of the project far in advance of their occurrence. Frequently this results in the uncovering of tasks which were not previously recognized as necessary.
2. Interrelationships between tasks are described more clearly than with any other planning technique, thus permitting early analysis of future bottlenecks.
3. Attention is focused on those parts of a project that are most critical to complete on schedule. This focusing takes place early enough so that corrective action can be taken. It also reveals those activities from which resources can be diverted.
4. A framework is developed which can be used to test out alternative approaches to a project.

As the project implementation proceeds, PERT becomes an effective control device. Some of its advantages in this area include:

1. A running estimate is provided both as to the most probable time in which a project will be completed and as to the probability of its being completed on time. Management, thus, is kept up to date on a project's progress.
2. It identifies quickly those areas where time and cost overruns are endangering the project's success. This allows the manager to divert resources from the activities which have slack time to those that do not.
3. It provides a framework for analyzing proposed changes in the project's course during the project's implementation.

Limitations of PERT

1. PERT is not a panacea for ineffective management. It is only an improvement over former project planning devices such as bar charts and Gantt charts, although often it allows the generation of analytical information that was not previously available.
2. The introduction of PERT will probably increase costs. Consequently, the cost of introducing PERT into a specific situation must be evaluated against the increased benefits received from the addi-

tional information that may be available. This evaluation will by no means always favor the introduction of PERT.

3. PERT is generally limited to projects rather than continuous type activities. Development of weapons systems, building construction, introduction of a new product, and research and development are areas where PERT has been most successfully used.

4. Most cost accounting systems are not designed to accumulate the costs required for a PERT-COST system. Consequently, it is usually necessary to change the cost accounting and this can be very expensive if it is not done right.

5. Many human relations problems can be generated by the introduction of PERT. Some of these come as a result of adding new controls (almost everyone will resist having new controls placed over him.) Many human relations problems occur, however, because PERT is not used correctly by management. For example, if any deviation from plan is considered bad, regardless of reason, there could be some serious reactions to PERT controls.

Role of Computers

The mathematics of both PERT-TIME and PERT-COST are relatively simple, involving only the operations of addition, subtraction, multiplication, and division. Small networks (under 150 items) are actually faster and cheaper to work out by hand. For larger networks, however, a hand process can be very time consuming and subject to clerical errors. As a result, programs have been developed for a number of computers to handle PERT problems. One of the more sophisticated systems is the IBM 7090 PERT-COST program. It is capable of processing up to 100 networks of approximately 750 activities each. The program has such features as:

1) The ability to summarize the network up to seven levels of specificity. An engineering section chief may get a network of 150 activities which outline in detail the project's progress through his section. This entire network, however, may be summarized by one activity arrow on the network which is given to the vice-president of manufacturing.

2) A built-in accounting calendar which will handle Saturdays, Sundays, and holidays in any desired fashion.

3) A wide variety of output reports. These include PERT-TIME and PERT-COST listing, cost status reports, manpower outlook reports, manpower and cost curves, and a variety of other management summary reports which relate time and cost. These reports can be obtained for each of the seven levels of summarization.

4) The ability to generate a Pictorial Network Program. The entire PERT network will be printed out. In addition to depicting the

relationships between all the activities, it will contain the following information:

a) the latest allowable date for each event

b) the actual date or expected date for each event.[1]

Responsibilities of Project Manager

The benefits described earlier do not just happen. Unless the project manager becomes involved with, supports, and uses the PERT network, it will be just additional overhead.

The project manager should have a thorough understanding of the mechanics of PERT. The mathematical complexity of the PERT techniques is not so great as to require special mathematical backgrounds for the managers who seek to utilize them. One or two days' study should be sufficient to provide a satisfactory introduction to the subject's techniques. Adequate mastery of PERT to a point where it can be effectively utilized requires, however, far more than a knowledge of the mathematical techniques. These additional skills include:

1. The ability to define fully the project's objective event. Often, one of the hardest jobs facing a project manager is to define adequately all the objectives of the project, to a point where they can be expressed as concrete events.

2. The ability to gain the confidence of the managers and engineers involved in the project so that they will cooperate in providing the necessary information. Successful implementation of PERT in a project requires the complete cooperation of the project's personnel.

3. The ability to keep the size and complexity of the network reasonable. The analysis of a project into a series of identifiable activities can be a very complex task. The mass of detail associated with any project often makes this task very difficult. There is a natural tendency to incorporate as much of this detail as is possible in the network.

    One of PERT's great advantages is its ability to provide a detailed analysis of the project that will locate troubles at an early stage. When a plan becomes too detailed, however, computer processing and other costs begin to reach major proportions. Also, it becomes difficult to locate trouble spots because the weight of detail may obscure some important information.

In summary, the skills necessary for successful implementation of PERT are such that the responsibility cannot be delegated success-

[1]IBM 7090 PERT-COST Programs, An IBM Application Program Bulletin, International Business Machines Technical Publications Department, (White Plains, N.Y.: 1962).

fully to a low status clerk. Rather, it requires the active support and judgment of the project manager.

APPENDIX A

DEVELOPING A PERT-TIME NETWORK

The Quick-Sales Company

The following example demonstrates how a PERT-TIME network is developed. The Quick-Sales Company is considering the introduction of a new line of goods. After some consultation and analysis, the following steps and times have been estimated to complete the project.

Activities	Time in Weeks			
	t_o	t_m	t_p	t_e
Order stock from factory................	10	12	20	13.0
Design package........................	2	2	3	2.2
Set up packaging facility...............	7	11	15	11.0
Package stock.........................	3	6	7	5.7
Ship stock to distributor................	2	7	7	6.3
Organize sales office...................	4	5	10	5.7
Select distributor......................	7	8	14	8.8
Sell to distributor.....................	2	7	8	6.3
Hire salesmen.........................	2	2	3	2.2
Train salesmen........................	5	6	6	5.8
Select advertising agency...............	3	4	4	3.8
Plan advertising campaign...............	2	5	5	4.5
Conduct advertising campaign...........	5	7	9	7.0

The time relationships among these activities are as follows:

Order stock from the factory, design the package and organize the sales office can begin at once.

The stock must be received and the packaging facility set up before stock can be packaged.

The stock must be packaged before it can be shipped to the distributors.

Once the sales office has been organized, the selection of dealers, the hiring of salesmen, and the selection of an advertising agency can go on simultaneously.

You cannot sell to distributors before selecting them.

You cannot train salesmen before hiring them.

After the selection of an advertising agency, the advertising campaign is planned, and conducted in that order.

Figure 4–12 indicates the above relationships.

Earliest Expected and Latest Allowable Time

The next step in developing a PERT network is to calculate the *Earliest Expected* time. The *Earliest Expected* time is the earliest time that an *event* can take place. It is represented by the symbol T_E. T_E is equal to the summation of activity times through the longest time chain from the beginning of the project to the given event. (Note that the subscript is a capital "*E*" as contrasted to a lower case "*e*" for the expected time for the completion of a single event.) Thus in our example, T_E for Event 13 is 20.8 weeks because it is the longest time chain from Event 1 to Event 13. It is the time necessary to complete Event 1 + Event 5 + Event 11 + Event 13. The sum of these activity times is 20.8 weeks. It is the usual practice to place T_E's on a network in a square alongside of the event. Figure 4–13 shows the Quick-Sales Company's network with the T_E's on it.

After the *Earliest Expected* time is calculated, the next step is to calculate the *Latest Allowable* time for each event. This is the latest time that an event can occur without affecting the completion of the project's final event. It is represented by the symbol T_L. To start the calculation, you assign the final event (Event 14 in the example) a T_L equal to its T_E. Then you go backwards through the network, calculating T_L for each event by subtracting the T_e of the preceding activity from the T_L. Thus, in the following example, the T_L of Event 93 is 87.2.

$$T_L = ? \qquad\qquad\qquad T_L = 96.3$$

$$t_e = 9.1$$

$$\text{(93)} \qquad\qquad \text{(94)}$$

In our Quick-Sales Company example, T_L for Event 5 is 5.7. This is because the longest chain of t_e's from Event 14 to Event 5 is Event 14—Event 13 –Event 11—Event 5. The t_e's on this chain total 21.4 weeks which, when subtracted from Event 14's T_L of 27.1, gives Event 5 a T_L of 5.7. It is usual practice to put the T_L's in a circle alongside of the event. Figure 4–13 shows the Quick-Sales Company with the T_L's on it.

In a number of situations these calculations will be sufficient. For example, if 40 weeks were allotted to the completion of the Quick-Sales project and the calculation of T_E for Event 14 is 27.1, it indicates that the project is in no trouble. It will, in fact, be completed almost 13 weeks before management considers it necessary. Under these circumstances, no further analysis would be required. Under other circumstances, however, further analysis might be necessary. For example, if management wanted the project completed in 21 weeks, the location of project bottlenecks and pools of excess resources would be important.

Slack Time and the Critical Path

The next step is to calculate the slack time for each event and to identify the critical path. The slack time for each event is the difference between T_E and T_L. When T_L is greater than T_E the event's completion can be delayed the amount of the difference without delaying the project's completion. (This is why it is called "slack" time.) For example, in the Quick-Sales Company, the completion of Event 3 can be delayed 1.9 weeks without affecting the expected completion of Event 14, the objective event. Any delay, however, in the completion of Event 5, which has zero slack, will delay completion of Event 14.

The critical path is the path along the events where the T_L's equal the T_E's. Delays of activities along this path will result in delaying the completion of the project. In the example of the Quick-Sales Company it can be seen that the critical path is Event 1—Event 5—Event 11—Event 13—Event 14. The critical path analysis has two principal uses: first, it pinpoints the critical and near-critical activities upon which management should focus its attention if the project is to have its time schedule reduced; secondly, it shows the activities which are noncritical and therefore can be considered as potential pools of resources for diversion to more critical activities.

Method of Presentation

For programs larger than that of the Quick-Sales Company, two changes are made in the format of presentation to management. First, in addition to the preparation of a network, the results are also listed in tabular form for ease of analysis. Secondly, the *Expected Time of Completion* and *Latest Allowable Time* are translated into actual dates. Thus, the report for the Quick-Sales Company would appear shown in Figure 4–14.

FIGURE 4–12

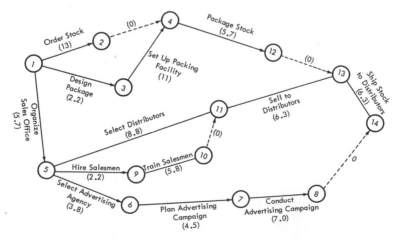

FIGURE 4–13

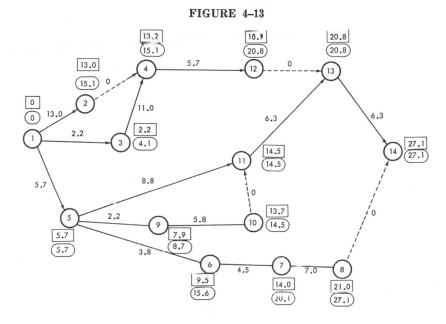

FIGURE 4–14

PERT SYSTEM

Event	Nomenclature	Expected Date	Latest Allowable Date	Slack
1	Start ordering stock & package design	5/ 7/63	5/ 7/63	0
2	Finish ordering stock	8/ 6/63	8/20/63	2.1
3	Start packaging facility	5/22/63	6/ 5/63	1.9
4	Start package stock	8/ 7/63	8/20/63	1.9
5	Start dist. sales, hire sales, select ad. agency	6/14/63	6/14/63	0
6	Start plans ad. campaign	7/11/63	8/22/63	6.1
7	Start conducting ad. campaign	8/13/63	9/24/63	6.1
8	Finish conducting ad. campaign	10/ 1/63	11/12/63	6.1
9	Start salesmen tng.	6/29/63	7/ 5/63	.8
10	Finish tng. salesmen	8/ 9/63	8/15/63	.8
11	Finish selec. distrib.	8/15/63	8/15/63	0
12	Finish pkg. stock	9/14/63	9/28/63	1.9
13	Finish selling to distributors	9/28/63	9/28/63	0
14	Finish shipping stock to distrib.	11/12/63	11/12/63	0

APPENDIX B

PROBABILITY OF COMPLETING PROJECT ON TIME

There are many situations in which it will be useful to assess the probability that the project will be completed on time. This is done as follows: It is assumed that the probable outcome for any activity can be represented by a normal curve which has t_e as its mean. You may recall from statistics that the degree of dispersion around the mean is described by the standard deviation (σ). The smaller the standard deviation becomes, the more concentrated is the dispersion. Figure 4–15 is a picture of the normal distribution.

FIGURE 4–15

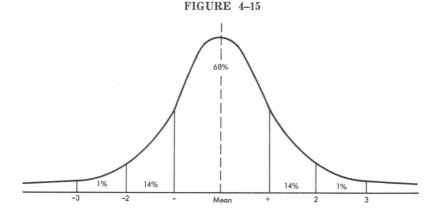

The normal distribution has the following characteristics which are relevant here:

1. 68% of its area lies between the mean and $\pm\ \sigma$
2. 96% of its area lies between the mean and $\pm\ 2\sigma$
3. 99% of its area lies between the mean and $\pm\ 3\sigma$

Earlier in the chapter it was stated that both the optimistic and pessimistic estimates were "1 in 100" occurrence. Thus, 98% of the time the actual activity time will fall between the limits of t_o and t_p. As a rough approximation we can then say that t_o and t_p are each located 3σ away from the mean. In PERT, therefore, the standard deviation for each activity can be approximated by the expression

$$\sigma = \cdot\frac{t_p - t_o}{6}$$

The variance of a distribution is defined as being equal to the square of the standard deviation. It can be proved mathematically that, when two numbers are added together, their variances may also be added together, and this new variance is the variance of the sum of the two numbers. For example, consider Activity A with a t_e = 6 and a standard deviation of 2. It is immediately followed by Activity B which has a t_e = 9 and a standard deviation of 3. It is desired to know the t_e of the sum of activities A and B and its variance.

	Activity A	Activity B
Standard Deviation	2	3
Variance	4	9
Variance of Activity (A+B) = 13		
Std. deviation of Activity (A+B) = $\sqrt{13}$ = 3.6		

Generalizing, the accumulated standard deviation of a series of n activities, which follow each other, can be expressed by the following formula:

$$\sigma \text{ series } = \sqrt{\Sigma\,(\sigma1^2 + \sigma2^2 + \sigma3^2 + \ldots \sigma n^2)}$$

This expression is used to calculate the probability of completing the project on time in the following way. First, the network's critical path is located. Then σ is calculated for each of the activities on the critical path. They are then squared and added to get the accumulated variance for the critical path. The square root of this number is then taken to get the accumulated standard deviation of the critical path which will be called $\sigma\,cp$. The value of the following expression is then calculated

$$Z = \frac{T_S - T_E}{\sigma cp}$$

T_S = the amount of time that has been *scheduled* for the completion of the project

T_E = the amount of time estimated by PERT network as *expected* for the completion of the project

Z = ratio figure to enter probability table.

You find the ratio Z on a table of values of the Standard Normal Distribution Function to determine the probability of completing the project on time.

The techniques just described will now be applied to the Quick-Sales Company problem. Assume that the scheduled date of completion is 30 weeks from the present. It may be recalled that the critical path is Event 1—Event 5—Event 11—Event 13—Event 14. Figure 4–16 presents the calculations leading to the determination of this path's variance.

FIGURE 4–16

Activity	t_o	t_p	$\sigma = \dfrac{t_o - t_p}{6}$	σ^2
1–5	4	10	1.0	1.0
5–11	7	14	1.16	1.35
11–13	2	8	1.0	1.0
13–14	2	7	.83	.69
				4.04

$$\sigma \; cp = \sqrt{4.04} = 2.01$$

$$Z = \frac{30.0 - 27.1}{2.01} = 1.44$$

Looking up $Z = 1.44$ in a table of Normal Curve indicates there is a 92% probability that the project will be completed on time.

APPENDIX C

EXAMPLE OF PERT-COST CALCULATION

The following network indicates the time dependence of the project's various activities; the table indicates the various time-cost relationships possible for the projects. The project's target completion time is 17 weeks.

FIGURE 4–17

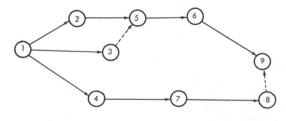

The first step is to develop the PERT network by identifying the critical path and comparing its estimated time to that of the project target time. Figure 4–18 represents the PERT network. Since the estimated time is greater than the project target time, the network must be reduced. The first step is to calculate the time/cost ratios for each activity (see Figure 4–19)

FIGURE 4–18

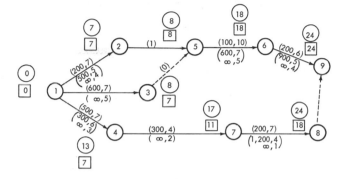

FIGURE 4–19

TIME-COST ESTIMATES FOR THE SEVERAL ACTIVITIES

Activity	Time (weeks)	Cost	Time/Cost Ratio
1–2	7	700	
	5	1,100	200
	4	1,600	500
1–3	7	800	
	5	2,000	600
1–4	7	500	
	6	1,000	500
	3	1,900	300
2–5	1	300	
5–6	10	1,500	
	7	1,800	100
	5	3,000	600
6–9	6	1,100	
	5	1,300	200
	4	2,200	900
4–7	4	800	
	2	1,400	300
7–8	7	800	
	4	1,400	200
	1	5,000	1,200

The critical path is Event 1—Event 2—Event 5—Event 6—Event 9. Thus, the total project time is 24 weeks and the total cost is $6,500. This is substantially above the project time of 17 weeks, so the following series of changes are made:

1. Activity 5–6 has the smallest time-cost ratio (100) on the critical path. It is, therefore, shortened by three weeks at a cost of $100 a week or a total of $300. The adjusted network now is as follows:

FIGURE 4–20

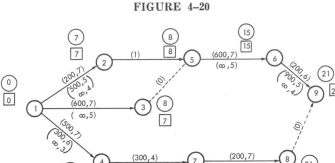

The critical path remains the same as before but the total project time is now 21 weeks. Because the project target time is 17 weeks, however, further reduction in the network is necessary.

2. Activities 1–2 and 6–9 have the smallest time-cost ratios (200) on the critical path. Because activity 6–9 has the shorter time reduction of the two activities (1 week), it is shortened one week at a cost of $200. The adjusted network now is as follows:

FIGURE 4–21

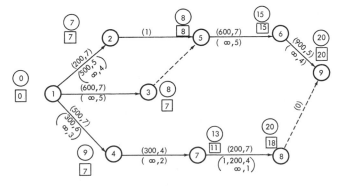

The critical path remains the same as before but the total project time is now 20 weeks. Still further reduction in the network is necessary.

3. Activity 1–2 has the lowest time-cost ratio (200) on the critical path. It is shortened therefore by two weeks at a cost of $200 a week or a total of $400. The adjusted network now is as follows:

FIGURE 4–22

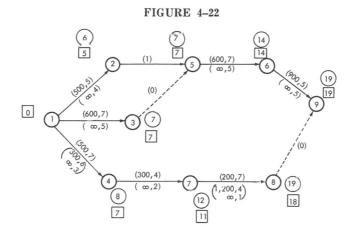

The critical path has changed to Event 1—Event 3—Event 5—Event 6—Event 9. The total project time is now 19 weeks, or 2 weeks more than the target project time of 17 weeks. Consequently, further reduction in the network is necessary.

4. Activities 1–3 and 5–6 have the lowest time-cost ratios (600) on the critical path. They also have the same time reduction (two weeks). In this case an arbitrary reduction of activity 1–3 will be made. It is shortened therefore by two weeks at a cost of $1,200. The adjusted network is as follows:

FIGURE 4–23

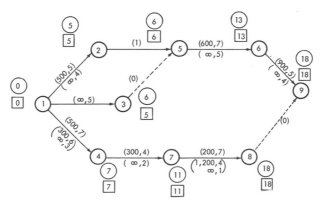

It can be seen that the network now has two critical paths. The first is Event 1—Event 2—Event 5—Event 6—Event 9. The second is Event 1—Event 4—Event 7—Event 8—Event 9. In this situation, the lowest time-cost ratio must be located for each path because they share no activities in common. (If they did share one or more activities, a cost comparison would be made as to the cost of reducing one of the shared activities as compared to the cost of reducing one event in each path.) The activities to be reduced are activities 1–2 (1 week at a cost of $500) and 7–8 (3 weeks at a total cost of $600). The adjusted network now is as follows:

FIGURE 4–24

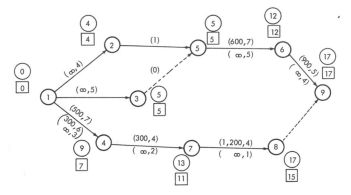

The project expected time of 17 weeks is now equal to the project target time. Consequently, the network need be reduced no further. It is assumed here that reducing T_E to the scheduled time T_S is sufficient. This provides a 50 percent probability of the project being completed on schedule or earlier. If a higher probability were required, further network reductions would take place. After each reduction the standard deviation would be calculated for each activity on the critical path, and, in the way described in Appendix B, the probability of completing the project on time would be computed. This process would continue until the probability of completing the project on schedule is equal to or greater than the desired probability.

The slack paths must now be analyzed, however, to shift slack activities to longer time-lower cost points where possible. In the example, the slack path is Event 1—Event 4—Event 7—Event 8—Event 9. It contains a total of two weeks slack which may be apportioned to any activity in the path. An analysis of this path indicates that at a cost of $600, a three week reduction was achieved in activity 7–8. In view of the slack now in the path, it is feasible to rescind this three-week reduction in activity 7–8 and, instead, take a one-week reduction in path 1–4 costing $500. This gives a net savings of $100. The selected times and costs for each activity are then printed out. For our example, the output would appear as follows:

FIGURE 4–25

Activity	Time (weeks)	Cost
1–2	4	$1,600
1–3	5	2,000
1–4	6	1,000
2–5	1	300
5–6	7	1,800
6–9	5	1,300
4–7	4	800
7–8	7	800
		————
		$9,600

Nonoptimum Solution

The method just described for preparing PERT-COST estimates is currently being advocated by the Department of Defense. It should be noted that this is not a technique for optimizing PERT networks. It will lead to good solutions, but not necessarily to the best ones available. This can be demonstrated with the example calculated above. In reducing the critical path from 19 weeks to 17 weeks, activity 1–3 was cut by 2 weeks at a cost of $1,200 and activity 1–2 was cut by 1 week at a cost of $500. Had, however, activity 5–6 been cut by 2 weeks, the same overall time reduction would have been achieved and the total cost of the reduction would have been only $1,200 instead of $1,700.

Further development work is currently being done in this area. If cost functions whose slope is always increasing (see examples below) are used exclusively, an application of linear programming techniques to this problem has been developed which will assure the achievement of an optimal solution to the problem. (This technique is quite complex and technical.)

FIGURE 4–26

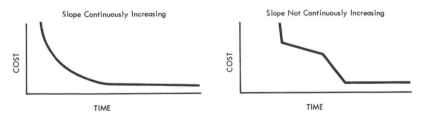

Slope Continuously Increasing   Slope Not Continuously Increasing

COST   COST

TIME   TIME

Chapter 5

Simulation

THE GENERAL BUSINESS SIMULATION

SIMULATION is a method of approaching a problem by constructing a model of a real situation, and then manipulating this model in such a way as to draw some conclusions about the real situation. Simulation, therefore, is not a specific technique at all but an approach to a problem. Consequently, simulation can take a multitude of forms and use many different techniques. (For example, the Link Trainer of World War II fame is a simulation model.)

In this chapter we are concerned with digital computer models that can be used to help management in strategic planning. We have called this type of model a "general business simulation." This has been defined by Jay Forrester in this book, "Industrial Dynamics" as follows:

> In business, simulation means setting up in a digital computer the conditions that describe a company's operations. On the basis of the descriptions and assumptions about the company, the computer then generates charts which show the performance of finance, manpower, product movement and so on over time. Different management policies and assumptions can then be examined.

The general business simulation is treated in a separate chapter because of its importance to management. Of all of the mathematical techniques, this is the one with which management should be the most familiar. This is so because:

1. It has the greatest possible potential for helping top management, whereas the other mathematical techniques apply principally to operating management.
2. Management judgment is needed in the development of the model because the typical model builder does not have an intimate enough

knowledge of the business to select the appropriate relationships for inclusion in the model.

3. If management is to use a simulation model, it must be aware of the principal assumptions that were made in its construction.

The mathematical techniques employed in the general business simulation are, for the most part, very simple. They are so simple in fact, that they never need prevent a manager from understanding a business model. This is very important to understand. A manager cannot excuse himself from becoming involved in a general business simulation on the grounds that he does not have enough mathematics. (He may, of course, excuse himself on other grounds.) This is not to say that building a general business simulation is easy. It is not; but the difficulties are not with complex mathematical formulations. The difficulties in building a general business model result from the following conditions:

1. The typical business is so complex that only a very complex model can come even close to approximating reality. The degree of complexity, in itself, makes model building very difficult.

2. Even the most complex model can include only a fraction of the things that are happening in a typical business. Consequently, it is necessary to simplify real life in nearly every part of the model. It takes considerable skill to simplify to the extent that is necessary in the typical model and still retain reality.

3. The model is only as good as the values that are placed on the coefficients of the equations. The determination of these values takes considerable skill.

As a result of these difficulties, it takes a man of unusual ability and experience to develop a general business simulation. This is important to understand. Because of the relative simplicity of the techniques, many people think they are capable of building a complex model. This is not true and, because the cost of such a model can be quite high, management would be well advised to consider carefully the personnel available before approving a project to develop a general business model.

Building a Simulation Model

Notation

One of the things that makes a simulation model appear to employ complex mathematics is the mathematical notation used. To most people not familiar with this notation, it looks formidable. Actually, it is not. Each element in an equation contains two parts; the first part contains a symbol that represents something in a business. For example: "I" could be inventory; "DS", dollar sales; "US", unit sales. The second part of each element describes the time of this element. There are many ways of expressing the time factor in an element but they are all similar. One way to do it is to let some time period = "t" and express all time relations from this. For example, t = May 1, then $t + 1$ would equal June 1, if "1" is made equal to a month. (If working in terms of weeks, the "1" would equal one week.) So, then, $I(t)$ would mean the amount of inventory on May 1; $I(t + 1)$ = inventory on June 1; $I(t - 1)$ inventory on April 1. The general expression "t" is used so that it can be made to equal different times for different runs of the model.

The "t" expresses a point in time. To show something over a period of time, a diagonal "/" is used between the beginning and end of the period covered. For example, suppose it is desired to symbolize Dollar Sales for May; this could be expressed as $DS(t/t + 1)$, or Dollar Sales between May 1 and June 1, which equals Dollar Sales for May. (Note that the "/" does *not* mean divide, as it does in some mathematical notations.) With this notation, we are now ready to develop some simulation equations.

Equations

There are three types of equations in a simulation model. These are explained below:

1. *Level equations:* These describe the level of resources (e.g. dollars or physical units) at a given time. The following is an example of a level equation:

    $I(t + 1) = I(t) + R(t/t + 1) - US(t/t + 1)$, where t = May 1 and "1" = one month

    $I(t + 1)$ = Inventory June 1
    $I(t)$ = Inventory May 1
    $R(t/t + 1)$ = Receipts of goods during May (from May 1 to June 1)

    $US(t/t + 1)$ = Unit sales during May.

2. *Rate equation:* These describe the rate at which resources are flowing through the business. The following is an example of a rate equation.

$VC\ (t/t + 1)\ =\ 3US\ (t/t + 1)$, where
$VC\ (t/t + 1)$ = variable cost incurred during May
$US\ (t/t + 1)$ = unit sales during May. In words, this equation says
that the total variable cost is equal to \$3 times the number of
units sold.

3. *Initial condition equations:* These describe the initial values of
parameters at the beginning of the simulation. For example,
it would be unrealistic to expect an operating company to
have no inventory. Therefore, the following equation would
probably appear.

$I\ (O)\ =\ 1{,}000$

This signifies that, at the beginning of the period being simulated by the model, one thousand items were in inventory.
Both rates and levels will require initial condition equations.

With these equations, we can now develop a simulation model.

RIGHTWAY DISTRIBUTORS

Rightway Distributors, Inc., is a small retailer of such items as
notebooks, pencils, and fountain pens. On May 1, 1965, Mr. Daniel
Newton, president of Rightway, was reviewing the company's less
profitable items. During his review, Mr. Newton was able to ascertain
the following information concerning one particular line as of May 1.

a) An inventory of 3,000 items was currently on hand. An order to
replenish inventory was sent out at the end of every month. The
size of this order was determined by multiplying the actual demand
for the item during the past month by 9/4 and then subtracting
the on hand inventory from this amount. Shipments were always
received five weeks after the order was sent. Thus, shipment on an
order sent out on April 30 would be received June 4.

b) Actual demand for the item was stimulated by two factors, marketing expenditure and price. \$100 spent on marketing induces sales
of an extra 25 units. The number of unit sales stimulated by the
price factor each month is represented by 5,000 ÷ price. The product is currently priced at \$10.00. Last month's marketing expendi-
tures for the item were \$20,000, and the expenditures two months
ago were \$18,000.

c) Actual sales of the item during the month can be approximated by
selecting the lower of the following two amounts:
1) Actual demand for item during month (as calculated in b)
2) Amount in inventory at the beginning of the month plus items
received during the month.

d)   Each item of the product incurs $3.00 of variable costs. The product line incurs fixed costs of $20,000 each month.
e)   The company's marketing expenditures on the product line observe the following pattern during the year. In January they are at a level of $14,000. They rise in increments of $2,000 each month through July. They then decline by increments of $2,000 each month until by the following January, the marketing expenditures are again at a level of $14,000.
f)   Orders had been placed as follows: March 31, 6,000 units; April 30, 7,000 units.

Required: Build a simulation model of the product line described above and simulate May's activity.

Notation

The first step is to decide upon the notation to be used. Any notation that you wish to use is all right. The main thing is to use notation that *you* can remember, without having to keep looking it up on a table. The following notation is suggested:

t = May 1
1 = one month
$I(t)$ = Inventory at time (t)
$R(t/t + 1)$ = Receipts during month
$D(t/t + 1)$ = Demand during month
$US(t/t + 1)$ = Unit sales during month
$DS(t/t + 1)$ = Dollar sales during month
$P(t/t + 1)$ = Unit price during month
$MC(t/t + 1)$ = Marketing costs during month
$VC(t/t + 1)$ = Variable cost during month
$FC(t/t + 1)$ = Fixed costs during month
$TC(t/t + 1)$ = Total costs during month
$O(t/t + 1)$ = Orders placed during month
$E(t/t + 1)$ = Earnings during month

Equations

(1) $I(t + 1) = I(t) + R(t/t + 1) - US(t/t + 1)$

Inventory June 1 is equal to the inventory May 1 plus receipts during May less unit sales during May.

(2) $D(t/1 + 1) = \dfrac{5,000}{P(t/t + 1)} + .25\ MC(t/t + 1)$

Demand during May is equal to 5,000 divided by the price of the items plus ¼ of a unit for each dollar of marketing cost.

(3) $US\ (t/t + 1) = D\ (t/t + 1)$ if $D\ (t/t + 1) \leqslant I\ (t) + R\ (t/t + 1)$ or $I\ (t) + R\ (t/t + 1)$ if $D\ (t/t + 1) > I\ (t) + R\ (t/t + 1)$

The unit sales during May will be equal to the demand (that is, customer orders) if the demand is equal to or less than the inventory on May 1 plus the receipts during May. The unit sales will equal the inventory on May 1 plus the receipts during May, if the demand is greater. In other words, the sales will equal the demand if there is enough in stock; otherwise it will equal the amount available for sale. (Note how this rather formidable looking equation expresses a very simple idea.)

(4) $DS\ (t/t + 1) = US\ (t/t + 1) \times P\ (t/t + 1)$

Dollar sales for May equal unit sales for May multiplied by the price.

(5) $VC\ (t/t + 1) = 3\ US\ (t/t + 1)$

Variable cost during May equals $3 multiplied by the units sold.

(6) $TC\ (t/t + 1) = VC\ (t/t + 1) + FC\ (t/t + 1) + MC\ (t/t + 1)$

Total costs during May equal variable costs plus fixed costs plus marketing costs.

(7) $E\ (t/t + 1) = DS\ (t/t + 1) - TC\ (t/t + 1)$

Earnings for May equal the dollar sales for May minus the total costs incurred during May.

(8) $O\ (t/t + 1) = 9/4\ US\ (t/t + 1) - I\ (t + 1)$

The orders placed for May equal 9/4 of the sales made during the month less the inventory on hand at the end of the month.

Simulation of May Activity

The next step is to solve these equations. This is done "recursively" or in a given order. This order is determined by the requirements of the equations. For example, you cannot solve equation (1) until you find the unit sales for the period. You cannot find the unit sales for the period until you find the demand. Consequently, the first equation to be solved is equation 2.

Initial Condition Equations and Given Values

$I\ (t)$ = 3000
$R\ (t/t + 1)$ = 6000
$P\ (t/t + 1)$ = 10
$MC\ (t/t + 1)$ = 22,000
$FC\ (t/t + 1)$ = 20,000

(2) $D\ (t/t + 1)\quad = \dfrac{5,000}{P\ (t/t + 1)} + .25\ MC\ (t/t + 1)$

$\qquad\qquad\quad = \dfrac{5,000}{10}\qquad + .25\ (22,000)$

$\qquad\qquad\quad = 500\qquad\quad + 5,500 = 6,000$

(3) $US\ (t/t + 1) = D\ (t/t + 1)$ if $D\ (t/t + 1) \leqslant I\ (t) + R\ (t/t + 1)$
$\qquad\qquad\qquad = 6,000$ if $6,000 \leqslant 3,000 + 6,000$
$\qquad\qquad\qquad = 6,000$ (demand of 6,000 is less than the 9,000
units available for sale)

Now we can solve equation (1)

(1) $I\ (t/t + 1)\quad = I\ (t) + R\ (t/t + 1) - US\ (t/t + 1)$
$\qquad\qquad\qquad = 3,000 + 6,000 - 6,000$
$\qquad\qquad\qquad = 3,000$

(4) $DS\ (t/t + 1) = US\ (t/t + 1) \times P\ (t/t + 1)$
$\qquad\qquad\qquad = (6,000)\qquad (10)$
$\qquad\qquad\qquad = 60,000$

(5) $VC\ (t/t + 1) = 3\ US\ (t/t + 1)$
$\qquad\qquad\qquad = 3\ (6,000)$
$\qquad\qquad\qquad = 18,000$

(6) $TC\ (t/t + 1) = VC\ (t/t + 1) + FC\ (t/t + 1) + MC\ (t/t + 1)$
$\qquad\qquad\qquad = 18,000 + 20,000 + 22,000$
$\qquad\qquad\qquad = 60,000$

(7) $E\ (t/t + 1)\quad = DS\ (t/t + 1) - TC\ (t/t + 1)$
$\qquad\qquad\qquad = 60,000 - 60,000$
$\qquad\qquad\qquad = 0$

(8) $O\ (t/t + 1)\quad = 9/4\ US\ (t/t + 1) - I\ (t + 1)$
$\qquad\qquad\qquad = 9/4\ (6,000) - 3,000$
$\qquad\qquad\qquad = 13,500 - 3,000$
$\qquad\qquad\qquad = 10,500$

See if you can simulate the June activity.

Some Comments on the Rightway Distributor

You will notice that the mathematical notation is merely a shorthand for expressing relationships, levels, and flow of resources in a business. This shorthand is necessary because:

(1) It represents an easy way of expression and one that the computer can handle efficiently.
(2) It represents a general situation that can easily be changed. For example, by changing a few parameters, it can be used for any month of the year.

Although Rightway was a very simple case, it represents exactly the type of mathematics used in even the most complex simulations.

If, instead of using only one product, we had simulated all of Rightway's products, immediately you would increase the size of the simulation many times. In general, more complex simulations differ from Rightway in three ways:

(1)   A much larger number of product lines are simulated;
(2)   The relationships between the equations are more complex;
(3)   The decision rules are more complex.

Nevertheless, it is only size and complexity that increase; the mathematics would be identical and no more difficult to understand.

Appendix A provides an example of a simulation where more complex decision rules are used.

Deterministic and Probabilistic Models

There are two general types of relationships which appear in simulation models. The first is the straight deterministic relationship. An example of this is the relationship between sales and advertising for the Rightway Distributors.

$$D\ (t/t + 1) = \frac{5,000}{P\ (t/t + 1)} + .25\ MC\ (t/t + 1)$$

These equations reflect average relationships that will be the same on every simulation run.

The second type of relationship incorporated in a simulation model is the probabilistic relationship. An example of this is the rate at which incoming orders are received in the mail each day. For example, assume the following relationships existed:

Probability of Receiving This Number of Orders per Week	*Number of Orders/Week*
.1	70
.2	80
.3	90
.2	100
.1	110
.1	120
1.0	

Each time the model simulates a week's activities, a table of random numbers is used to determine the number of orders received during the week. The results will simulate the probabilities shown on the table above. There will be a 10 percent chance of 70 orders, a 20 percent chance of 80 orders, a 30 percent chance of 90 orders, and so on. Thus, instead of a single relationship, representing the average number of orders, you have multiple relationships. The advantage of this, of course, is that it more closely simulates what is actually happening. The average number of orders rarely occurs in one week. (Remember the story about the man who drowned in a river that averaged one foot in depth.) Consequently, you will have a more realistic simulation by using these probabilities.

When a model utilizes these types of relationships, it should be noted that no two calculations of the simulation will produce exactly the same results, even when the structure of the model has not been altered. Consequently, it is necessary to make several simulation runs, so that a range can be established. Where there are several difficult-to-predict interrelated elements in a real-life situation, the use of probability distributions to provide a value for these elements makes it possible for the model to provide management information never available before. It is nearly impossible, in many instances, to estimate the possible total effect of some of these interrelated variables. When these elements are included in a simulation on a probabilistic basis, it is possible to obtain a general idea of the range of likely outcomes.

The use of probabilistic models does not require including a complex probability function in the computer program. Only a finite number of points, similar to the above example, are needed. It has been found that about eight points are all that are required to obtain a reasonable fit for most probability distributions.

The disadvantage of a probabilistic model is the necessity of always having to make a number of runs to obtain a distribution of results. Clearly, this can be very expensive in computer time. Most probabilistic models, therefore, are designed in such a way that the average values can also be used. That is, these models are built in such a way that they can be used as either deterministic models or probabilistic models, depending on the purpose of the simulation run.

Static and Dynamic Models

A simulation model is usually not calculated for just one period but is recalculated for a number of successive periods. This is useful in highlighting trends and showing the extent to which significant fluctuations may appear as a result of changing the model's input or structure. If the model is designed to cover only one period of time, it is called a "static" model. If, however, the model is designed to continue over a number of periods, it is called a "dynamic" model. Each time period in a static model is treated independently of any other time period. In a dynamic model, however, certain outputs for one period, such as inventory levels, are inputs for the next period. All general business models are dynamic, but many simulations of operating problems are static.

Testing the Validity of the Models

Once the model has been built, the final step before using it is to test its validity. This is usually done by using historical data (say, for the past two years) as input and seeing how close the model comes to what actually happened during the period. If the results of the model differ significantly from what actually happened, the model is "calibrated" (that is adjusted) to provide a closer approximation to reality. (When a model approximates reality, it is said to "fit".) When a reasonable fit is obtained, the model is ready for use.

There is one very important point for management to understand about the testing of the general business simulation. This is, *the test, no matter how good the fit, does not prove that the model will give an accurate representation of real life.* There are two main reasons for this. First, most models are so complex that one is never sure which assumptions should be changed if the model does not fit well. (If the model fits well on the first test, one cannot be sure that there are not several off-setting errors.) For example, the model might show that the company earned a higher profit than it actually did. It is an easy matter to reduce the earnings of the model; but it is very difficult to know which of the hundreds of elements that affect profits is incorrect. In calibrating the model, it may be made less accurate in the future by adjusting the wrong element. In fact, the model can always be calibrated to fit historical data closely; but if the good results are because of off-setting incorrect assumptions, the future accuracy of the model is questionable. The second reason why the test does not prove accuracy is that the firm's structure and environment is constantly changing. Thus, a useful model in 1964 may have considerably less value when used in 1966 because its structural elements are no longer good simulations.

It is important for management to understand that the accuracy of the model cannot be proved. It is necessary, then, to understand how the model was built, what the principal assumptions were, and what the major simplifications were. It is only in this way that the manager can reasonably assess the significance of the model's results. The business simulation is not like an engineering simulation that can be proved. All management needs to know, in that instance, is that it has been tested and found to be reliable. Management then gives approval to the engineer to use the model. In the general business simulation, top management must use it as a tool; and only top management has a sufficient understanding of all of the intricacies of the business to evaluate the validity of the model.

MANAGEMENT CONSIDERATIONS OF SIMULATION

Simulation and Strategic Planning

The general business simulation is uniquely different from nearly all other computer-dependent mathematical techniques in that it is designed to help *top management in strategic planning.* (It may also help operating management, e.g., in inventory control policy.) Consequently, the implications of simulation to management are much more important than most other computer applications. The typical computer application provides a better way of performing an operational job, or a cheaper, faster, or more accurate way of handling data; whereas simulation has the potential for improving the strategic decision-making ability of top management.

A wide difference of opinion exists among business executives, operations research personnel, and simulation experts as to the ultimate potential of the general business simulation. At one extreme are the people who seriously believe that within a few years no company of moderate size or larger can afford to be without a simulation model. They picture a computer as being a part of all boards of directors meetings: the computer is interrogated on a wide variety of problems and the answers to the questions are immediately flashed upon a screen in the directors' room.

On the other hand, there are many people who believe that simulation is just a "fad" and will never offer any real assistance to management in making strategic decisions. They point out that the output of a simulation program is only the result of information fed into the computer and that the answers will be only as good as the assumptions that went into building the model. Moreover, some believe that business is so complex that it will never be possible to simulate it accurately enough to provide a basis for dependable decisions. As in most cases of this kind, the answer is probably somewhere between these two extremes. At the present writing, simulation is still in its early development and consequently it is impossible to know how great its ultimate impact will be on business. Needless to say, the development of this technique should be watched carefully by all businessmen.

Some Generalizations on Simulation

Although the ultimate impact of simulation on business is, at present, an unknown quantity, a few generalizations can be made:

1. General business models have proved to be useful in the following areas:
    (a) Business games.
    (b) As a laboratory method for studying management decision-making techniques.
    (c) As a means of analyzing complex business interrelationships.
2. Almost without exception, companies that have attempted to build a general simulation model have found that they have benefited indirectly in that the simulation study has brought out areas where information systems can be improved. (Remember, however, that this can be an expensive way of examining current information systems.)
3. A real conflict is a possibility when an attempt is made to use a simulation model for strategic decision making:
    (a) The accuracy of the model cannot be proved; yet management must have confidence in the model if it is to be used as a basis for making strategic decisions.
    (b) The model is most valuable when it results in management taking some different action from that which would have been taken without the model, i.e., by relying on management intuition.
    (c) The simulation's most valuable contribution will be, therefore, when it indicates different action from that indicated by management intuition.
    (d) In the light of (a), the action indicated by the model may meet serious management resistance.
4. The use of a simulation model in improving strategic decision making will be dependent upon the number of important variables that must be considered in a particular problem. If only one or two variables influence the entire result, it is evident that the answer provided by the simulation will be directly dependent on values placed on these variables. In introducing a new product line, for example, the key variable is usually the volume of sales. The assumptions concerning what sales volume is dependent on will, in effect, determine the answer.

5. Simulation models appear to have a greater potential for businesses with predictable growth and competitive conditions, such as public utilities.
6. It appears likely that, at least for the near future, simulation models will be limited to relatively large companies. Small businesses do not have the resources to pay for the high cost of developing a business simulation model.

Management Responsibility for Simulation

A simulation model is designed to improve the quality of top management decisions. Management participation in the construction of this model is vital for two reasons:

(1) Management judgment is required in developing the equations that make up the model.
(2) If management is to use the model, it must have confidence in its results. This confidence will only exist when the manager has an intimate knowledge of how the model is constructed, what assumptions and simplifications have been made, and how the estimates of the variables were made.

Although some management participation is usually necessary for any successful computer application, the degree of management participation required in developing a general business simulation model is of an entirely different order of magnitude from other computer applications. *This is an extremely important characteristic from a management point of view.* If management is unwilling or unable to spend the time, it is a waste of money even to start the project.

THE "SYSTEMS" APPROACH TO PROBLEM SOLVING

Closely associated with simulation is a method of problem solving called the "systems" approach. (One has to be careful in reading the literature, however, because the term "systems" is used to mean several different things.) The purpose of this section of the chapter is to describe this approach to problem solving.

Any problem, no matter how simple, can have an infinite number of variables, and the solution to the problem can result in an infinite number of effects, if all variables and all effects were to be considered. For example, take the problem of deciding which of two people to promote to a supervisory job. There are nearly an infinite number of characteristics that could be evaluated. Also, the *total* effect of promoting one over the other will result over the years in an infinite number of differences in the way things are done within the business. Most of these characteristics and effects are very minor and it is necessary to consider only a few of the major items. Problem solving ability is dependent upon picking out the critical variables and evaluating the possible effects of these variables. In other words, it is the intelligent simplification of reality.

Some problems are so complex that when they are simplified to the point where they can be solved by manual methods, they are really different problems. When you solve the simplified version, therefore, you are not really solving the original problem. The computer, together with the new mathematical techniques (simulation, in particular, but also techniques such as linear programming and statistical decision theory), makes a more complex formulation of problems possible. Consequently, one can solve problems now in a way that was not possible before. The use of these techniques can be considered to be the "systems" approach because it allows consideration of a wider range of variables and effects than was possible heretofore.

The "systems" approach, then, consists of freeing ourselves from the restraints inherent in manual methods of solving problems. A great deal of confusion has resulted because the systems approach is often considered to be only the inclusion of a greater number of relevant items in the solution of a problem. People are apt to believe that it is nothing new and say, "This is the way intelligent people always solved problems. Why would any problem solver limit himself to just one aspect of a problem?" There is a great deal of sentiment, therefore, to the effect that the systems approach is "old wine in new bottles." We believe that this sentiment is not justified. When properly done, better solutions can now be obtained than were possible before; and the "systems" approach is a way of thinking about problems to see if better solutions can be obtained from broader examination of problems. Inevitably, as a result of this way of thinking, a better solution will often be obtained without the use of computers and related techniques.

Limitations of "Systems" Approach

There appear to be three limitations in employing the systems approach to business problems. These are:

(1) Many problems do not lend themselves to this approach. This is particularly true of "people" problems—or any other problems, for that matter, where it is not practical to quantify the relevant con-

siderations. Many people will argue that if a problem must be solved it is better to try to quantify the elements of the problem than to rely on human intuition and judgment. In answer to this, one can only say that, with the present state of the arts, this approach is far from operational in the typical business. If a company has money to spend on research in this area, and time to wait for the results, perhaps they should try it. The payoff, however, is more likely in solving problems with a reasonable degree of quantification.

(2) Most problems can still be solved best by present manual methods. One of the dangers of becoming enthusiastic about the systems approach is the tendency to set up overly complex solutions to relatively simple problems.

(3) Where speed of solution is required, complex formulations are frequently not possible. For example, the time required to develop and test a simulation model can be considerable. If an answer to a problem is required in a day or two, it may not be possible to use simulation. As a general rule, it is safe to say that the complex formulation requires considerably more time than more simple manual formulations.

Management Considerations of the Systems Approach

From a management point of view, the systems approach will have its greatest impact in strategic planning. Although this approach is still in its infancy, it appears that better solutions to complex problems involving the forward strategy of the business will be possible. In fact, we expect to see many companies establishing small groups of people who are expert in using computers, simulation, and other techniques in the solution of complex problems. As we see it, these people will not be the "grand strategists" of the business, but they will aid management in the solution of certain types of problems.

Even if no formal group is set up, the systems approach can be of value to management as an approach to problems solving. It requires an explicit consideration of the broader aspects of a problem, and therefore could result in a better solution which might have been overlooked in a narrower approach.

APPENDIX A

All-Purpose Tire Store Simulation

The All-Purpose Tire Store is located in Kingswood, Vermont. A small store, all its tires are sold at a price of $16 apiece. It is solidly established in the region and for a number of years has been getting 15%–20% of the region's tire business. The Vermont tire business is somewhat seasonal in nature with sales peaks in October and April. Sales decline sharply in January and July. These peaks and troughs are roughly 35% above and below the year's average tire sales. This has caused severe fluctuations in both the company's tire inventories and cash position during the year. The company's inventory policy has been to have enough tires on hand at all times to satisfy sales demand for two months. Two months' sales demand is determined by adding up the sales of the past 13 weeks and multiplying the figure by two-thirds. The number of tires to be ordered from the manufacturer is then determined by subtracting the actual number of tires in inventory from this figure. This is the amount ordered during the week. It always takes exactly six weeks for the tires to be delivered after the order has been placed. All deliveries are COD and cost $10 per tire. The manufacturer has always delivered promptly and it is expected that he will continue to do so. All other operating costs are fixed.

Management is concerned by the sharp rises and falls in the cash and inventory balances during the year. Inventory stockouts followed by problems of storing excess inventory were hampering the company's operations. Questions began to be raised by management as to whether their inventory ordering rule was the best under the circumstances and whether changing to another manufacturer who could deliver tires two weeks after the order was sent would be a good idea. At this point it was decided to build a model of the company's operation for purposes of exploring the long-range effect of some of these decisions. The following sets of equations were developed to describe the company's operations:

The amount of cash generated through operations each week is given by the following equation:[1]

(1) TSR $(t - 1/t) - CTP$ $(t - 1/t) - FC$ $(t - 1/t) = CC$ $(t - 1/t)$,
     where:

     TSR $(t - 1/t)$ = Tire sales revenue for the week
     CPT $(t - 1/t)$ = Cash paid for tire purchase by company during the week
     FC $(t - 1/t)$ = Company fixed costs during the week
     CC $(t - 1/t)$ = Increase or decrease in the company's cash position during the week.

---

[1]Note that, in this example, "t" is the *end* of the week and the "1" represents a week.

The company's actual cash position at the end of the week is expressed by the following equation:

(2) $CP(t) = CP(t-1) + CC(t - 1/t)$, where:

$CP(t)$ = Company's cash position at the end of the week.
$CP(t-1)$ = Company's cash position at the end of the previous week.
$CC(t - 1/t)$ = Increase or decrease in company's cash position during the week.

The following two equations simply identify the initial value of the company's cash position and its weekly fixed costs:

(3) $FC(t - 1/t) = 1,000$
(4) $CP(t-1) = 100,000$

The equation given below states the company's weekly dollar sales:

(5) $TSR(t - 1/t) = ASL + WSI(t)$, where:

$TSR(t - 1/t)$ = Tire Sales revenue during week
ASL = Annual sales level smoothed evenly over 52 weeks
$WSI(t)$ = Amount by which this week's sales level is either above or below the annual level.

The following equation represents the behavior of the weekly sales level. It should be noted that it has been assumed that the company's sales pattern conforms to that illustrated in Figure 5–1 rather than that illustrated in Figure 5–2. It is not difficult to write an equation which will simulate a pattern similar to that of Figure 5–2. The equations are somewhat more complex, however, and it is more difficult to grasp their intuitive significance. For the purpose of clarifying the explanation, the sales pattern of Figure 5–1 has been assumed.

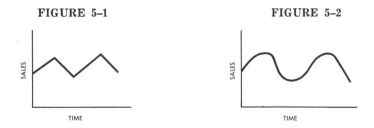

FIGURE 5–1   FIGURE 5–2

The following equation represents the calculation of the weekly increment to the average weekly sales level:

(6) $WSI(t) = WSI(t-1) - A$, when $TSR(t - 2/t - 1) \geq D$
$WSI(t) = WSI(t-1) + A$, when $TSR(t - 2/t - 1) \leq C$
$WSI(t) = WSI(t-1) - A$, when $D > TSR(t - 2/t - 1) > C$,
    and $WSI(t-1) < WSI(t-2)$

$WSI\ (t)\ =\ WSI\ (t-1)\ +\ A$, when $D > TSR\ (t-2/t-1) > C$, and $WSI\ (t-1) > WSI\ (t-2)$, where:

$WSI\ (t)$ = Amount by which this week's sales level is either above or below the annual level

$WSI\ (t-1)$ = Amount by which last week's sales level is either above or below the annual level

$WSI\ (t-2)$ = Amount by which two weeks' ago sales level is either above or below the annual level

$TSR\ (t-2/t-1)$ = Tire sales revenue last week

A = The increment that either increases or decreases a week's sales level from that of the preceding week

D = Maximum weekly sales level attainable under present operations

C = Minimum weekly sales level attainable under present operations.

The following equations represent the values of the constants and the initial values of the variables for the last two equations:

(7) $ASL = 5{,}000$

(8) $D = 6{,}750$

(9) $C = 3{,}250$

(10) $A = 270$

(11) $WSI\ (t-1) = 0$

(12) $WSI\ (t-2) = -270$

These equations may appear formidable, but they really are not. They are designed to increase the volume of sales by a fixed increment (A) each week until a maximum weekly sales volume (D) is reached. Then the sales are decreased by (A) each week until a minimum sales volume (C) is reached. Then, the sales volume begins to increase again and this pattern continues for as many weeks as the simulation is run. Incidentally, these equations demonstrate how involved putting even simple mathematics into equation form is when decision rules are involved.

The preceding sets of equations have defined the company's pattern of cash generation. Now a group of equations which will satisfactorily define the company's inventory and ordering cycle must be developed.

The following equation defines the company's tire inventory. (The figures represent the number of tires on hand rather than their dollar value.)

(13) $IT\ (t) = IT\ (t-1) - TS\ (t-1/t) + TRM\ (t-1/t)$, where:

$IT\ (t)$ = Tire inventory at end of week

$IT\ (t-1)$ = Tire inventory at end of previous week

$TS\ (t-1/t)$ = Total number of tires sold during the week

$TRM\ (t-1/t)$ = Tires received from the manufacturer during the week

The next two equations relate TS $(t - 1/t)$ back to equation 1:

(14) $TS \ (t - 1/t) = \dfrac{TSR \ (t - 1/t)}{TP}$, where:

   $TS \ (t - 1/t)$ = Number of tires sold during the week
   $TSR \ (t - 1/t)$ = Tire sales revenue for the week
   TP = Selling price of a tire

(15) $TP = 16$

(16) $IT \ (t - 1) = 2,000$

The company's desired level of inventory at the end of the week can be expressed by the following equation:

(17) $TID \ (t) = 2/3 \displaystyle\sum_{a=1}^{13} TS \ (t - a)$, where:

   $TID \ (t)$ = Tire inventory desired at the end of the week.

   $\displaystyle\sum_{a=1}^{13} TS \ (t - a)$ = Number of tires sold over the past 13 weeks

   $TID \ (t) = 3,450$

The following equation defines the number of purchase orders that are sent out each week:

(18) $TPOR \ (t - 1/t) = TID \ (t) - I \ (t)$, where:

   $TPOR \ (t - 1/t)$ = The number of tires ordered from the manufacturer during the week
   $TID \ (t)$ = Tire inventory desired at the end of the week
   $I \ (t)$ = Actual tire inventory on hand at the end of the week.

The next equation defines the number of tires being received each week:

(19) $TRM \ (t - 1/t) = TPOR \ (t - 7/t - 6)$, where:

   $TRM \ (t - 1/t)$ = Tires received during week
   $TPOR \ (t - 7/t - 6)$ = Tires ordered six weeks ago.

The next two equations relate the number of tires purchased back to the cost of tires item mentioned in equation (1):

(20) $CPT \ (t - 1/t) = TRM \ (t - 1/t) \times TC$, where:

   $CPT \ (t - 1/t)$ = Cash paid for tires during the week
   $TRM \ (t - 1/t)$ = Tires received during week
   TC = Cost of an individual tire

(21) $TC = 10$

(22) $TPOR\ (t - 7/t - 6) = 300$
       $TPOR\ (t - 6/t - 5) = 300$
              *   *
              *   *
       $TPOR\ (t - 2/t - 1) = 300$

This completes construction of the model. Running through one week's operation will indicate how it can be used to generate useful information. (The technical term for this is hand simulation.) No attempt will be made to arrange the equations in their optimal order for computer solution. This solution will merely indicate one way of arranging the equations for a solution.

The first equation in the model to be solved is equation 6, which reveals how much the week's sales are above or below the year's average. Equation 11 indicates $WSI\ (t - 1) = 0$ and equation 12 indicates $WSI\ (t - 2) = -270$. Therefore, $WSI\ (t - 1) > WSI\ (t - 2)$. Comparison of equations 8 and 9 with $TSR\ (t - 2/t - 1)$ indicates that $C < TSR\ (t - 2/t - 1) < D$. Therefore, the option of equation 6 which should be used is the one which says $WSI\ (t) = WSI\ (t - 1) + A$. Since equation 10 indicates that $A = 270$, it follows that $WSI\ (t) = 0 + 270 = 270$.

Taking the results of equation 6 and equation 7, equation 5 calculates total tire sales revenue as follows:

$TSR\ (t - 1/t) = 5,000 + 270 = \boxed{5,270}$

The next equation to be presented for solution is equation 19, which indicates the number of tires to be received during the week. Equation 22 says $TPOR\ (t - 7/t - 6) = 300$ so $TRM\ (t - 1/t) = 300$. Then, since equation 21 indicates that $TC = 10$, equation 20 can be solved to show how much cash was paid for tires during the week:

$CPT\ (t - 1/t) = 300 \times 10 = \$3,000$

Equation 17 is then solved to find the desired tire inventory:

$TID\ (t) = 3,450$

Attention is next directed to the solution of equation 13. Using the result of equation 5 ($TSR\ (t - 1/t) = 5,270$) and equation 15 where $TP = 16$, equation 14 indicates that 330 tires were sold during the week. Using the results of equation 16 [$IT\ (t - 1) = 2,000$], equation 14 [$TS\ (t - 1/t) = 330$], and equation 19 [$TRM\ (t - 1/t) = 300$], equation 13 indicates that tire inventory at the end of the week is 1,970 tires.

Using the result of equation 17 ($TID\ (t) = 3,450$) equation 18 indicates the number of tires ordered from the manufacturer at the end of the week would be 1,480.

Equation 1 can now be solved. The results of equation 20 [$CPT\ (t - 1/t) = 3,000$], equation 3 [$FC\ (t - 1/t) = 1,000$], and equation 5 [$TSR\ (t - 1/t) = 5,270$] indicate that $CC\ (t - 1/t) = +1,270$. Equation 2 can then be solved with the aid of equation 4 [$CP\ (t - 1) = 100,000$] to give the result $CP\ (t) =$

$101,270. At this juncture the simulation model has completed one week's operation.

If this problem were being solved on a computer, the following changes would be made preparatory to beginning calculations for the second week:

(1)   Amount in location CP (t) would be moved to location CP ($t - 1$) (updating equation 4).

(2)   Amount in location WSI (t) would be moved to location WSI ($t - 1$) (updating equation 11).

(3)   Amount in location WSI ($t - 1$) is moved to location WSI ($t - 2$) (updating equation 12).

(4)   Amount in location IT (t) is moved to location IT ($t - 1$) (updating equation 16).

(5)   Amount in location TS ($t - 12$) is moved to location TS ($t - 13$), amount in location TS ($t - 11$) is moved to location TS ($t - 12$), etc. This allows equation 17 to be updated.

(6)   Amount in $TPOR$ ($t - 6/t - 5$) 15 is moved to location $TPOR$ ($t - 7/t - 6$), amount in location $TPOR$ ($t - 5/t - 4$) is moved to location $TPOR$ ($t - 6/t - 5$), etc.

The model would then go through the same series of computations for the second week of operations. This process can be continued for as many weeks of operations as desired. The output figures concerning cash balances and inventory can either be listed tabularly or plotted graphically.

The All-Purpose Tire Store management must then decide whether this output appears realistic in terms of the company's actual experience. If it is satisfactory to them, the model can be accepted as having captured many of the essentials of the environment which the model is simulating. Otherwise, the equations must be modified and possibly some new ones added.

When it is complete, it can be used to analyze the effect of making certain alterations in the model. Some of the areas that management might want to test include:

(1)   The effect of using an ordering rule which recognizes the seasonal nature of the company's business.

(2)   The effect of responding more slowly (or more quickly) to changes in sales pattern as far as ordering more or less in inventory. A decision rule which would cause the company to make its ordering pattern respond more quickly to the changes in sales pattern would be the following rule. Desired inventory level at the end of a week should be 7 times as great as the week's sales. This could be accomplished by introducing the following change into the model:

Change equation 17 to:

$$TID\ (t) = 7\ TS\ (t - 1/t)$$

(3)   The effect of reducing the time lag between the time the product is ordered and the time it is delivered. Reduction of this time lag from six to two weeks could be accomplished by introducing the following change into the model:

Change equation 19 to:

$$TRM \ (t - 1/t) \ = \ TPOR \ (t - 2/t - 1)$$

Chapter 6

Information Retrieval

An information retrieval system consists of a set of procedures for
storing items in a file in an organized way, so that they can be found
in the future by people who are interested. A corollary to the definition
is that items will not be located by someone who is not interested in
their contents. The items might be facts, words, sentences, or documents. The file is constantly updated by the addition of new or more
reliable information and by the deletion of obsolete, incorrect, or
unreliable information. Retrieval systems are necessary whenever
data is stored and the exact requirements and timing of its ultimate
uses are not known.

The ease of defining information retrieval does not mean that the
underlying theory and the problems with which it is concerned are
simple ones. Quite the converse is true. Some of the most complex
problems which face logicians, scientists, and linguists today are
information retrieval problems. The statement of the problem is
simple, but its solution is complex.

Although tremendous research activity in the field of information
retrieval during the past ten years has resulted in the publication of

many papers treating the problem in various professional journals, unfortunately, nearly all this activity has been by scientists and operations research specialists. Most of these papers are too technical to be of value to the businessman. The subject, of course, has not been completely ignored in business publications. Several articles have appeared that were very enthusiastic about the long-range potential of information retrieval for business problems. A 1960 *Fortune* magazine article even suggested that information retrieval in 1960 occupied the same position as EDP did in 1950. It expected that by 1965 expenditures in the United States for information retrieval equipment would jump to $100 million a year (from a level of $2 million a year) and would double every three years thereafter.[1]

Progress in the technical development and large-scale marketing of information retrieval systems has proceeded at a slower rate, and its ultimate impact appears to be more limited, than anticipated above. In our opinion, however, the nature of information retrieval problems and the tools for resolving them are sufficiently important that they should be understood by businessmen. This chapter therefore, has two objectives:

(1) To present a description of the nature of information retrieval systems and the general types of problems they are designed to handle.

(2) To describe some of the specific types of business problems which information retrieval techniques may be able to solve.

Requirements of Effective Information Retrieval Systems

The equipment and techniques used in an information retrieval system will vary widely, depending on the characteristics of the environment. Some of the more important of these characteristics are:

(1) Number of items in the file

(2) Number of requests for items from the file received each day

(3) The nature of the requests (does the user know precisely what items he wants or does he need a considerable amount of assistance in locating the particular items relevant to his interests?)

(4) Funds available to support the file's operations.

Despite the varying structures of different information retrieval systems, however, the effectiveness of any individual system must be judged by how well it manages to meet the following five criteria:

---

[1] Francis Bello, "How to Cope with Information," *Fortune*, September, 1960.

(1) Does the IR system retrieve stored information within a satisfactory time? Once the user has decided he needs a set of facts, very little time should pass before the system can locate them for him. For example: in a library, once the librarian is given the specific code number of a book, it should take only a short time for it to be located (providing, of course, that it is in the library). Thus, for many proposed IR systems, a Random access file attached to a computer may be necessary because of the importance of having rapid access to randomly selected items.

(2) Does the IR system effectively correlate information to a desired degree of specificity, considering the character of its user's needs? For example, if you want information on electric air coolers, the system should be set up so that you will not have to search all the literature on electricity, air, and coolers to find the relevant information.

(3) Does the system contain valuable information and provide methods for screening out that which is less valuable? In other words, does it have some form of quality control? Several different problems are involved here:

   (a) Material should be excluded from the system that has little substantive content.

   (b) As material becomes obsolete, it should be removed from the system.

   (c) The system should be indexed in such a way that a user can be quickly directed to those items which are relevant to his needs.

(4) Where appropriate, does the system provide access to expert human assistance? In many circumstances, the advice of an expert will be of far more value than information gathered by searching currently available literature.

(5) Is the cost of the system reasonable in the light of its accomplishments? The degree to which the first four objectives should be achieved must be balanced against the cost of the system. The economies of operating the system place a definite upper limit as to the speed and thoroughness of retrieval that it is practicable to include in the system.

Research in Information Retrieval

This section describes the areas of information retrieval in which particularly important research is currently being carried out. Its purpose is to clarify the nature of the problems that information retrieval techniques can be useful in solving.

Theory

The principal thrust of the work in information retrieval theory has been directed to the problem of indexing. The purpose of an indexing system is to maximize the "precision" and "recall" ratios for each user of the file.

$$\text{Precision ratio} = \frac{\text{Number of relevant documents retrieved}}{\text{Total number of documents retrieved}}$$

$$\text{Recall ratio} = \frac{\text{Total number of relevant documents retrieved}}{\text{Total number of relevant documents in the collection}}$$

An ideal system would provide the user with a value of one for both ratios. In practice, current systems never achieve this, although constant efforts to improve their nature are being made.

When an indexing system must be selected for a particular collection of material, there are several different systems from which to choose. The most common of these include:

a) *Random Indexing.* Each item is placed in the file as it is received. When information is desired, the entire collection must be searched. This is adequate for small collections, where search time is somewhat less than a minute.

b) *Classified Indexing.* This is what is found in most library catalogue systems. Each item is classified under one heading such as author, title, or subject. This system makes it very difficult to locate the specific items which are relevant to a particular topic. For example, a book whose title is the "Theory of Systems" might have some excellent chapters on PERT. This indexing scheme, however, would never classify it in such a way that a person interested in PERT literature could spot its applicability from the index. This type of index has a low "precision" ratio.

c) *Hierarchical Indexing.* Each *item* (book, set of facts, and so forth) is represented by *one* card. The items are classified by a series of subject headings which are ordered from a broad level of meaning down to a very specific level. For example, in a collection of business literature, one classification category might be *marketing.* Within this category, items might be arranged into subcategories such a pricing, promotion, and competition. Each of these subcategories might be further subdivided. It is a difficult task to define these categories so that they contain the appropriate items. Often particular items will contain information relevant to several subcategories. A set of rules must be developed to handle these situations. Thus, the users must be very familar with the system's organization before they can make effective use of it. These indexes also tend to have low "precision" and "recall" ratios.

d) *Inverted Indexing.* This recently developed technique is considered particularly useful for automated information retrieval projects. Instead of preparing one index card for each document, a card is prepared for each concept contained in the document. A concept refers to a single idea. All documents which contain information relevant to this concept will have their document number punched into an index card. These cards are called descriptor cards. Depending on the degree of depth desired in the indexing system and the document's contents, the document number will be punched on one or more descriptor cards. Preliminary research has indicated that the most complex documents can be completely indexed by 100 or less descriptor cards. To prevent the problem of synonyms (several descriptor cards containing the same concept expressed in different words; an example of this might be "ferric oxide" v. "iron rust"), a thesaurus that lists all synonyms is developed concurrently with the system.

As the system becomes larger, such things as homonyms and the grammatical use of words must be identified to allow the item to be properly handled. For example, the index should distinguish between "rubbing alcohol" and "drinking alcohol." Also, the different uses of the word "man" must be distinguished in the following two sentences:

1) A *man* is sailing the ship.
2) We are going to *man* the ship.

In this case the grammatical use of the word "man" will indicate how the sentence should be classified.

One of the characteristics of this system is that the number of descriptors does not increase proportionately with the number of items. For example, it has been shown that a file containing 10,000 items will require a little more than 5,000 descriptors, while a file of 100,000 items will require less than 10,000 descriptors.

Inverted indexing has several advantages over the other indexing systems:

1) Items relevant to the user's interest can be located quickly. The user merely selects the concept cards that interest him and checks to see which document numbers appear on all or most of the descriptor cards.
2) It is easy to add new items to the system.
3) The index does not grow indiscriminately. The more documents that are added to the system, the slower the growth in the number of descriptors.

Further research in developing more powerful indexing techniques is being carried on in a number of places. For example, the National Science Foundation is sponsoring a project at the Association of Special Libraries and Information Bureaux of London. Eighteen thousand documents in the field of aeronautics were selected and classified in four different ways. It is planned to search these indexes with more than 1,000 questions to obtain significant data on the efficiency of the various factors involved in indexing technical documents. Particular attention will be paid to the incremental results which can occur from greater depth in indexing.

The second problem involved in indexing is how to index an item once the indexing scheme has been determined. An example of the type of research in this area is the work being done by Peter Luhn at IBM. He is developing various mechanical and statistical ways of indexing documents (using descriptors) and then preparing abstracts of these documents. His work is based on two key assumptions:

1)   There is a very small probability that the same word is used to reflect more than one notion in any single paper.
2)   There is a very small probability that an author will use different words to describe the same notion in a single paper.

The contents of the document are key punched onto IBM cards. The information on the cards is then transferred to magnetic tape for processing on a computer. The computer then counts the number of times each word appears. Through comparisons with a tape of "noise" words, words such as "and," "the," are eliminated from the analysis. The articles can then be indexed by the ten or fifteen remaining words which appear most frequently in the text.

To prepare an abstract of an article the computer then computes a packing power fraction (defined below) for each sentence.

$$\text{Packing power fraction} = \frac{\text{(Number of descriptor words in the sentence)}}{\text{Number of significant words in a sentence}}$$

Descriptor word—One of the 15 or 20 most frequently appearing words in the text (excluding noise words).
Significant word—Any word in a sentence that is not a noise word.

The abstract is then prepared by writing out the eight or ten sentences with the highest Packing Power Fraction. Preliminary results with this technique have been very favorable, and it is being developed further. The essential problem being tackled here is to find a way to reduce the time-consuming and costly process of having people do the indexing and abstracting.

These are but a few of the specific research projects in the field of information retrieval theory. The overall direction of this research is to develop better (both in efficiency and cost) means of describing a particular item so that an unknown user can decide from its indexing whether the item is relevant to his needs. These research projects will continue to focus heavily on both the structure of the English language and the characteristics of the human associative function.

Technology

The second important field of information retrieval research is in equipment development.

Large files of information can be efficiently searched by high-speed computers. The storage capacity of random access and magnetic tape units plus the processing speed of today's computers appear to be adequate to handle current information retrieval projects. Further developments in this field, therefore, are not likely to improve significantly the information retrieval process, except in so far as rental costs of the equipment are reduced.

The critical area of research is to improve the speed and cost of getting the information onto magnetic tape. The volume of detail involved in the typical IR project makes a breakthrough here mandatory before many large-scale IR projects can be implemented. The key punch is an expensive way to convert information retrieval data into a form suitable for machine processing. Assuming an operator rate of 5,000 strokes/hour, operator wages of $1.80 an hour, and keypunch machine rental of $60 a month, the cost per stroke is $.0004. For information that is highly compact, such as payroll or inventory control data, this cost is not prohibitive. However, information retrieval schemes such as the one by Peter Luhn require enormous amounts of data to be key punched. The machine then searches it for a few relevant items. Converting the data for processing in this fashion, where only a few items will be of interest, is decidedly uneconomic.

Developmental work is being done on optical scanners at several companies including Farrington, IBM, and Bell Laboratories. These machines will automatically translate the contents of a page to either punches in punched cards or spots on magnetic tape, thus bypassing the key punch machine. A beam of light is shone on a piece of paper and the pattern of the reflected beam is compared to patterns previously stored in the machine's memory to identify which letter or number is being examined. It is believed that optical scanners will ultimately be able to read at a rate of faster than 1,000 characters a second. Currently few of these machines are on the market. One of them is the IBM 1428 optical character reader. It is capable of optically reading alphabetic and numeric data at a rate of up to 480 characters a second. This machine when connected with a 1401 computer can read information directly into memory. Useful as it is, it is still subject to some important limitations:

1) It can only read information at a rate equivalent to 360 cards/ minute. The 1402 card read unit can read 800 cards/minute.
2) It can only handle documents ranging in size from 2¾" high x 5⅛ wide to 3⅔" high and 8¾" wide.
3) The input data must be typewritten in IBM 407 font.
4) Monthly rental is $3,000.

The basic physical principles for handling optical scanning have been developed; they have not, however, been refined technologically so that they are economically feasible for many applications.

Technical research is also helping in reducing the time required to locate an item physically, once it has been identified as being desired. The current research in microfilming and microminiaturization is particularly relevant here. Documents can currently be reduced in size by a factor of 1,000. Through using these developments, files have been considerably reduced in size and access time has been shortened.

One project undertaken at IBM has carried this development to an advanced stage. Project Walnut resulted in the development of a machine which stores documents on 0.9 by 15.5 inch strips of film. An index provides the storage location in the machine of the particular items that are desired. Using random access principles similar to those found in a random access file, the machine quickly produces the necessary strips of film for the user. Significant improvements are expected in the next five years as a result of this research.

In addition to the above areas, a number of other fields in technical research may have important side effects for information retrieval systems. These include the development of hybrid analog-digital computers, development of high-speed access memory devices, and improved magnetic tape.

Business Applications of Informal Retrieval

Of the types of business information listed in Chapter 1, information retrieval techniques apply principally to documentary, non-recurring, historical, nonaction information. First, since only documentary information can be stored and retrieved, all nondocumentary information is eliminated. Second, there is no retrieval problem with recurring information; it is simply given regularly to the people who require it. (There may be a problem if there is an occasional demand for previously published recurring information; this, however, is then nonrecurring information.) Third, nonrecurring action information is used principally in strategic planning and, consequently, requires special studies. It is very difficult to anticipate what information these special studies will require, and, in general, a retrieval system for this type of information is uneconomic.

From the foregoing, it can be seen that modern information retrieval techniques are not vital to most businesses. In some companies, however, the efficient retrieval of certain types of information can be very valuable. In other companies, modern information retrieval techniques, although not vital to the welfare of the business, can provide improved methods for storing and handling certain kinds of data.

The following are some of the areas of a company's operation where information retrieval techniques may be of assistance:

a) Classification of published research developments. The effectiveness of research and development activities can be improved through better classification of material in technical journals or in research papers prepared by people within the company. This must be accomplished at both the industry and company level. Time and money are frequently wasted by duplicating research that has already been done, and the results published in some journal. Finding the place where these results were published, however, is often difficult. For example, the research director of a large company recently estimated that if it cost less than $100,000 to do a particular item of research, it was cheaper to proceed directly with the research than to attempt a literature search to find an article that would be pertinent to the particular problem. A well developed technical literature index could be invaluable for this situation.

   The costs of developing and maintaining such a file are not inconsiderable. An alternative under experiment in several industries is to have a number of companies in the industry contribute to the development of an independent library, the contents of which would be available to the participating companies.

b) Storage of financial and operating statistics. When statistical data about past operations are needed, the IR system will be able to provide the necessary details. This could eliminate a considerable amount of file space and should facilitate the communication of information throughout the company. An adjunct to this system has been developed by one large company. Not only will this system ultimately provide detailed factual information, but it will also be able to show what elements went into the creation of the particular piece of information.

c) Profile of people's activities and interests. Profiles of people's activities and interests are developed and maintained in a file and updated every three months. This would serve the following two purposes:

1. As the library acquires more information, it can review periodically the profiles of the people against the index description and selectively distribute abstracts of the material to people who might be interested in it.

2. In large companies, the problems of locating people who can best give advice on a particular subject can be quite critical. Such a file could be of use in allowing the company to take fuller advantage of its human resources.

d) Information retained for legal reasons. When a large number of items must be kept for several years because of legal reasons, simple information retrieval techniques may be helpful. Microfilming much of the material may prove to be cheaper than maintaining a large warehouse of obsolete paper. Similarly, the introduction of a simple indexing system may reduce the search time on the infrequent occasions when specific items in the file are needed.

e) Storing of blueprints. Some companies, such as automobile manufacturers, produce literally millions of engineering drawings yearly. Since many of these drawings can be used for several years, a system of filing and classification can save the cost of redrawing a blueprint already in existence.

Although modern information retrieval techniques are not as important to business as many other computer uses, information retrieval has great potential in other fields, such as law, medicine, and government. Consequently, a considerable number of new developments, both in theory and technology, are expected in information retrieval within the next few years.

Section III

CASE STUDIES

BLACKWELL AND MASON

In January 1964, Mr. Harold McGowan, manager in charge of the data processing section at Blackwell and Mason, was reviewing a recent top management decision to put the monthly "Sales Report" on a mechanized basis.

A medium-sized manufacturer of ball bearings, Blackwell and Mason had recently installed a number of IBM punched card machines for use in mechanizing their payroll and inventory control report systems. Blackwell's initial experience with punched card equipment was considered highly successful by top management and efforts were made to discover other applications of the machines. One of the applications discussed and approved was the preparation of the monthly sales report.

SALES REPORT

Every month the sales department issued a report showing:

1. The inventory number of each item sold during the month.
2. The number of units of each item sold during the month.
3. The total revenue received from the sale of each type of inventory item.
4. The total cost of each type of item sold during the month.
5. The contribution to overhead and profit made by each inventory item.

The monthly reports are summarized into quarterly reports at the end of each quarter. Also, a year's end report is prepared which presents the same information for each item, broken down by quarters. These reports are considered an integral part of the company's decision-making process and it is hoped that their mechanization will lead to both more rapid preparation and further accuracy.

All of Blackwell's sales transactions are recorded on a standard sales slip which contains, among other things, the following items:

1. Inventory numbers of the items sold. (Blackwell and Mason used an inventory coding classification which required the use of five digits for each inventory item style.)

2. Number of units of each item sold (a typical sales order contained a request for 50 pieces of a particular style. To date no individual request for more than 2,000 pieces had been received, nor in McGowan's opinion was this likely to occur.)
3. Sales price and sales total of each item. For nearly all items the sales price was somewhat under $1,000 and the items sales totals typically varied between $100 and $200,000.
4. Document number of the sales slip (these numbers were six digits in length).
5. Date.

The sales department receives the sales slips from its salesmen and batches them in groups of fifty. Attached to each batch is an adding machine tape which shows both the total number of items sold on the fifty sales slips and also the total dollar amount of sales.

NEW PROCEDURE FOR PREPARING THE SALES REPORT

Mr. McGowan was considering adopting the following procedure to prepare the report:

(1) The data processing section would receive the batches and edit them for completeness. After the documents were edited, the detail cards would be punched from the data on the sales slips. A batch control card would be prepared from the adding machine tape which contained the following information:
   a. The batch number—each batch processed by the sales department would be assigned a number for control purposes.
   b. The date.
   c. Total number of items sold in batch.
   d. Total dollar sales amount in batch.
   The purpose of this card would be to prepare a zero balance report, the function of which will be explained shortly.
(2) After the information was key punched and verified, the detail cards would then be merged with a deck of inventory master cards. This deck of inventory master cards would contain one card for each inventory number and item per unit cost (this cost varied between $20 and $3,000). As changes occurred this deck would be updated.
(3) After the detail cards were merged with the inventory master cards, the cost per unit would be gang-punched (interspersed gang-punching) into the detail cards. The detail cards would then pass through a calculator which would multiply the number of units sold by the unit cost and punch the product in the card. Then the detail cards would be merged with the batch control cards and a zero balance report would be prepared.
   The zero balance report would take the total of units and sales dollars in the detail cards and subtract from it the total of units

and sales dollars in the batch control cards. The result should be zero. If the balance was zero, it could be safely assumed that no detail cards had been lost and no cards had been mispunched in the units or sales dollars columns. If it was not zero, the section would be able to take steps to rectify what mistakes might be there.

(4) After the accuracy of the detail cards had been proved by the zero balance listing, the monthly sales report would be prepared. The detail cards would then be filed away. In order to save filing space in the data processing section and to speed preparation of the year-end report, Mr. McGowan was planning to attach a reproducer to the accounting machine and punch out a summary card for each item of inventory at the time of the preparation of the quarterly reports. This card would summarize the total units sold, the total sales revenue, and total cost incurred for each item of inventory during the period. The old cards could then be shipped out for storage and ultimate destruction.

IBM MACHINES USED IN PREPARING THE REPORT

In view of the management's interest in the system and the likelihood of being assigned more projects of this nature, Mr. McGowan considered it important to ascertain approximately how many hours of machine time for each type machine would be utilized by the project; and also, roughly, how soon after the end of each month, quarter, and year, he would be able to have the reports ready. He knew it would take approximately five business days after the end of the month for the last sales slips to be routed through to the data processing section. He also knew that during the course of a month, an average of 1,000 different inventory item styles were sold and that 20,000 sales slips were prepared, each containing an average of four different item styles on it. (There are 10,000 different parts in inventory.)

In making the calculation he decided he could plan on the use of the following equipment:[1]

3	026	key punches
3	056	verifiers
1	088	collator
1	082	sorter
1	519	reproducer
1	407	accounting machine
1	604	calculating punch

[1]Certain cost and operating characteristics of these machines are described in the Appendix.

Finally Mr. McGowan was concerned with the problem of deriving some cost figures for management for the operation. He knew that the average machine operator earned $1.81/hour, and that overhead was being charged to his department at the rate of 100 percent of direct labor. He decided that because of the nature of this operation and the machines that were being utilized, he could assume that all machines required a full-time attendant except for the 407, which would take up a third of an operator's time. IBM cards cost $2.30/thousand.

QUESTIONS

1. Design the following cards:
   a) Daily Detail Cards
   b) Batch Control Cards
   c) Inventory Master Card
2. Prepare an operational flow chart for the monthly procedure. (Make any changes that you wish in Mr. McGowan's procedure.) Be sure to consider the necessity for use of such machines as collators and sorters.
3. How many hours of machine time will be required each month to complete the sales report? How long after the end of the month will the report be available?
4. What will be the annual cost of preparing these reports? (Assume that the machines will be rented.)

APPENDIX

Key Punch

This machine transfers information available in written form on documents into punched holes on a card. This is accomplished by an operator hitting keys on a keyboard, similar to that of a typewriter, which cause the punching of the proper letter, digit, or special character in a card column.

The machine also duplicates cards and gang-punches (see paragraph on *collator* for definition of gang-punching) information into a deck of cards. Because of the relative slowness of this machine compared to the *reproducer*, these later functions are usually only done by a key punch on a replacement basis—i.e., when a card is mutilated to the extent that it cannot run through one of the higher speed machines (usually a relatively small nick on one of the edges will be sufficient to cause this), or when only a small number of cards is to be processed.

The speed of these machines is a function of the efficiency of the operator and the difficulty of interpreting the source document. Six thousand punching strokes an hour, however, is fairly close to maximum achievable level. The 026 key punch rents for $60 a month.

Verifier

Card verifying checks the accuracy of the original key punching. An operator verifies the original punching by depressing the keys of a verifier while reading from the same source data. The machine compares the key depressed with the hole already punched in the card. A difference causes the machine to stop, indicating a discrepancy between the two operations, and consequently the existence of an error. The speed of the machine is similar to the 026 key punch. The 056 key verifier rents for $50 a month.

Sorter

This machine arranges punched cards into numerical or alphabetic order. The machine operator is told which columns compose the field for sorting purposes. (For example, card columns 10–13 might compose a field by which the cards should be sorted.) The machine sorts one column at a time. Therefore, to sort a deck of cards by a four column numerical field would require the entire deck of cards to be sent through the machine four times, one time for each column they are to be sorted on. For a four column alphabetic field, it is necessary to run the cards through the sorter eight times (two for each letter).

Sorting permits
1) Arrangement of data in numerical or alphabetic order;
2) Arrangement of cards into groups;
3) Selection of desired cards from a large group of cards;
4) Arrangement of a group of cards in such a way that by use of a collator, they can be merged into another deck so that the completed deck will be in a desired sequence.

Machine	*Monthly Rental*	*Cards/Min.*
082	$55	650
084	$250	2,000

Collator

This machine performs five primary functions.

1. *Sequence Checking.* The collator can check a deck of cards to determine whether or not they are in order. As the deck passes through the machine the desired columns of one card are compared with that of the card ahead, and if it is out of sequence, the machine stops.
2. *Primary Card Selection.* The machine will select a particular card or cards from those which are run through the machine. For example, the machine could be made to set aside all cards which have the number 26 punched in columns 10 and 11.

3. *Merging.* The machine can merge two decks of cards already in sequence into a single ordered deck.
4. *Matching.* The machine compares two decks of cards to determine that there is a card or group of cards in one deck to match each card or group of cards in the other deck. ("Matching" means that they have identical punches in a specified field of the card.) After the machine has compared the cards it sends them to different places in the machine depending on whether they do or do not have a matching card.
5. *Merging with Selection.* The machine compares two files of cards and merges the matching pairs into a single file. Unmatched cards in either or both files are selected and form separate files.

Machine	Monthly Rental	Cards Min.
085	$125	240–480—depending on operation
088	$415	650–1,300—depending on operation

Reproducer

This machine will perform the following functions:
1. *Reproducing.* In this operation, all or any selected parts of the information punched into one deck of cards can be punched into another deck of cards.
2. *Gang-punching.* This is the automatic copying of punched information from a card into one or more succeeding cards. To illustrate, let us assume that it is desired to punch the number 22 into columns 50 and 51 of all cards in the new deck of cards. Through the operation of gang-punching this may be achieved. Gang-punching may be either done separately or in conjunction with a reproducing operation.

   The reproducer will also do interspersed gang-punching. Here there are a number of cards called master cards, each of which has information to be transferred to one or more subsequent cards. Each master card immediately precedes the cards to which the master card's information is to be transferred. Information in the master card is automatically punched into all following cards until a new master card is read (the master card has a special punch in it that enables the machine to recognize it as a master card). The punching pattern then changes to conform with the new master card.
3. *Mark Sensing.* In this operation information recorded in the form of pencil marks on IBM cards is automatically transcribed as punched holes in these cards.
4. *Summary Punching.* The reproducer can be attached to an accounting machine (type 402, 403, or 407) by means of a cable. Whenever the accounting machine produces a total or subtotal the reproducer

will produce a summary card containing this and any other relevant information

Machine	Monthly Rental	Cards Min.
514	$125	100
519	$135	100

Interpreter

This machine reads the information punched into a card and prints this information onto the card. Interpreting is advantageous when punched cards are used as documents on which additional information is written or marked, or wherever reference to filing operations is involved.

Machines	Monthly Rental	Cards Min.
552	$270–305	100
557	$270 305	100

Accounting Machine

The accounting machine has two functions.
1. To print alphabetic and numerical data from punched cards onto paper in an orderly and meaningful fashion.
2. To total data by proper classification.

The machine can do two different types of printing.
1. *Detail Printing:* The printing of information from each card as the card passes through the machine. This is used to prepare the reports that show complete detail about each transaction.
2. *Group Printing:* Summarizing data on groups of cards and printing the total on a report. This is used in preparing reports requiring summarized totals.

These machines can produce three types of totals—major, intermediate and minor. For example, the same report could give the total company sales, sales by territory and sales by the individual salesman within each territory. This same report could not, however, further break down each salesman's sales by product line.

Machine	Monthly Rental	Cards Min.
402, 403, 407	$220–420	100–150

Calculating Machine

This is the most powerful machine discussed here and lies just below the small computer range. The IBM 604 adds, subtracts, multiplies and divides amounts punched in the same card or in successive cards. It performs these operations repetitively and in combination as required for punching results for all general types of calculating problems. Up to 21 digits may be read for calculating from a card and up to 29 digits can be punched for results.

Information can be simultaneously gang-punched with the results of the calculation. Straight gang-punching or interspersed gang-punching can be performed, either in combination with calculation or as an independent operation.

Machine	*Rental Price Range*	*Purchase Price Range*	*Cards 'Min.*
604	$330–550/mo.	$20,200–25,900	150

J. L. CARVER CO. (A)

The J. L. Carver Co. manufactured and sold supplies and equipment to bakeries, soda fountains, ice cream and confectionery manufacturers, restaurants and institutions in 13 northeastern and eastern states. The majority of the 8,850 items in the product line were purchased for resale, but the company manufactured ovens and other bakery equipment and more than 100 varieties and flavors of food products.

The firm was founded in 1877 when Mr. J. L. Carver set up shop in Boston as a wholesale grocer. A few years later he withdrew from the grocery field to serve the bakery trade exclusively. In the early 1880's his concern made the first commercial pie filling used in this country. Other fillings, jams and jellies were added in subsequent years.

The Carver items were divided into three product groups as follows:

Group A
Products made by the company (25% of total sales)

A–1	Jams, jellies, pie fillings and bakers' specialities
A–2	Soda fountain and ice cream supplies
A–3	Extracts
A–4	Powders and icing bases

Group B
Products purchased by the company (70% of total sales)

B–5	Pie fruits, dried and glacéd fruits and nuts
B–5S	Staple wholesale groceries (shortenings, cocoa, dessert preparations, tea, etc.)
B–6	Specialities (powdered milk, molasses, malt, spices)
B–7	Canned goods (fruits and vegetables)
B–8	Frozen goods

Group C
All products purchased by the company except C–9 (5% of total sales)

C–9	Ovens and other equipment
C–10	All small equipment and utensils
C–11	Motor driven machinery
C–12	Bakery furniture (showcases, tables, etc.)

The J. L. Carver Co. had done business with a substantial number of its 12,000 customers for many years and had attained an annual sales volume of about $12,000,000. The 54 salesmen had regular routes and called on city accounts once a week, others either biweekly or monthly. They were paid "drawing accounts," which actually were minimum salaries, plus commissions based on gross profits from their sales. Forty-four salesmen operated out of Boston, while 10 salesmen were in the New York office. All sold the company's entire line.

In addition to the salesmen, a service staff of four specialists helped customers with their problems. A trained dietician worked with restaurants and institutions. The other three were experts in problems encountered by either ice cream manufacturers, soda fountain operators or bakers.

The nature of the company's operations was reflected in the number of persons in the various types of jobs. Sixty-two worked in manufacturing, which was all done at the Boston plant. Fifty-one were in warehousing and shipping. The company maintained warehousing facilities in both Boston and New York. A complete stock of all items was carried in the Boston warehouse and a 5-day stock was maintained in New York. Fifty-four were salesmen and 11 drove delivery trucks. The remaining 107 persons had administrative and clerical duties and accounted for 40 to 45 percent of the payroll. Wages and salaries represented about 50 percent of the company's total expense.

Three generations of the Carver family have furnished company presidents. Upon the death of the founder in 1930, his son, Mr. W. T. Carver succeeded to the presidency. He became well known also for his active participation in church, civic, philanthropic and business groups. In July 1964, he became chairman of the board of directors of J. L. Carver Co. and his son, Mr. W. T. Carver, Jr. was elected president. The latter had been a salesman, sales manager, vice president in charge of sales and advertising, and a director since joining the company in 1945. He was in charge of the New York office for the three years immediately preceding his election to the presidency. Eight executives currently reported to him. Exhibit 1 contains a company organization chart.

In July 1964, the J. L. Carver Co. installed a punched card accounting and inventory control system, primarily to provide more detailed sales and profits analyses on the 8,850 different items[1] of supplies and equipment sold to company customers.

The punched card system, which used International Business Machines Corporation equipment, was adopted soon after the J. L. Carver Co. had moved into a new building. The latter included a warehouse arranged and equipped for the most efficient handling of merchandise. The use of punched cards, with the new warehouse, promised important inventory and merchandise selection economies. The new system also appeared to offer other advantages over the methods formerly employed for processing orders, maintaining records, and preparing invoices.

THE OLD SYSTEM

Before punched cards were used, most of the operations connected with handling orders and preparing reports were performed manually. Upon taking an order, the salesman filled out an order blank, original and three copies. Descriptions of the items were written by hand.

The salesman forwarded the order to the company's office in Boston. The routine procedure leading to the shipping of goods and the preparation of the invoice and sales reports follows:

1. *Mail Desk.* Between 400 and 500 orders each day were received, sorted and routed.
2. *Register Desk.* A register number was placed on the original and first copy of the order and entered in a running record. The first copy of the order was filed.
3. *Credit Department.* All orders were either approved or rejected for credit. For each new customer, credit information was entered by the salesman on the special form printed on the reverse side of the order blank.
4. *Pricing Desk.* Prices which had been filled in by the salesman were checked. Orders for merchandise on which special prices had been quoted by the salesman, and orders involving contracts, were sent to the appropriate product department head for approval. The original and two copies of the order were sent to the shipping department for use in the selection of the merchandise in the warehouse.
5. *Shipping Department.* Merchandise was selected and shipped on either the same day the order was received or the day following.

---

[1] An item consisted of a shipping unit. Usually there were several shipping units of an individual product, one for each size of container.

If any items ordered could not be sent because of out-of-stock conditions or other reasons, a note to that effect was made on the order form so that it constituted a record of what actually was shipped.

The original and two copies of the order were sent to the billing department.

6. *Billing Department.* The invoice was prepared in triplicate, price extensions were checked, and the bill of lading was prepared. The original copy of the invoice was mailed to the customer. The first copy was sent to the sales department, where it was filed by customer in the permanent duplicate bill file, after the sales total had been pasted to a Kardex record of sales by salesman by accounts. The second copy went to the costing department.

7. *Costing Department.* The cost of the merchandise ordered was filled in on the second copy of the invoice. In this connection, changing prices of goods bought for resale created a problem of timing changes in cost figures. The costing department did not know exactly when the goods bought at the old price were cleared from inventory and when merchandise bought at the new price was being used to fill orders. Estimates were made which were subject to error but believed to be reasonably accurate in most cases.

Totals from the costed invoices were tabulated manually to prepare daily reports of sales by departments and by salesmen, and monthly breakdowns of sales and gross profit by departments, by salesmen, and by salesmen by departments. When the system ran smoothly, daily sales reports were available three to four days after the orders were received. However, delays in this schedule were frequent.

The above reports were distributed to the chairman of the board, president, vice president in charge of merchandising, vice president in charge of the equipment division, vice president in charge of manufacturing, treasurer, sales manager, operations manager and the 15 product department heads who had merchandising and buying responsibilities.

Procedures outlined above had been used for about 25 years with only minor modifications from time to time. An advantage of the system was that little paper work was required before the shipment of an order, thus permitting prompt shipment. Also, an order was easy to locate if it became necessary to make additions after processing had started. The system was flexible enough so that a rush order could be expedited.

The smooth operation of the system was disrupted by various difficulties. Illegible orders sent in by salesmen caused much trouble in the office and delayed shipping and billing. Out-of-stock conditions often held up orders. No perpetual inventory records were kept;

instead, periodic sight checking was relied upon for inventory control. Frequently the first indication a buyer received of an exhausted inventory was a note saying that a certain item had been omitted from a shipment of an order.

THE NEW SYSTEM

Under the new system, writing up an order was a simpler task. Only the original and one copy were required, and code numbers replaced handwritten descriptions of merchandise. Credit and other customer information were filled in on the front of the order blank. The quantity, price and code number of each item ordered were recorded on the reverse side of a form designed so that all entries easily could be made in code number sequence. The salesman ascertained prices and code numbers from his price book.

Processing of orders at the company office involved the following steps:

1. *Mail Desk.* Orders were received, sorted and routed.
2. *Order Desk.* Telephone orders were received in addition to the orders from the mail desk. Invoice numbers were placed on both the original and the copy of each order. The duplicate was placed in the register file and the original was sent to the credit department.
3. *Credit Department.* All orders were either approved or rejected for credit. Approval by the treasurer was required on all new accounts.
4. *Pricing and Editing.* Each order was checked to see that it was filled out correctly. When special pricings made by the salesman and contracts were involved, the order was sent to the appropriate product department head for approval. Department heads also handled requests for items not carried in the product line. Examples were bleach water and aspirin tablets which sometimes were included in orders received from summer camps. Such orders had been accepted in the past as a service to customers. An errand boy would be sent out to buy the special items and they would be included with the shipment of the remainder of the order. After the punched card system was installed, the company attempted to discourage the special requests because they slowed down the processing of orders. Some orders of this type still came in, however, and they were serviced to retain goodwill of established accounts.
5. *IBM Register.* Each order was returned to the order desk. Its invoice number was entered in a register to show that it had cleared the preceding steps and was ready for the IBM room. In subsequent steps, punched cards were involved.
6. *Preparation of the Invoice.*
   a. The customer's name and address and routing cards were pulled

from the master file (Exhibits 2 and 3). These cards were pre-punched with various information, some of which was printed later on the invoice. The customer's name and address and account number were printed from the name and address card, and the means of shipment and the salesman's number were printed from the routing card.

b. An invoice card was key punched to contain the following information which was later printed on the invoice: shipping basis (Boston or outside of Boston), date of order, date of invoice, invoice number, and special instructions pertaining to the individual order (Exhibit 4).

c. Commodity detail cards were pulled from the unit inventory control file or "tub file." This file in effect was a miniature warehouse in that each card should represent a shipping unit of merchandise actually in the warehouse. Cards were added to the file when merchandise was received and removed when goods were shipped. The tub file was divided into sections, one for each item. Each product was identified by a code number printed in large numerals across the end of the card. As items were listed on the order blank in code number sequence, the selection of commodity cards from the tub file was facilitated.

A commodity card (Exhibit 5) was prepunched with the following information about the item it represented: the number of the product department to which it belonged, item code number, warehouse slot number which indicated the item's location in the warehouse, the quantity represented by the card, the shipping unit, the alphabetical description of the item including its pack and size, the cost, f.o.b. price, delivered unit price and gross weight.

d. Commodity cards were "mark sensed" if changes had to be made in prepunched information. This frequently was necessary because of price changes. In mark sensing a card for a price change, a special mark was made with an electrographic pencil over the appropriate numbers representing the new price. The mark sensed card then was run on a reproducing machine which read the mark sensed information and automatically punched the new price into the columns reserved for this purpose. When the card was run on a tabulating machine in subsequent operations, the prepunched price was ignored by the machine and the new price was picked up instead.

e. The salesman's number, a customer's number and designation of type of customer were gang-punched from the name and address card into the commodity cards pulled for the order.

f. Commodity cards were sorted and arranged in warehouse slot number sequence.

g. The invoice card, customer name and address card, customer routing card, and the commodity cards were run on a tabulating machine which automatically prepared a combination invoice and shipping authorization (original and 3 copies) (Exhibit 6).

In the body of the invoice, lines representing more than one shipping unit of a single item were printed by the machine after it had totaled the number of commodity cards pulled for that item. For instance, five commodity cards were necessary to make the first entry, "B/A lemon pie fill," in Exhibit 6. Only one commodity card was used for the second entry, "B/A baking powder," because only one shipping unit of that item was ordered. The tabulating machine was equipped with a special device for listing single cards for any line and accumulating totals for multiple-card lines.

At the bottom of the invoice, totals were printed for the dollar amount and gross weight (right-hand columns, Exhibit 6). At the same time the totals were printed, a summary card was punched with various totals for use later in preparing a register of shipments and statistical analyses. The summary card contained the salesman's number, customer's number, customer's name, cost of the merchandise listed on the invoice (to be posted in the general ledger), selling price of the merchandise (to be used in making up accounts receivable), and gross profit on the order (to be used in computing the salesman's commission).

h. The original of the invoice was held in the IBM room until a check had been made to determine whether all items actually were shipped. Then the invoice was mailed to the customer. The three copies went to the warehouse to be used in the selection and packing of merchandise for shipment. As the items were listed on the invoice in warehouse slot number sequence, merchandise could be selected continuously from the first item to the last and all back tracking by the selector was eliminated. When this step was completed, the copies of the invoice were returned to the IBM room where they were matched against the original order and the customer copy. Any changes were noted. If changes were necessary, a new invoice had to be prepared. One copy then was attached to the original order and filed. The other two copies comprised the bill of lading set.

REPORTS UNDER THE NEW SYSTEM

Daily reports of sales by product departments were prepared for Carver's Boston operation and the New York house. The reports gave sales today, sales for the month to date, and gross profit today (Exhibit 7). In another column, total sales for the month to date a year ago were entered by hand.

The mechanical steps involved in making up these reports included sorting the commodity cards used in processing the day's orders and arranging them in department number sequence. The cards then were run on a tabulating machine which printed department totals for sales and gross profit. Department totals for sales to date this month were printed at the same time. The only difference was that the totals for the month prior to "today" were added from departmental summary cards prepared for this purpose. As the daily sales report was printed on the tabulating machine, a new month-to-date summary card, which combined the totals for "today" and for the month prior to "today," was punched automatically for each department. The new month-to-date cards were used in preparing the next day's sales report.

Another daily report gave sales today, sales this month to date, and gross profit today for each salesman (Exhibit 8). The steps involved in preparing this report were similar to those described above, except that the commodity cards were sorted by salesman instead of by product department.

Daily reports were to be available one day following the day they covered. This schedule had not been met, however, because of various difficulties. Early in November, there was a six-day delay, but this was considered to be a temporary condition.

A monthly report was prepared for each salesman showing his sales and gross profit by customer. Invoice summary cards were used in making up this report. They were first sorted by salesman. Next the cards for a given salesman were sorted by customer. The cards were run in customer number sequence, and sales and gross profit information for each card was listed by the tabulating machine.

Only the above reports had been made available. However, other reports, which had been prepared regularly under the old system, were being examined to determine whether they should be reinstated. In addition, the treasurer planned to undertake the following analyses in the future:

1. Sales and gross profit by customer.
2. Sales and gross profit by item for each salesman.
3. Sales and gross profit by item for each customer.
4. Sales and gross profit by item for each department.
5. Inventory turnover by item.

INVENTORY CONTROL

In addition to the sales and profit analyses, the punched card system was expected to provide effective inventory control, so that stock balances would be available for use in costing, buying and shipping. A perpetual inventory was kept to reflect each stock movement, unit by unit. Therefore, information was to have been readily available on what was received, what was shipped and what was on hand.

The tub file of commodity cards was designed to give a quick picture of the stock situation in the warehouse. The file was divided into many sections, one for each item in the product line. Cards were placed in the file end-up, so that the code numbers and serial numbers printed across one end could be read. A code number identified all cards representing the same item. Serial numbers running from one up were printed when cards for a given item were prepared on the receipt of an incoming shipment of merchandise. The cards were placed in the appropriate tub file section so that the lowest numbered card was in front. New cards representing later receipts were inserted in front of the cards already on file. Therefore, each section of the file might contain several groups of cards for the same item, each serially numbered. The groups were separated by high divider cards. When a card was needed for the filling of an order, the one at the back of the section was taken.

When only one shipment group of cards was in the file for a given item, the inventory could be read simply by referring to the highest numbered card. If several groups were present, the highest numbers of each of the groups were added to give the inventory. The current inventory reading subtracted from the previous inventory total plus any receipts gave the quantity shipped during a period.

"Time to buy" signals, consisting of "minimum," "danger," and "out-of-stock" cards of different colors, were inserted at selected points in each division of the tub file. The signal cards were removed when they were encountered as commodity cards were pulled to fill orders. The signal cards were either sent to the buyer directly or listed by a tabulating machine to prepare a time-to-buy report for the buyers.

The punched card inventory control system had been installed for all Carver items except equipment.

The tub file on the New York stocks was maintained in Boston. After shipping an order, the New York house sent the order form to Boston for processing and billing. The Boston and New York offices were in contact with each other daily by telephone.

ACCOUNTS RECEIVABLE

The company was not preparing accounts receivable statements directly from punched cards, although it planned to do so after some of the problems connected with installing the new system had been solved.

As of November 1964, accounts receivable posting was done manually from daily records of shipments which listed for each invoice the salesman, customer and invoice numbers, customer's name, gross profit, the date, and the total price. The daily listings were prepared from the summary cards which were automatically punched when totals were printed on the invoices.

If statements were to be printed from punched cards, the invoice summary cards would be placed behind customer name and address cards in an accounts receivable file and used in the maintenance of customer accounts. If credit was issued for returned merchandise, a card would be key punched for the amount of the credit and placed in the file. As payments were received, the cards for invoices on which payment had been made would be withdrawn and listed to prepare a register of cash received and to establish control totals. Customer statements would be prepared monthly from the cards remaining in the open item file. The statements would show all open items, credits and balance due.

The company did not plan to use the punched card accounting system for either accounts payable or the payroll.

QUESTIONS

1. Draw a flowchart of the two systems.
2. What are the principal differences between the two systems? What advantages does the IBM system offer?
3. What problems do you expect J. L. Carver to encounter under the new system?

EXHIBIT 1

ORGANIZATION CHART

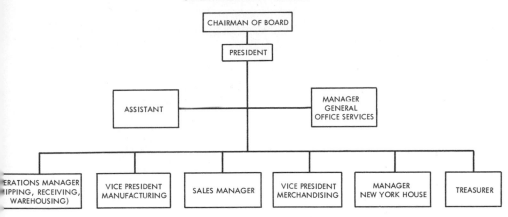

EXHIBIT 2

CUSTOMER NAME AND ADDRESS CARD

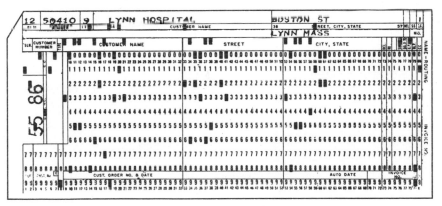

Columns	Information Contained
1–2	Salesman's number
3–7	Customer's number
8	Designation of type of customer
9–32	Customer's name
33–52	Customer's street address
53–72	Customer's city and state
73	Price class designation
74–75	Blank
76–77	"Skip X's" to control vertical spacing of heading information
78	Heading card "X"
79	Multiple line print code
80	Heading card sequence code

EXHIBIT 3

CUSTOMER ROUTING CARD

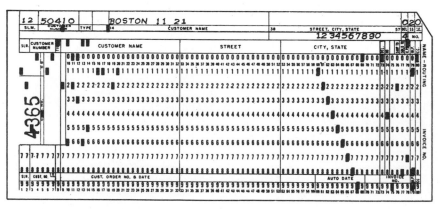

Columns	Information Contained
1–2	Salesman's number
3–7	Customer's number
8–32	Means of shipment
33–52	Special billing information (C.O.D., duplicate invoices requested, bill with goods etc.)
53–72	Blank
73	Price class designation
74	Routing card code
75	Blank
76–77	"Skip X's" to control vertical spacing of heading information
78	Heading card "X"
79	Multiple line print code
80	Heading card sequence code

EXHIBIT 4

THE INVOICE CARD

EXHIBIT 4—*Continued*

Columns	Information Contained
1–2	Salesman's number
3–7	Customer's number
8	Invoice card code
9–32	Shipping basis, date of order and order number
33–52	Special instructions pertaining to the order
53–72	Blank
73–78	Invoice number
79	Multiple line print code
80	Heading card sequence code

EXHIBIT 5

COMMODITY CARD

Columns	Information Contained
1–2	Salesman's number
3–7	Customer's number
8	Designation of type of customer
9–10	Product department number
11–15	Commodity code number
16–19	Slot number
20	Quantity
21–22	Shipping unit designation
23–48	Alphabetical description of pack and size
49–53	Cost
54–58	F.O.B. unit price
59–63	Delivered unit price
64–69	Special unit price (mark sensed into card)
70–76	Special price extension (mark sensed into card)
77–79	Gross weight of item
80	Commodity card code

The "350" at the left end of the card is the item or commodity code number. Cards for each item also were serially numbered. The serial number, (normally appearing near the item code number) was omitted from the card used in this exhibit.

EXHIBIT 6

MANUFACTURERS AND DISTRIBUTORS OF FOOD
PRODUCTS AND EQUIPMENT

CUST ORDER NO AND DATE	**BOSTON 11/21**			MO. DA. YR. 112651	INVOICE NO. 49287	6305
SOLD TO AND OR						
SHIPPED TO	**LYNN HOSPITAL BOSTON ST LYNN MASS·**			ACCOUNT NO. 5 410		
SHIPPED VIA	**OUR TRUCK DUP**			SM. NO. 12	TERMS 1% 10 DAYS NET 30	

LOCATION	QUANTITY	UNIT	DESCRIPTION	PACK & SIZE	UNIT PRICE	TOTAL	
8062	5	CS	B/A LEMON PIE FILL	6/10	7.25	36.25	250
J999	1	CN	B/A BAKING POWDER	1/7LB	1.26	1.26	
94	5	CS	DIETETIC RA CHERRY	24/2	6.40	32.00	185
96	5	CS	DIETETIC FR COCKTL	24/2	6.50	32.50	185
103	5	CS	DIETETIC YC PCH SL	24/2	5.35	26.75	185
102	1	CS	DIETETIC Y C PCH HV	24/2	5.65	5.65	
380	5	CS	DIET PEAS	24/2	5.05	25.25	190
377	5	CS	DIET SPINACH	24/2	4.50	22.50	175
420	5	CS	B/A DICED GR PEPPER	24/2	5.70	28.50	185
421	7	CS	B/A DICED RED PEPPER	24/2	5.70	39.90	259
	1	JR	BEEF BULUN CUBES	1/100	1.35	1.35	
	1	JR	CHICK BULUN CUBES	1/100	1.35	1.35 ●	
						253.26	1614

ALL SALES SUBJECT TO TERMS ON BACK OF INVOICE
SELLER REPRESENTS THAT WITH RESPECT TO THE PRODUCTION OF THE ARTICLES AND/OR THE PERFORMANCE OF THE SERVICES COVERED BY THIS INVOICE IT HAS FULLY COMPLIED WITH SECTION 12 (A) OF THE FAIR LABOR STANDARDS ACT OF 1938, AS AMENDED.   PAY THIS ● AMOUNT

EXHIBIT 7

DAILY SALES BY DEPARTMENTS—AUGUST 29

Carver (Boston)	Sales Today	Sales for Month to Date	Gross Profit Today	Sales for Month to Date Last Year
A 1	$1,691.03	$52,593.26	$556.83	
A 2	292.60	14,007.96	107.21	
A 3	750.00	39,357.58	289.63	
A 4	1,006.27	13,966.71	131.08	
	3,739.90	119,925.53	1,084.75*	
B 5	4,889.66	148,975.88	645.75	
5 S	1,376.89	30,826.62	187.08	
B 6	897.05	41,654.65	183.70	
B 7	1,748.93	57,396.78	300.33	
B 8	2,813.88	26,454.52	518.52	
	11,726.41	305,308.45	1,835.38*	
C 9		7,668.79		
C 10	463.42	19,791.69	180.78	
C 11	13.50	5,596.74	6.75	
C 12		513.45		
	476.92	33,570.67	187.53*	
Manuf. Goods	423.31	14,401.83	226.99	
Resale Foods		109.84		
Ret. Cherries	31.20	96.41	12.24	
Murray Equip.		104.90		
Coca Cola	7.20	803.55	1.08	
	461.71	15,516.53	240.31*	
	$16,404.94	$474,321.18	$3,347.97*	$608,090.45

(Similar reports were prepared for the New York house)

EXHIBIT 8

DAILY SALES BY SALESMEN—AUGUST 29

Salesman's Number	Salesman's Name	Sales Today	Sales This Month to Date	Gross Profit Today
1	Benson	$252.11	$7,850.93	$49.48
2	Bickford	630.58	10,527.18	129.45
3	Bicou	266.33	6,032.95	56.35
4	Bingham	228.75	10,405.52	25.68
5	Bossman		10,606.99	
6	Clear	434.77	13,503.66	81.26
7	Cosgrove	163.38	9,408.04	28.94
8	Dinsmore	313.93	16,575.43	75.66
9	Elliott	2,074.31	17,234.97	349.44
10	Farrell	462.67	22,412.80	162.97
.	.	.	.	.
.	.	.	.	.
.	.	.	.	.

J. L. CARVER CO. (B)

In November 1964, executives of the J. L. Carver Co. reviewed their experience with a new punched card accounting and control system to determine whether it should be retained.

INSTALLING THE NEW SYSTEM

The introduction and operation of this new system was the responsibility of the treasurer. To prepare himself for this task, he attended a one-week course in IBM accounting for wholesale distribution given by IBM's department of education in Endicott, N.Y.

A few weeks prior to the changeover, a one-hour meeting was held on company time to announce plans for the introduction of punched card procedures to the 200 salesmen, office, warehouse and shipping people whose jobs would be affected by the change. The program included an IBM movie on how punched cards were used and talks by the treasurer of the company and a representative of IBM. The program was repeated, 100 employees attending each session.

None of the Carver employees was experienced in punched card methods or equipment. In addition, it developed that a number were not suited to this type of work, which differed considerably from the clerical tasks they had performed for many years. In installing the new system, the company found it necessary to change a number of job assignments, and to hire six new people who had worked with IBM machines. In addition, several girls were sent to a two-week school for key punch operators. No employee was to be dismissed because of the changeover.

Two IBM representatives worked with the company during July, the first month under the new system. They returned several times in later months to try to help solve various operational problems.

PROBLEMS UNDER THE NEW SYSTEM

The company encountered many problems as it tried to get the punched card system to function smoothly. Many errors were made in handling orders. Customer dissatisfaction mounted. So did work pressure and tension within the company's offices as executives and employees sought effective control over the new procedures.

Pacifying irritated customers occupied much of the time of executives and salesmen. Complaints arose from errors in merchandise shipped, errors in billing, delays in shipments and delays in the receipt of bills. Business suffered because of the customer dissatisfaction.

In analyzing the troubles, one executive noted several classes of errors as follows:

1. *Number Errors.* Incorrect figures appeared in invoices due to salesmen's mistakes on the original order, the pulling of the wrong cards in the IBM room, incorrect key punching and, occasionally, typographical errors in code numbers appearing in the salesman's price book.

2. *System Errors.* Some errors were believed to have been caused by the nature of the system. Lost orders were a problem, especially during the first month or two. Some orders disappeared for a day or so after they had started to be processed. A few lost orders were never found. Explanations were difficult to make. The product department heads were responsible in some cases because they failed to return promptly the orders referred to them for approval of special prices or contracts. But this difficulty had been largely corrected. Lost orders prompted complaints because they meant delayed shipments.

Special instructions, which accompanied about 10 percent of the orders, were an important source of errors. Sometimes customers asked that their bills be prepared on special forms instead of the usual invoice blank. The majority of special requests, however, were shipping or delivery instructions which were to be reproduced on the invoice. Lengthy instructions had to be edited to fit into the space allotted for them on the invoice card. Editing errors sometimes changed the meaning. For example, a New York City restaurant which did most of its large business during the lunch hour rush had made this request on its order: "Don't deliver between 12 and 2 p.m." In preparing the invoice card, the key punch operator omitted the first word. As a result, the instructions printed on the invoice read: "Deliver between 12 and 2 p.m." In attempting to carry out the orders, the truck driver met angry resistance. The restaurant manager promptly made his displeasure known to the Carver company in a one-sided telephone conversation.

3. *Shippers' Errors.* Mistakes in selecting and packing mer-

chandise occurred occasionally, but they could not be blamed on the punched card system. Presumably, the use of slot numbers in the warehouse should reduce errors of this kind.

4. *Billing Errors.* Incorrect prices on invoices were a major source of trouble and came in for special attention. They resulted from mistakes in decimal points and price extensions, failures to note that certain orders called for special prices, and failures to use the proper discounts granted to the various classes of trade.

The procedure for handling discounts differed somewhat depending upon the item involved. Category A items had four classes of discounts. Prices for each class were punched into the commodity card. A code number appeared by each item on the order blank to designate what discount the customer should receive. An operator was to act on this information and mark sense the proper columns of figures on the card so that the correct price would be picked up by the machine as it printed the invoice. There was less chance for discount errors on category B orders, but they occurred nevertheless. Category B products had two prices, one for f.o.b., Boston, and the other for shipments outside of Boston. The customer name and address card contained information to show which price the customer should receive. If operations went smoothly, the accounting machine read this information and automatically selected the proper set of prices from the commodity card for use on the invoice.

The recently hired machine operators had previously worked with IBM equipment, but they were not familiar with the customary shipping units and prices of products sold by the company. The other employees had worked for Carver for some time. They were acquainted with the business details but were not experienced in punched card operations. The lack of background contributed to the making of errors.

Night work frequently was necessary in the IBM room to complete the processing of a day's orders. This was true in spite of the fact that the workload was only about one half of the rated capacity of the equipment. Because the machines were tied up most of the time handling orders, the daily reports were delayed and the more elaborate sales and profit analyses had not yet been attempted.

The company received about 500 orders a day. This meant that 6,000 punched cards were run on the IBM machines daily in the preparation of invoices. The total included 500 customer name and address cards; 500 routing cards; 500 invoice cards; 4,000 commodity cards (one for each shipping unit of a product ordered and an average of four per order); and 500 summary cards (one per invoice). The commodity cards were involved in two machine runs, one for sorting by slot number and the other for the printing of the invoice.

Actually the daily card volume handled by the machines was higher than indicated above, because many invoices had to be rerun. The number of reruns had declined somewhat, but was 20 percent of the total in November 1964.

Out-of-stock conditions in the warehouse were a major cause of reruns. Equipment had not yet been placed under punched card inventory control. Therefore, commodity cards in the tub file did not represent warehouse supplies. Frequently, orders were put through for merchandise not on hand. When this happened, the warehouse noted the fact on the invoice and returned it to the IBM room, where a new invoice was prepared to cover only the merchandise actually shipped.

The company also experienced much difficulty with the inventory system where it was in use. The tub file often was inaccurate for any one of several reasons. Sometimes receipts of goods by the warehouse were not reported promptly, or commodity cards were not added to the tub file soon enough to prevent an out-of-stock condition from being shown when goods were available. As a result, shipments were either unnecessarily delayed or orders were shipped short.

It also was common for the tub file to show items as being in the warehouse when an out-of-stock condition existed. One explanation was that demand for a number of the products manufactured by the company was so great that very little inventory had been built up. Some items virtually were shipped "hot." When orders for such merchandise were received and the tub file showed no stock on hand, it was customary to ask manufacturing how many units would be ready later that day. If the answer was 10 for a given item, that number of commodity cards was added to the tub file and orders were processed on that basis. However, the manufacturing estimate sometimes proved to be inaccurate. Perhaps only 5 instead of 10 units actually reached the warehouse. In the meantime, 10 orders for the product may have been processed. This meant that 5 were either delayed or shipped short. In the latter event, new invoices were required.

Call order business also led to inventory discrepancies. About 25 orders a day were received from customers who personally called at the plant for the merchandise. These orders were filled promptly from warehouse stocks and did not go through the usual punched card processing. As the number of call orders was small, they had been allowed to accumulate before being forwarded to the IBM room. This meant that the tub file was "long" on some items in the interim.

Reruns of invoices also were due to various errors which were not discovered until the invoice had been printed, and to the fact that weights for a number of items shipped in bulk were not known until the shipping unit had been packed. Examples of the latter were jellies. The standard sized barrels varied in weight even for the same jelly. For such cases, the correct weights were noted on the copy of the invoice in the warehouse after packing. The invoice was then returned to the IBM room where it was rerun after a commodity card for the item had been punched with the correct weight.

Reruns complicated the difficult job of scheduling work in the IBM room. Orders were received throughout the day, so it was impossible to have only one large machine run on invoices in the morning. Instead, several smaller runs were necessary to keep the workload reasonably even in the warehouse and shipping room and to assure prompt shipment of merchandise. With the machines busy most of the time processing orders, it was difficult to find time to make runs for the daily record of shipments as well as the various sales reports. Delays resulted. The November 1 bills were not sent out until November 27, and the end-of-the-month figures for October were not available to company executives until November 28.

A major cause of complaints was the absence of price per pound information on the invoice. The unit price and weight were given, but the unit usually was a barrel, pail, or some other shipping container of more than one pound of merchandise. Many customers demanded that the price per pound be included so that they would not have to compute it.

CHANGES IN ORGANIZATION

Shortly after punched card operations had begun in July, Mr. W. T. Carver Jr., who had been head of the New York house, was elected president. He succeeded his father, who became chairman of the board. The executive vice president retired August 1 upon reaching his 65th birthday. These top level moves and the introduction of punched card methods gave rise to other changes in personnel and job responsibilities which affected principal executives in the next several months.

The assistant manager in New York was made head of that office. The company's sales manager became a temporary assistant to the president to work on operational problems which had become of major importance under the new system. He later was to take over the territory of the senior salesman upon the latter's retirement. The head of a major product department was named sales manager.

The executive in charge of the company's manufactured goods became senior vice president in charge of merchandising. Later in the year the credit manager was promoted to a new post as head of general office services.

The treasurer and the operations manager, the other two executives who reported to the president, continued to serve as heads of finance and shipping, receiving and warehousing, respectively. The details of their duties were materially altered by punched card operation, however. The treasurer had direct responsibility for the new system.

COST OF NEW SYSTEM

The punched card installation, as it originally was proposed, would consist of the following IBM machines on which the company would pay a monthly rental of $1,230.

No.	Machine	Rental
3	Alphabetic key punch machines, $60 each	$180
1	Alphabetic interpreter	$270
2	Sorting machines, $55 each	$110
1	Collator	$125
1	Reproducing and gang-punching machine with summarizing and mark sensing units and card counting devices for serial numbering	$125
1	Multiple line print tabulating machine	$420
		$1,230

According to the original proposal, only nine employees would be needed to do the same work which had been performed by twelve persons under the old system. Monthly depreciation charges on equipment used with the old procedures were $100 a month.

Five months after the introduction of the new system, the company was using the equipment itemized above plus another reproducing and gang-punching machine, which brought the total monthly rental up to $1,355. Fifteen persons were employed in the IBM room instead of nine, as had been proposed. They included an assistant manager of the system, four key punch operators, two machine operators, three card selectors and five persons who had various clerical duties.

Office expense connected with the processing of orders and the preparation of sales reports was expected to remain about the same in the future. Some saving in clerical expense should accompany the extension of punched card operations to the handling of accounts receivable. However, if the new system were to pay for itself, it would have to do so largely through better directed selling efforts and warehouse and inventory economies.

The president believed that inventories eventually might be reduced as much as 30 percent from the $1,700,000 total. More efficient buying, made possible by better inventory control, presumably would contribute to this result. Also, the president thought that studies of sales and profits by products might lead to a cut of up to 20 percent in the number of items in the product line. Insurance costs would be lower with smaller inventories. The president also was hopeful that the more efficient merchandise selection methods of the new system, along with reduced inventories and the advantages of the new warehouse, might in the long run make possible a reduction of fifteen persons in the warehouse staff.

EXECUTIVE COMMITTEE MEETING

Members of the executive committee met in November 1964 to decide the future of the punched card installation.

The treasurer believed that the system could be made to work satisfactorily and favored its retention. He emphasized that the company's gross profits had been declining because of rising freight costs and expenses. More knowledge about the business was essential, he believed, if the profit level was to be protected. He pointed out that the company did not know whether it was making a profit on all items or on all customers, or whether the salesmen were giving the proper attention to the different products in the line. The use of punched cards, he said, made it feasible to get answers to these and other important questions.

The vice president in charge of merchandising also favored retaining the installation. He recognized that the salesmen, who had to deal directly with the customer complaints, did not like the system, but he was hopeful that the difficulties that had led to errors could be eliminated. He believed that the additional information which the punched card system promised would be very valuable in directing and coordinating sales and merchandising efforts.

The operations manager had not come to a definite conclusion. On the one hand, he favored the system because it facilitated the selection of merchandise and eliminated much clerical work in the warehouse. These advantages allowed the company to get along with five fewer warehouse employees. On the other hand, the operations manager feared that the new system would tend to destroy the firm's close relationships with its customers. He said that over the years the company had developed a warm, friendly personality and a reputation for personalized service. He believed that punched card operations introduced a highly impersonal quality which was objectionable. To illustrate his point, he criticized the new invoice for being too impersonal in tone. Entries often were difficult to understand because of the extensive use of abbreviations. He believed that the invoice, as well as other paper work connected with the system, suggested that the customer was regarded as just another number rather than as an individual concern in which Carver had a friendly interest.

The vice president in charge of manufacturing believed that the company would be better off with its former methods of handling orders and keeping records. The punched card system was not flexible enough, he said, to meet the needs of the firm's business, which regularly involved special prices to customers, rush orders and call orders. Also, it had proved to be more costly than the old procedures because it had been necessary to do much night work and to hire several additional persons with IBM experience.

In his opinion, the system had not produced important information which management needed for control and planning. While daily reports were prepared on sales by departments and by salesmen, they often were late and they did not include comparable figures for the previous year. He desired a daily report on all company sales combined, in addition to the separate reports which were issued for Carver, Boston; Carver, New York. Of greatest importance, he said, was the loss in sales which had resulted from customer dissatisfaction over the many errors in shipping and billing. He opposed risking a further loss of business. The cost, he believed, would exceed the benefits the company could hope to realize from the new procedures. He moved that the punched card system be abandoned.

QUESTIONS

1. What action should J. L. Carver take with respect to the new punched card system?

STATE CONSUMER REPORTING BUREAU

On June 1, 1962, Mr. Robert Markson, president of the State Consumer Reporting Bureau retained two consultants to assist him in developing methods for handling State's information processing needs. In their initial session with Mr. Markson, the following information was presented which the consultants felt was particularly relevant.

COMPANY OPERATION

Founded in December 1962 by Mr. Robert Markson, State Consumer Reporting Bureau is a customer collection agency. Various retail stores in Metropolitan Boston give them delinquent accounts receivable. Through a combination of collection letters, telephone follow-ups and, in a few extreme cases, personal visits, the company's collection department attempts to collect the overdue amounts. In about 50 percent of the cases they are successful. The other 50 percent are either dropped, if the amounts involved are less than $35, or are turned over to the attorneys in the legal department, who file suit against the customer and legally press the matter to a conclusion. The company is paid a fixed percentage on every dollar collected. This percentage increases if legal action must be taken on an account. Currently the company is trying to collect on approximately 4,000 accounts. New customers' accounts are received at a rate of 500 a month. The firm employs two attorneys, six collectors, and three secretaries, in addition to Mr. Markson.

Collection Department. When new customer accounts arrive at State Consumer, a collection card is prepared by a secretary. This is given to Mr. Irwin Gannich, the company's attorney. Considering such things as the amount due, the store where the sale was made, the elapsed time since the last payment on the account, and previous collection action taken by the store, he decides if immediate collection action is necessary or whether the collection department should be given the account.

If the account is sent to the collection department, the collection card is given to a secretary, who automatically mails the delinquent account the first of the company's four collection letters. Designed to frighten the customer into paying, these letters are printed up by a local printing company. The secretary takes the letter and types the following information in the proper places.

(a)   The customer's name and address
(b)   The store where he incurred the bill
(c)   The amount of the bill.

The secretary types up an envelope for the letter and mails it. The collection card is then routed to one of the six collectors in the collection department.

State Consumer Reporting Bureau

In general, each collector is responsible for a certain section of the alphabet. Cards of customers whose last names begin with the letters A-E would be given to collector #1, etc. For certain stores, however, continuity of approach makes it desirable that the same collector handle all accounts for this store. Thus collector #1 is responsible for customers whose last names begin with letters A-E plus all accounts of the Central Garden Florist Shop.

Upon receiving a collection card, a collector takes no action on it for five days. At the end of this period, if no payment is received, he telephones the customer. At his discretion, he may also order the mailing of the second, third and fourth collection letters. A record of all telephone conversations, letters mailed, promises made and payments given is kept on the collection card. Mr. Markson, in speaking of the collection card, noted:

. . . This record of information is our collection department's most important tool. They use the customer's past performances as a guide in effective bargaining. When a customer knows you are acquainted with his past activities he takes you more seriously. Past addresses too may give clues on slips (people who move to another location, leaving no forwarding address). Take away their history record and collection effectiveness is reduced by 60 percent. Any information processing system must be designed around the preservation of this information for the collector.

Many of these cards are completely covered with notations and have a second one stapled to them.

These collection cards are filed alphabetically in a box on the collector's desk. If after 45 days the customer shows complete inaction, the collector automatically turns the card over to the legal department. Similarly, if the collector feels payments are dragging too slowly, he refers the account to the legal department.

In talking about the collectors, Mr. Markson said:

. . . the role of the collector at State is similar to that of a blue collar assembly worker. He is the company's primary revenue producer, and it is the effectiveness with which he accomplishes his task that keeps us in business. It is similar to a detective game and they view it as a contest between themselves and the customer.

Collections. The collector negotiates a payback agreement with the customer. In some cases the customer will make a lump sum payment. The majority of the time, however, an installment payback scheme is worked out, sometimes stretching over six or more months.

The collections may be received in three different ways.

(1) The customer comes to the office and makes payment. He is given a receipt and the money is placed in an envelope with his name on it.

(2) The customer mails his payment to State (about a third of these payments are cash). The envelopes are checked to make sure the customer's name is on the outside.

(3) The customer makes payment at the store where the purchase was acquired. Within six days after the payment the store sends a notice to State Consumer, giving the customer's name, amount of payment and date it was made. This is placed in an envelope with the customer's name on the outside.

Each day these envelopes are taken to the collection room and a secretary gathers the necessary collection cards. She first posts the amount and date of payment on them. Then she lists the customer's name, date and amount of payment on a yellow collection sheet (separate ones for each store) for payments made to State and on blue collection sheets (separate ones for each store) for payments made to the store. The secretary then returns the collection cards to the collection room and files them in the individual collector's box.

The collection sheets are filed away until the end of the month. They are then gathered and each store is mailed a copy of its collections, together with a summary stating how much it collected and how much State collected. This information is used to calculate State's commission.

The legal collections are handled separately from those of the collection department, and separate, more complete statements are sent by the legal department to the stores. Presently the company has two attorneys. They divide the legal business between themselves and initiate a series of letters and telephone calls which culminates in the customer being brought into court if he takes no payment action.

When payments are received at State, in most cases the secretary can quickly sort the legal payments from the collection department payments. This is because State supplies return mail envelopes to the customers which are stamped legal if it is an account in legal. About 20 percent of the legal mail is not identified as such and is sent to the collection room. If the collection card is not found there, the envelope is forwarded to legal.

Information Processing Requirements. Mr. Markson then made the following remarks which seemed particularly relevant to the two consultants:

I am not worried about our ability to operate efficiently at the current level of operations. Our current performance from both a cost and efficiency viewpoint is satisfactory. What concerns me is our internal capacity for handling growth. If I thought we could handle it, within six months we would be receiving new customer accounts at the rate of 5,000 per month. Organizing and expanding the collection staff is not a major problem. Neither do finances pose a real threat. What is worrying me is the fear of drowning ourselves in a flood of paper work so that we could neither service the accounts nor produce timely statements for the stores. This could do lasting harm to the firm's prospects. Before we get this business we must be set up to handle it. I have had two companies in here who have submitted proposals for remedying the situation (see Appendixes A and B). Frankly, I don't know whether they have any value or not. That's your job.

You have the run of the office. Ask anyone any question you want. Probably you will want to talk to the two companies who made proposals. I have made arrangements for you to do so, if you so choose.

This is important. In two years I will be deeply committed to whatever system we select and it will be both difficult and costly to change. I hope you are going to introduce me to concepts and ideas that I never dreamed existed.

Mr. Markson then introduced the two consultants to Miss Duncan, the office manager. During the course of the morning she made the following comments:

The present system seems to work all right. The only real bottleneck is finding out where a customer's card is. When we get a telephone call I don't always know whether the card is in the collection room, legal, or with the man on the road. . . . Yes, we have our man out collecting all the time. Every Monday I give him 50 collection cards. I mark them down so if someone calls I won't spend all day trying to find a card that isn't in the office. Mr. Markson is sold on the idea of automation so it is coming. It is only a matter of time. I'll do my best . . . a lot of people don't care for the idea. They have been in the collection business for 30 years and never seen anything like it.

APPENDIX A

Transcript of IBM Proposal

A.   Acquisition of the following equipment is recommended. Members of the IBM Series 50 family. They are rebuilt older machines where both speed and rental have been reduced.

1. *The IBM 526 Printing Summary Punch*—can serve as a summary punch, card punch, interpreter, and gang punch. Whether used solely for summary punching or for its value as a utility machine, it is a practical machine for almost any punched card installation. Monthly rental is $100; it summary punches at 17 columns/sec.

2. *The IBM 82 Sorter*—Groups all cards of similar classification, arranging such classification in numerical or alphabetic sequence. Alphabetic sorting is accomplished by the double sorting of each column. Monthly rental is $55; it sorts 650 cards per minute.

3. *The IBM 77 Collator*—Designed for the requirements of small business, performs many card filing and selection operations. It can simultaneously feed two sets of IBM punched cards, merging the matched cards and selecting the unmatched cards. During this processing, the machine can also check the sequence of the primary file of cards. Monthly rental is $80; it operates at 120 to 240 cards per minute.

4. *The IBM 403 Alphabetical Accounting Machine with Multiple Line Printing*—Prepares reports and records from punched IBM cards. It is a versatile unit whose flexibility and other features make it a fast production machine. The 403 reads 80-column cards, records details, and/or subtracts to print any desired combination of totals. Monthly rental is $320; it detail prints at 80 or 100 lines per minute and accumulates totals at 80 or 150 cards per minute.

B.   It is recommended that this equipment be used in the following way:

1. Receive List of Accounts
   from Client. Keypunch and
   Duplicate.

   (new clients only)

   a) name   )
   b) city   )   Client
   c) street   )   Master
   d) client number)   Card
   e) cycle code   )

   a) Client Number)
   b) Claim Number)
   c) Debtor Name   )   Debtor
   d) Street   )   Master
   e) City   )   Card
   f) Amount of Claim)
   g) Age Code   )
   h) Cycle Code   )

2. Duplicate Client and
   Debtor Masters are
   sorted, then filed
   alphabetically for
   coding reference

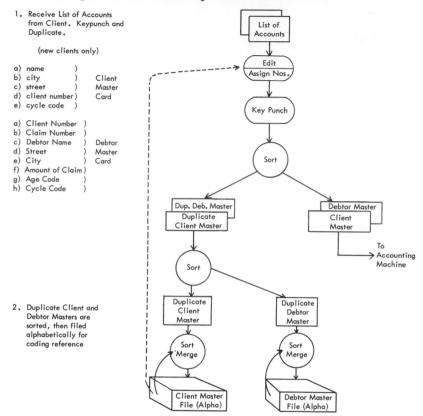

3. Client and Debtor Master Cards put through Accounting Machine. Acknowledgment Report sent to client.

4. Client totals summary punched and put through an accounting machine to establish control totals.

5. Client and Debtor Masters sorted and numerically filed within cycle.

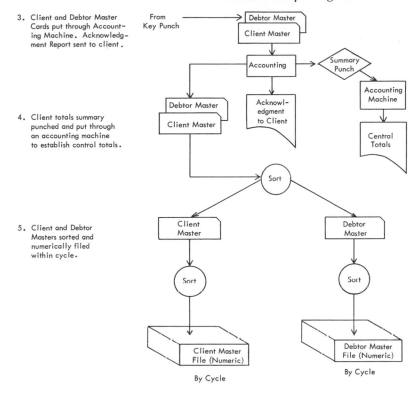

From Key Punch

Debtor Master
Client Master

Accounting

Summary Punch

Accounting Machine

Debtor Master
Client Master

Acknowledgment to Client

Central Totals

Sort

Client Master

Debtor Master

Sort

Sort

Client Master File (Numeric)

By Cycle

Debtor Master File (Numeric)

By Cycle

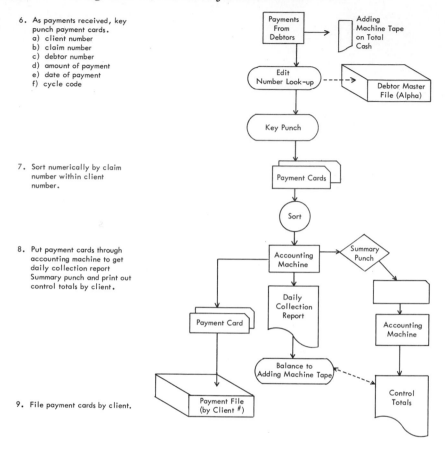

6. As payments received, key
   punch payment cards.
   a) client number
   b) claim number
   c) debtor number
   d) amount of payment
   e) date of payment
   f) cycle code

7. Sort numerically by claim
   number within client
   number.

8. Put payment cards through
   accounting machine to get
   daily collection report
   Summary punch and print out
   control totals by client.

9. File payment cards by client.

10. At the end of each cycle,
    the following files are
    merged:
    1) Client Masters
    2) Debtor Masters
    3) Old Balance Forward
    4) Payments

11. The collated cards are put
    through the accounting
    machine to produce an aged
    trial balance report show-
    ing status of each claim
    by client.
    1. Client name and address
    2. Debtor name and address
    3. Opening balance
    4. Payments this period
    5. New aged balance, e.g.,
       30,60,90,120 days
    6. Total amount collected
    7. Total amount out-
       standing

12. Summary punch new balance
    forward cards. Sort out
    zero or negative balance
    cards representing paid
    up or overpaid accounts.
    Use to purge outstanding
    Debtor Master File.

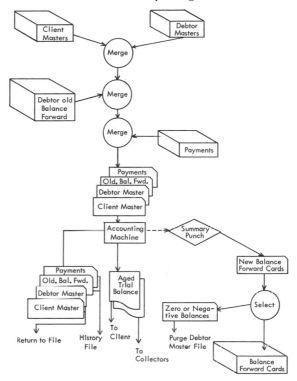

C. The following is a transcript of an article that appeared in the December 1960 issue of *Associated Credit Bureau of America Management*.

"Within a recent six-month period, our volume of new business entered for collection increased sixfold—from $500,000 to $3 million yearly! Our solution for handling this sudden increase of collection business was a punched card data processing system.

"With this system, actual dollar collections for the first six months of operation doubled those for the same period the previous year—based on only a small proportionate increase in volume. And this increase in business has not required a proportionate increase in employees.

"Prior to installing the punched card system, 12 clerks handled about 2,000 new collection accounts per month. Now, 14 clerks can handle new accounts at the rate of 5,000 or 6,000 per month.

"Our bureau might have handled this volume without the data processing system, but this would have entailed hiring a staff of from 30 to 35 clerks, moving into larger quarters, purchasing additional filing equipment and purchasing additional office equipment to accommodate a larger staff.

Automation's Assets

"When we decided that some form of automation was necessary, investigation indicated that cost of such equipment would make the system financially prohibitive. However, through the efforts of the International Business Machines Corporation, a unique, efficient punched card system was devised to handle processing of our collection accounts; and we were able to install it on a rental basis. The rental cost, incidentally, is only about half the cost of one good clerk-typist.

"Basically, the IBM punched card system gives us: *automatically typed acknowledgement notices for our clients;* automatic preparation of collection notices; an accurate and current follow-up procedure; automatically printed forwarding notices (when accounts are sent to other agencies for collection); increased capacity, and a higher percentage of collections per dollar value.

"The system also enables *one* girl to handle 1,300 new accounts in two days. This includes preparation of work cards, acknowledgement lists, original notice and the alphabetizing of the work cards for filing.

Collection Steps

"New accounts are turned over to a machine operator, who key punches the work cards. This key punch, an IBM 26 Printing Card Punch, prints key identification and basic information on the cards.

"Simultaneously, an IBM Document Writer prepares the acknowledgement list. Essentially an electric typewriter with an automatic carriage, the document writer operates electronically through the key punch. A separate keyboard is used to key-in static information, such as date and filing and follow-up codes.

The Writer and the Sorter

"When the operator has completed the punched work cards (and acknowledgement list) for the 1,300 new accounts, they are put through the document writer again for preparation of the original collection notices. The notices are return-mail envelopes attached to perforated continuous forms. Information includes date, creditor's name or number, balance due, and the debtor's name and address. The name and address are so printed that the return-mail envelope can be inserted into a window envelope for mailing. The IBM document writer can prepare up to 600 of these notices per hour.

"The final step is to put the work cards through an IBM 82 Sorter, which alphabetizes them, ready for filing in tub files.

"At the end of each day, the entire file of collection accounts is processed through the sorter to give us our work file for the following day. Using the code, the sorter drops out all cards that are to receive follow-up notices. These cards are further divided into groups which are to receive second, third, and final notices on that day.

"Among collection services, the nation's average for collection is 36.7 percent. Because of our new automated system, our collection average has increased to 54 percent, ranging as high as 85 percent for certain client categories. And perhaps as important as any advantage: this collection system has reduced our cost per dollar collected."

APPENDIX B

Friden—Data Processing Inc. Proposal

This proposal was made jointly by Friden, Incorporated and by Data Processing, Incorporated. Friden would install a Flexowriter at State Consumer. This produces a punched paper tape which once a week would be sent to Data Processing, Incorporated for processing on their computer.

A Flexowriter is very similar to a typewriter. The operator types at normal typing speed and regular copy is produced. As a by-product of this operation, a tape punch records the typing on paper tape in the form of various codes. A code is a combination of punched holes aligned across the width of the tape.

This paper can be used:

1. To operate the Flexowriter. It will type the information as many times as required at approximately 100 words per minute. A code can be punched in the tape at any point to stop the Flexowriter automatically so manual fill-ins can be made.
2. As input data to a digital computer.

Friden Proposal

1. *Advantages of Flexowriter*
   a. Low initial investment.
   b. Equipment and services on a pay-as-you-earn basis.
   c. No special training required.
   d. Operation handled by clerical people.
   e. Prepunched, proofed information entering into the system. Minimum of manual entries.
   f. Flexowriter used to create personal letters when not engaged in payment and promise entry. This will result in a higher return on investment.
   g. Readily expandable system.
   h. Installation and systems work carried out by qualified people.

2. *Account Entry*
   Accounts are received from store, checked, assigned numbers, and put through the Flexowriter which prepares:
   a. Acknowledgement for store.
   b. A tape for Data Processing at Data Processing, Inc.
   c. An edge card for the heading of notices and Flexowriter input is produced. This card is a master card and filed by account.

3. *Payments*
   A payment is received from the account. The Account Master Card is put through the Flexowriter. Produced automatically are:
   a. A journal.
   b. Bank deposit slip.
   c. Tape for Data Processing.

4. *Promises*
   When a promise of payment is extracted, the master card for the account is put through the Flexowriter. Produced automatically are:
   a. An inside journal.
   b. A tape for Data Processing—this is used to set up the Payment—Expected History.

5. *Equipment Required*
   The equipment required by your organization which would be best suited for the job is:

   Flexowriter SPD with Auxiliary equipment $6,285.00
   6% Federal Excise Tax 377.10

   _____

   $6,662.10

Lease Plans

Five Year Lease . . . .$146.56 per month
Three-Year Lease . . . .$219.85 per month

Options

1. Renewal of Lease . . . .$333.10 per year
2. Purchase of equipment $666.21

Data Processing Inc.

. . . As we discussed in your office, the basic input for the system would be furnished as a result of your use of a Friden Flexowriter. By using prepunched master account cards and various other aids that are a part of the Flexowriter system, a punched paper tape will be produced which can be fed directly into our computer. We plan a system with the proper controls, checks, and balances so that the financial data we receive will at all times be under *your* control for auditing purposes.

It is our present intention that the procedure would involve the following steps:

1. The Flexowriter would have in it a master recording form on which all transactions going through the agency would be recorded for complete auditing and inspection by the agency at any time they may desire. This form will be designed so that it will have provision for —

   a. receipt of payments from accounts.
   b. receipt of accounts from clients.
   c. Entry of promise information as a result of telephone calls.
   d. Any other pertinent data required by the system.

2. Upon receipt of a new account from a client, a name and address master edge punched card will be prepared on the Flexowriter with whatever pertinent information is required. We are contemplating the possibility of utilizing the edge punched card to be mailed to the account for the record card of payments.

3. Upon receipt of a payment from the account, the edge punched card that accompanies the payment or the appropriate account prepunched master card would be removed from a tub file. This card would be inserted into the Flexowriter reading head which would automatically type the account number and name. The account number would be coded so that the client would be part of the number and readily discernible for future reporting. The amount of the payment would be entered manually by the Flexowriter operator and an appropriate code entered to indicate whether the payment was received directly from the client or by other means such as direct from the account, or by collector.

4. Any promise that is received by a telephone solicitor would be entered into the Flexowriter, utilizing again the master name and address card and entering the promise date and amount in the appropriate column on the journal sheet that is always in the Flexowriter carriage.

5. All the data that is typed into the Flexowriter will simultaneously be punched onto punched paper tape. Once a week the tape will be sent to Data Processing for entry into our high speed computer.

6. As a result of the tape input, the computer will store in its memory all pertinent details concerning both the account and the client. As a result of the promise information that is entered and various other data, weekly dunning lists will be printed and returned to

the agency. The dunning lists will be prepared by client, showing all accounts that are delinquent for that week. The list will show by account number sequence the name and telephone number of the delinquents. The original balance, the present balance, the last payment date and amount, the promised payment date and amount, the next to last previous payment date and amount, and the second to last previous payment date and amount will be shown on this sheet. In this way the telephone collector will have available to him all the information necessary to solicit the account by phone. Any accounts that have met their promises, or are maintaining their payments as agreed will not be printed out, so that the collector need only concern himself with those that require his attention.

7. At the end of the month Cash Receipts Journals will be prepared for each client, showing by account number all collections for the month for that client. The date of the payment, the amount, whether it was a direct payment from the client or received by other means, the new balance and the original balance of the account will be shown on this report. As a result, the tedious hand posting now required at the agency will be completely eliminated.

8. As a result of controls that will be instituted, the balances, cash receipts, and other financial data will constantly be under proper audit controls by the agency to easily prove out all the figures.

A procedure will be designed into the computer program so that, when desired, an account can be removed from the computer file and a complete detailed statement printed out for use by the Legal Department in enforcing collections. An additional procedure will list out each week all accounts that have become completely paid up so that they can be removed from the agency active files as well as from the computer active files.

We believe that the above procedure will afford a complete and economical system for use by the agency. Obviously, the exact details of the procedure will have to await a detailed study by Data Processing, Inc. and Friden engineers. However, the general outline of the procedure should be substantially as described above.

Costs of Data Processing

Based on the information we received during our conference and the number of transactions that will be involved, we have established costs of data processing on a weekly basis at our Service Center to be as follows:

1. There will be a minimum running charge of $80 per week which will include up to the first 1,500 active accounts in the file.

2. A weekly charge of $3\frac{1}{2}$ cents per active account above the first 1,500.

3. There will be a one time charge of 25 cents per account entered into the system to cover initiation of the master file and the prorated cost of magnetic tape necessary to maintain the account file.

4. There will be a charge of 25 cents per account that is removed from the active file for the Legal Department. This charge will cover the

appropriate cost of punching message cards here at Data Processing, Inc. and the cost of preparing a detailed printed statement of the account activity.

Setup Charges

In order to properly design the system and program the operation of the computer, our engineers will make a detailed and complete study of the agency's operations. In order to properly prepare the procedure to assist in training the personnel to write the computer program, debug it, and monitor its installation, there will be a one-time setup charge of $750, payable upon the acceptance of this proposal.

Conclusion

We believe that the system outlined herein will economically and simply take care of the requirements of the agency. Furthermore, expansion of the agency can readily be handled for known processing costs. The capacity of our computer installation is such that it is inconceivable that the agency could ever expand to the point where there would be any kind of problem. The only additional equipment that we can foresee for the system would be the possibility of an additional Flexowriter sometime in the future when the load becomes excessive for the one piece of equipment. . . .

THE WILLIAM CARTER
COMPANY (A)

In late December 1960, Edward Marzo, manager of the Methods Department at the William Carter Company, was considering a proposal made by the International Business Machines Corporation that the company acquire an IBM-1410 computer. A large manufacturer of knitwear clothing, the Carter company was not a newcomer to the field of automatic data processing. Prior to December 1958, the company had had over 30 years of satisfactory experience with punched card equipment. In 1956, the company had become interested in the acquisition of a computer and after extensive investigation had ordered a Univac File computer. It was installed on December 10, 1958.

When the computer had been ordered, the following applications had been planned:

1. The entire processing system for customers' orders.
2. Production scheduling for the company's seven plants.
3. Sales statistical analyses not currently available for the sales forecasting department, together with several other statistical reports.

Despite some unanticipated delays, by December 1960, the entire order processing function was being done on the computer. The extra work involved in correcting the delays, however, had caused work on the production scheduling system to fall behind. At that time some 70 to 80 percent of the systems analysis for the production scheduling application had been completed, and the detailed flow charting had been started; no work had yet been done on writing the programs. Some progress had been made toward achieving the system's third objective, both in terms of systems work and actual programs (25–50 percent of potential realized).

In a recent report to top management, Mr. Marzo had described himself as being basically satisfied with the performance of the computer and the features of the operating systems. The relatively slow operating speed of the machine, however, had had two consequences:

1. The costs of operating the system were higher than had been anticipated.
2. The computer was currently operating two shifts a day to handle the work volume generated by the order processing system. Management believed that the computer should not be scheduled for more than two-shift operations, so as to retain flexibility in case of machine breakdown and also to retain a safety margin for the peak loads of the summer season. This policy meant that, with the current setup, there was no time to install and operate the production scheduling system or the work on the sales forecasts.

Recalling that the original reason the Carter company had gone into data processing was to achieve benefits in the production area, Mr. Marzo still felt that considerable benefit might accrue to the company from mechanizing this area. He believed that mechanization would result in a better utilization of space and equipment and in a reduction of production lead times, with consequent inventory savings and less obsolescence of fabric. Also, he felt that recent developments in forecasting techniques indicated that a study should be made of the possibility of using the computer for sales analysis and forecasts.

Recognizing this capacity problem as one that was likely to assume serious proportions in mid-1959, Mr. Marzo asked Remington Rand to see if it could develop a core memory to replace the machine's drum memory. He believed that this would speed up the machine sufficiently so that installation of the other systems could be feasible. Although there were repeated indications that Remington Rand would undertake this project, final approval of it and prices were not received until December 16, 1960. Exhibit 1 presents a comparison of the physical features of the machine before and after the installation of the magnetic core memory. Remington Rand said that the unit would be ready for delivery late in December 1961 and could be hooked up to the machine over a weekend. No revision of the company's present programs would be required.

In the meantime, during 1960, several other computer manufacturers had approached the Carter company in an attempt to convince it that it should adopt their equipment instead. As a result of several months' study by company officials and a large consulting firm, it was decided that the most feasible of these proposed systems was the IBM 1410, a medium-sized solid state computer produced by the International Business Machines Corporation. Exhibit 1 presents a listing of its key physical features compared to those of the

Univac File computer, both before and after the addition of the core memory.

In his November presentation to the Carter management, the IBM salesman, in addition to remarking on some of the contrasts indicated in Exhibit 1, made the following remarks concerning the IBM 1410:

Every position of memory can be operated on arithmetically. This means that data do not have to be moved to a separate location, called an accumulator, saving program steps and simplifying programming. . . . The machine has 15 index registers. Index registers assist in program modification, thus reducing the number of instructions, conserving space and simplifying programming. . . . There are no control panels. Because of the fast internal speeds, and powerful operation codes, such as the editing commands, all arrangement of input and output data is performed in core memory. This reduces setup time between operations. . . . There is no fixed record length on tape. The features of variable length tape records, combined with the high recording density of 556 characters per inch, offer several systems advantages. In handling, there will be fewer tape reels. Many reels will be considerably smaller. Fewer tapes mean fewer changes in setups. This saves the time of the operators and the system. It also minimizes operator errors in filing, selecting, and handling. There should also be a really significant savings in tape cost. . . . Earlier this year we installed four large-scale computers near your office. They were delivered and installed on or prior to their target dates. . . Included in the programs currently being developed for 1410 customers are the following:

1. Autocoder. By using 1410 Autocoder a programmer will use a symbolic language that is simpler to learn and easier to use than machine language. Meaningful names for data and instruction locations are used. In addition, programming is simplified through the use of macro-instructions, which generate an entire sequence of appropriate machine instructions from a single statement. Typical macro-instructions pertain to arithmetic operations, logical decisions, and data movement in storage.
2. Input/Output Control System. A high percentage of instructions in any program are related to input-output operations and provide a set of routines that efficiently schedules all input-output operations.
3. Fortran. The Fortran language, which is applicable to the IBM 650, 704, 705, 709, 1620, 7070, 7080, and 7090, as well as the 1410, provides facilities for expressing problems in a symbolic source-language similar to the language of math.
4. Sort and Merge Program. Generalized sort and merge programs for various configurations of 1410 units, including one for a 1410 RAMAC with a single tape unit will be available.
5. Utility System. This set provides frequently needed routines to assist in the testing and operation of your programs.

Included are the following:
a. Disk-to-tape and tape-to-disk.
b. Clear disk storage.
c. Clear core storage.
d. Storage print.
e. Trace program.

. . . The 1410 system machine time will be provided to you before the actual installation. Forty hours of test time are provided and test time for 90 days following installation is not considered use. . . . Special representatives of IBM Applied Science department are highly trained and experienced in mathematics and the physical sciences and have a thorough knowledge of our equipment. They are available to consult with your people at any time in the areas of linear programming and operations research. Their contribution will be especially helpful in planning for the production scheduling application.

The original IBM price estimate (see Exhibit 2) indicated that the total rental for the machine would be $12,740 a month. For several reasons, Mr. Marzo believed that this was conservative.

1. The IBM proposal included provision for only four tape drive units. In nearly all cases, four units would be sufficient for handling the actual programming. Experience with the Univac File computer, however, had indicated that tape units were the part of the machine most likely to encounter mechanical failure. At present, with the five Remington Rand units, 15 to 20 percent of the time one or more was inoperative. In the past, the record had been even more unsatisfactory. Therefore, Mr. Marzo believed that a fifth tape unit was essential.

2. Secondly, he felt that an off-line printer would be useful to achieve additional flexibility and speed of operation.

To get some feel for the speed differential between the IBM 1410 and the installed Univac File, Mr. Marzo, in conjunction with an IBM salesman, recorded part of the present order processing system so that it could be run on the IBM 1410 computer. The theoretical processing time for each step was then calculated and added up. This figure was then compared with the known processing times for this operation on the Univac File, and the figures were extrapolated to cover the rest of the operations. On the basis of this study it was estimated that the IBM 1410 was three to four times faster than the Univac File and that it would take 70 hours of running time a month to handle the order processing work. A large consulting firm that had worked closely with the Carter company on this effort concurred with these estimates.

Mr. Marzo believed that converting the present set of Univac programs to the IBM 1410 would cost around $75,000. He anticipated that it would take two man-years each by two programmers, which would cost around $40,000. The remainder would be attributed to the supervisor's time and actual clerical conversion costs (e.g., key punching new programs). Because of the reprogramming problems and also because of the long lead time required for an IBM 1410, Mr. Marzo concluded that December 1962 would be the earliest feasible date for installation. He anticipated that once the machine was installed, it would be in use for at least six years before it would need replacement. He anticipated, also, that if a decision were made to acquire the 1410, the central processing unit with its extra features would be purchased over a five-year period and the rest of the equipment would be rented. (The central processing unit would be depreciated over a five-year period.) He also estimated that, because the 1410 was entirely internally programmed, it would be up to 30 percent faster to program new projects than was the Univac File with its wired control panel. He also thought that the 1410 would not require as high a caliber of programmer as did the Univac File.

In the face of this competition, Remington Rand made three proposals, each of which provided a price cut to meet the stiffening competition.

1. *Rental Plan:* If the Carter company agreed to rent the computer for three years (1961–64), Remington Rand would install the cores at no additional cost. The basic rent would be $16,740 a month (this included maintenance service and insurance). Second shift rental would be computed at 50 percent of the first shift rental on an hourly basis. Thus, if Carter spent an average of one hour a day during the month operating on the second shift, its bill would be increased only by one sixteenth.

2. *Four-Year Deferred Payment Purchase Plan:* Carter would purchase the file computer on a monthly payment basis, with the magnetic core memory being installed in December 1961. Monthly payments would be $12,224 in 1961 and $15,187 in 1962–64. In addition, down payments of $19,254 and $5,126 would be made on January 1, 1961, and January 1, 1962. This was based on the following cost figures.

   A. For equipment now installed:
      1. Current net purchase price (gross price less credit for one half of rentals already paid) . $385,092
      2. Total carrying charge, 4 years at 6% of remaining balance after each monthly payment . . . . $ 46,564
      3. Maintenance contract . . . . $ 3,633/month

    4.   Overtime maintenance.................$10/hour
    5.   Insurance...........................$300/year
B.   For 2000-word magnetic core memory to re-
     place 1000-word high speed drum memory in
     December 1961:
    1.   Total purchase price..................$102,529
    2.   Total carrying charge, 3 years at 6% of re-
         maining balance after each monthly pay-
         ment................................$ 9,271
    3.   Additional maintenance.................None
3. *Five-Year Deferred Payment Purchase Plan:* The details of this plan
    were similar to those of the four-year plan except that the payments
    for the computer (less the magnetic core memory) would be spread
    out over five years, and the payments for the magnetic core memory
    would be spread out over four years. This would result in monthly
    payments of $10,506 in 1961 and $12,779 in 1962–65.

    In each of the purchase contracts, the machine would be depreci-
    ated on a straight-line basis during the period 1961–64, down to
    scrap value equal to 3 percent of its original purchase price. The
    magnetic core memory would be depreciated during the period
    1962–64 in a similar manner. Carter would be obliged to cover the
    insurance on the machine as well as to pay for a maintenance con-
    tract. Exhibit 3 summarizes the relevant cash flows stemming from
    the several alternatives.

In presenting the case for acquisition of the cores, the Remington
Rand salesman made the following points which seemed particularly
relevant to Mr. Marzo:

Further benefits will accrue as follows:
1.   Present successful systems concepts can be retained.
2.   Present programming can be retained.
3.   The investment in the installation of equipment and the training
     of personnel will be protected.
4.   Continued operation of the File Computer will result in additional
     management benefits in the shortest possible time.
There are further benefits to be gained by retaining your present equipment during the development phases of your production scheduling application. When your complete requirements are clearly defined, you may
then take advantage of technological developments in the computer art
by writing your requirements in COBOL (Common Oriented Business
Language) and selecting equipment on the basis of actual performance of
your data processing problem. Since COBOL is a common language, it is
applicable to equipment of vendors participating in this program.

In November 1960, the assistant manager of the production department unexpectedly left the company. Mr. Marzo was quick to

feel his loss, because he had been the man in the production area who was really behind the automation of production scheduling and had handled all the liaison work with the data processing department. At approximately the same time, the more experienced of the two programmers working on the production scheduling project left Carter's to take another job. Mr. Marzo was still looking for a suitable replacement.

QUESTIONS

1. If you were president of the William Carter Company, would you acquire an IBM 1410 or would you add memory capacity to your Univac File Computer?

EXHIBIT 1

COMPARISON OF OPERATING CHARACTERISTSCS OF IBM 1410, UNIVAC FILE WITH DRUM MEMORY, AND UNIVAC FILE WITH CORE MEMORY

Characteristics	Univac File with Drum Memory	IBM 1410	Univac File with Core Memory
1. Solid state....................	No	Yes	No
2. Power requirements.................	75 KVA	27.3 KVA	75 KVA
3. Floor space......................	1,400 sq. ft.	500 sq. ft.	1,400 sq. ft.
4. Air conditioning equipment needed....	60 tons	5 tons	60 tons
5. Fixed or variable word length........	Fixed (12 digits per word)	Variable	Fixed (12 digits per word)
6. Size of machine memory.............	1,020 words	10–40K digits	2,000 words
7. Access time (internal storage)*.......	3.100m	4.5u	4u
8. Add time (6 digit factors)...........	8.6m	.24m	2.3m
9. Multiply time......................	33.9m	1.6m	8.9m
10. Divide time.......................	40.0m	6.0m	10.5m
11. No. of instruction..................	23	190	23
12. External wiring board...............	Yes	No	Yes
13. Addresses/inst.....................	3	1–2	3
14. Random access capacity.............	1,800,000 char.	10,000,000 char.	1,800,000 char.
15. Maximum access time to random access memory...........................	34m	160m	34m
16. Punched cards,** input/output.......	150R 150P	800R 250P	150R 150P
17. Printer...........................	600 lines/min.	600 lines/min.	600 lines/min.
18. Magnetic characters per second read..	10,000	20,000	10,000
19. Length of reel.....................	2,400 ft.	2,400 ft.	2,400 ft.
20. No. of blockettes or records per reel...	20,000 fixed length	variable length	20,000 fixed length

Notes: The Univac system records of magnetic tape always are of the same size. The IBM 1410 records are variable depending on the material. For example, on Univac tape, a sales report record for an invoice with 2 styles would take as much space as a record for an invoice with 4 styles. On IBM tape, the 2-style invoice would only take one-half as much room as the 4-style invoice.

*m = one thousandth of a second (millesecond);
u = one millionth of a second (microsecond).
**P = Punch; R = Read.

EXHIBIT 2

IBM 1410 Cost Proposal

Machine	Description	Monthly Rental Cost Component	Unit
1402–2	Card—Read Punch.......................... Read 800 CPM Punch 250 CPM	$ 615	$ 615
1403–2	Printer—600 lines per minute, 132 print positions	775	775
1405–1	Disk Storage (10 million characters)...........	965	
	Additional Access Arm......................	400	
	Disk Storage Control.......................	400	1,765
1411–2	Processing Unit (20,000) positions core memory..	4,550	
	Card Read Punch Adapter...................	35	
	Disk Storage Adapter......................	30	
	Processing Overlap.........................	200	
	Tape Input-Output Adapter (2 required).......	110	
	Dual Synchronizer Adapter...................	325	5,250
1414–2	Input/Output Synchronizer for 7330 Tape Units (2 required)...............................	1,000	1,000
1414–3	Input/Output Synchronizer for card read punch & printer...............................	675	
	Synchronizer storage printer.................	550	
	Additional.................................	60	1,285
1415–1	Console...................................	250	250
7330–1	Magnetic Tape Units (4)...................	1,800	1,800
	Total Monthly Rental...........................		$12,740

EXHIBIT 3

Annual Costs Accruing to
The William Carter Company under Various Proposals

Univac 4-Year Deferred Payment Purchase	1961	1962	1963	1964	1965
A. Capital Investment					
1. Down Payment for Computer.......	$ 19,254				
2. Down Payment for Cores...........		$ 5,126			
3. Annual Installments for Purchase of Machine......................	83,419	88,565	$ 94,027	$ 99,827	
4. Annual Core Purchase Installments..		30,545	32,428	34,429	
Total Capital Investment......	$102,673	$124,236	$126,455	$134,256	
B. Cash Expenses					
1. Computer Carrying Charge.........	$ 19,680	$ 14,536	$ 9,082	$ 3,275	
2. Magnetic Core Carrying Charge.....		5,018	3,129	1,130	
3. Regular Maintenance Contract......	43,596	43,596	43,596	43,596	$ 43,596
4. Overtime Maintenance (3 hrs./day 1962, 7 hrs./day other years) rate of $10/hr......................	17,500	7,500	17,500	17,500	17,500
5. Insurance......................	300	300	300	300	300
Total Cash Expenses...........	$ 81,076	$ 70,950	$ 73,607	$ 65,801	$ 61,396
C. Depreciation					
1. Chargeable Depreciation on Machine (st-line).........................	$ 88,715	$ 88,715	$ 88,715	$ 88,715	
2. Chargeable Depreciation on Cores (st-line)......................		34,176	34,176	34,176	
Total Noncash Expenses.......	$ 88,715	$122,891	$122,891	$122,891	

EXHIBIT 3 (Continued)

Univac 4-Year Deferred Payment Purchase	1961	1962	1963	1964	1965
D. *Calculation of Tax Credit*					
1. Cash Expenses Plus...............	$ 81,076	$ 70,950	$ 73,607	$ 65,801	$ 61,396
2. Depreciation Equals..............	88,715	122,891	122,891	122,891	
3. Total Expenses....................	$169,791	$193,841	$196,498	$188,692	$ 61,396
4. Tax Credit (50% Exp.)...........	84,895	96,920	98,249	94,346	30,698
E. *Calculation Cash Flow*					
1. Capital Investment Plus...........	$102,673	$124,236	$126,455	$134,256	
2. Cash Expenses Equals............	81,076	70,950	73,607	65,801	$ 61,396
3. Total Cash Outflow Minus.........	$183,749	$195,186	$200,062	$200,057	$ 61,396
4. Tax Credit Equals................	84,895	96,920	98,249	94,346	30,698
5. Cash Drain.......................	$ 98,854	$ 98,266	$101,813	$105,711	$ 30,698

Univac 5-Year Deferred Payment Purchase	1961	1962	1963	1964	1965
A. *Capital Investment*					
1. Down Payment for Computer.......	$ 19,524				
2. Down Payment for Cores..........		$ 5,126			
3. Annual Core Purchase Installments..		22,112	$ 23,588	$ 25,064	$ 26,540
4. Annual Installments for Purchase					
of machine....................	63,883	68,443	73,123	77,803	82,483
Total Capital Investment......	$ 83,407	$ 95,681	$ 96,711	$102,867	$109,023
B. *Cash Expenses*					
1. Computer Carrying Charge.........	$ 21,000	$ 16,440	$ 11,760	$ 7,080	$ 2,400
2. Magnetic Core Carrying Charge.....		5,172	3,696	2,220	744
3. Regular Maintenance Contract......	43,596	43,596	43,596	43,596	43,596
4. Overtime Maintenance (3 hrs./day					
1962, 7 hrs./day other years)......	17,500	7,500	17,500	17,500	17,500
5. Insurance........................	300	300	300	300	300
Total Cash Expenses...........	$ 82,396	$ 73,008	$ 76,852	$ 70,696	$ 64,540
C. *Depreciation*					
(Same as 4-Year Plan).............	$ 88,715	$122,891	$122,891	$122,891	
D. *Total Expenses*......................	$171,111	$195,899	$199,743	$193,587	$ 64,540
Tax Credit (50% Expenses)...........	85,555	97,949	99,871	96,793	32,270
E. *Calculation Cash Flow*					
1. Capital Investment Plus...........	$ 83,407	$ 95,681	$ 96,711	$102,867	$109,023
2. Cash Expenses Equals............	82,396	73,008	76,852	70,696	64,540
3. Total Cash Outflow Minus........	$165,803	$168,689	$173,563	$173,563	$173,563
4. Tax Credit Equals................	85,555	97,949	99,871	96,793	32,270
5. Cash Drain.......................	$ 80,248	$ 70,740	$ 73,692	$ 76,770	$141,293

Univac Rental Plan					
1. Basic Rent (12 x 16,740)...........	$200,880	$200,880	$200,880	$200,880	$200,880
2. Overtime (3 hrs./day 1962, 7 hrs./day					
other years)...................	87,880	32,960	87,880	87,880	87,880
Total Expenses................	$288,760	$233,840	$288,760	$288,760	$288,760
3. Tax Credit.......................	144,380	116,920	144,380	144,380	144,380
4. Cash Drain.......................	$144,380	$116,920	$144,380	$144,380	$144,380

IBM Proposal	1961	1962	1963	1964	1965
A. *Capital Investment*					
1410 Central Processor.............			$ 46,104	$ 46,104	$ 46,104
B. *Cash Expenses*					
1. Univac File Rental................	$259,680	$259,680			
2. 1410 Rental as Proposed by IBM 1410			89,760	89,760	89,760

EXHIBIT 3 (Continued)

IBM Proposal	1961	1962	1963	1964	1965
3. Maintenance on 1410 Central Processor..........................			1,236	1,236	1,236
4. Extra Features...................			14,700	14,700	14,700
Total Cash Expenses...........	$259,680	$259,680	$105,696	$105,696	$105,696
C. *Depreciation*........................			$ 46,104	$ 46,104	$ 46,104
D. *Total Expenses*......................	$259,680	$259,680	$151,800	$151,800	$151,800
Tax Credit (50% Expenses)...........	129,840	129,840	75,900	75,900	75,900
E. *Calculation Cash Flow*					
1. Capital Investment Plus...........			$ 46,104	$ 46,104	$ 46,104
2. Cash Expenses Equals.............	$259,680	$259,680	105,696	105,696	105,696
3. Total Cash Outflow Minus.........	$259,680	$259,680	$151,800	$151,800	$151,800
4. Tax Credit Equals................	129,840	129,840	75,900	75,900	75,900
5. Cash Drain......................	$129,840	$129,840	$ 75,900	$ 75,900	$ 75,900

THE WILLIAM CARTER
COMPANY (B)

In early January 1961, Mr. Edward Marzo, methods department manager at the William Carter Company, was reviewing data concerning a proposal that Carter's production scheduling be done on the company's Univac File computer. In 1956, when Carter's first considered the possibility of acquiring a computer, a well-known consulting firm was engaged to help them formulate their thinking as to possible applications for EDP. On August 13, 1956 the consulting firm submitted a report, in which they indicated potential EDP applications in the production area. These included:

1. Determination of schedules in response to forecast changes for:
   a. sewing
   b. cutting
   c. finishing cloth
   d. knitting
   e. yarn and trim purchase.
2. Preparation of production performance reports.
3. Preparation of usage reports for raw materials and in-process materials.
4. Preparation of material requirements.

By late 1960, sufficient progress had been made in other areas that Mr. Marzo could turn his attention towards the proposed mechanization of production planning. He realized this was an enormously complex task, and that a large amount of preliminary systems work must be completed before a workable approach to the problem could be developed. He felt, however, that a preliminary survey of production planning and scheduling operations could provide useful guidelines for directing this system's work.

COMPANY ORGANIZATION

The William Carter Company manufactures high-quality knitwear for men and boys, as well as underwear and outerwear for infants and small children. Included in its product line are infants' shirts, gowns, toddlers' polo shirts, sleepers, dresses, topper sets, brief- and boxer-type undershorts, pajamas, and T-shirts, all made in a variety of styles, fabric types, colors and sizes. The company has maintained a position of industry leadership since its founding in 1865. It annually sells about 40 million garments.

Carter's main office is located in Needham Heights, Massachusetts. Its manufacturing operations are scattered throughout the country. The manufacturing plants process cotton or synthetic fiber yarns into finished goods by knitting, bleaching, printing, dyeing, cutting and sewing. Exhibit 1 indicates the location and general nature of the operations carried out at each plant. After manufacture, the garments are inspected and bundled for shipment by truck to the large central warehouse in Needham. In Needham the goods are packaged in attractive "see-through" Pliofilm bags and stored in cardboard boxes awaiting shipment to leading department stores and specialty shops throughout the nation. Seconds (garments with defects) are sold by a store in Needham and to regular accounts on a selective basis.

PRODUCTION

Purchasing

Carter's manufacture of knitted garments is integrated back through the production of fabric. It does not produce its own yarn. All yarn purchases are made by the yarn purchasing department in Needham. Approximately 8 million pounds of yarn, in 300 different styles, are purchased each year. In recent years approximately 10 percent of these yarn styles have been dropped in a year and replaced by other yarn. These new yarns account for a very small fraction of the company's total yarn needs. Of the remaining 270 yarn styles, 40 are stocked on a perpetual inventory basis. The remaining yarns are ordered to fill specific production schedule commitments. Delivery times vary between three and six weeks. The yarn is stored in a warehouse in Barnesville, Georgia, near the company's only knitting mill.

Knitting

Carter has 300 knitting machines of various sizes which knit about 90 percent of the company's cloth requirements. (These machines knit plain and fancy fabrics in different weights and widths.) They run about 24 hours a day, 6 days a week. Prior to the knitting of a particular type of fabric a great deal of time (up to several days) may be spent in making mechanical adjustments to set up the knitting machine. Once these initial adjustments are made, however, it is relatively easy to operate the machine, and one operator is usually responsible for between 3 and 10 machines.

After 150 yards (approximately 40 pounds) has been knit on a machine, the operator cuts the cloth, removes the loaded spool, and replaces it with an empty one. The removed spools are then placed on a conveyor belt. They are carried to a weighing station where they are weighed and then sent to a greige storage room where they are stored awaiting further processing.

These 150-yard rolls are too short for efficient processing in the bleaching, dyeing and printing areas. They are, therefore, sewn together in the laying-out room to form continuous pieces, several thousand yards in length. The quantity of cloth joined together is limited only by the size of the order or the capacity of the kier to be used for boiling, whichever is smaller. It is then led to a kier where it is boiled in a weak alkaline solution. This removes any grease, oil or natural impurities in the cloth. If bleaching is desired, it is then sent to the bleach room, where the cloth is run through a chlorinated soda solution.

If it is desired to dye the cloth, it is passed and repassed through a series of baths which contain the dyes and various other solutions. The makeup and arrangement of the baths is determined by the types of dyestuffs being used, the shades desired, the nature of the fabric and several other factors.

For printing, the process is quite expensive. Large machines have to be carefully set up and considerable cost is involved in engraving the desired pattern on the surface of a print roller.

Cutting Room

At the conclusion of these operations, some of the cloth is sent to the cutting room at Barnesville, while the rest is sent to the mills at Senatobia, Springfield, and Thomaston, which also have cutting rooms. Here the cloth is stored until needed. Because of the variations in color between rolls of the same color description, considerable care is taken to combine the most closely shaded rolls on each cutting ticket. The warehouse boy carries the rolls to the cutting room. The spreader lays the cloth flat on a large cutting table, using a buggy to carry the weight of the roll the length of the table. After one layer is placed flat, the cloth is folded back and the buggy is again pulled the length of the table, placing another layer on top of the first. When completed there may be 72 layers of cloth, one to two yards wide and 50 to 60 yards long.

If it is a regular volume article that is being cut, a perforated marker is placed on top of the cloth. This is prepared by the pattern department. It is a layout of how the cloth is to be cut so that a minimum amount of cloth will be wasted. The marker is made of paper and is designed so that where the cloth is to be cut there are perforated holes in the paper. After the paper is placed on the cloth, it is dusted with blue chalk dust, which will fall through the perforations in the paper and leave the desired pattern on the cloth. The marker is then rolled up and stored until needed again.

If it is a special one-run item, markers are prepared which are the size of the items to be cut. These are placed on the cloth and blue chalk is run around their outside edges to indicate the cutting lines.

Power cutting tools are used to cut along these pattern lines. The pieces thus cut are bundled together and sent to the sewing room, where they are distributed to operators.

Sewing Room

Here, by use of electric sewing machines, the various cut pieces of cloth are sewn together into finished garments. The operators receive four types of material to construct the garment.

1. Cut pieces of cloth from the cutting room.
2. Trims from the trim department. This would include such things as buttons, snaps, lace, etc.
3. Stays from the stay department. These are ribbons of cloth varying in width from one to two inches. They are extensively used in reinforcing seams, making collars, etc.
4. Thread for the sewing machine.

The room is set up so that work progresses from one operator to another. Each operator is responsible for one operation, such as attaching cuffs, sewing on a collar, putting buttons on, etc. After the garment is finished, it is taken to the inspection department, where it is inspected, folded and shipped to Needham.

PRODUCTION PLANNING DEPARTMENT

Located in Needham, the Production Planning Department (see Exhibit 2 for organization chart) has responsibility for organizing the overall planning, scheduling, and controlling of fabrics and garment manufacturing for all mills. Mr. Richard Kirchner, the department manager, outlined the department objectives as being:

1. Give good service to the sales effort. Arrange for delivery of goods when ordered or if delay is unavoidable notify customer when goods can be shipped.
2. Reduce manufacturing expenses to lowest possible cost level.
3. Minimize capital investment (example—careful development of fabric producing plans will lead to better machine utilization and reduce the number necessary for Carter's to own).
4. Smooth out level of production (example—steady production levels keep workers employed year round and consequently reduce turnover and training costs).

Continuing, he had said:

. . . the basic responsibility of our department is to take the estimates of the sales planning department and allocate garment production among the various sewing mills in such a way as to achieve the optimal systemwide production level. We try to peg their activity within 15 percent of capacity or so but because of the geographical separation we are not in a position to do their detailed scheduling. We provide the necessary data for them to handle their short-range production planning . . . we are constantly caught in a time squeeze. On the one hand, sales planning wants to delay as long as possible in giving us information so that they can get the very latest market estimates and thus avoid production runs that may be difficult to sell. On the other hand, the mills are constantly on our backs to give them early production data so they can plan more effectively their production schedules . . . .

Garment Planning Group

The basic information input to the department is the sales plan which is received from the sales planning department. Carter's garment manufacture falls into two broad categories.

1. *Staple garments.* These are sold and manufactured on a continuous basis. Examples of these are infants' shirts, children's pants and men's shirts.
2. *Style garments.* Individual garment styles are manufactured and sold over a limited period, and then they are discontinued and replaced with another style. Examples of these are toddlers' polo shirts and girls' gowns.

For staple garments, the sales planning department issues the next year's sales plan three months prior to the peak sales month of the current plan. Thus a staple item sales plan for 1962 would be issued in June 1961 if the peak sales month is September. The sales plans for style garments are issued twice a year—one group for the spring line and a second group for the fall line. Spring plans are issued in June—covering sales deliveries from January through June of the following year. Fall plans are issued in December—covering sales deliveries from July through December of the following year. The sales plan contains the best estimate of the total sales during the period broken down into monthly requirements. A separate sales plan is prepared for each style-color combination, of which approximately 600 are produced during a year. These plans are not static, and typically are revised on an average of 2½ to 3 times before the year is ended, as different marketing data is absorbed. At any given time there are approximately 150 seasonal items and 300 staple items in production.

On the basis of the sales plan, a production plan and control report is prepared. This involves the following steps:

1. Determination of the seconds rate (percent of manufactured garments that will contain defects) and utilization of this to figure total production requirements by style and color. This is done by a subjective analysis of what past experience has been on this type of garment and the relative degree of proficiency of the operators. This normally runs between 3 and 5 percent.
2. Determining actual number of weeks available to produce garment.
3. Assignment of garment to a specific mill for manufacturing. In general certain mills are responsible for making certain types of garments. Because of the large amounts of certain garments that are required, however, some flexibility must be retained here. Thus several mills may be engaged in the manufacture of T-shirts. After a mill has been selected to produce a style it is consulted to determine the operator learning curves for each style so an expected rate of production can be established.

Using this information, a production plan and control report is developed. The planned production is then listed on the sales plan and cumulative production is checked against cumulative sales to make sure it covers each period. If deficiencies exist, either the production plan is changed or the sales planning department is consulted and the sales plan is altered.

This procedure is followed for approximately 60 percent of the sales plans. However, the sales planning department is often unable to issue sales plans when needed. Therefore, to aid the mills in making their plans, the production planning department estimates what the remaining 40 percent of the sales plans are likely to be and uses this guess to prepare an initial production plan and control report for the item. The information for this guess is derived partly from past experience and partly from informal contacts with personnel in the sales planning department.

When the production plan has been prepared, a check is made to determine whether the assignment of garments by mill and department are correct. Then rough time standards are used to see whether any mill has been overloaded under its present condition of absenteeism and number of operators. If the work assigned to a mill is higher than the operators on hand can perform, additional operators are hired if space is available; if not, the work is reassigned to another mill where operators and space can be found. The mill will do its own study of operator requirements and sewing machine requirements in more detail.

The next step is to prepare cutting plans to support the production plans. The first cutting must be made four to ten weeks prior to the time the finished garments are scheduled to be shipped from the mill. This time is needed to sew the garments together, inspect them, and assemble them for shipping. The cuttings are plotted by color to cover the planned sewing programs. Consideration is given to the effect on material requirements, so cuttings are usually staggered and balanced as well as possible throughout the season. The schedule is arranged so that 50 percent of the season's production in fall and spring lines will be cut and sewn in the Needham warehouse shortly after July 1 and January 1 respectively. In developing the schedule, special time allowances must be made for items which are cut and then sent out for special application (such as plastic coating) before sewing.

Six to eight weeks prior to the first cutting date, on the basis of the *cutting plan*, the production planning department will request and get the first round of *cutting sheets* from the sales planning department. This allows them to make a final decision as to the number of each garment size that should be cut. When the garment scheduler receives the cutting sheet, its number and the total dozens are posted to the cutting plan to show that the planned dozens have actually been authorized. The cutting sheet is then sent to the mill in triplicate. When the actual cutting has been made this information is returned to Needham so that it can be posted to the cutting plan. This enables the department to keep a close watch on all garment styles and to request corrective action where necessary.

When a garment is first introduced to the market, the sales planning department carefully analyzes its pattern of incoming orders to verify the accuracy of the initial sales plan. Frequently this sales plan turns out to be inaccurate. In these situations, the sales planning department issues a sales plan revision. The Garment Planning Group analyzes these changes and attempts, in coordination with the Trims and Fabrics Planning Groups, to implement the requested change. Because of the size of the manufacturing lead times involved, it is frequently not possible to implement increases fast enough to provide the garments in time to meet the company's sales needs. This is a function of the size of the increase, the availability of raw materials, production capacity in the cutting and sewing mills, and the time in the selling season that the request is made.

Fabric Planning Group

A copy of the sales plan is given to the fabric planning group. They first determine the total amount of cloth required for the production program by mill, fabric, color and yarn size. To do this, the *Official Notice* issued by the merchandising department covering each new style is consulted. This designates:

1. The type of fabric used in the garment.
2. The estimated number of pounds or yards required of each fabric per dozen of the garment.

The mill cutting department will advise the fabric planning group as to the most economical cutting width for each garment part. The cutting widths are then checked with the fabric producing mill (Barnesville) to determine the knitting machines which will be used and make sure they are not overloaded. With this data, the total fabric requirements for six months are calculated. These figures serve four purposes:

1. As a basis for yarn purchasing.
2. For overall control and reference purposes by Fabric Planning when ordering fabric.
3. Checking knitting mill capacity utilization.
4. Determining knitting mill employee requirements.

To determine actual weekly fabric production, a copy of the cutting sheets, released each week by sales planning, is given to the fabric planner who prepares a machine loading chart for all style items. This indicates the type of cloth to be knit on each machine for the next few weeks. In developing the chart, the following criteria are used:

1. Select a schedule which will minimize changeover time.
2. Postpone production of style merchandise fabrics as long as possible to take maximum advantage of sales forecast revisions.
3. Insure that adequate amounts of cloth are available to cover cutting sheet requirements.
4. Utilize economic lot size for each production center where possible:
    Knitting—setup time.
    Dye—tub capacity.
    Printing—minimize print run.

Since the timing element is less critical for staple merchandise items, the Fabric Planning Department merely indicates total needs for the next three-month period, and Barnesville actually schedules the work into the machines. This division of machine scheduling responsibility is feasible since very few machines .are used to manufacture both style and staple merchandise cloth. Each week a set of *Knitting Orders* is sent to Barnesville to indicate the particular cloths to be knit two weeks hence for the style items.

In order to keep abreast of fabric status, inventory cards are set up for each fabric, color, and yarn size. As the cutting sheets are received, their amounts are added to the fabric required and a notation is made as to the date that this cloth is scheduled to be knit. As cloth is received, the required balance is reduced. Therefore, at any time information is available as to:

1. What is the mill scheduled to cut?
2. What can be cut?
3. What cuttings are not covered by stock?

Each man reviews his own inventory cards to determine their fabric status. If the mill is running late, it is queried as to the cause and further asked when the orders will be processed and shipped. When a delay cannot be avoided, the cutting mill is notified, and fabrics for other styles finished in the same cutting mill are rushed to minimize lost production time. Also, as cutting sheets are returned to Needham after the cutting has been done, the actual fabric usage is checked against the estimated fabric requirements. If a variance is noted, the mill is checked as to the reasons for the variance. When actual usage is found to be correct, cloth orders are adjusted.

Exhibit 3 indicates Carter's spring production seasons for the various departments and the lead times required to manufacture a garment.

Springfield

The Springfield plant is Carter's oldest operation. Employing approximately 300 people, the plant both cuts the cloth for and sews infants' and toddlers' outerwear. These are one-season style items, and twice a year the plant is reengineered to produce an entirely new line of garments.

Most of the plant's employees are paid through an incentive wage system. Their wages run from a base of $1.30 per hour to $2.50 per hour. The plant's work force is unionized under the International Ladies Garment Workers Union. Management considers company-union relations to be excellent.

The mill produces the fall line of garments from April 1 to September 30 and the spring line of garments from October 1 to March 31. Preparation for a season's production commences with the receipt of the *Official Notices* from the merchandising department in Needham. These contain detailed descriptions of the garments that will be produced by the mill during the coming season. They are all at the mill by December 15 for the fall season and by June 16 for the spring season. Their primary use is to assist the methods and standards department in developing production techniques and standards, and to act as a reference bill of materials. Approximately a week later, a rough estimate of the total planned production of each style is sent to the mills.

This data enables work to be begun on planning the factory layout and other technical details for the season. Work is begun in the engineering department to prepare the numerous special jigs and fixtures that will be necessary.

In mid-January the *production plan and control report* for the fall season is received from the production planning department in Needham. This presents an initial forecast of required production by the mill of each style-color combination. During the next six months it will be refined and altered many times as the sales planning department in Needham adjusts its sales forecasts to coincide more closely with the latest market estimates. This report is used by the production control department at the mill, in conjunction with the *Official Notice*, to prepare tentative production schedules and otherwise organize for the coming season.

Because of holidays and the time the plant is inoperative while it is being reengineered for a new line (one week), it is estimated that each season has 22.6 producing weeks in it. To give a margin for unexpected delays and additions to the schedules, work is initially scheduled over a 19-week period. The total required production for each style-color combination is then divided by 19 to give the weekly required production for each item. The items are then analyzed so garments containing similar sewing operations are placed in the same department. (The plant has 3 sewing departments. Each department is equipped to complete all sewing on the garments assigned to it.) This helps provide steady production volume and optimum operator utilization. The complexity of this task has increased considerably in Springfield in the last four years as Carter's has been moving steadily towards producing more styles and manufacturing less of each. Concurrent with this scheduling effort is the preparation of cutting patterns, development of forms and codes to handle the new trims and cloths, and the preparation of sales samples. Exhibit 4 presents a rough estimate of the timing of these steps.

During the middle of February, the first cutting sheets for the fall season arrived at the mill. Despite the preparation of tentative sewing schedules by the mill and the fact that cloth is in the storeroom, no cutting may be done until the cutting sheets are received from the production planning department in Needham. This is of particular importance since the economics of the manufacturing process are such that once the cloth is cut, the garments should be sewn into finished garments, even if they have to be sold at substantial discounts.

Each week the production planning department in Needham releases 50–100 cutting sheets in quadruplicate to Springfield. Typically they will call for the cutting of between 50 and 350 dozen of each style-color combination. Three copies of the cutting sheets are sent directly to Springfield. The fourth goes first to the printing office in Needham, where the job order tickets are prepared (one ticket for every five dozen required), and is then routed on to the mill with the job order tickets.

The cutting sheets are then used to post cloth and trim requirements to the various inventory cards. These inventory cards provide detailed information on stock status. The job order tickets accompany the cut goods and trims as they move through the factory from the time of initial cutting to final sewing.

Stubs are detached from the job order ticket and forwarded to the plant's production control room three times during the manufacturing process:

1. When the cloth has been cut for the job.
2. When the garments have been sewn.
3. When the garments have been shipped from the plant.

This permits the progress of each order to be checked.

No attempt is made by the plant's production control office to schedule the work by machine and operator. Each sewing supervisor is responsible for keeping production moving in her department. To guide her scheduling decision, each day a *weekly production record* is issued by the production control department. This indicates the number of dozen of each style-color combination required to be manufactured daily if the mill is to meet its schedule, and how they have performed so far this week relative to these requirements. Depending on production problems and *sales plan* changes, weekly production will be altered from week to week during the production season. The performance aspect of this report is prepared on the basis of the ticket stubs received each day from the cutting, sewing (finishing) and shipping departments.

Mr. Kent, Springfield's Production Manager, stressed the importance of this decentralized control, noting that:

. . . . this type of production operation requires on-the-spot decision making. Ann (department supervisor) has been with us for 15 years. She knows these girls and what they can and cannot do. When you have a girl turning out a dozen items every three minutes and a machine breaking down two times a day, you have a situation where a detailed schedule by machine becomes so cumbersome as to be almost totally ineffective. The problem becomes even more complex when you realize that there are over 15 different types of sewing machines in each department, each of which requires very different sewing operator skills to run. Each operator is usually very proficient on one or two machines and far less on the others. Often, in fact, she can perform certain kinds of jobs on a particular machine far better than others. A quick-thinking supervisor can save you a lot of money here as she juggles her schedule around.

A second control document is the monthly *production plan and control report* which is broken down into a *weekly production finishing plan and control report*. This compares desired production of each style-color combination against actual shipments of completed garments to Needham. This is reviewed each week by Mr. Kent and Mr.

Spellman, the plant's assistant superintendent. Discrepancies are analyzed to spot the bottlenecks. Expedite orders are then sent to appropriate mill department supervisors or to Barnesville if cloth shortage is the bottleneck. This process is backed up by an in-process inventory book, and inventory stock status card files concerning cloth and trims raw materials. This enables them to answer frequent inquiries about the production cycle, and the status of particular orders.

Finally, every morning Mr. Kent holds a conference with his supervisors in which special instructions are given and the supervisors have an opportunity to discuss their problems and to work out a solution which is mutually satisfactory.

EXHIBIT 1

DESCRIPTION OF CARTER'S PHYSICAL FACILITIES

Plant Location	Principal Activity	Number of Employees
Springfield, Mass.	Cutting and sewing: infants' outerwear, toddlers' outerwear, play pajamas, infants' sun-suits, women's and children's gowns and pajamas.	21 (cutting) 265 (sewing)
Needham, Mass.	Central warehouse and administrative offices.	1,065
Forsyth, Ga.	Sewing: children's sleepers, children's shorts.	320
Barnesville, Ga.	Knitting, dyeing, printing, cutting and sewing—children's pajamas, children's sleepers, boys' and men's pajamas, infants' shirts, gowns, kimonos, sacques.	90 (bleach) 25 (print) 85 (knitting) 50 (cutting) 502 (sewing)
Thomaston, Ga.	Cutting and sewing: toddlers' polo shirts, infants' crib sheet and towel sets, misc.	25 (cutting) 500 (sewing)
Senatobia, Miss.	Cutting and sewing: T-shirts, girls', men's and junior figure pants.	15 (cutting) 370 (sewing)

EXHIBIT 2

PRODUCTION ORGANIZATION

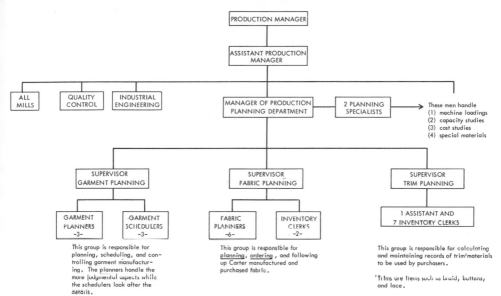

This group is responsible for planning, scheduling, and controlling garment manufacturing. The planners handle the more judgmental aspects while the schedulers look after the details.

This group is responsible for planning, ordering, and following up Carter manufactured and purchased fabric.

This group is responsible for calculating and maintaining records of trim¹ materials to be used by purchasers.

¹Trims are items such as braid, buttons, and lace.

EXHIBIT 3

PRODUCTION CYCLE FOR THE FALL SEASON

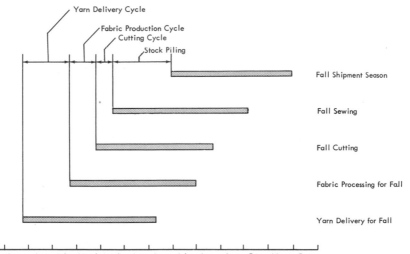

EXHIBIT 4

PRODUCTION SCHEDULING—TIMING

Fall Program
Weeks Ending

December 15	Official Notices released. Initial sales plan completed. Trim and fabric for sales samples ordered. Assignment of styles to mills—with rough production estimate on each.
January 6 13	Patterns—final measurements to mills. Mills develop forms and codes. Mills to complete operation sequence.
January 20 27	Cutting mills furnish cutting quantity—yarn sizes, etc., cutting widths. Initial check on fabric and trim deliveries for sales samples. Production planning establishes requirements—initial purchase.
February 3	All trims and fabrics in mills for sales samples. Mill and advance samples complete. Mills to present initial sewing plans.
February 10	Start cutting sales samples. Review of mill sewing plans by purchasing and sales plan by production planning.
February 17	Solidify production plans. Production planning starts issue of cutting sheets.
February 24	Cutting sheets checked by sales planning. Check delivery fabrics and trims for first two weeks to mills. Job order tickets printed.
March 10	All trims and fabric in mills for first two weeks.
March 17	Sales and office samples completed. First production cut.
March 24	End of production—previous season. Mills set up machines in sewing department.
March 31	First cuttings—new season into sewing.

NEGEA SERVICE CORPORATION*

NEGEA Service Corporation is a subsidiary of New England Gas and Electric Association, an investor-owned utility system with headquarters in Cambridge, Massachusetts.

The company made an extensive study of how it could use electronic data computer equipment in its operations. Possible accounting applications included customer billing and accounting, payroll, general accounting, and stockholder records. Possible engineering applications included work on complex problems related to power station operation, system expansion, distribution scheduling, load forecasts, cost reduction, and research. As a result of this study the decision was made to acquire new IBM 1410 and 1401 electronic computers.

The company now must decide whether to acquire the computer equipment by purchase or by lease. The Comptroller's Department prepared a schedule of the estimated costs for a nine-year period if this oquipmont wao purchasod for an original cost of $734,110 (see Exhibit 1).

The report of the Comptroller's Department commented on the trade-in value of the computer equipment as follows:

IBM's current trade-in policy provides for applying the trade-in value of purchased equipment against:
1. The purchase of new IBM data processing machines.
2. The purchase of installed rented machines on a purchase option plan.
3. The rental cost of machines not installed as of the date of a trade-in commitment.

The trade-in allowance is subject to change and is based on the schedule in effect at the time of the delivery to IBM. The schedule and trade-in value in effect at this time is shown as follows:

Age of Machine (Years)	Trade-in Value	
Original cost $734,110	Percent	Amount
1	48	$352,374
2	36	264,280
3	24	176,186
4	12	88,093
5	6	44,047
6	3	22,023
7	0	—

*Copyright by Chauncy Beagle, Associate Professor of Accounting, University of Colorado. Reproduced here with his permission.

If the computer equipment was leased from IBM under a standard rental contract, the annual rental payment would be $176,580. After the first year the rental contract could be canceled by the company upon giving three months' notice of cancellation to IBM. If the computer equipment was leased, it could be purchased at any time at its depreciated value. Depreciation would be computed at 10 percent a year. However, the minimum depreciated value would be 25 percent. (If leased equipment was purchased, accelerated depreciation would not be used because the equipment would be considered to be "used" equipment.)

Leased equipment also could be purchased under a purchase option plan up to 24 months after the date of delivery. (Once again, accelerated depreciation probably could not be used because the equipment might be considered to be "used" equipment.) Under this plan 65 percent of the rentals paid (with one minor exception) would be applied to the purchase price if the option was exercised. Also, if the option was exercised, a required deposit of 1 percent of the purchase price would be refunded.

If the computer equipment was leased under the standard 176-hour use contract offered by IBM, a charge would be made for overtime at 40 percent of the hourly rate for the prime shift for the actual hours used in excess of 176 per month. If the equipment was purchased, the only charge for second- and third-shift use would be maintenance.

The comptroller was concerned about the rapid obsolescence of computer equipment. The report prepared by his department identified three kinds of obsolescence; physical obsolescence, technological obsolescence, and system obsolescence. The report commented on equipment obsolescence as follows:

1. *Physical Obsolescence* refers to the potential for NEGEA Service Corporation to outgrow the physical capabilities of the equipment. We have made timing tests using the estimated machine requirements for the present customer accounting application as a base of 100 percent and have found that the equipment utilization would be as follows:

	Chargeable		Hours Per Day Including Setup and Handling	
Work Load	1410	1401	1410	1401
100% (customer accounting).......	4.1	8.2	5.4	9.5
200............................	8.3	16.5	10.5	19.0

It is very difficult to estimate the machine requirements for applications beyond customer accounting because of the wide and varied use made of computers by many utilities. An estimate of approximately 60 percent of the customer accounting work load for the remaining accounting, payroll, and stockholder records would, however, generally be considered conservative.

This test would indicate that substantial additional capacity in second-shift operations is available on the IBM 1410 for processing additional volume or applications not considered above, such as transformer load studies and other engineering procedures. In addition, third-shift and weekend use also offer substantial periods of available computer time.

2. *Technological Obsolescence* relates to the potential that the 1410 and/or 1401 would be replaced by a faster machine at lower cost in the future. There is, of course, no assurance that such a situation would not take place in the next two to five years, particularly if the experience of the last five years can be used as a basis. However, the 1410 and 1401 are very recent computer announcements and reflect substantial reduction in cost over the previous models. Future announcements would have to be very substantial to make them sufficiently attractive to NEGEA Service Corporation to support the heavy costs resulting from reprogramming and conversion to a new machine.

3. *System Obsolescence* refers to the possibility that (1) more advanced systems concepts might make the equipment under consideration less ideal, and (2) the system being designed for the 1410 might not function up to anticipation because the 1410 did not achieve its announced specifications. With regard to the first point, the system being developed will be designed with the latest techniques available, in line with economic considerations and will therefore be as modern as the equipment.

The comptroller pointed out that the method of financing the purchase of the computer equipment was a separate question which would need to be solved if the decision was made in favor of purchasing rather than leasing. Schedules were prepared to estimate the cash flow gain or loss if the computer equipment was purchased (see Exhibits 2 and 3). The estimated cash flow gain, if purchased, of $186,220 was based on the assumption that the parent company, New England Gas and Electric Association, would finance the purchase of the computer equipment and that the equipment would adequately serve the company's purposes for a nine-year period.

The consolidated financial statements for 1961 and 1962 are summarized in Exhibits 4 and 5.

One of the notes to the consolidated financial statements in the

1962 Annual Report commented as follows about the construction and financing plans for 1963:

The construction program of the operating subsidiaries is estimated at $12 million for the year 1963. New capital requirements are estimated at $3 million and are expected to be financed initially by bank loans which, together with loans of $4,500,000 presently outstanding, will be permanently financed through the issuance of long-term debt securities. Present plans call for issuance of $5 million of such subsidiary long-term debt securities late in 1963 or in 1964.

EXHIBIT 1

NEGEA Service Corporation

Estimated Costs if the Computer Equipment Were Purchased

Year	Depreciation*	Maintenance	Interest at 6%	Total
1........	$183,526	$ 10,338	$ 39,780	$233,644
2........	137,646	10,338	32,003	179,987
3........	103,234	10,338	25,535	139,107
4........	77,426	11,127	20,092	108,645
5........	58,069	11,127	15,379	84,575
6........	58,069	11,127	10,985	80,181
7........	58,069	12,621	6,591	77,281
8........	58,071	12,621	2,197	72,889
9........	—	12,621	—	12,621
Totals...	$734,110	$102,258	$152,562	$988,930

*The depreciation computations are based on using the double declining balance method until the fifth year and then changing to the straight line method.
Source: Report of the Comptroller's Department.

EXHIBIT 2

NEGEA SERVICE CORPORATION

Cash Flow under Financing through New England Gas and Electric Association

	Total	1	2	3	4	5	6	7	8	9
					Year					
Repayment of loan (equivalent to depreciation and deferred income taxes from accelerated tax depreciation) (Exhibit 3)	$ 734,110	$142,233	$146,598	$ 98,072	$ 83,878	$ 73,232	$ 73,232	$ 73,232	$ 73,233	$ —
Annual maintenance	102,258	10,338	10,338	10,338	11,127	11,127	11,127	12,621	12,621	12,621
Total purchase cash flow	$ 836,368	$152,571	$157,936	$108,410	$ 95,005	$ 84,359	$ 84,359	$ 85,853	$ 85,854	$ 12,621
Payments under rental from I.B.M.	1,589,220	176,580	176,580	176,580	176,580	176,580	176,580	176,580	176,580	176,580
Cash gain (or loss) from purchase, excluding interest and before income tax effects	$ 752,852	$ 24,009	$ 49,244	$ 68,170	$ 81,575	$ 92,221	$ 92,221	$ 90,727	$ 90,726	$163,959
Interest charge (payments by NEGEA Service Corporation to New England Gas and Electric Association at 6% on average invested capital)	152,562	39,780	32,003	25,535	20,092	15,379	10,985	6,591	2,197	—
Cash flow gain (or loss) from purchase before tax effects	$ 600,290	($ 15,771)	$ 17,241	$ 42,635	$ 61,483	$ 76,842	$ 81,236	$ 84,136	$ 88,529	$163,959
Effects of income taxes, at 55% tax rate: Tax reductions if purchased— Depreciation (from Exhibit 3)	$ 403,760	$100,939	$ 55,775	$ 56,778	$ 42,584	$ 31,938	$ 31,938	$ 31,938	$ 31,940	$ —
Maintenance	56,241	5,686	5,686	5,686	6,120	6,120	6,120	6,941	6,939	6,943
	$ 460,001	$106,625	$ 61,391	$ 62,464	$ 48,704	$ 38,058	$ 38,058	$ 38,879	$ 38,879	$ 6,943
Tax reduction under rental from I.B.M., at 55% tax rate	874,071	97,119	97,119	97,119	97,119	97,119	97,119	97,119	97,119	97,119
	($ 414,070)	$ 9,506	($ 15,723)	($ 34,655)	($ 48,415)	($ 59,061)	($ 59,061)	($ 58,240)	($ 58,240)	($ 90,176)
Net cash flow gain (or loss) after taxes if purchased	$ 186,220	($ 6,265)	$ 1,513	$ 7,950	$ 13,068	$ 17,781	$ 22,175	$ 25,896	$ 30,289	$ 73,783
Cumulative cash flow gain (or loss)	186,220	($ 6,265)	($ 4,752)	$ 3,228	$ 16,296	$ 34,077	$ 56,252	$ 82,148	$112,437	$186,220

Source: Report of the Comptroller's Department.

EXHIBIT 3

NEGEA SERVICE CORPORATION

Loan Payment Schedule

	1	2	3	4	5	6	7	8
Unpaid Balance of Loan at Beginning of Year .	$734,110	$591,877	$474,879	$376,807	$292,929	$219,697	$146,465	$ 73,233
Payment on Loan:								
Depreciation—straight line (8 years)......	$ 91,763	$ 91,763	$ 91,763	$ 91,763	$ 91,763	$ 91,763	$ 91,763	$ 91,763
Deferred tax on accelerated depreciation..	50,470	25,235	6,309	(7,885)	(18,531)	(18,531)	(18,531)	(18,530)
	$142,233	$116,998	$ 98,072	$ 83,878	$ 73,232	$ 73,232	$ 73,232	$ 73,233
Unpaid Balance at End of Year............	$591,877	$474,879	$376,807	$292,929	$219,697	$146,465	$ 73,233	$ —
Interest Earned on Average Invested Capital at 6% Annually......................	$ 39,780	$ 32,003	$ 25,535	$ 20,092	$ 15,379	$ 10,985	$ 6,591	$ 2,197
Depreciation:								
Tax basis at beginning of year............	$734,110	$550,584	$412,938	$309,704	$232,278	$174,209	$116,140	$ 58,071
Accelerated depreciation deduction........	183,526	137,646	103,234	77,426	58,069	58,069	58,069	58,071
Tax basis at end of year....	$550,584	$412,938	$309,704	$232,278	$174,209	$116,140	$ 58,071	$ —

Source: Report of the Comptroller's Department.

EXHIBIT 4

NEGEA SERVICE CORPORATION

1962 Operations in Brief Compared with 1961
(New England Gas and Electric Association and Subsidiary Companies)

WE RECEIVED:	*1962*	*1961*
From our electric, gas and steam customers for service	$61,890,506	$58,442,721
As interest, dividends, and rents	1,035,565	898,403
Total	$62,926,071	$59,341,124

WE USED IT:		
To buy fuels for our boilers and gas generators	$ 6,351,354	$ 6,073,982
To purchase electricity and gas for resale	13,307,403	12,607,230
To pay our employees and provide benefits for them	12,805,695	12,081,167
To buy materials, insurance, and other items	6,049,746	6,070,807
To support federal, state and local governments by taxes	12,513,280	11,208,254
To pay interest to those who have loaned us their money	2,785,325	2,696,864
To provide for recovery of original cost of property, plant and equipment (depreciation)	4,038,674	3,859,705
To pay our investor-owners for the use of their funds	3,349,795	3,173,490
And the remainder we have held in the business to meet future needs	1,724,799	1,569,625
Earnings per average common share outstanding	2.01	1.88
Annual dividend rate	1.32	1.24
Bid price range—high	35⅞	36⅝
low	27¼	24½

Source: 1962 Annual Report.

EXHIBIT 5

NEGEA Service Corporation

Our Financial Position
(New England Gas and Electric Association and Subsidiary Companies)

WE OWNED:	1962	1961
Property, plant, equipment and construction funds (less provision for recovery of original cost)	$112,033,938	$105,437,807
Cash and U. S. Government Securities	8,961,084	9,908,327
Investment in Algonquin Gas Transmission Company	4,856,100	4,856,100
Miscellaneous investments and funds deposited for special purposes	2,796,897	2,935,322
Amounts receivable from others	9,203,586	8,415,889
Materials and supplies on hand	2,384,619	2,706,836
Amounts paid in advance to others and deferred items	1,215,447	1,100,874
	$141,451,671	$135,361,155
WE OWED:		
For money borrowed	$ 75,711,000	$ 73,437,000
For materials, supplies, and services	4,312,644	3,720,114
For accrued taxes	4,848,118	4,920,887
For interest and other accrued expenses	1,039,921	938,008
For dividends declared	856,509	832,892
Customers' deposits	809,564	761,720
Deferred items:		
Reserves for deferred income and franchise taxes	4,246,873	3,029,172
Other	735,457	480,607
	$ 92,560,086	$ 88,120,400
BALANCE—SHAREHOLDERS' OWNERSHIP:		
Amount paid in for Association shares	$ 31,932,238	$ 31,932,238
Minority interest in a subsidiary	8,160	82,129
Retained earnings	16,951,187	15,226,388
	$ 48,891,585	$ 47,240,755

Source: 1962 Annual Report.

BOOTHBY
MANUFACTURING COMPANY

In the spring of 1956, the Boothby Manufacturing Company[1] was preparing for the installation of an electronic data processing machine. This device, the company's first computer, introduced a number of new problems in the company's operations, many of them having personnel ramifications.

The Boothby company, one of the nation's oldest corporations, had been engaged principally in the production of basic consumer goods since the mid-1800's. Certain of its products had found industrial applications, however, so that by 1956 sales were made not only to household consumers but also to other manufacturing concerns. Throughout its long corporate history, the company had experienced depressions and booms and had continued to progress in both circumstances. Its record of dividend payments had helped win wide respect in business circles for the company's management, and its reputation for quality products had made its name well known to consumers. The company had taken numerous pioneering steps within its industry, notably leading in matters such as product packaging and display and in the "styling" of products in which fashion had previously been generally regarded as inconsequential.

Executive offices were maintained in Philadelphia for corporation officers of the purchasing department, the insurance department, the traffic department, the office of the vice president in charge of advertising, the general accounting office, and a special sales office which sold the company's products to particular industries and could also contract to purchase products outside the company for resale to those industries. The general sales office of the company, which served as headquarters for the vice president in charge of sales, was located in New York City and was complemented by nine additional sales offices throughout the United States. The general sales offices

[1]All names have been disguised.

provided facilities for the product sales managers, the director of market research, the director of product research, an order processing department, a sales accounting office and a mill department, the latter furnishing production control and liaison between sales and the production plants. Manufacturing plants, of which there were nine, were located chiefly along the East Coast. Total employment of the company numbered about 9,000, while the sales volume amounted to nearly $100 million in 1956.

Although there was no single director of personnel for the company who might serve as a coordinator of overall personnel programs,[2] the company had laid down certain personnel policies and practices to be followed throughout its organization. Generally, up-to-date personnel practices were observed, with an extensive concern for employees being evidenced notably in the brochure distributed to new members of the Philadelphia office. In this brochure, a brief history of the company and descriptions of its principal products were followed by employment policy statements, information on insurance programs, vacations, hours of work, payroll records, company tearoom service and similar matters. The company had a limited profit-sharing plan in operation. Other employee benefits included physical examination, financial help with certain education courses, and a library of company books and business information.

Each of the plants had a personnel manager, reporting directly to its plant manager, whose functions dealt chiefly with matters affecting the productive work force. Labor relations were particular concerns of these men, not only in the unionized plants in the North, but also in the nonunionized plants in the South. Where plants were unionized, contract negotiations were conducted by the plant manager, permanently retained (outside) legal counsel and the personnel manager. The plant personnel managers acted fairly independently of centralized authority.

In the New York office, where 125 to 150 persons were employed, most personnel administration functions were handled by line executives. The sales department controller had responsibility for most of the clerical personnel in the New York office, including the recruiting

---

[2]During a discussion group meeting of second-level executives a suggestion was made by a plant personnel manager for yearly conferences of personnel officials. This suggestion was incorporated in the executives' report to the policy committee (president, sales vice president, advertising vice president, and the retired treasurer), but no action on it had been taken at the time the case was written.

and interviewing of such personnel. If a vacancy occurred in a merchandise department, the final hiring decision rested with the departmental supervisor. The hiring of supervisory employees and salesmen was generally done by the coordinator for sales. No central source dealt with hiring other members of the supervisory force; the usual practice was for a department head to deal with such matters through inquiries in the trade, calls on executives' employment agencies, and similar means. New jobs of a supervisory nature required the approval of the company president before the position could be established, and it would then become the duty of the supervisor to find the man for the position.

The Philadelphia offices similarly followed a decentralized pattern of personnel administration. A total of about 100 persons were employed in these offices, most of them performing tasks in the general accounting office. This office maintained centralized accounts receivable, accounts payable, and companywide statistical records. No overall personnel officer, as such, was employed in the executive offices, and personnel matters for this office generally devolved upon the company controller, Mr. Bruce, whose department was numerically the largest. Mr. Bruce was familiar with many personnel policies and procedures, but time limitations prevented his conducting a large-scale personnel program. In his opinion, there would have been insufficient work for a full-time director of personnel, although he believed that such a position might advantageously be filled as a part-time function.

Among his personnel duties, Mr. Bruce served as a coordinator for the hiring of clerical personnel for the executive offices, departmental requests for such personnel being routed through his office. It then became his task to find and screen suitable applicants, who would be referred to their future supervisors for approval. For vacancies occurring above clerical levels, the employment process would fall to the supervisor of the proposed job, unless this vacancy occurred in Mr. Bruce's departments. In the latter case, Mr. Bruce had full responsibility.

For all company positions over a salary level of $4,000 a year, the company president maintained a personal history file. The president himself passed on the promotions and salary increases of such persons, though he generally followed the recommendations of the immediate supervisors. The president's office also kept on file the scores registered on a well-known "temperament test" which was given to all personnel, and which was used as a guide in employee selection and in considering personnel for promotions. These tests were administered by the president's secretary and by the treasurer of the company, both of whom had been qualified by the designer of the test to interpret the results. In addition, the president's office approved recommendations for new supervisory positions.

In considering the purchase of a computer, Boothby first conducted a detailed feasibility study. A "Survey Committee," consisting of Mr. Bruce, the director of operations research, and a cost accountant from one of the company's plants, was established to investigate exhaustively specific operations that could be appropriately adapted to electronic processing. Systems and procedures were analyzed, and the possibilities- for programming the machine were explored. In essence, the committee was to determine which machine, if any, to obtain. A comprehensive study of the electronic processing equipment field ensued. After studying machines of all manufacturers, the conclusion was reached that the company should rent, with an option to buy, a medium-sized computer. Cost factors, displacement of personnel, and personnel training for the new operations were all included in the committee's considerations.

Personnel planning for the computer was considerably complicated by a location factor. The machine was actually to be installed in the New York offices of the company, but most of its work would supplant tasks being performed currently in the general accounting office in Philadelphia. Moreover, there was no real "mechanization" of office functions in the New York office, while the Philadelphia offices were well mechanized with adequate tabulating, key punch, and similar equipment. It was clear that a certain measure of employee displacement would follow, to the extent that the jobs of some of the Philadelphia employees would be eliminated.

The decision to locate the computer in New York was made in compliance with the president's desire for accelerated service to the sales department, especially in the development of information not presently available. Initially, computer applications would concentrate on keeping track of orders and inventories for the sales department: what had been ordered, delivery dates, what the company needed to sell, and what it needed to manufacture.

The survey committee, in a final report submitted to the president and the treasurer of the company, recommended that steps be taken to reassure employees who were in danger of losing their jobs, in order to maintain employee morale. In the committee's opinion, it was desirable to say that "no employee was to lose his job" because of the advent of the computer and either to state or imply that normal turnover and attrition would take care of personnel reductions. Although the committee felt that normal turnover *would* compensate for displacements, it was thought that the company might have to request employees to transfer to other jobs. In any event, the committee believed that its recommended policy of reassuring employees could be followed easily by simply not replacing employees who left in the normal course of business.

This recommendation, however, was not followed. Top management took the position that it was unrealistic to provide employee reassurances: jobs *were* to be eliminated and "this fact should be faced by the company."

Subsequently, the employees were told that (1) the company had ordered a computer; (2) the computer would be in New York and would perform functions currently executed in Philadelphia; (3) the company would make every effort to see that employees who were affected were offered other work within the company if suitable openings existed, and, where no openings existed, efforts would be made to help the employees to locate elsewhere; and (4) the company expected no jobs to be affected during the coming 12 months, the present personnel were performing satisfactorily, and they would be needed for at least an additional 12 months' period.

This message was transmitted to the employees by means of a bulletin, in which it was stated also that the company would lease the computer which would perform functions in the ordering, sales analysis, accounts receivable, and inventory record keeping areas. Following distribution of this bulletin, Mr. Bruce personally talked to the employees of the two departments to be most affected, telling them substantially what was outlined in the bulletin. This talk was given after supervisors had reported unrest and discontent concerning possible effects of the computer. It was Mr. Bruce's opinion that earlier timing of his talk would not have helped dispel such unrest and that only specific reassurances would have been of real value.

The effects of these decisions and announcements upon the general accounting office were not long in appearing. Actual installation of the computer and the commencement of its operations were not scheduled until a year later; but following the announcement of the plans, morale in the department dropped appreciably, according to

Mr. Bruce. This drop in morale was evidenced by diminished work efficiency, a more careless and unconcerned attitude, and a general feeling of "I'm not going to be around here long, anyhow." There was no immediate *mass* upsurge of resignations, but the company felt reasonably sure that some employees began to look for other employment. Exit interviews were not a practice of the company, and, accordingly, it was not possible to be certain of precisely which resignations were due to the computer. It was estimated by Mr. Bruce, however, that, over a period of about one year, some 10 resignations were tendered as a result of the computer planning.

Vacancies occurring after such resignations were very difficult to fill. Applicants were reluctant to accept jobs that in all probability would not be permanent, while supervisors felt handicapped because they had less of a future to offer a new employee. Shortages of adequate personnel compounded the department's difficulties, requiring longer hours of work, overtime pay, delays in data handling, and progressively lower employee morale. Furthermore, the introduction of changes in methods and systems in order to prepare for the computer became quite difficult. The usual problems of getting clerical personnel to accept changes were complicated by lowered morale deriving from a sense of the futility of "learning a new job for only one year." This situation, Mr. Bruce believed, was one which would have to be "lived with" until the computer actually commenced operations.

The precise number of persons who would be released because of the change in operations could still not be determined. In some instances, it appeared possible that initial computer operations would reflect the desirability of returning to some manual operations. For a time, it was certain that there would be a need for parallel systems of data processing, until the new computer center was thoroughly "proved out."

In looking forward to terminations the company expected a gradual "phasing out" process to release the pressure of wholesale eliminations of jobs. (The company's termination policy, as stated in the *Employee's Handbook*, is given in Exhibit 1.) It was anticipated that terminations would not be made by seniority but in inverse ratio to merit. With only one exception, no one who would be released was near retirement age, and this one exception had already exceeded the retirement age that was to become compulsory in 1960. The usual termination policy had been modified in the case of four supervisory level employees, by reaching agreement with them that they would receive their regular pay until they found other employment, up to a maximum of six months, in the event that their positions were eliminated.

In preparing for the computer, the survey committee had given consideration to the training that would be provided by equipment manufacturers to those persons selected for operators. All members of the survey committee had attended equipment manufacturers' schools, and it was expected that the computer manufacturer would train personnel to the company's satisfaction.

The first step in the selection of computer personnel was to find a man who would be in charge of the installation, reporting to Mr. Bruce. Recommendations for the position of supervisor were made by the survey committee. The final selection was made by the company president. A former plant manager with no previous knowledge of computers was finally chosen, primarily because of his administrative ability. This man was designated the "chief of the computer center."

The second step involved the selection of programmers who would study systems and actually write the instructions for the machine. Plant managers were asked for names of personnel who might be suitable; and recommendations also were received from the Philadelphia and the New York offices. Nominees first were interviewed by Mr. Bruce and the chief of the computer center and then given a series of tests. These tests included the "temperament test," previously referred to, given by company personnel; an arithmetic test for logic and accuracy, developed by a West Coast manufacturer; and an aptitude test for electronic data processing machine operators. This last test, prepared for a manufacturer of computers, was designed essentially to test the applicant's ability to follow instructions, to read series of numbers, and to think logically. Following the tests, the nominees were told that, if they finally were selected, they would have to move to New York at company expense, and what the salary would be. This salary was considerably higher than that presently being earned in most instances. No other promises were made, but the advantages of higher salaries and the opportunities of entering a new and interesting field were emphasized. The fact that the computer would be located in New York City had to be taken into consideration in interviewing employees.

From the overall group, nine persons were finally selected to be sent, with the chief of the computer center, to the first training course.

These nine were told that four of them would ultimately be chosen, based on their performance in the training course as evaluated by the computer center chief and the teachers of the course. It was pointed out, however, that all nine were honored by being selected for the course and that by no means would the five not finally chosen be considered "black sheep." Of the four selected, two came from one of the Northern manufacturing plants, one from the New York office, and one from the Philadelphia office.

Courses in the manufacturer's school included programming, theory of electronic data processing, logical operations, and "flow-charting." The courses were generally satisfactory, except in the area of flow-charting, where it was felt that a more extensive treatment would have been justified. Added training here was subsequently given by Mr. Bruce and the director of operations research, using their experience gained in this field in another manufacturer's school.

After this course was completed, the Boothby company held one-day sessions for most of top management, to outline what could be expected from the computer installation. These sessions were scheduled as a part of regular quarterly meetings.

In the new installation, the computer center chief and the four programmers were to be joined by four or five key punch operators and probably two tabulating machine operators, one of the latter being a working supervisor. The key punch and tabulating machine operators were to be new employees, as there was then no tabulating or similar machinery in the New York office. In addition, a systems and procedures man, employed from outside the company, was temporarily assigned to the computer installation, in view of the systems problems arising there. Although competition for programmers was expected to become keen in the future, the company up to then had no problems in retaining its personnel. It was aware of the possibility that other companies might ultimately seek to draw away such trained personnel, but it expected higher salaries to help guard against this possibility.

EXHIBIT 1

BOOTHBY MANUFACTURING COMPANY

Statement of Termination Policy*

Termination, Resignation, or Retirement

If, under ordinary conditions, the company finds it necessary to terminate your employment, two weeks' notice or salary will be given to regular employees with at least three months' regular full-time employment unless termination is due to misconduct or illegal action. Severance pay in unusual circumstances is left to the discretion of management.

If, for any reason, you should resign, the company expects to receive reasonable notice.

All Philadelphia or New York office employees who retire on or after January 1, 1957, and who at the time of retirement are at least 65 years of age, will receive from Boothby one week's salary (base rate only, at the time of retirement) for each full year of service with Boothby. Years of service will be determined by Boothby. After the total of past service credit has been determined, payments to the retired employee will be made semimonthly until a total of 24 equal payments have been made. These payments will be continued even though the retired employee may have secured other employment.

You should consult with the insurance department before leaving to insure proper handling of your Blue Cross-Blue Shield and life insurance.

*From the *Employee's Handbook*.

UNITED TOOL COMPANY (A)

On October 15, 1958, John Flynn, vice president in charge of United Tool Company's Springfield plant was reviewing initial steps taken at Springfield to determine its data processing requirements. He had recently received a Computer Feasibility Study (reproduced as Appendix A) from the Data Processing Committee and was uncertain as to what action it warranted.

United Tool Company was founded in 1891 for the purpose of making small hand tools. Over the years its activities expanded enormously through both profitable operations and mergers, and it diversified its activities into such areas as high-precision machine shop work and the manufacture of electronic components. It had plants in 31 states and employed over 100,000 persons.

Its Springfield plant was extensively used for basic research and experimental production runs. Roughly one third of the facility was devoted to research, engineering, and administrative uses. Basic research in metallurgy, heat transfer, elasticity, etc., was carried on here. New techniques of assembly and prototype construction were developed in the engineering department. If one of the projects was successful, it was then turned over to another plant which developed it for commercial application. The rest of the plant's area consisted of foundries, machine shops, and assembly areas. The plant had available certain unique equipment which rendered it the logical supplier of many large, closely machined components. As a result, approximately one half of its activity was in the form of job shop machining. The plant's work force was in excess of 3,000.

United Tool Company was organizationally decentralized, with the head of each plant having broad responsibilities for the plant's overall operation. (See Exhibit 1.) Control was achieved through the submission of a number of cost, production, and other reports which were sent regularly to headquarters in New York for analysis. In addition, New York had responsibility for approving major capital investments. Acquisition of a computer was defined as a major capital investment, and New York already had rejected one proposed installation at another plant, on the grounds that the initial research had been "superficially carried out."

COST AND GENERAL ACCOUNTING

The accounting information generated at Springfield was dictated by requirements from New York and was covered by appropriate operating regulations. For job orders, performance was measured against established standards, and significant deviations were highlighted for management attention. Direct costing was used internally. The system culminated in a cost of performance budget which was submitted to New York. In the laboratories and engineering departments efforts were made to control expenditures by maintaining detailed records on the status of each project.

Detailed records were kept on the status of work-in-process inventories, and the administration of purchases and accounts receivable collections were handled there.

PRODUCTION PLANNING AND CONTROL

The production planning and control system provided a detailed record of the progress of a part through Springfield's production centers, and accounted for it as it was completed. This was accomplished by breaking the system down into two separate portions, the planning phase and the operations phase.

In the planning phase, customers' orders were broken down into a list of materials necessary to produce the orders. The various lists of materials were then sorted to get a series of reports showing common materials in different subassemblies of one order as well as materials common to different orders. A master production delivery schedule was then developed.

In the operation phase, work was scheduled to be produced during the following week, and two- and four-week predictions of the future workload were made. In addition, there were workload forecasts provided for the machines in each department as well as for all machines of a particular type. Completed production was recorded in a daily production report, and for the foundry in a weekly production report.

Since Springfield's production was basically that of a job shop which produced small orders of complex parts, little inventory of finished goods-in-process was maintained. Advance planning was essential to such a system in order to keep setup time at a minimum and to produce orders on time.

SCIENTIFIC RESEARCH

The data processing requirements of the research, development, and engineering divisions resulted from the need to calculate design specifications from data obtained through experiment and research. An example of the type of computation required is as follows:

Investigation in the field of applied mechanics involved the elastic stress analysis of notched specimens, cracks, and multiholed plates. The approach to these problems involves determining the coefficients of a complex mapping function and then solving a system of linear equations. The generation of the coefficients of the linear system is accomplished through use of a recursive technique based on the geometry and loading of the experiment. Manual computation of coefficients requires two to three weeks. The resulting system of simultaneous linear equations usually exceeds 25 equations in 25 unknowns and is solved by an iterative technique which requires in excess of three to five days if done manually.

ORIGIN OF FEASIBILITY STUDY

For a number of years Springfield had had several punched card machines that had assisted in the development of the payroll and some cost accounting information. In 1956 there had been some interest shown in the possibility of acquiring a Univac File Computer. At that time, however, the New York office believed that the field was so new that it was unwilling to invest much in it.

During late 1957 and early 1958, members of Springfield's top management held a series of meetings which reopened the possibility of Springfield's attaining benefits from EDP. In April 1958 a presentation was made to Mr. Flynn by several members of the comptroller's office which recommended a computer feasibility study. Impressed by their arguments, in May 1958 he authorized the feasibility study for the installation of automatic data processing equipment. Despite opposition from certain of the research personnel, it was decided at the outset that only a computer capable of meeting both the scientific and commercial interests of the Springfield plant should be considered.

A data processing committee, composed of the comptroller, an assistant to the comptroller, and the assistant manager of systems design (the systems design manager reported directly to the comptroller) was appointed to handle the responsibility of completing the feasibility study. Each department designated one or two men to work with the committee. A scientific subcommittee made up of a solid-state physicist, a mathematician, and an operations research man was formed to advise the committee on scientific requirements.

The data processing committee developed a plan consisting of five major phases:

(1) Training for the committee and other personnel.
(2) A survey of areas to which electronic data processing might apply and the gains which would accrue from computer application.
(3) An application study, preparing specifications for manufacturers, reviewing manufacturers' proposals, and then selecting equipment.
(4) Preparation training, developing systems, changing, programming, and debugging.
(5) Conversion to the electronic system.

Training

The initial training consisted of a two-week course called "Automatic Data Processing Systems for the Systems Analyst," conducted by the New York headquarters. This course covered computer characteristics, programming techniques, and practical problems in systems analysis. Two other courses given by consultants were taken. The first covered the feasibility study, programming, and the systems approach pertaining to substitution of equipment or integration of systems. The second included consideration of the organizational placement of EDPS, selection of and training of personnel, and problems involved in installation of computers. All committee members attended these courses, as well as other courses given by consultants. The personnel assigned to work with the committee attended the two-week course in New York.

The Feasibility Study

The feasibility study covered a preliminary evaluation of the computer requirements in selected areas, notably those areas then served by the punched-card system. The report of the data processing committee on the feasibility study outlined the activity of the committee and its conclusions. It is presented in full as Appendix A.

EXHIBIT 1

ORGANIZATION CHART—SPRINGFIELD

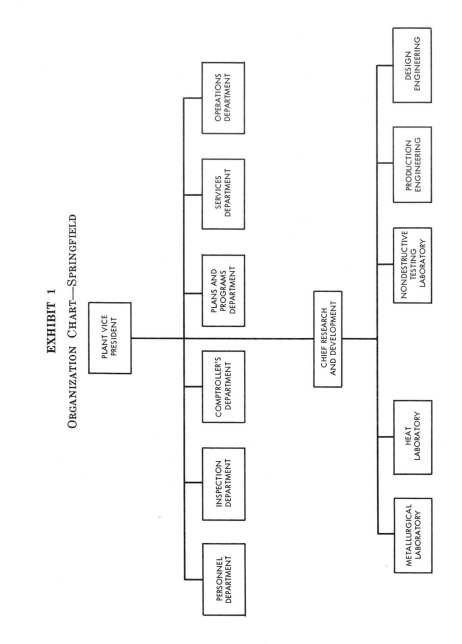

QUESTIONS

1. What are the principal facts brought out by the study?
2. Do you agree that these facts are supported by adequate evidence?
3. As manager, what action would you take as the result of this study?

APPENDIX A

FEASIBILITY STUDY FOR ADPS EQUIPMENT AT SPRINGFIELD

Section I

Business Data Processing

1. **Present Methods of Processing Data:**
   Data are processed either manually or by use of a punched card Remington Rand system utilizing a 120 Univac Computer.
2. **Utilization of Present Data Processing Equipment:**
   A. The following systems are at present being processed either partially or in whole through our punched card system.
   - (1) Payroll.
   - (2) Personnel files.
   - (3) Stock accounting, both standard and nonstandard material.
   - (4) Inventory control, both standard and nonstandard material.
   - (5) Material cost and distribution.
   - (6) Cost accounting.
   - (7) Consolidated project cost.
   - (8) Production control.
   - (9) Customer order accounts.
   - (10) Maintenance and manufacturing control.
   - (11) New York reporting system.
   - (12) Miscellaneous reporting for production control, accounting, and maintenance.
   B. Springfield's policy is to reduce the clerical cost of data processing as much as possible through adapting manual systems to electric accounting machine processes. This practice has resulted in savings of approximately $100,000 a year in the comptroller's area alone. However, the utilization of the "Machine Room," now operating on a three-shift basis, has now extended beyond its capacity to the point where it is necessary to use the Remington Rand Service Bureau once a quarter in order to meet reporting requirements of New York. The release of many reports is delayed, and the consideration of issuing a new one involves the choice of dropping some present report or not issuing the newly requested

data. Thus the saturation point of a data processing system which requires the handling of great volumes of cards through sorters, collaters, computer, and printer before reports are released has been reached. The situation is further aggravated by a high personnel turnover rate in the Data Processing Branch along with the difficulties involved in finding suitable replacement personnel.

3. **Data Requirements of Springfield:**
    A. In order to carry out daily operations more effectively and to meet New York's reporting requirements there exists a requirement for Springfield to process and record data. Types of systems which must be provided are:
        (1) Production planning, engineering, and control.
        (2) Accounting reports.
        (3) Budgets.
        (4) Program progress reports.
        (5) Inventory accounting and control.
        (6) Payroll.
        (7) Personnel data.
        (8) Standard costs and material control.
        (9) Customer order accounting.
    B. Future data processing equipment will involve an extention of the principle of standard costing and standard labor and material control to other than those in the Operations Division. This will include support organizations such as Plant Facilities Office and Materials Office. The integrated approach to systems work available with automatic data processing will enable the utilization of a system of comprehensive accounting in which the accounting records will be maintained so as more closely to tie in workload, manpower, and cost data, and evaluate the effectiveness of each against a standard or a budget. The implementation of the concept of comprehensive accounting would build flexibility into the system and make fluctuating data requirements of higher headquarters more easy to obtain.

4. **Sample Cost of Processing Data at Springfield:**
    A. In order to determine what Springfield is paying for the processing of data, a few selected areas were investigated. These areas were Production Planning and Control, Accounting, and Supply. This information was gathered from the 1959 budget revised August 1, 1958.

Labor Budget, 1959 (adjusted for leave and retirement)

Production Planning and Control and Production Engineering	$854,747
Finance and Accounting Office	459,854
Program Analysis Branch	81,286
Data Processing Branch	143,000
Supply Branch	161,662
Rental and Maintenance Budget	33,832
Total	$1,734,381

B. The above figures are presented only to show the magnitude of our present data processing costs, and are not intended to reflect total savings. However, the types of functions performed by these areas are compatible with ADPS processing, and these costs should be reduced considerably upon converting to ADPS techniques.

5. **Timeliness of Data Transmission and Reporting under Our Present EAM System:**

Because of the high volume of integrated data processing systems now using our punched card equipment, the following general conditions exist as to the timeliness of the reports being furnished. In spite of the best effort in its efficient utilization, the present equipment is inadequate to meet the requirements of Springfield. A few selected areas were studied and the following specific examples are given:

A. *Financial Statements.* Scheduled date for receiving this information from data processing branch permits the preparation of statements and closing of books so that financial statements can be issued at the close of the month following the last month being reported, that is, statements as of July 31 are issued August 31. This schedule is the earliest possible one with the present equipment and system. Any speedup of the processing time required for the preparation of these statements would have significant results in the timely analysis of the data and the ability to take prompt corrective action.

B. *Billing.* Monthly billing tapes are scheduled for the fifteenth work day after the close of the month. It takes about one week after receipt of the billing tape to prepare the bills, and about two to three weeks more to receive payment. This means that approximately 4 to 4½ million dollars are tied up. Each day saved on this cycle frees approximately $100,000.

C. *Line Item Cost Data for Manufactured Items.* Because of the limitations of our present equipment, line item costs for manufactured parts are being furnished 30 to 60 days after the item is completed, and in some cases as long as 90 days. This means that on short-run production orders the cost of the part is not received until the complete product on order is made and delivered. This does not permit us in all cases to take positive corrective action in order to control costs at the line item until it is too late.

D. *Production Control Reports.* The data processing for production control operations is at the present time one of the major applications for EAM. "Daily Production Reports," a weekly two-week schedule, an "Unfinished Work Report," and a "Master Production and Delivery Schedule" are examples of some of the reports prepared. With the exception of the Unfinished Work Report there are considerable delays in submitting the reports in production control. This difficulty is particularly evident in the handling of crash work route sheets, which are released at the same time as the items get into the shop. These actually never get into the two-week schedule because of the length of time it takes to process these items.

SECTION II

SCIENTIFIC APPLICATIONS

1. **Present Method of Processing Scientific Data at Springfield:**
    A.   The Univac 120 is used to a very limited extent for the processing of scientific data. Springfield laboratories use it occasionally as an aid in performing certain numerical phases in arriving at a solution to selected mathematical problems. However, the restrictions due to the computer's capacity have allowed only infrequent use of it as an assistance in computation work in the research area.
    B.   Computers located outside the installation are utilized to solve a number of scientific problems which develop in the research area. The Materials Lab uses the IBM 704 located at Hartford to solve certain problems. The Heat Lab uses an IBM 650 located in the Boston area to work problems involving the foundry. These problems involve a method of linear programming and a method of furnace chargings.
2. **Need for a Computer:**
    A.   The phenomenal benefits that have resulted from the application of high-speed electronic analog and digital computers to the research area are well known. These benefits have been realized in areas of research in which Springfield is engaged. In certain fields of applied mechanics for example, in studies in elasticity, particularly as applied to the "thin shell theory," the utilization of an electronic computer has had enormous effect.
    B.   The lack of computer facilities at Springfield has deterred those working in this area from working on certain problems related to their field, and has forced the finality of certain solutions to problems to be left in general form. Lack of computer facilities makes it difficult for those in applied mechanics to keep up with advances made in certain fields.
    C.   At the present time in the Metallurgical Laboratory there is under way a long-range program that involves the study of atomic displacement and characteristic temperatures of certain alloys. Future plans call for the expansion of the above program and the start of the analysis of structural factors of material in the study of single crystals. The present program is slowed down by the lengthy computations necessary to reduce data to desired parameters. There are other problems that have not been considered, because of the computation involved in their study. The computer is much needed in this branch to free personnel from present laborious computations and to speed up and extend present programs outlined above. Not only this, but it will permit expansion into allied fields in which research outside the installations has advantageously used data processing equipment.
    D.   Again, in the Nondestructive Testing Laboratory there are at-

tempts being made to discover and develop nondestructive testing methods for material and equipment. Development of these methods depends upon the evaluation of data. The data consist of many parameters, and their combinations under various conditions are of such magnitude and kind as to necessitate the use of an electronic computer. Future plans will create an even greater demand for such equipment.

SECTION III

CONCLUSIONS AND RECOMMENDATIONS

1. **Conclusions:**
   A. *Data Processing.* As a result of the study thus far devoted to electronic digital computers, it is apparent that a medium-scale computer would be extremely beneficial. As these computers process data at extremely high speeds and have the ability to update and prepare a number of reports with one pass of the basic data, it is believed that a computer would enable Springfield to receive appreciable managerial benefits through improvement in the timeliness and quality of data.
   B. *Scientific Application.* As a result of this preliminary examination into the need for a computer in the research area, it is apparent that our research efforts are being hindered because of the lack of modern computational facilities.
2. **Recommendations:**
   A. That this committee proceed with a detailed application study of a Production Planning and Control System, and a comprehensive accounting system for the entire plant, excluding research, which will include both quantitative and monetary data. The express purpose will be to design these systems for computer application and submission to manufacturers for estimates in terms of time and costs for processing on their equipment. From this the economies and benefits can be measured and a computer selection made.
   B. That further study into the specific requirements of our research area be made and incorporated as a separate section in the application study and be evaluated as the overall computer requirements of Springfield.

SECTION IV

POTENTIAL AREAS OF COMPUTER APPLICATION UPON INSTALLATION

1. Production Planning and Control (scheduling, forecasting, workload, manpower, machine loading, efficiency reporting, unloading schedule).
2. General Accounting.
3. Cost Accounting.

4. Headquarters Reporting.
5. Maintenance Scheduling and Reporting.
6. Budgeting.
7. Payroll.
8. Materials Inventory.
9. Production Control.
10. Personnel Files and Reports.
11. Application of Material and Time and Motion Standards.
12. Literature Searching.
13. Delivery Status Report Processing.

Section V

Estimated Costs and Benefits

The estimated costs and direct benefits for a complete study and installation of automatic data processing equipment are detailed in Exhibit 1 by expense classification and by quarters in which the expense is incurred. The quarters start with June 1958, when the feasibility study began, and ends with March 1961.

The process of studying and acquiring a computer falls naturally into six phases as follows:

(1) Feasibility Study . . . . June '58 through October '58
(2) Application Study . . . . November '58 through June '59
(3) Preparation . . . . July '59 through April '60
(4) Installation . . . . May '60
(5) Conversion . . . . June '60 through July '61
(6) Operation . . . . August '61

The training expense consists of costs incurred for tuition or fees for courses offered by consultants. The cost of evaluation of equipment consists of expenses incurred in travel and per diem in attending approximately a week's seminar in programming given by the manufacturers of equipment under consideration.

The committee is dissolved after the submission of the Application Study and the formal ADPS organization is established in July 1959. However, a firm basis for the organization is attained through having programmers and analysts work under the guidance of the committee during the application phases of the study.

Personnel costs are those that would be involved in any special testing that may be necessary to guide in the selection of the most highly qualified personnel.

Installation cost is based on the best estimate that can be made without knowing definitely which computer will be installed and the exact location of the installation. A possible location was used in making the estimate and a vacuum tube type computer was selected in order to be on the high side of such cost.

The computer rental cost includes necessary input and output equip-

EXHIBIT 1

Estimated Cost and Direct Benefits
For a Complete Study and Installation of ADP Equipment

	First Year								Second Year								Third Year							
	1 Qtr Jun 58		2 Qtr Sep 58		3 Qtr Dec 58		4 Qtr Mar 59		1 Qtr Jun 59		2 Qtr Sep 59		3 Qtr Dec 59		4 Qtr Mar 60		1 Qtr Jun 60		2 Qtr Sep 60		3 Qtr Dec 60		4 Qtr Mar 61	
	P	$	P	$	P	$	P	$	P	$	P	$	P	$	P	$	P	$	P	$	P	$	P	$
A Training		1,270		1,350																				
B Travel (other than evaluation)		2,126		1,744		1,600		1,600																
C Evaluation of equipment				561		1,329		366		2,476														
Salaries:																								
D Committee	3	7,400	3	7,400	3	7,400	3	7,400																
E Associated	2	380	2	600																				
F Administration			1	1,250					6	8,116	9	12,174	9	16,194	9	16,194	9	16,194	9	16,194	9	16,194	9	16,194
G Analyst					1	1,689	4	5,067	4	7,269	4	7,269	4	7,269	4	7,269	4	7,269	4	7,269	4	7,269	4	7,269
H Programmers					1	1,689	4	5,067	4	7,269	4	7,269	4	7,269	4	7,269	4	7,269	4	7,269	4	7,269	4	7,269
I Operators											1	1,878	3	8,256	7	10,416	7	12,576	10	12,576	10	14,730	10	15,852
J Personnel Selection						1,000		1,000																
K Installation cost																20,000								
L Computer rental																1,500		45,000		45,000		45,000		45,000
M Material																		300		300		300		300
Total expense		11,176		12,925		14,707		20,500		25,130		28,590		38,988		62,648		88,608		88,608		90,762		91,884
Savings:																								
N Personnel												2,936		2,936		2,936		2,936		38,823		53,787		91,355
O Equipment rental																				2,190		4,380		6,570
Total savings												2,936		2,936		2,936		2,936		41,013		58,167		98,125
Net expense		11,176		12,925		14,707		20,500		25,130		25,654		36,052		59,712		85,672		47,595		32,595		(6,241)
Cumulative net expense		11,176		24,101		38,308		59,308		84,438		110,092		146,144		205,856		291,528		339,123		371,718		365,477

P = People $ = Expense

ment based upon the situation as it looks at the time of preparing this study. Of course, the application study will refine these estimates.

Direct savings are determined on the basis of the best estimates in the areas listed in Section I–4, and are phased in at the time they may occur.

The anticipated direct savings resulting from a decrease in the needs of personnel in affected areas and the release of equipment at present on hand amount to quarterly net savings of $49,000. The break-even point, where the savings have amortized the computer expense, will occur during December 1962 or January 1963.

It is believed that these estimates are on a conservative basis, and through an integrated approach to computer utilization and application, additional savings may accrue.

Only the direct benefits with respect to cost savings are detailed in Exhibit 1 page 227. However, while such direct savings should accrue and are the most readily measured savings, there are others that are of the utmost importance and that are the real motivating factors in determining the need for a computer. As a result of a well-integrated system, the computer should result in a definite improvement in management control through supplying management with meaningful information that is more accurate and more timely as well as impossible to obtain without a computer.

The computer system is also flexible, in that it can be expanded and contracted to meet rather permanent or long-range adjustments in workload.

UNITED TOOL COMPANY (B)

On October 22, 1958, John Flynn, vice president in charge of the company's Springfield plant, gave approval to the plans laid out in the Data Processing Committee's Feasibility Study. [See United Tool Company (A)]. The data processing committee then turned its efforts toward developing an Application Study. Three members of the committee worked full time on the project for a year, and a total of approximately one man-year of effort was received from other people in the plant. As the report's preparation was drawing to a close in August, the committee received a memorandum from Mr. Flynn requesting more detailed information than it had planned to present. This caused a substantial delay, and the final draft of the study was not submitted to Mr. Flynn for approval until January 8, 1960. After Mr. Flynn's approval it would be sent to company headquarters in New York, where a final decision would be made.

Mr. Flynn, therefore, was anxious both that the study reach a reasonable decision and that his decision be well substantiated by material in the document.

A partial transcript of the study appears in the following Appendix. Most of the omitted sections are mainly technical in nature, and a resume summarizing their important points has been substituted. The detailed cost analyses and logic leading to selection of a specific equipment configuration are contained in the United Tool Company (C) case.

APPENDIX

APPLICATION STUDY FOR USE OF EDP EQUIPMENT AT SPRINGFIELD

1. **Scope of Application:**
   The data processing system will be used in the scientific and business areas of Springfield.
   A. *Scientific Areas.* The scientific applications will include the solution of problems in molecular theory and solid state physics. This will involve calculations on problems resulting from the use of a nuclear reactor. It will be used to determine the feasibility

of using mathematical relationships to correlate physical properties of metals with process histories. Other scientific applications will concern themselves with buckling behavior of certain configurations, analysis of the dynamic response of systems, conformal mapping and studies of atomic displacement.

    B.   *Business Areas.*

       (1) The initial business applications will include those system areas which may be readily integrated and which contain the most urgent need for improvement. These areas are production control, cost accounting, top management reporting, material inventory control; and two related systems, payroll and personnel records.

       (2) Subsequent areas which will be integrated into the data processing system as rapidly as possible thereafter include the balance of top management reporting, aspects of general accounting not included in the initial application, fixed asset accounting, and additional budgeting systems.

       (3) Other applications are planned but will require additional research work. These include the application of material and time standards and literature searching in connection with scientific reports.

2. **Objectives Which Will Be Achieved:**

    A.   *Scientific Areas.*

       (1) Will enable the scientific staff to attack problems too difficult to resolve without computer facilities.

       (2) Problems on which a great deal of manual calculation is presently required will be solved more rapidly and enable more efficient utilization of scientific personnel.

       (3) Scientific work in which the finality of certain solutions to problems had to be left in general form can now be resolved with the availability of adequate computer facilities to tabulate data.

       (4) Computer techniques are, of course, now widely used in all scientific research work. Without computer facilities it is difficult to keep abreast of all developments applicable to the scientific areas of interest at Springfield.

    B.   *Business Area.*

       (1) Makes available new management control data such as product line item costs, a value for work-in-process inventory, departmental costs; as well as improved processing in automatic billing, payables, and disbursements.

       (2) Reduces cost of data processing through reduction in personnel cost involved and through processing more data per unit of time and per dollar of cost.

       (3) Improved management control through timely and accurate reporting.

       (4) Increased flexibility in modifying EDP procedures.

(5)   Capability of expansion with relatively small increase in cost.
(6)   Further integration of system through use of a computer.
(7)   Ability to solve problems which involve mathematical or logical sequences which are too complex or lengthy for other types of data processing.

PART I—SCIENTIFIC REQUIREMENTS FOR COMPUTER FACILITIES AT SPRINGFIELD

(This section consisted of a description of 36 specific scientific areas where the computer could be of service. A detailed discussion followed of how two particular problems would be prepared for solution on the computer. This included developing the problems' equations and showing how they could be programmed.) The part closed as follows:

Summary

1.   Springfield employs approximately 530 personnel in its scientific and engineering areas. Of these, approximately 170 professionals and 80 nonprofessionals are engaged in scientific or engineering projects. About 50 of these personnel will be concerned with problems which either demand rapid large-scale computational ability for their solution or would appreciably benefit from its availability.

2.   The requirement that rapid large-scale computational facilities be available to scientists at Springfield is evident from this exposition of the research mission and scientific activities. These are areas where the use of an electronic computer can result in significant improvements; this is further documented by a review of the appropriate technical literature, where widespread use of computers in these areas is evident.

3.   Mr. Hoffman, United Tool's vice president of production, in a speech on October 3, 1959, stressed the urgent need to increase research efficiency. The availability of a computer of the capacity selected will provide a much needed "tool" to accomplish this result. It permits solution of additional problems: first, by eliminating the time spent on repetitive and monotonous computations; and second, by increasing the researcher's ability in certain areas, by making available to him programs and solutions developed by competent persons with similar interests in other organizations. The availability of an electronic computer increases one's ability to communicate with researchers in many areas where substantial contributions have resulted from computer applications.

4.   The areas of research in which the computer will be used are detailed in Exhibit 1. This exhibit shows the estimated hours per month that are spent on manual calculation and the estimated time it would take to accomplish this work with the recommended computer facility.

EXHIBIT 1

ESTIMATED SCIENTIFIC COMPUTER UTILIZATION

	Hours per Month			
	A	B	C	D
Elastic Stress Analysis	36	3	2	5
Diffraction Patterns	9	1	3	4
Plastic Stress Analysis	8	2	3	5
Thermal Problems	7	1	3	4
Ionization Chamber	84	3	4	7
X-Ray Diffraction	50	2	4	3
Nondestructive Testing Evaluation	36	1	2	3
Bending Beam Studies	40	3	3	6
Linear Programming	28	0	1	1
Vibration Analysis	11	1	½	1½
Heat Transfer Studies	16	1	½	1½
Vacuum Furnace	11	1	1	2
Nuclear Reactor	0	0	2	2
Management Gaming	0	0	2	2
Production Simulation	3	0	3	6
Operations Research	0	0	2	2
Experimental Management	0	0	5	5
Miscellaneous Heat Lab	88	5	4	9
Miscellaneous Metal Lab	54	4	4	8
Miscellaneous NDT Lab	36	3	3	6
Total	517	31	52	83

A—Present manual calculations
B—Computer Equivalent of (A)
C—New work.
D—Total Computer Hours.
Assumes compiling and interpretive routines.
Includes debugging time.

PART II—BUSINESS APPLICATIONS FOR THE COMPUTER AT SPRINGFIELD

SECTION A

Present Method Used

Springfield's data is processed, at present, either manually or by a punched card system which utilizes a Univac 120 calculator. All applications possible within the limitations of time available and equipment capabilities, in the areas of production control, accounting, payroll and personnel records utilize the electrical accounting machines and the Univac 120.

To evaluate fully the present production control, cost accounting, and payroll systems, a detailed study was made. The accomplishment of this task during the application phase of the study not only allowed the present systems to be better evaluated, but also furnished the necessary data on which to base a closely integrated cost accounting, production control, payroll and personnel record maintenance system. It was felt that the detailed systems study will be useful as a simple starting point in modifying the systems for the computer.

This study of the present systems in production control and cost accounting revealed basic conditions which could be corrected by an integrated electronic digital computer system. These deficiencies and examples are:

1. The Electronic Accounting Machines card system does not allow sufficient flexibility to derive both internal and external reports simultaneously.

This particular condition is evident in the New York headquarters system reporting. These reports should be derived simultaneously from internal reporting runs. Current conditions, however, require the manual consolidation of data from various EAM runs as well as numerous manual reports from operating officials before these external reports can be prepared.

In the production control system considerable inflexibility exists because the large operations file (up to 62,000 cards) requires extensive sorting and handling to produce the currently available control reports. This lack of procedural flexibility and speed has made it impossible to readily gather costs at each of the numerous operational and assembly levels and develop product line costs.

2. The delay in producing the required management control reports both in the production control and cost areas has minimized their usefulness and resulted in a duplication of effort.

In the collection of direct costs and in the preparation of bills, costs are collected for labor, material and other charges from EAM cards. These are processed at various intervals depending on the type of charges. Repeated handling of cards and elaborate controls delay issuance of reports whose prompt delivery would tighten management control.

The "Expenditure Control Report" which is used to forecast the future financial position of customers' orders is prepared from large volumes of EAM cards from the budget, production control and accounting sections. The variety of necessary card processing and volume have, with the other urgent work load in the EAM operations, resulted in issuing reports too late to attain close and proper control of expenditure against customer orders.

A by-product of an integrated production control and cost accounting system should be a cost report by product line. Procedures were established to obtain such information. However, because of the overload in EAM operations, much of the work is of necessity accomplished manually and submitted so late as to reduce its effectiveness as a product cost control report.

Production Planning and Control personnel have in some cases had to revert to costly manual methods when the machine room had to drop, or couldn't absorb more, data processing, because of capacity limitations.

3. Issuing reports on a less frequent basis than desired is often necessitated by an overloaded EAM operation.

At the present time the "Overhead Cost Report" is prepared quarterly. This cycle is necessary because of the numerous processing cycles in EAM and the manual cost distribution and computations which are required.

The quarterly issuance of this report reduces its effectiveness as a medium of control.

4. Time consuming manual methods are used which often make it difficult to readily determine the status of accounts.

Processing the payroll through the Univac 120 still involves considerable card handling, and many manual controls are needed to match payroll with labor cost. Also many long clerical hours are required each month to post to individual pay and leave records, and to manually prepare and sort checks for delivery.

5. Limited use can be made of exception-type reporting within production control and cost accounting. The already overloaded EAM operations are not able to accomplish the card processing required for such reports; and also, the limitations of the equipment make it difficult to accomplish readily this timely and important type of reporting.

SECTION B

Proposed Method

The proposed method includes an integrated system of production control, cost accounting, payroll and personnel file maintenance made possible through the use of a high speed general purpose digital computer with magnetic tape storage. This computer has the large internal storage capacity and rapid internal computing speeds necessary for efficient data handling, integrated file maintenance and reporting.

The proposed integrated system of production control, cost accounting, payroll and personnel file maintenance is outlined in detail later in this report. This proposed system will overcome fully all the deficiencies outlined in the previous section. It will accomplish tasks which are not now possible and realize an appreciable saving in operations as well as savings resulting from a better informed management.

The deficiencies outlined in the previous section will be relieved or overcome as follows:

1. Internal and external reporting may be derived simultaneously from the integrated files established. Since these master files will be currently updated, information may be extracted readily from the master file for both reports.

2. Management reports will be available at the required time and all duplication of effort will be eliminated.

In the proposed cost accounting system, costs will be collected and files updated on a daily or weekly basis as required. Because of the integration of required data on single files, complete billings can be automatically produced with service-type orders being billed automatically on costs incurred.

Daily updating of costs and analysis of customer order status internally within the computer will enable Springfield to forecast each customer order position on a timely basis.

Product line costs will be available weekly, and more often if the need arises; also, costs will be available at each assembly level. Current work-in-process data, finished parts cost and cost variance reports will be available as required.

3. The frequency of issuance of management reports will be as desired by management.

The weekly updating of the cost file will make readily available the operation and maintenance of facilities data for headquarters. Under the proposed system the overhead cost report will be prepared monthly, which will give closer control over overhead rates, and more accurate cost of idle facilities.

4. Manual methods will be reduced to only those procedures which can be accomplished most efficiently and economically by this method, and the status of accounts will be available on a current basis.

Purchase orders, receipts, invoices and payments will enter the system daily. The accounts payable, cash disbursements and unliquidated obligation files will be simultaneously updated. The accounts payable and disbursement journals will be printed out automatically, thus producing books of original entry. Analysis of their accounts can be accomplished rapidly, to give management better information for control. The unliquidated obligations will be available merely by printing out the master file at the end of the year.

5. Exception-type reporting—as, for example, the Unfinished Work Report—will be readily available; since, with the integrated files, conditions can be built into the computer program to print out when particular conditions exist.

Section C

Other Methods of Processing Data Which Have Been Investigated and Reasons Why They Were Not Selected

1. The four basic methods of data processing—manual, bookkeeping-type machines, electrical accounting machines, and electronic digital computers—were considered.

2. Manual methods, of course, are now being used, and will continue to be used where this method is the most efficient and economical, as it is in some types of processing. However, the method has proved an inadequate and costly data processing technique.

3. Bookkeeping types of machines were considered in selected areas and a detailed study was completed. They provided no basic improvement over the methods presently used. This type of equipment would not be able to realize the objectives stated in the introduction.

4. An electrical accounting machine, the Remington Rand Univac 120, is now used, and the inadequacies of this system were detailed previously.

Section D

Workload, Cost, and Other Data Relating to Both the Present and Proposed Systems.

1. The monthly workload volumes in the areas of business application—namely, production control, cost accounting, payroll and personnel

file maintenance—consist of 251,428 input messages per month, 335,938 master reference records, 34,164 working file records, and 383,627 output messages per month. The breakdown of these volume figures is in an exhibit (not included here) that contained a detailed listing of all records used in the system and the volume per month requirements.

2. Cost:
    (a) The comparative monthly cost of the present system and the proposed system, including equipment rental and operating personnel for the areas under consideration, are as follows:

    Present System............................ $64,826
    Proposed System.......................... 48,274

    Monthly Operating Savings................. $14,552

    (b) Details of these comparative system costs and resultant saving are in Section I [reprinted here as an Appendix to United Tool Company (C)].

Section E

Summary of Makes and Equipment Evaluated Selection and Justification

(A more detailed analysis is made in Equipment Selection Section.)

Invitations to submit a proposal to meet the digital computer requirements for Springfield were sent to six manufacturers. They recommended the following systems:

    RCA.......................501
    Burroughs.................205
    Remington Rand...........Univac 80 with magnetic tapes
    IBM......................1401
    National Cash.............did not submit proposal
    Philco...................did not submit proposal

The RCA 501 was selected as the computer to recommend for installation at Springfield. This computer was selected for the following reasons:

The equipment met all specifications required[1] and was capable of accomplishing economically and efficiently both the business and scientific data processing requirements.

The equipment made maximum use of computer speed and capabilities by accomplishing all data processing within the computer system, with no time-consuming peripheral EAM equipment with its concomitant requirement for additional personnel.

The 501 system is extremely flexible and can readily expand or contract to meet changing requirements.

---

[1]Each manufacturer was sent a volume, very similar in nature to Volume 2 of this application study, which outlined the present system as it now operates and indicated the areas where automation was considered to have potential. Detailed figures were given concerning the number of transactions in each area that occur each day, week or month. Indication was also given as to the size of files that would have to be stored on tape or in memory.

All critical reporting requirements can be accomplished on a one-shift basis.

The computer is compatible with the larger RCA 501 system recently installed in New York. Compatibility will be of value in program assistance which New York can give if required, and use of the equipment on which to process scientific problems which require a larger machine.

Internal computing speed is rapid (15 microsec. access time). This is advantageous to scientific work and helpful to business; the system may be easily modified to give computer speed up to four times as fast, if required.

Delivery time is adequate—January 1961.

SECTION F

Personnel and Cost Distribution Implications

1. *Personnel:*
    A. Twenty-five people are required to staff the EDP organization, including systems analysts, programmers, and operators. Details of staffing pattern and organizational structure are in Section G.
2. *Cost Distribution Implications:*
    A. As it is recommended that the equipment be rented, no special capital expenditure is required. The rental charges will be distributed on the basis of actual or planned hours of use. Usage which can be identified with a specific customer order will be charged directly to that order at actual cost. The remaining costs will be distributed to customer orders as a portion of the predetermined overhead rates established on the basis of planned hours of use.
    B. The planned installation site requires only minor alterations. The equipment requires a limited amount of air conditioning, and adequate power facilities are already in the building; therefore, the site preparation cost is estimated at $71,500.

SECTION G

Preparation Phase of EDP Operation

1. *Organization, Staffing and Training:*
    A. The Automatic Data Processing System Organization will be established as a branch of the comptroller's office. The present data processing organization will be replaced by the new organization during the conversion phase. An organization chart indicates the branch will require 25 persons.
    B. Technical training of personnel will be accomplished by the computer manufacturer at Springfield and at the manufacturer's facilities. It will consist of both formalized classroom and on-the-job training. Preliminary training of personnel may be supplemented by courses of instruction in EDP which are given at New York.
    C. Upon completion of the necessary training, personnel of this installation will immediately begin programming our applications

As each application is completed, the program will be tested and debugged at the manufacturer's service center.

2. *Site Preparation:*
   A. The site proposed for the computer operation is located on the first floor of the main administration building.
   B. The plant facilities office, Springfield, has prepared a cost estimate for the inside site preparation. This cost is summarized as follows:

Air Conditioning System	$19,522
Sprinkler System	1,936
Plumbing	8,775
Raised Floor	9,614
Metal Pan Ceiling	3,097
Insulated Metal Partitions	6,405
Structural	3,388
Painting	552
Heat Absorbing Glass	978
Excavation	575
Electrical	16,712
Total	$71,554

Section H

Plans To Safeguard System

1. A statement of planned procedure will be developed to assure continuity of operations in the event of loss of magnetic tapes, paper tapes, cards, etc., or the equipment itself by fire or accident.

2. The RCA 501 system recommended for Springfield is completely compatible with the 501 system now installed at New York. In case of damage to the equipment, the equipment at New York would be available. RCA has advised us that between March and August 1960 a 501 system will be available at its Springfield office.

3. The master files will all be on magnetic tape. Programs will be both on paper tape and magnetic tape; data will be on a paper tape. Magnetic tapes and paper tapes will be retained as back-up as far as the "grandfather." These grandfather tapes will be filed in a vault in a building some distance from the computer room.

Part III—Summary

This backs up the previous part with a very detailed treatment of the payroll, cost accounting, and production control systems. The inputs and outputs of each of these systems are first isolated. Then, a flow-chart is drawn which indicates in detail the steps by which the input data are transferred into output form. The average number of characters that will be processed through each step is then multiplied by the time necessary to complete this step. In this way, statistics are generated which indicate the amount of machine processing time required to handle the problem.

It also indicates potential bottlenecks as far as month- and year-end data processing requirements are concerned.

The net result of this section is to define the system's requirements in such a way that the machine's capacity to handle the problem is closely analyzed and a realistic estimate of the amount of slack time left can be made.

UNITED TOOL COMPANY (C)

The United Tool Company (B) case presented portions of an Application Study which recommended installation of an RCA 501 computer at the United Tool Company. The Appendix to this case contains the portions of the Application Study relating to detailed cost analysis of the proposed EDP operation and evaluation of the different equipment proposals.

APPENDIX

Cost Analysis

The cost phasing of the planned Automatic Data Processing System at Springfield was dependent upon the preliminary scheduling of the pre-installation workload and the phasing of the various applications onto the computer. The work summary chart (Exhibit 1) illustrates the time at which the various phases will begin. Separate scheduling for production control, cost, payroll and personnel records is not shown, since they are so interrelated that separate scheduling is not feasible.

These phasing schedules were also based upon the final number of personnel needed to operate the ADPS conversion, in order that the number of people required during the conversion phase would be kept close to a minimum.

The cost of operating the present system, as shown in Exhibit 2, is $64,826 per month. This includes direct, support, and other costs. Also included are personnel costs in cost centers which will be directly affected by EDPS. To these personnel costs are added supplies, depreciation and maintenance on the presently owned EAM equipment. These costs for the present system are detailed in Exhibits 3, 4 and 5.

The cost of the proposed EDP operation as applied to business is $48,274 per month (Exhibit 6). The rental cost of the computer is applied to the business operation on the basis of planned hours of use. Planned utilization of the computer for business operations is 49 percent of one shift and utilization for scientific operations 51 percent of a one-shift operation. This readily illustrates the economic advantage accruing to both business and scientific operations as a result of both utilizing the same computer, since each is obtaining a computer which will completely fulfill its individual requirements at a reduced cost of operations.

EXHIBIT 1

WORK SUMMARY CHART

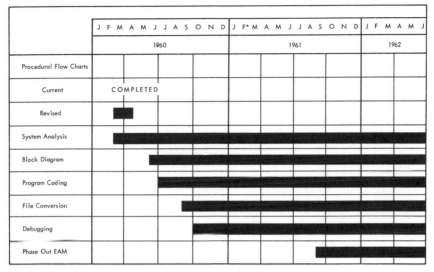

	J F M A M J J A S O N D	J F*M A M J J A S O N D	J F M A M J
	1960	1961	1962
Procedural Flow Charts			
Current	COMPLETED		
Revised	■		
System Analysis	████████████████		
Block Diagram	███████		
Program Coding	███████		
File Conversion	█████		
Debugging	████		
Phase Out EAM		███	

*Computer Installation.

EXHIBIT 2

COST OF PRESENT SYSTEM

Personnel—Direct (Data Processing Dept.)	31 People	$10,893 per month
Support	12	3,383
Other (Employees of other departments)	100	45,867
Supplies (Exhibit 3)		924
Depreciation (Exhibit 4)		532
Maintenance (Exhibit 4)		613
Machine Rental (Exhibit 5)		2,614
	Total	$64,826

EXHIBIT 3

PRESENT AND PROPOSED COST OF SUPPLIES

Present   Cards........$ 6,109
            Paper......... 4,899
            Ink–Payroll....   84

$11,092 ÷ 12 = $924 per month

Proposed Paper Tape....$ 180
            Cards........ 1,000
            Paper......... 4,899
            Ink–Payroll....   84

$ 6,163 ÷ 12 = $514 per month

EXHIBIT 4

PRESENT MONTHLY DEPRECIATION AND MAINTENANCE

	Depreciation	*Maintenance*
Key Punches (4)..............	$ 21	$111
Sorter......................	30	29
Interpreter..................	61	61
Collator–Reproducer..........	106	101
Verifier.....................	36	17
Tabulator....................	278	294
Totals..................	$532	$613

EXHIBIT 5

PRESENT MACHINE RENTAL COST

Key Punch......................	2 @ $40	$ 80
Tabulator........................		484
Sorters.........................	2 @ $85	170
Collator........................		125
Computer........................		1,570
Cardomatic Punch................		95
IBM Key Punch..................		40
IBM Verifier....................		50
		$2,614

EXHIBIT 6

COST OF PROPOSED SYSTEM PER MONTH
CHARGEABLE TO BUSINESS USES

Personnel—Direct................	$13,726	25 people
Support...............	3,424	10
Other................	24,607	52
	$41,757	87
Supplies (Exhibit 3)..............	514	
Machine Rental (Exhibit 7)........	6,003	
Total............	$48,274	

EXHIBIT 7

MACHINE RENTAL COST PER MONTH FOR BUSINESS APPLICATIONS

		Cost per Month
Computer	Central Processing Unit (includes Paper Tape Reader, Monitor Printer, Tape Selector and Buffer and Power Supply)	$ 5,400
	High Speed Memory (16,384 digits)....	2,400
	Magnetic Tape Stations (5)...........	2,325
	On Line Printer....................	1,300
		$11,425
Peripheral	IBM Key Punch...................	$ 40
	IBM Verifier......................	50
		$11,515
Flexowriter Rental............................		$ 735
		$12,250
Less 51% applicable to Scientific Utilization.......		$ 6,247
		$ 6,003

A recap of the monthly operating cost of the proposed and present business systems is as follows:

	Present Method	*Proposed Method*	*Gain*
Personnel.................	$60,143	$41,757	$18,386
Machine Rental...........	2,614	6,003	(3,389)
Miscellaneous.............	2,069	514	1,555
Totals...............	$64,826	$48,274	$16,552

The monthly saving should be realized in full in April 1962, which is two months after the conversion to EDP is scheduled for completion. The personnel savings, amounting to $18,386 per month, results from the planned elimination of functions which will be placed on the computer which are now performed by 56 people.

The summary of estimated cost in dollars (Exhibit 8) shows the phasing of cost by quarter, beginning with the third quarter of fiscal 1961, when the computer is planned to be installed and placed in operation. Non-recurring costs are detailed in Exhibit 9.

The monthly direct cost (Direct ADPS personnel, machine rental and supplies) for the EDPS operation will be $20,663. During August 1963, all expenses will be recovered and the operation will break even.

Schedules for the release of EAM equipment and personnel are shown as Exhibits X and Y. [Not shown here. These included detailed schedules of personnel requirements before and after the computer installation as well as schedules showing when various personnel would be released. The same type of schedules were presented to indicate the disposal of present equipment.]

EXHIBIT 8

SUMMARY OF ESTIMATED COST BY QUARTER

	1961 1st Quarter	1961 2nd Quarter	1961 3rd Quarter	1961 4th Quarter	1961 TOTAL	1962 1st Quarter	1962 2nd Quarter	1962 3rd Quarter	1962 4th Quarter	1962 TOTAL	1963 1st Quarter	1963 2nd Quarter
1. Current System (Base)	$194,478	$194,478 ·	$194,478 ·	$194,478	$777,912	$194,478	$194,478	$194,478	$194,478	$777,912	$194,478	$194,478
2. Total Project Cost (3 + 4)	489,386	225,034	187,685	168,703	1,070,808	150,778	146,098	146,098	146,098	589,072	146,098	146,098
3. Current System (Phased Out)												
Direct Data Proc. Personnel	$ 21,568	$ 17,732	$ 11,286	$ 6,204	$ 56,790	$ 9,184	$ 953			$ 10,137		
Support Personnel	7,755	2,186			9,941							
All Other Personnel	118,884	108,177	67,970	37,570	332,601	1,665				1,665		
Machine Rental	7,682	5,980	5,185	4,665	23,512							
Supplies	2,772				2,772							
Depreciation	1,596	1,596	1,553	939	5,684	313				313		
Maintenance	1,839	1,839	1,615	1,050	6,343	350				350		
Total	$ 162,096	$ 137,510	$ 87,609	$ 50,428	$ 437,643	$ 11,512	$ 953			$ 12,465		
4. ADP System (Phased In)												
Direct ADPS Personnel	$ 41,178	$ 41,178	$ 41,178	$ 41,178	$ 164,712	$ 41,178	$ 41,178	$ 41,178	$ 41,178	$ 164,712	$ 41,178	$ 41,178
Support Personnel	2,394	6,213	7,524	7,524	23,655	7,524	7,524	7,524	7,524	30,096	7,524	7,524
Flexowriter Personnel	2,763	2,763	2,763	2,763	11,052	2,763	2,763	2,763	2,763	11,052	2,763	2,763
All Other Personnel	16,251	16,558	27,799	45,998	106,606	66,989	72,868	73,821	73,821	287,499	73,821	73,821
Machine Rental												
Computer	11,370	17,065	17,065	17,065	62,565	17,065	17,065	17,065	17,065	68,260	17,065	17,065
Input	2,205	2,205	2,205	2,205	8,820	2,205	2,205	2,205	2,205	8,820	2,205	2,205
Supplies	1,542	1,542	1,542	1,542	6,168	1,542	1,542	1,542	1,542	6,168	1,542	1,542
Site Preparation	71,554				71,554							
Nonrecurring Cost	178,033				178,033							
Total	$ 327,290	$ 87,524	$ 100,076	$ 118,275	$ 633,165	$ 139,266	$ 145,145	$ 146,098	$ 146,098	$ 576,607	$ 146,188	$ 146,188
5. Net (Cost) or Saving (1-2)	$(294,908)	$ (30,556)	$ 6,793	$ 25,775	$ (292,986)	$ 43,700	$ 48,380	$ 48,380	$ 48,380	$ 188,840	$ 48,380	$ 48,380
Cumulative Gain or (Loss)	$(294,908)	$(325,464)	$(318,671)	$(292,896)	$ (292,986)	$(249,196)	$(200,816)	$(152,436)	$(104,056)	$(104,056)	$(55,676)	$ (7,296)

EXHIBIT 9

NONRECURRING COSTS

Systems Analysis and Programming...........	$111,125
Magnetic Tapes—60 reels @ $56.............	3,360
Storage Equipment........................	1,000
Freight Charges..........................	1,000
Feasibility and Application Studies...........	61,548
	$178,033

Input Media

1.   Preparation of input data for the computer from source documents was an area the EDP Committee desired to investigate. With the phenomenal increase in computer speeds and efficiency, it appeared that the techniques used in the input area should match computer efficiency as closely as possible. If this were not done, significant portions of the gain accruing from a computer operation would be lost by inefficient methods of input preparation and processing. Thus, the objective of the study was to determine if the time and cost of data preparation could be reduced while at the same time improving accuracy, speed, and efficiency both in the preparation of the input data and in processing the data into the computer. The ease of converting from EAM to EDP operation was also a consideration.

2.   Cards and punched paper tape were the two techniques considered. Remington Rand "90" column cards are presently used at Springfield. The "80" column cards were used as input for those computer manufacturers who recommended cards. Thus, any system selected required a conversion from the current "90" column card input to another medium.

3.   In considering the ease of conversion, a number of factors were evaluated. During the conversion phase, when parallel runs are necessary, a temporary addition of personnel is required. It was advisable to keep this increase to a minimum both from economic and personnel space considerations. The conversion period will last approximately one year. As some phases of the Univac 120 system would be in operation during this period, it would be necessary to have both "80" column and "90" column cards created from the source document if cards were used. This would require approximately six more key punch operators and would make the input data more susceptible to errors. This consideration, plus the fact that one computer manufacturer, RCA, recommended an extensive paper tape system, led to the investigation of punched paper tape systems.

4.   This investigation consisted of a careful study of the paper tape system recommended by RCA, studying actual paper tape systems at installations using this technique, discussing problems with manufacturers of paper tape producing equipment, viewing demonstrations of equipment, and conducting a test run on an actual planned operation at Springfield.

5.   In reviewing the RCA proposal, it seemed evident that there were many advantages in using punched paper tape as data input. This medium seemed suitable for a well-balanced data processing system. The speed of

input (1,000 characters per second) helped utilize the computer more efficiently. No peripheral equipment was necessary, so that the total processing time on the computer was the total time to complete each task without the necessity of having off-line operations such as sorting, collating, etc. This simplified work scheduling. By using the computer for all operations, source data could be entered in random sequence and processed internally, which would take full advantage of computer speeds. The reduction of steps outside the computer would reduce the probability of error. In many cases punched paper tape would be the by-product of typing operations. With no peripheral equipment needed, personnel requirements could be reduced by possibly six people in the ADPS office. This would include both tabulating machine operators and key punch operators. While the net savings might be only three personnel spaces (since all paper tape preparation would not be a real by-product of current operations) other important gains would be realized. Key punch operators are a critical classification in this area. The turnover rate for them is extremely high and it is very difficult to retain trained personnel. Flexowriter operators, on the other hand, are typists who are comparatively stable employees and require less training than key punch operators. All of these factors offer real advantages to a punched paper tape system.

6.   Members of the EDP Committee visited three separate installations where paper tape was used or being developed for use in a computer system. All seemed enthusiastic about its use.

7.   Commercial Controls Corp. and Underwood Corp. gave demonstrations on the Flexowriter and Data-Flow equipment, respectively. Both used the same type of basic equipment, which included a special electric typewriter, a paper tape punch, or paper tape reader and programming devices. Each is designed to permit the use of the "Building Block" principle of assembling and increasing number of equipment units into a single integrated system. One basic difference between the two types of equipment was the technique used in programming or controlling the operation of the system. The Underwood Data-Flow system uses a 550 step plug board which is wired for a series of predetermined operations. The Flexowriter uses a programmed paper tape that controls the system.

8.   The Production Control Route Sheet preparation was used in the test operation on both the Flexowriter and on the Data-Flow. The purpose of the test was to determine, based on an actual potential application, the accuracy, flexibility, economy, ease of handling, and acceptability of the paper tape to the computer under consideration.

9.   In the test, a manuscript copy of the route sheet was to be typed, producing copies of the route sheet plus two paper tapes. One tape was to capture all information on the route sheet except variable data which would include date, work order, lot number and total pieces. The other tape was to capture selective data, all of which would be used to update the master file on magnetic tape.

10.   From the test, it was demonstrated that punched paper tape provided a very flexible input medium. The length of fields was not limited to

80 or 90 digits of data. While changes to paper tape, after the tape was finished, could not be made as readily as with cards, routines were available to make such changes. Corrections or changes desired while the tape was being punched were easy to accomplish.

11. One of the main factors which we wished to determine in the test was the accuracy of the paper tape. All data that were typed and programmed for inclusion in the by-product paper tape were recorded in exact duplication. Both vendors stated that many banks were using punched paper tape without need for verification. However, there were a number of verification procedures available if required. Both vendors incorporated parity checks. The accuracy of punched paper tape and error correction techniques were very adequate.

12. Paper tape is easier to store than punched cards and does not take up as much storage space.

13. The main economy would result from the paper tape being simply a by-product of a necessary operation. This would occur in a number of areas. It is anticipated that punched paper tape would be used in the following areas.

a. Job Control Center
b. Inventory Control
c. Personnel Management
d. Methods (Production Control)
e. Procurement
f. EDPS Operation

14. Equipment requirements and costs are estimated in the proposal as follows:

```
6 Flexowriters......................  $433.62 per month
6 Auxiliary Punches...............    139.20
1 Adding Machine.................     23.32
2 Flexowriters....................    121.26
8 Stands.........................     17.38
                                     _____
       Total......................  $734.78 per month
```

15. This rental cost is approximately $345 per month less than the peripheral equipment requirements of a card system, including an estimated $185 per month saving in cost of paper tape over card supplies. Two converters with the ability to go from card (90 column) to tape and tape to card would be required during the conversion period. These rent for $110 per month each.

Equipment Selection

Prior to requesting the manufacturers to submit a proposal, detailed system specifications were developed based upon the analysis of the present system and management's requirements. These presentations were specific as to the system requirements which had to be satisfied, and included the following:

A. Input:
Method by which data will be received or developed.
Format, message length and alpha-numeric requirements.
Daily volume.

B. Maintenance of Information:
    Volume of records.
    Method of files.
    Record lengths.
    Alpha-numeric requirements.
C. Data Handling:
    A detailed description of the updating action that was required
    for each record.
D. Output:
    Type of output.
    Volume.
    Format.
    Reporting frequency.
E. Special Requirements:
    Ability to perform scientific requirements.
    Ability to meet expansion requirements.
    Assistance from manufacturers in training personnel.
    Assistance from manufacturers in getting initial programs de-
    veloped.
    Ability to process 80 column cards if cards are used.

After development of the specifications, invitations to submit proposals
were extended to six manufacturers:

International Business Machines Corporation
Sperry Rand Corporation
Radio Corporation of America
Burroughs Corporation
National Cash Register Corporation
Philco Corporation

With the exception of National Cash Register Corp. and Philco Corp.,
both of whom requested to be excused from submitting a proposal, all
others prepared and submitted their bids within the time limit specified.
During the preparation of the proposals by the manufacturers the committee members made themselves available to each of the manufacturers
for any clarification or detailed explanation of the specifications.

The computer system proposed by each of the equipment manufacturers was as follows:

Burroughs Corporation "205"
International Business Machines "1401"
Radio Corporation of America "501"
Sperry Rand Corporation "Univac 80"

Each of the proposals received was carefully reviewed by the committee
to determine whether or not all of the specifications of the system were
satisfied. With the exception of one manufacturer's submission, all the
specifications were fulfilled adequately.

One of the basic specifications given to the computer manufacturers
was that the computer have the capability of processing both the business

and scientific requirements of Springfield. A scientific subcommittee was established to work with the company's representatives, in order to familiarize them with the details of this requirement.

In recommending the "1401," IBM stated in its proposal that the 1401 was designed specifically as a data processor. It has limited use in scientific problem solving. Because of this scientific capabilities limitation, IBM recommended that a service bureau be used for scientific work beyond the capabilities of the 1401. Since the specifications called for a computer which would enable both the scientific and business personnel to process data efficiently and accurately, IBM, in recommending the 1401, only partially met the specifications. This deficiency outweighed such advantages of the 1401 as its low price, reasonable installation cost and ease of programming. After complete evaluation of all factors, the 1401 was not considered to be the best computer for the desired application.

There were two basic system approaches proposed: one, random access; the other, sequential record processing. The committee believed that the basic system concept should be examined first to determine which concept was the best for Springfield. If there were a significant benefit in either system concept, this would be a strong factor in consideration of the computer.

Upon further careful review and evaluation of data requirements, the committee could not find that there was any significant reason for updating records as soon as the transaction was completed, and neither was there a requirement to make inquiries into the status of a record such that the answer had to be forthcoming within minutes. Based upon this, and the fact that our specifications called for daily updating of detail records, we came to the conclusion that random access by itself was not a major requirement.

It was apparent that all four proposals were in equal contention from a systems design standpoint. The next consideration was to evaluate whether all would accomplish our business data and scientific data processing requirements within the allotted one-shift rental. As mentioned above, the IBM 1401 did not have the capabilities to satisfactorily meet the scientific specifications. The Burroughs 205 was unable to do the business data processing within a one-shift basis during peak loads, that is, when daily and weekly reports had to be processed at the same time. Since these two computers had important limitations, it was necessary then to evaluate the two which did meet the basic specifications against other criteria of selection.

These criteria included, of course, the time to do both the scientific and business data processing, both on-line and off-line (if applicable); rental cost of the equipment; potential for expansion needs; and any benefit which would accrue to Springfield with a particular computer.

Based on consideration and analysis of all the criteria of selection, the EDP Committee, in conjunction with the scientific subcommittee, unanimously agreed that the RCA 501 computer system would best satisfy the requirements of Springfield for both business data and scientific application.

The RCA 501 system offered many advantages over the other computers which were proposed. The equipment configuration recommended met all specifications and was capable of accomplishing economically and efficiently both the business data and scientific processing requirements of Springfield.

The 85.7 hours per month (Exhibit 10) total time for use as a business data processor—including 15.1 hours for debugging, reruns and errors—was the lowest time of the three computers which met the specifications. These hours of business processing time are the total time to do the complete task. Off-line EAM equipment is not involved since the source input data are ready for the computer when it arrives at the computer center. Thus, the efficiency and speed of the computer are used to process all data and print out all reports. Other computer systems under consideration took approximately 75 hours a month to sort, collate, interpret, etc., the input data (cards) for preparation prior to entering the computer. Although this is an off-line operation and does not take computer time, it does require peripheral equipment and their operators (estimated two). This reduction in equipment requirements will save personnel spaces within the organization and will result in a somewhat more economical operation.

The cost of the equipment configuration of RCA is $580 per month more than that of the Univac 80; however, the cost of processing per unit message on the 501 is $.0012 less than that of the Univac (Exhibit 11). In addition, the difference in cost is more than recovered by the savings in personnel operating cost for peripheral equipment operators required by the Univac system. These advantages of the 501 make it decidedly the best computer for Springfield.

In any electronic digital computer system programming is a major cost. If changes in equipment configuration become necessary because of expansion or contraction of data processing requirements, equipment cost is only one factor involved in making a change. Programming effort is the other major cost factor. The RCA 501 system is the most flexible of any under consideration. Although only one module of memory (16,384 digits) is necessary at the present time, additional modules up to a total of four may be added without adding another main frame. The magnetic tape stations can be changed from 22,222 to 33,333 characters per second, read and write speed, or to 66,666 characters per second if additional processing time were required; also, the 503 main frame can be made into a 504 main frame by the simple addition of a unit. This would further increase the speed of the data processing operation. Each of these changes could be made without disrupting the computer operation, although additional rental costs would be required. However, only minor programming changes would be necessary. If it were necessary to reduce the size of the system, magnetic tape stations might be eliminated. With the computer being used for both science and business this flexibility in computer capacity without the necessity of reprogramming is a real asset.

EXHIBIT 10

EQUIPMENT TIME AND COST EVALUATION CHART, HOURS PER MONTH

	IBM 1401	Burs 205	RCA 501	Rem Rand 80
Primary Application:				
Production Control				
Process	23.9	57.5	18.6	29.0
Setup	4.7	15.7	10.7	6.3
General Accounting				
Process	30.1	31.8	13.1	18.3
Setup	7.2	10.0	12.4	16.1
Payroll				
Process	2.1	3.5	4.0	3.4
Setup	.5	.7	.7	.7
Personnel File Maintenance				
Process	—	.3	6.8	—
Setup	—	.4	4.3	—
Totals				
Process	56.1	93.1	42.5	50.7
Setup	12.4	26.8	28.1	23.1
TOTAL	68.5	119.9	70.6	73.8
Debugging, Reruns, etc.	15.1	15.1	15.1	15.1
Total Business	83.6	135.0	85.7	88.9
Balance—Science	88.4	37.0	86.3	83.1
Total Hours Per Month	172	172	172	172
Installation Cost	$4,000	$ 7,361	$ 4,070	$ 3,762
Rental Cost Per Month	8,165	13,439	11,515	10,935
Rental Cost Per Hour	48	77	66	63

EXHIBIT 11

COST PER INPUT MESSAGE

	IBM 1401	Burs 205	RCA 501	Rem Rand 80
Total Processing Time	56.1	93.1	42.5	50.7
Rental Cost Per Hour	$48	$77	$66	$63
Total Processing Cost	$2,693	$7,169	$2,805	$3,194
Number of Input Messages	←———251,428 ———————→			
Cost Per Message	$.018	$.0285	$.0112	$.0123

This computer is compatible with the larger RCA 501 system recently installed at New York. With recent restrictions on personnel spaces and the problem of obtaining trained programmers, the compatibility with New York takes on an additional importance. With similar equipment at both installations there is a source of trained and experienced personnel in the data processing group at New York—available to give assistance as required during the preparation and conversion phase of the operation.

The compatibility feature has another decided advantage to both business and science. New York could act as a back-up in case of an emergency at Springfield, and Springfield could possibly act as a partial back-up for New York since the equipment could be expanded without interrupting operations.

The larger computer system at New York can also be advantageous to the scientific effort, since occasionally a problem may be developed which could use four modules of memory more effectively than one. Thus, with a relatively low-cost system at Springfield, the compatibility at New York would allow tremendous potential problem solving power.

GREAT PLAINS
NATIONAL BANK (A)

The Great Plains National Bank, located in a large Midwestern city was one of the nation's larger banks. A major part of the bank's business was its trust operations, consisting of the management of property for individuals, corporations, institutions, and charitable organizations. These activities were divided between Personal Trust and Corporate Trust accounts, the former comprising some 85 percent of its trust business. The bank had trust funds amounting to nearly $2 billion under its investment supervision.

Great Plains served as executor, trustee, agent, or investment advisor in managing the property of individuals, and there were some 7,000 personal accounts, all of which contained a variety of securities and all of which involved various transactions over the course of a year. Securities were bought and sold, dividends were paid, tax records were maintained, and so forth. As agent for its corporate customers, the major portion of the bank's work was in maintaining the current stockholder lists, effecting the transfer of their securities as they were bought and sold on the stock market, and issuing dividend and interest checks to the current holders of these securities. The bank also provided commercial banking services, but these were set up chiefly to facilitate the handling of funds for trust and agency customers, and for the convenience of individual corporate accounts.

In the summer of 1961 George Mathew, head of the General Administration Division of the bank, began to investigate the question of whether or not there were profitable computer applications at the bank. To assist him, the bank's president requested a consulting firm to make an initial study, and if results indicated it was worthwhile, to make a further detailed study of possible computer applications.

The consulting firm sent an associate and his assistant, who began their study in September, and completed it in November, 1961.

PHASE I STUDY

The consultants' report on Phase I was some fifteen pages in length and contained an outline of the proposed systems and estimates of systems costs. Pertinent excerpts from this report follow.

Objective

The objective of Phase I was general identification of opportunities for improving the timeliness, cost and efficiency of the services provided by the Great Plains National Bank through the use of advanced data processing equipment, and to determine whether a detailed computer feasibility study appeared warranted.

Scope

The scope of this study included all data processing activities now engaged in by the company's various divisions and departments.

Approach

This study included:

1.   Initial interviews with Messrs. Mathew, Preston[1] and Stoddard[1] to gain a general understanding of the bank's operations.
2.   Subsequent interviews by both bank and consultant personnel in those areas included in the scope of the study, including:

General Administration Division	Securities Department
Trust Investment Division	Tabulating Department
Trust Administration Division	Trust Accounting Department
General Services Department	Banking Operations Department
Probate Department	Order Department
	Tax Department

3.   Preparation of general systems flow charts and analysis of the content and usage of filed reference records which might be maintained by a computer.
4.   Assembly of volume and activity statistics together with estimated growth factors.
5.   Collection of personnel, equipment, and other cost data. Estimates of future costs were developed from bank projections of anticipated growth.
6.   Analysis of these data in terms of the currently available data processing equipment. A possible general computer solution to the bank's data processing problems was devised.
7.   Preparation of a 10-year projection of the personnel and equipment requirements of this possible solution.

---

[1] In charge of the punched card operations.

8.   Review of this information with the president of Great Plains and the senior officers of the General Administration Division.

The consultants then described a system envisioned for the Personal Trust Accounting and also the Corporate Trust Accounting departments, the two departments they felt could best utilize a computer. These systems were based on magnetic tape files which were to be updated, sorted, and processed as required by the various tasks. This computer system would take over all tabulating department functions and eliminate or drastically change the operations of such departments as Trust Bookkeeping.

Following a ten page list of advantages of the proposed computer system, the report went on to specify the disadvantages:

Disadvantages

The computer system has two possible disadvantages.

1.   Inasmuch as the various hard copy files would be combined in the magnetic tape files, no source of visual reference to customer data would be available.

2.   The rapid evolution of computers would seem to favor the delaying of a computer installation for a few years in order to take advantage of future advances in equipment capabilities.

The first of these disadvantages can be answered by including in the system a machine-generated hard copy file which would be designed to meet the bank's reference needs. Regarding the second disadvantage, it should be remembered that the advantages from installing a computer lie primarily with the systems. The computer is merely the tool necessary to implement these systems. Thus, the availability of more modern equipment would probably not change these systems, and would affect the bank only to the extent it might reduce equipment cost. Since this possible reduction would probably not outweigh the savings which would be forfeited by delaying installation, the second disadvantage would not appear to be valid for the bank.

System Costs

The acquisition of a computer would result in substantial one-time and continuing costs for Great Plains. These costs would, however, be recovered in about 4½ years after the actual installation of the computer, through offsetting savings from reduction in present staff and office equipment costs. The bank's net personnel would decrease by an estimated 46 positions, and about 10 pieces of the present punched card equipment would become excess.

[Detailed cost breakdowns by department followed in support, as well as estimates of installation, programming costs, etc.]

Expenditure Recovery

As the tabulated data show, the computer system could result in a reduction in annual operating cost of approximately $135,000, beginning in 1965, and increasing gradually each year thereafter. Furthermore, the increase in expenditures required for the computer system through 1964 would be fully offset before the end of 1968, and by the end of 1973— about 10 years after installation—the computer system could be expected to have resulted in a cumulative savings of close to $1,000,000.

The report's final recommendation was as follows:

The foregoing analyses indicate that there are some major advantages, which could be realized from the installation of a computer at Great Plains and, further, there are no major disadvantages foreseen for such an installation. Thus the bank should proceed with the second phase of this study—a detailed feasibility study which would include both design of a computer system and consideration of possible equipments.

The consultant who had drawn up this report went over it with Mr. Mathew and together they presented it informally to the president. A decision was reached immediately to go ahead, and Mr. Barr was sent in by the consulting firm to undertake the Phase II study. Mr. Barr was familiar with the Great Plains National Bank, since he had worked there on a previous project. He worked very closely with staff members of the bank—including Mr. Mathew, with whom he had been previously associated—and the Phase II report was completed by August 1962. Neither Mr. Barr nor Mr. Mathew had much contact with the president on computer matters during this time, although there was considerable interaction with the staff as Mr. Barr collected the data he required. Mr. Barr, in fact, spent much of his time obtaining his information and projection figures from the staff members who he felt were best placed to estimate such information.

In August 1962, Mr. Barr drew up his study in a 28-page report, which formed the basis of the presentation made to the president and the management advisory committee at the end of the month. This committee consisted of the eight division heads, who were vice presidents, and the two senior department heads, and was chaired by the president. Copies of the report were distributed at the meeting, and Mr. Barr with two of his superiors from the central office made a presentation to the group. This presentation was based entirely on the Phase II report, pertinent extracts of which appear as an Appendix.

In connection with this report Mr. Barr had stressed to Mr. Mathew on several occasions that the basic approach they used in their report was to design a system best suited to Great Plains without any regard to hardware. He felt that the only valid approach was first to design the best possible system to meet the bank's requirements and then to determine what equipment was available to satisfy such a system.

Mr. Barr had not asked the equipment manufacturers for proposals; he had sent the exact equipment configuration to the manufacturers and had asked for price quotations. The appropriate configuration for any one manufacturer was determined on the basis of his past experience with their equipment.

This report was accepted by the committee. The questions after the presentation mostly concerned the systems details, although a few members did question the advisability of not using IBM equipment, since IBM had had such extensive banking experience. The committee agreed that a computer would be economically justified and that a Honeywell 400 should be acquired. On the matter of lease or buy, it was generally felt that purchase was the best course, although no decision was made.

A few weeks later Mr. Mathew gave the president a further set of financial data and the decision was made by the president, on Mr. Mathew's advice, to purchase rather than lease the H400. An order was placed for the purchase of an H400, and delivery was promised for July 1964.

Mr. Barr then was hired by the Great Plains National Bank and spent his first months on a roving assignment relating to improvement of customer services and data processing. Mr. Mathew, meanwhile, had decided to accept an attractive offer made to him by a consulting firm and resigned his position in December 1962 at Great Plains. Mr. Barr was promoted to vice president and head of the General Administration Division.

APPENDIX

Phase II Report
Objectives of Phase II Report

The objectives of the Phase II study were five:

1. Identification of specific functions in the bank suitable for further mechanization.

2. Design of a system for handling these functions on an electronic computer.

3. Determination of the electronic computer best suited to the needs of the bank.

4. Preparation of detailed cost estimates and projections.

5. Development of a plan and timetable for installation of the computer and conversion to the new system.

Scope

The Phase II study concentrated on the bank's Personal Trust Accounting and Corporate Trust Accounting operations.

From the systems design it was determined that the equipment necessary to handle the personal trust and corporate trust accounting systems would be a medium-sized computer.

Equipment Evaluation

The personal trust and corporate trust accounting systems were analyzed in order to determine the equipment which would best satisfy their requirements. The specifications of various currently available electronic computers were evaluated in terms of performance, cost, capacity for expansion and installation support.

A description of this evaluation process and of the conclusions reached is recorded below.

Equipment Considered

The bank's system requirements were reviewed in the light of experience with similar studies, and an equipment configuration was developed which would be capable of meeting these requirements. The recommended configuration centers around a general-purpose, high-speed electronic computer. Attached to this computer are a card input device which can read data from punched cards, and five magnetic tape transports to be used in transferring data into and out of the computer.

A variation on this magnetic tape-oriented system was developed to take advantage of the card random access memory (called CRAM) available with the National Cash Register Company computer. This CRAM configuration differs from the tape configuration in that it would substitute two CRAM units for three magnetic tape units.

Analysis of system requirements and of overall equipment capabilities indicated that the monthly rental of computers capable of meeting the bank's needs would probably range between $9,000 and $14,000. The manufacturers approached and the equipment proposed are shown in Exhibit 1. Each computer was then evaluated in terms of performance, cost, capacity for expansion, and installation support.

Performance

Estimates were developed of the running times and associated equipment setup times required for each computer to handle the proposed personal trust accounting and corporate trust accounting systems. Timing figures were adjusted to reflect probable time lost through reruns, operator delays, and equipment downtime. The figures were also adjusted to reflect the anticipated growth in the number of accounts over the next seven years. These estimates were provided by Mr. Mathew, a vice president.

Cost

Cost figures for the equipment, if rented, were developed by adding to the basic monthly rentals of the equipment the costs resulting from any extra-shift use of the equipment and the added cost of the personnel involved in such extra shifts, as determined from the time requirements described above. Purchase costs for the equipment were adjusted to include maintenance charges and extra-shift personnel costs only, since no charge for use of the equipment on the extra shifts would be incurred if the equipment were purchased by the bank.

Capacity for Expansion

Consideration was given to the anticipated growth in number of accounts over the next 12 years and the effect which such growth would have on equipment times. In addition, each machine was examined to determine its capacity for expansion to a size great enough to handle a growth rate substantially greater than that now anticipated by the bank. The capabilities considered necessary to provide such expandability included the ability to increase magnetic tape speeds, the ability to increase computer memory size, and the ability to add a second printer to the equipment configuration.

Installation Support

Each manufacturer was asked to submit a proposal outlining the support which he would provide to an installation of his equipment at the bank. Special emphasis was placed on three kinds of support:
   a) Systems assistance, which included the assignment of systems personnel to work with the bank, the training of bank personnel in equipment programming and operation, the furnishing of programming aids, and service routines.
   b) Equipment maintenance, which included the assignment of maintenance personnel.
   c) Equipment back-up, which included designation of the equipment which would be available for emergency use in the event of failure of the bank's machine for an extended period. In addition, special consideration was given to each manufacturer's performance in the computer field to date and to his future plans.

Results of Equipment Evaluation

The results of each of the steps in equipment evaluation are shown in Exhibit 2. They can be summarized as follows:

Performance

Daily required equipment times for personal trust accounting and corporate trust accounting range between a low of 6.74 hours and a high of 13.20 hours in 1964, and a low of 7.40 and a high of 14.77 hours in 1968. The GE 225 and the H400 would both handle 1964 volumes within the seven and one-half hours available in the bank's workday, but only the H400 would do so under anticipated 1968 volumes. The other machines would require personnel and/or equipment overtime.

Cost

Average monthly costs of some equipment would differ considerably from quoted monthly rentals because of the personnel and/or equipment overtime charges. Average monthly costs range from $9,765 for the H400 to $14,560 for the IBM 1410 (729II). The H400 and the NCR 315 (CRAM) would be the least costly of the nine kinds of equipment.

Capacity for Expansion

On the basis of the expansion capabilities cited previously and listed in the exhibits, the B200, IBM 1401 and RCA 301 all lack adequate capacity for expansion, chiefly because of their relatively small memories.

Overall Ranking

When the machines are ranked in order of desirability in terms of performance, cost, and capacity for expansion, the H400 is first, the GE 225 second, the NCR 315 (CRAM) third, and the IBM 1410 (7330) fourth. The B200, the IBM 1401 and the RCA 301 can be eliminated from consideration because of their relatively poor standing in all three categories, while the IBM 1410 (729II) and the NCR 315 (Tape) can be eliminated because of their comparatively high cost.

Installation Support

Analysis of the installation support proposals reveals that Honeywell and IBM are especially well equipped to support an installation at the bank, while GE and NCR are less well equipped to do so.

Honeywell has a distinct advantage, in terms of installation support, since it has a particularly strong regional office near the bank, and the personnel and facilities of this office would be available to the bank. Honeywell has had computer experience with another bank and can provide nearby equipment back-up. Its proposals for systems assistance and equipment maintenance were considered satisfactory.

IBM, the acknowledged leader in the computer industry, can also provide nearby equipment back-up, and can point to long years of experience with local banks. Furthermore, IBM has had a long-time relationship with the bank and has provided satisfactory service to Great Plains' punched card installation. The systems assistance and equipment maintenance proposed by IBM were not considered satisfactory, however, because the systems assistance would be part time, with equipment maintenance on an on-call* basis. IBM's installation support could not be considered satisfactory unless it were changed to assure the bank of full-time, on-site assignment of IBM personnel.

So far, GE has not had experience with local banks with the equipment proposed, and its back-up equipment would be at some distance from the bank.

NCR also has not had experience in local banks with the equipment proposed, and does not have a back-up machine installed or on order in the area.

Conclusion

On the basis of its excellent performance, cost, and capacity for expansion, in terms of the bank's personal trust accounting and corporate trust accounting system requirements, and because of the ability of its manufacturer to provide satisfactory installation support in the area, the Minneapolis-Honeywell H400 is recommended as the equipment best suited to the bank's needs.

Impact on Personnel Requirements

[The personnel requirements were broken down by department in the report, but in summary are as in Exhibit 3.]

Projection Comments

Projections shown in Exhibit 3 are based on the bank's estimate of an annual growth in number of accounts. Present system personnel requirements reflect the company's estimate that the number of personnel will grow at a slower rate than the number of accounts because of the increased efficiency anticipated from management improvement programs now in progress or contemplated. Thus, personnel requirements in the affected cost centers would increase annually by approximately 4 percent if the present system were to continue in operation, to handle the projected annual increase in number of accounts.

As a result, present system personnel requirements would increase from 264 to 439 during the period from 1962 through 1973. Under the proposed system, present system personnel requirements would continue unchanged in 1962, 1963 and 1964, since the present system would still be operating in those years. In 1965, however, as conversion to the new system is completed, 99 positions can be dropped. It has been assumed that half of the

---

*"On-call" maintenance involved a regular maintenance schedule; any breakdowns in between regular service calls involved telephoning for a service man and a subsequent 30 minute to 1 hour delay.

position eliminations will take place in 1965 and the balance in the period from 1966 through 1968.

Partially offsetting these eliminations are the additions of computer personnel to prepare for, install and operate the computer. Under the proposed system, the added computer personnel requirements would amount to 6 persons (the programmers) in 1962; to 14 persons in 1963, as some of the control and equipment operating personnel are added to the staff; and to 22 persons in 1964, as staffing is completed.

Of the $50,600 annually being spent on IBM tabulating equipment, some $30,738 could be cut after the installation of the H400.

[Details of such equipment followed.]

Other Charges

These were estimated as follows:

Other Costs	1962	1963	1964	1965
Site Preparation..............	—	$ 35,000	—	—
Programming Expenses.........	$ 5,000	5,000	—	—
Tax Cost Research Expenses....	—	5,000	$ 5,000	—
Conversion Expenses...........	—	25,000	35,000	$ 5,000
Assistance from Others.........	72,000	99,000	90,000	84,000
TOTAL.................	$77,000	$169,000	$130,000	$89,000

Charges for assistance by others covers the cost of the assistance required from operating departments in preparing for the installation of the new system, as well as the cost of outside assistance. Operating department heads and other supervisory personnel will be called upon to assist in design of the new system, development of new operating procedures, actual system conversion, development and implementation of retraining programs, reorganization of operating units and similar activities vital to the successful installation of the computer system. Operating departments will also be asked to provide such services as assembling data for files, checking computer input and output during parallel operations and so forth. Further, the consultant has been requested to advise the Systems Planning Department and the various operating departments in fulfilling their respective roles in the computer installation. To cover the cost of this interdepartmental assistance, and the consulting fees involved in this study and estimated for future counsel, the computer project has been charged with $72,000 in 1962, $99,000 in 1963, $90,000 in 1964, and $84,000 in 1965.

Cost Comparisons

The personnel, equipment and other costs just described are shown in Exhibit 4 for the present and proposed systems during the period from 1962 through 1973, assuming that the computer is purchased and depreciated over a 10 year period. Personnel costs include an average annual increase in salary. As indicated in the exhibit, proposed system costs would be greater than present system costs during the period from 1962 through 1965, and less in subsequent years. Initial investment in the proposed system would be recovered by 1969, and by 1973, the return to the bank after all costs had been recovered would amount to $2,984,000.

An analysis similar to that in Exhibit 4, for the situation where the computer is rented, indicates that proposed system costs are less than present system costs beginning in 1966. Investment recovery would occur in late 1969, and by 1973 the return to the bank would amount to $2,391,200. Other annual cumulative expenditure recovery figures for this situation are shown on the bottom line of Exhibit 4.

Purchase versus Rental

Several noneconomic considerations should be weighed before a decision to purchase a computer is made. These include: (1) the computer's capacity for expansion, (2) its operating life, and (3) its susceptibility to technological obsolescence.

The H400 can handle personal trust accounting and corporate trust accounting volumes anticipated for ten years from the date of installation within a single shift of operation, leaving the second and even a third shift available for increases in volumes far in excess of those now anticipated. Furthermore, the machine's tape speeds can be increased, its memory can be enlarged, and multiple printers can be added to the installation. It is reasonable to say, then, that the H400's *capacity for expansion* is more than adequate.

The H400 installation experience to date indicates that it performs well with relatively little maintenance required. A regular program of continuing preventive maintenance, including parts replacement, is performed. It therefore seems likely that, even though field experience to date with the H400 and similar solid-state computers is relatively short, the *operating life* of the machine should be more than acceptable.

Constant improvements in electronic computers and their components have characterized the data processing industry in the past five years. However, the models of equipment being announced at the present time appear to offer relatively small improvement over existing models. The H400 selected by Great Plains is a modern, powerful machine, and should compare favorably with other machines for at least the next few years. Further, even if a more attractive machine were announced five years from now, the cost and time involved in reprogramming the system to fit the new machine could—on the basis of past experience—exceed any benefits that such a machine might offer.

It would therefore seem that there are no major noneconomic reasons why the bank should not purchase the H400.

The data in Exhibit 4 reveals that the return to the bank is considerably greater from a purchased computer installation than a rented one. These figures, of course, include neither the cost of money nor the federal tax implications of rental versus purchase.

EXHIBIT 1

EQUIPMENT CONSIDERED IN THE STUDY

Manufacturers	Equipment Proposed
Burroughs Corporation	B200
General Electric Company	GE 225
Minneapolis-Honeywell Regulator Company	H400
International Business Machines Corporation*	IBM 1401
	IBM 1410 (729II)
	IBM 1410 (7330)
National Cash Register Company†	NCR 315 (Tape)
	NCR 315 (CRAM)
Radio Corporation of America	RCA 301
Sperry Rand Corporation‡	Did not respond

*Two configurations of the IBM 1410 were proposed, one using Model 729II magnetic tape transports and the other Model 7330 magnetic tape transports.

†Two configurations of the NCR 315 were proposed, one using magnetic tape throughout and the other a combination of magnetic tape and CRAM.

‡Sperry Rand Corporation did not answer the proposal request and therefore was eliminated from the study.

EXHIBIT 2

RESULTS OF EQUIPMENT EVALUATION

	B200	GE225	H400	IBM 1401	IBM 1410 (729II)	IBM 1410 (7330)	NCR 315 (Tape)	NCR 315 (CRAM)	RCA 301
Performance									
Estimated Daily Equipment Hours*									
1964 Average	13.20	7.16	6.74	10.36	7.57	8.55	9.60	7.85	10.68
1968 Average	14.77	7.87	7.40	11.52	8.35	9.48	10.67	8.82	11.88
Cost									
Rented Equipment (1964–68)									
Average Monthly Cost	$ 12,260	$ 11,360	$ 9,765	$ 13,970	$ 14,560	$ 12,360	$ 13,570	$ 10,050	$ 12,480
Purchased Equipment (1964–68)									
Quoted Purchase Price	$357,255	$509,220	$444,675	$499,800	$696,875	$589,675	$497,250	$488,250	$438,650
Capacity for Expansion									
Capabilities									
Increase Magnetic Tape Speeds	No	Yes	Yes	Yes	Yes	Yes	Yes	Yes	Yes
Increase Memory	No	Yes	Yes	No	Yes	Yes	Yes	Yes	No
Increase Number of Printers	Yes	Yes	Yes	Yes	Yes	Yes	Yes	Yes	Yes
Adequate?	No	Yes	Yes	No	Yes	Yes	Eliminated	Yes	No
Overall Ranking	Eliminated	2	1	Eliminated	Eliminated	4		3	Eliminated

*Estimates made by the consultants on the basis of their experience.

EXHIBIT 3

IMPACT OF PROPOSED COMPUTER INSTALLATION ON PROJECTED POSITION REQUIREMENTS

	1962	1963	1964	1965	1966	1967	1968	1969	1970	1971	1972	1973
Present System Position Requirements	264	275	286	300	315	328	342	357	376	396	417	439
Total Proposed System	270	297	316	273	258	256	254	265	278	292	307	322
Present System Positions Eliminated				(50)	(25)	(12)	(12)					
Proposed System Positions Added	6	22	30	23	23	24	24	25	25	26	27	27
Net Increase (or Decrease) from Installation of Proposed System	6	22	30	(27)	(57)	(72)	(88)	(92)	(98)	(104)	(110)	(117)

EXHIBIT 4

COMPARISON OF PRESENT AND PROPOSED SYSTEM COSTS IN AFFECTED COST CENTERS (IF COMPUTER IS PURCHASED)

1962 through 1973 (Figures in 000's)

	1962	1963	1964	1965	1966	1967	1968	1969	1970	1971	1972	1973
Total Present System Costs	$1,489	$1,596	$1,709	$1,844	$1,994	$2,135	$2,291	$2,462	$2,669	$2,892	$3,134	$3,596
Personnel Costs	$1,438	$1,543	$1,653	$1,785	$1,931	$2,071	$2,224	$2,391	$2,594	$2,814	$3,052	$3,310
Equipment Costs	$ 51	$ 53	$ 55	$ 59	$ 63	$ 64	$ 67	$ 71	$ 75	$ 78	$ 82	$ 86
Total Proposed System Costs	$1,607	$1,900	$2,092	$2,059	$1,816	$1,821	$1,868	$1,963	$2,112	$2,279	$2,461	$2,562
Personnel Costs	$1,479	$1,678	$1,862	$1,862	$1,733	$1,739	$1,785	$1,879	$2,028	$2,193	$2,374	$2,562
Equipment Costs	$ 50	$ 53	$ 99	$ 108	$ 83	$ 82	$ 83	$ 84	$ 84	$ 86	$ 87	$ 89
Computer Purchase Amortized	$ —	$ —	$ 33	$ 44	$ 44	$ 44	$ 44	$ 44	$ 44	$ 44	$ 44	$ 44
Other Costs	$ 78	$ 169	$ 131	$ 89	$ —	$ —	$ —	$ —	$ —	$ —	$ —	$ —
Annual Net Gain (or Loss) through Proposed System	$ (118)	$ (304)	$ (383)	$ (215)	$ 176	$ 314	$ 423	$ 499	$ 557	$ 613	$ 673	$ 745
Cumulative Expenditure Recovery	$ (118)	$ (422)	$ (805)	$(1,020)	$ (846)	$ (532)	$ (109)	$ 390	$ 947	$1,560	$2,233	$2,979
Cumulative Expenditure Recovery for Case Where Computer is Rented	$ (118)	$ (422)	$ (849)	$(1,123)	$(1,008)	$ (755)	$ (392)	$ 46	$ 541	$1,092	$1,702	$2,386

GREAT PLAINS
NATIONAL BANK (B)

The Great Plains National Bank was engaged in preparation for its H400 computer, which it had decided to purchase on the basis of a report made to it by its consultant in September of 1962. The machine was scheduled for delivery in August 1964, and preparations were under the direction of William Barr, vice president in charge of the General Administration Division. Mr. Barr had made the initial computer feasibility studies as a member of a consulting firm and subsequently had been hired by Great Plains. The consultants had been requested to make progress reports to the president and top management of Great Plains in March 1963 and 1964, in addition to their regular monthly visits for general advice and assistance.

The March 1963 report indicated that progress on the training program was satisfactory, as was the programming phase of the installation, although the report noted, "work progress is difficult to measure since a detailed programming schedule has only recently been completed."

It had been recommended in the Phase II report that scheduling and control could best be done with the aid of a PERT chart. The consultants noted that this had just been completed, the delay having been caused by priority accorded this project. "As yet no formal project control features have been developed, and no mechanism yet exists for posting progress." The consultants concluded that "scheduling and control of the computer project must be termed unsatisfactory."

The financial analysis section of this first progress report contained current estimates of the various costs involved. Great Plains personnel had given their latest best estimates of growth, personnel fringe benefit allowances, etc., to the consultant, and Exhibit 1 was drawn up. The category of "other costs" in Exhibit 1 was developed as follows.

Other Costs	1962	1963	1964	1965	1966
Computer Site Preparation...	—	$35,000	—	—	—
Programming Expenses......	$ 5,000	5,000	—	—	—
Conversion Expenses........	—	15,000	$45,000	$ 5,000	—
Assistance from Others......	68,500	44,900	42,000	40,100	$38,200
Total.................	$73,500	$99,900	$87,000	$45,100	$38,200

The financial analysis section concluded as follows:

1. By 1973, annual operating costs would be $532,000 less under the computer system than under the present system.
2. Cumulative investment in the computer project would be recovered by 1970, and by 1973 the excess of recovery over investment is estimated at $1,876,700.

The progress report was summed up in the conclusion which stated:

On the basis of performance to date and plans for the future, the computer project appears to be progressing in a satisfactory manner.

This report was distributed to management, and Mr. Barr met with the president and went over various points with him. The president was well satisfied with progress and requested Mr. Barr to issue a series of bulletins to the staff to keep them all informed of progress and the impact of the program on the bank.

In March 1964—one year later—the consultant again issued a progress report to management. The report, organized as before, made the following points:

The training program was considered satisfactory and generally effective. The programming schedule estimates were revised during the report preparation period and were now listed as in Exhibit 2.

The financial analysis section of this progress report, after presenting the cost figures in Exhibit 3, was summarized as follows:

The cumulative expenditure recovery of $1,416,000 now expected by 1973 is $463,000 less than the cumulative expenditure recovery figure reported in Installation Progress Report I. This difference can be attributed mainly to the lower estimated savings in personnel costs in those positions affected by the computer system.

Recent projections by the bank of the growth in the number of personnel indicates that, by 1973, under the present system only 110 persons would be in positions affected by the computer system, as compared with the 126 persons estimated in the first progress report.

The estimated savings figures have also been reduced by the delay in the conversion schedule. Cumulative savings are lower, since savings in personnel and equipment costs have been delayed.

The consultants discussed the report with Mr. Barr at some length and he in turn went over it with the president, explaining the measures that were being taken to put the project back on schedule. The president was satisfied with developments and asked Mr. Barr to prepare a section on the company's data processing activities for inclusion in the annual report.

In December 1963 Minneapolis-Honeywell announced its new H200 computer. Great Plains had had no prior knowledge of this announcement, and as the machine seemed to have several interesting features, Mr. Barr requested the consultants to do a detailed comparison of the two machines.

The two-man consulting team checked with Mr. Barr at the end of January, and as a result of their discussions made one change in their report: instead of only assuming a fixed computer staff and a flexible timetable, they added the alternative of a fixed timetable and flexible staffing to absorb the impact of changing machines.

The comparison report (reproduced in its entirety in the Appendix) was given to Mr. Barr in the middle of February.

Mr. Barr examined the report with care and concluded that several major intangibles were not given in the report.

He felt that there was widespread commitment at the bank to the H400. A major fundamental step had been taken with the introduction of the H400 and a whole new system had been designed for the company—a system that involved radical organizational changes. Plans had been set up for this change on the basis of the H400, and to change machines at this point would be a very delicate process. The line people in the organization had been educated, everybody in the company was aware of the impending arrival of the H400, and to change machines suddenly might well give an impression of instability, which would have damaging repercussions for the future of the whole system.

This consideration seemed particularly relevant to Mr. Barr since the H400 was adequate for expansion. There seemed to be little advantage, as far as he could see, in trading in the 1963 model for a 1964 model if the 1963 would do the job. He also felt that if he did wait for the 1964 model, he might have exactly the same problem in relation to the 1965's. Hardware was always improving, and he had to draw the line somewhere.

He believed that the apparent advantages of the H200 were offset by two intangible factors:

1.   The systems and programming staffs were familiar with H400 and its programming language and their morale was high. Any change now might throw them severely off stride.

2. There was a strong commitment and involvement to the H400 on the part of the staff, and in addition, the board of directors, the president and the stockholders were expecting the H400.

With this background, Mr. Barr felt that he was in a position to evaluate the question and recommend a course of action to the president.

APPENDIX

Honeywell 200 (H200) and Honeywell 400 (H400)

A: Comparison of Equipment

The two equipment systems were compared on seven factors—timing, equipment-related costs, site, delivery, support, expansion, and intangible considerations.

Timing

Timing for the H200 and H400 systems would be identical for runs that are limited by card reading, card punching and printing. The peripheral unit speeds are identical for both systems. Where magnetic tape speeds limit the processing speed, the H200 would be about 30 percent faster; it would use 44 KC (alphanumeric) one-half inch tapes instead of 32 KC (alphanumeric) three-quarter inch tapes used on the H400. Specific time differences for reading or writing varying record lengths of information to or from magnetic tape on the H400 and the H200 are shown below:

Characters per Record	H400	H200	Percent by Which H200 Is Faster Than H400
	(Milliseconds per Record)		
200	20.2	13.8	21.7%
500	29.5	20.4	30.9
1,000	45.0	31.4	30.3

An additional difference with the H400 is that computing time is not overlapped[1] with tape time, whereas it is almost completely overlapped in the H200 except for two microseconds per character during reading or writing.

If an operation is compute-bound, Honeywell estimates that overall the H200 will be about 25 percent faster than the H400. To test this estimate, we used a set of sample computer problems, weighted according to their average use. We found the H200 without multiply and divide logic to be 46 percent faster than the H400 with the logic, while the H200 with the multiply and divide logic would be 143 percent faster than the H400.

---

[1] The H200 can perform computations while simultaneously either writing on or reading from tape.

Our sample problems involved the use of add, subtract, multiply, divide, move and test operations. Honeywell could supply us only with estimated multiply and divide times for the H200, and these estimates were used in our calculation.

The memory sizes of the computers being considered for the bank are 24,576 alphanumeric characters for the H400 and 32,768 alphanumeric characters for the H200. The H200 therefore has one-third more memory capacity.

There are significant advantages to the H200 that permit more efficient use of its greater memory capacity. Since the H200 is a character-oriented computer, it can handle variable length records more efficiently than a word-oriented computer like the H400. A character computer uses the specific number of characters required by a record rather than the nearest multiple of fixed word lengths. An instruction for the H200 is two-address and requires an average of five characters, while instructions for the H400 are three-address but always require eight characters. In addition, the H200 would not need the considerable editing of input that is required in the H400 because of significant differences in the design of the hardware, thereby saving on the number of program instructions required. The effect of the larger memory capacity of the H200, together with the programming economies inherent in the design of the equipment, is such that a significantly smaller percent of the available memory would be required for the estimated number of program instructions for the Security Side programming (see Exhibit 4).

Equipment-Related Costs

Equipment

The planned H400 installation is quoted by Honeywell to sell for $444,675. A similar configuration of the H200 is quoted at $394,565. This represents a hardware saving of $50,110. This comparison is based on similar configurations and does not account for a possible decision to purchase an H200 without the multiply and divide feature, which would sell for $383,315 and result in a hardware saving of $61,360. Consideration of the H200 without the multiply and divide feature is largely dictated by the unavailability of the feature on the H200 until the second quarter of 1965.

Maintenance

The difference between the maintenance costs for the H400 and the H200 (without the multiply and divide feature for the reason mentioned above) would represent a savings of $2,113 with the H200 for each of the first three years; $1,797 each year for the next three years; and $1,439 a year for the following three years.

Site

While the computer site planning of the bank may be already committed for the H400, a comparison of some of the specific site requirements is significant. Similar configurations of the H200 and the H400 would have the following site requirements:

	H200	H400
Space	300 sq. ft.	700 sq. ft.
Raised floor	Yes	Yes
Electrical power	18 KVA	26 KVA
Air conditioning	5 tons	6 tons

Delivery

Honeywell has scheduled the bank's H400 for delivery in July 1964. While Honeywell will deliver its first H200 this summer, Honeywell would not commit itself to deliver the H200 configuration required by the bank before March 1965.

Support

Honeywell support for the H400 and the H200 has been explored from various standpoints:

Applications

The H400 would have a customer representative and a full-time resident applications man. The H200 would have a customer representative and on-call systems support for programming and systems design. While the actual contributed value of the Honeywell full-time support should be weighed, we feel that Honeywell would continue to give either installation the support necessary for its success.

Maintenance

The equipment maintenance contract for a purchased H400 would provide on-site maintenance. For the H200, Honeywell quotes on-call maintenance 24 hours a day with a response time of about one hour. The manufacturer feels that on-call maintenance would be completely satisfactory for the H200 with the reliability that has been designed into it.

Test and Assembly

Honeywell would allow 60 hours of free test time with the H400 and 48 hours with the H200. Test time would be made available on compatible computer configurations outside the bank before the delivery of its own computer. If its computer installation is delayed beyond the limit of this free test time (about 3 months for the H400 and 2½ months for the H200) additional computer test time would be available for about $65 an hour. We estimate that each month of delay would require about 20 hours of additional outside test time.

Equipment Back-up

The need to call on an off-premises computer to back up a computer installation is fortunately quite rare. However, if required, Honeywell states that the bank's configuration of the H400 or the H200 would be backed up by a compatible system in the area.

Schools

The bank personnel have already been schooled in the H400. For the H200, a one-week programmers' school and a one-week operators' training course are both currently available in the local area at no cost.

Programs

The software library available now for the H400 would meet the bank's requirements. Honeywell states that it expects to have an equivalent software library for the H200 system available in the fourth quarter of 1964, except for COBOL, which will not be field tested until the first quarter of 1965. Since the specifications for the H200 programs are available now, programming for the H200 could proceed without delay.

Expansion

The main memory of the H400 can be expanded to a maximum of 4,096 words (32,768 alphanumeric characters) of core storage. The main memory of the H200 is currently limited to a similar maximum of 32,768 alphanumeric characters, but Honeywell has indicated that the H200 will have a greatly expanded memory at a later date, and its programming capability allows for this.

The H200 and the H400 both have capacity for expanding the peripheral complement that can be handled by the central processor. The H400 is limited to one printer and one card reader/punch on line, but the H200 could handle up to eight printers or eight card reader/punches. The H400 is limited to eight magnetic tape units, whereas the H200 could handle up to 64 units. Both computers operate with similar peripherals except for magnetic drums and one-half inch magnetic tapes, which can be handled only by the H200.

Intangible Factors

The H400 is a thoroughly tested and proved computer that is in successful use today. Its installation should entail a minimum of problems with hardware, software, delivery or support. As a new computer, the H200 will be subject to more problems in the early models. Its installation thus runs a greater risk of delay and frustration. However, the Honeywell organization is now concentrating most of its major talent on the H200.

The H200 appears to be easier to program, especially for inexperienced programmers. This may enable faster progress to be made on programs written for the H200. In addition, the H200's logic is similar to that of the popular IBM computers on which many programmers received their early training—a factor which might make it easier in the future to hire experienced programmers.

Testing of programs before installation presents no problem with the H400, since Honeywell already has equipment available for this purpose.

However, a computer capable of testing some of the bank's large H200 programs will not be available until December 1964. Thus, while smaller configurations of the H200 will be available earlier for training purposes and testing of some of the small programs, the testing of the larger programs will be delayed.

The ability of the H200 to read IBM magnetic tapes would enable the bank to use outside services (e.g., Standard and Poor's statistics available on IBM magnetic tape), and to provide data processing services (e.g., account reconciliation) to customers who process with IBM magnetic tapes.

Delivery limitations on the H200 would not permit the bank to install an H200 with multiply/divide logic without waiting some additional months. Honeywell has made no provisions for a field retrofit of the logic; hence the multiply/divide operations would have to be handled by a standard subroutine program.

Finally, the dollar costs of any delays in the installation of a computer should be measured against the savings in earnings from invested capital that would be realized from delayed payment for the equipment.

B: Comparison of Annual Costs and Cumulative Expenditure Recoveries, H200 versus H400

Approach to the Comparison

This analysis assumes:

(1)   Four and one-half calendar months will be required to retrain the programmers and machine operators on the H200, and to revise existing block diagrams and item designs to conform with the H200 code structure. An H200 of the required configuration will be available by December 1, 1964, to assemble and test the bank's programs.

(2)   An H200, without multiply/divide hardware, can be installed on the bank's premises by March 1, 1965.

Comparison of Costs

Comparative costs of the two computer systems include both one-time costs and the recurring costs. Possible differences in the cost of preparing the installation site and in the charges for electricity and air conditioning were ignored, since they are small in relation to the difference in personnel and equipment costs. It would also be difficult to assess these costs accurately, since the bank plans to make a showpiece of its installation, no matter which computer is purchased. It has also been assumed that no extra-shift personnel costs will be incurred with the H200, since it is faster than the H400, which is scheduled to process the anticipated volume of work in less than one shift per day.

The bank may find it necessary to assemble and test its programs at a Honeywell Data Center, since it would not expect to install an H200 on its premises before March 1, 1965. If one hour per day is assumed for testing, then approximately 60 hours would be required between December 1, 1964, the date on which testing time is first available, and March 1, 1965. Since the first 48 hours of testing time are free, the cost to the bank would amount to about $780 at a rate of $65 per hour.

The most important comparisons are the anticipated personnel savings, the equipment costs and the maintenance charges for the period 1964 through 1973 for the two computer systems. These have been made for two possible courses of action—namely:

1. Hiring additional programmers to absorb the four and one-half month delay in the conversion of the personal trust system caused by the need to retrain personnel and to revise work.

2. Accepting the four and one-half month delay in conversion.

First Course of Action

The first course of action assumes that fewer personnel will be required in 1964 as control clerks and machine operators because of the later installation of the H200 equipment, and that additional programmers will be hired to absorb the four and one-half month delay in conversion of the personal trust system.

Exhibit 5 shows that the expected cumulative expenditure recovery by 1973 for the H200 would be $98,000 greater than for the H400. This difference results from savings in control personnel and operator costs (offset in part by additional programmer costs), and from savings in equipment costs and maintenance charges. The savings in equipment costs and maintenance charges would more than offset the cost of the additional programmers required to overcome the schedule delay.

Second Course of Action

This course of action also assumes that fewer personnel will be required in 1964 as control clerks and machine operators because of the later installation of the H200 equipment, but does not assume that additional programmers will be hired to absorb the four and one-half month delay in conversion. Thus the difference in anticipated savings would result mainly from differences in equipment costs and maintenance charges, and from differences in anticipated reductions in personnel costs in the period 1965 through 1969.

Calculations similar to those in Exhibit 5 show that for Alternative 2, the expected cumulative expenditure recovery by 1973 for the H200 system would be $40,500 less than for the H400. This difference results from a loss in anticipated savings of $138,000, offset in part by a saving of $97,500 in equipment costs and maintenance charges. However, if the difference between the conversion dates for the two computer systems could be reduced (this is possible, since the H200 computer may be easier to program than an H400 computer), the cost comparison would improve rapidly in favor of the H200 computer, since the loss in anticipated savings would be reduced while the savings in equipment costs and maintenance charges would remain the same. Thus the final difference in the cumulative expenditure recoveries would be determined mainly by the difference in conversion dates for the two computer systems.

C: Conclusion

We conclude from our analysis that while either computer system could serve the bank's data processing requirements, the H200 would serve them more effectively. The outstanding advantages of the H200 would be its lower cost, its greater speed and capacity, its ease of programming, its more recent design concepts, its greater capacity for expansion and its compatibility with widely used IBM equipment.

If the decision is made to change to the H200, two possible courses of action have been outlined for the bank:

1.   Hiring two additional programmers to absorb the four and one-half month delay in converting the personal trust system caused by the need to retrain personnel and to revise work.

2.   Accepting the four and one-half month delay in conversion.

We recommend the first alternative as the better choice, since it will permit the conversion to remain on schedule and will result in a greater cost saving to the bank.

EXHIBIT 1

COMPARISON OF COMPUTER AND PRESENT SYSTEM COSTS
1962 THROUGH 1973

(Figures in 000's)

	1962	1963	1964	1965	1966	1967	1968	1969	1970	1971	1972	1973
Computer System Costs												
Personnel Costs	$3,623	$4,010	$4,289	$4,420	$4,538	$4,660	$4,896	$5,181	$5,552	$5,956	$6,410	$6,896
Equipment Costs	$ 51	$ 53	$ 85	$ 108	$ 83	$ 82	$ 83	$ 84	$ 84	$ 86	$ 87	$ 89
Other Costs	$ 74	$ 100	$ 87	$ 45	$ 38	—	—	—	—	—	—	—
Total Computer System Costs	$3,748	$4,163	$4,461	$4,573	$4,659	$4,742	$4,979	$5,265	$5,636	$6,042	$6,497	$6,985
Present System Costs												
Personnel Costs	$3,578	$3,844	$4,037	$4,310	$4,612	$4,912	$5,226	$5,573	$5,982	$6,420	$6,908	$7,430
Equipment Costs	$ 51	$ 53	$ 56	$ 59	$ 62	$ 65	$ 68	$ 71	$ 75	$ 79	$ 82	$ 87
Total Present System Costs	$3,629	$3,897	$4,093	$4,369	$4,674	$4,977	$5,294	$5,644	$6,057	$6,499	$6,990	$7,517
Annual Net Gain (or Loss) through												
Computer System	$ (119)	$ (266)	$ (368)	$ (204)	$ 15	$ 235	$ 315	$ 379	$ 421	$ 457	$ 493	$ 532
Cumulative Expenditure Recovery	$ (119)	$ (385)	$ (753)	$ (957)	$ (942)	$ (707)	$ (392)	$ (13)	$ 408	$ 865	$1,358	$1,890

Assumptions:

1. Average clerical salary of those affected by the computer is $3,630 a year.
2. Average salary of control personnel and operators is $5,000 a year.
3. The volume of data processing work will grow as the number of accounts grow.
4. The fringe benefit % will not change over the period of the projection.
5. Personnel cost will increase at a moderate rate each year.

EXHIBIT 2

REVISED PROGRAM ESTIMATE

Estimates Made on March 9, 1964, Provide Actual and
New Anticipated Completion Dates as Follows:

	May 1963 *Estimate*	*March 1964* *Estimate*
Personal Trust System, Security Side		
System Design	October 7, 1963	November 20, 1963
Research	March 9, 1964	April 30, 1964
Programming	July 13, 1964	November 9, 1964
Conversion Planning and Programming	June 8, 1964	July 27, 1964
Conversion and Test	October 19, 1964	January 11, 1965
Personal Trust System, Account Side		
System Design	March 22, 1965	July 12, 1965
Research	August 2, 1965	November 22, 1965
Programming	October 4, 1965	January 24, 1966
Conversion Planning and Programming	September 27, 1965	January 17, 1966
Conversion and Test	October 4, 1965	January 24, 1966
Corporate Trust System		
System Design	March 16, 1964	May 11, 1964
Research	August 10, 1964	October 5, 1964
Programming	April 12, 1965 (Entire system)	April 12, 1965 (Entire system)
Conversion Planning and Programming	September 14, 1964	November 9, 1964
Conversion and Test	April 26, 1965 (Entire system)	April 26, 1965 (Entire system)

EXHIBIT 3

COMPARISON OF COMPUTER AND PRESENT SYSTEM COSTS
1962 THROUGH 1973

(Figures in 000's)

	1962	1963	1964	1965	1966	1967	1968	1969	1970	1971	1972	1973
Computer System Costs												
Personnel Costs	$3,458	$3,750	$4,024	$4,317	$4,438	$4,511	$4,658	$4,841	$5,142	$5,493	$5,879	$6,285
Equipment Costs	$ 51	$ 51	$ 31	$ 113	$ 108	$ 81	$ 82	$ 83	$ 83	$ 85	$ 86	$ 87
Other Costs	$ 73	$ 48	$ 174	$ 66	$ 57	—	—	—	—	—	—	—
Total Computer System Costs	$3,582	$3,849	$4,279	$4,496	$4,603	$4,592	$4,740	$4,924	$5,225	$5,578	$5,965	$6,372
Present System Costs												
Personnel Costs	$3,411	$3,670	$3,887	$4,149	$4,391	$4,662	$4,918	$5,199	$5,552	$5,922	$6,336	$6,769
Equipment Costs	$ 51	$ 51	$ 52	$ 54	$ 57	$ 60	$ 63	$ 66	$ 70	$ 73	$ 77	$ 81
Total Present System Costs	$3,462	$3,721	$3,939	$4,203	$4,448	$4,722	$4,981	$5,265	$5,622	$5,995	$6,413	$6,850
Annual Net Gain (or Loss) through Computer System	$ (120)	$ (128)	$ (340)	$ (293)	$ (155)	$ 130	$ 241	$ 341	$ 397	$ 417	$ 448	$ 478
Cumulative Expenditure Recovery	$ (120)	$ (248)	$ (588)	$ (831)	$(1,036)	$ (906)	$ (665)	$ (324)	$ 73	$ 490	$ 938	$1,416

Assumptions:
1. Average 1964 clerical salaries are $4,030 for those affected by the computer system, $6,490 for programmers and $5,180 for machine operators and control personnel.
2. Fringe benefits will not change substantially.
3. Personnel costs will increase a small amount each year. The exact amount of this figure was determined by examining the personnel cost growth for the period 1959–63.

EXHIBIT 4

COMPARISON OF PERCENTAGE OF MEMORY USED BY INSTRUCTIONS
FOR THE H400 VERSUS THE H200 TO HANDLE
THE SECURITY SIDE PROGRAMMING

	H400		H200		
Run	*Estimated Number Of Instructions*	*Percent Available Memory Used (a)*	*Estimated Number Of Instructions (b)*	*Adjusted To Characters (c)*	*Percent Of Available Memory Used (d)*
1	2,000	65	600	4,500	14
3	2,000	65	1,760	13,200	40
4	50	2	50	375	1
5	500	16	200	1,500	5
6	50	2	50	375	1
7	3,400	111	2,720	20,400	62
8	3,000	98	2,600	19,500	60
9	50	2	50	375	1
10	500	16	500	3,750	11
16	50	2	50	375	1
17	300	10	200	1,500	5

(a) 3,072 word memory (24,576 alphanumeric characters).
(b) Totals equal H400 instructions less the estimated saved edit instructions using the H200.
(c) H200 instructions multiplied by 1.5 to equal 3-address capability of the H400, then multiplied by 5 (average characters per instruction for the H200) to arrive at total instruction characters per run.
(d) 32,768 alphanumeric character memory (33 percent larger than the H400 memory).

EXHIBIT 5

COMPARISON OF H400 AND H200 COMPUTER SYSTEM COSTS
UNDER THE FIRST ALTERNATIVE

1964 THROUGH 1973

(Figures in 000's)

	1964	1965	1966	1967	1968	1969	1970	1971	1972	1973
Personnel Costs										
H400 Computer System	$4,289	$4,420	$4,538	$4,660	$4,896	$5,181	$5,552	$5,956	$6,410	$6,896
H200 Computer System	$4,250	$4,437	$4,556	$4,660	$4,896	$5,181	$5,552	$5,956	$6,410	$6,896
Annual Difference Between The H400 And H200 Computer Systems	$ (39)	$ 17	$ 18	—	—	—	—	—	—	—
Cumulative Increase Or (Decrease) Over The H400 Computer System Through Installation Of The H200 Computer System	$ (39)	$ (22)	$ (4)	$ (4)	$ (4)	$ (4)	$ (4)	$ (4)	$ (4)	$ (4)
Equipment Costs										
Total H400 Computer Cost	$ 85	$ 108	$ 83	$ 82	$ 83	$ 84	$ 84	$ 86	$ 87	$ 89
Total H200 Computer Cost	$ 56	$ 100	$ 75	$ 76	$ 75	$ 76	$ 77	$ 78	$ 79	$ 81
Cumulative Increase or (Decrease) Over The H400 Computer System Through Installation Of The H200 Computer System	$ (29)	$ (37)	$ (±5)	$ (51)	$ (59)	$ (67)	$ (74)	$ (82)	$ (90)	$ (98)

CURWEN
ELECTRONICS COMPANY

On January 2, 1964, James Phillips, manager of the Curwen Electronics Company's Data Processing Center, was reviewing the procedures used to evaluate and control the overall performance of the Data Processing Center (DPC) and its individual employees. He wondered whether the present procedures provided the most useful measures of performance or whether some other scheme of evaluation would be more meaningful.

BACKGROUND

The Curwen Electronics Company was a wholly owned subsidiary of the Porter Corporation, a nationwide manufacturer and distributor of electronic components and assemblies. The Curwen Electronics Company manufactured and distributed Porter Corporation products exclusively in the Southern states. The Curwen Electronics Company had eight manufacturing plants at various locations throughout the South and a central office located in Atlanta, Georgia. At each plant, there also was a warehouse from which products were distributed. The Curwen company had annual sales of about $250,000,000 a year and employed about 25,000 people.

The data processing requirements of the company were extensive. Payroll preparation, customer billings and collections, and disbursements to suppliers were the major large-volume EDP tasks. Curwen Electronics had nine data processing units; eight of these units (one at each plant location) were responsible for the routine, repetitive, high-volume tasks described above. Their work was carried out satisfactorily with a small staff and machine operators who had little or no previous training or experience. No programming was done at these units.

THE DATA PROCESSING CENTER

The ninth unit, the Data Processing Center (DPC), was located in the central office at Atlanta, and its work was quite different from that of the other eight units. This work consisted principally of many small, difficult, one-time jobs rather than high-volume, repetitive jobs. The unit was primarily concerned with providing management information reports requested by various departments of Curwen Electronics. Some of this work, however, was routine, because some jobs were required by the customer departments on either a monthly or quarterly basis. At any given time during the year, the center was responsible for nearly 300 projects.

Organizationally, the DPC was evaluated as a separate cost center and reported as a line group to the Accounting Department. Although job costs were compiled, the DPC did not charge customer departments for its services. To make sure, however, that only those jobs in the company's best interests were undertaken, Curwen Electronics had established a headquarters staff group called the Mechanized Procedures Staff group (MPS). Its function was to examine all proposals, to evaluate their usefulness from the company's viewpoint, and to correlate them with the present schedule of the DPC. If the MPS group felt that a job was to the overall advantage of Curwen Electronics, it was discussed with the DPC, and a joint agreement was reached as to whether or not to run the job in the center.

A company spokesman noted:

> It is a real advantage to have someone with a knowledge of operating conditions, coupled with knowledge of Curwen Electronics' other data processing units throughout the country, examine each job to insure that Curwen Electronics' best interests are met. For example, there are a number of small jobs which require a great deal of programming and debugging time with little resultant machine time. Under the present system of internal evaluation, it is clearly not in the DPC's best interests to take these jobs—even though the company as a whole might be benefited.

The MPS staff also helped to arbitrate situations where the DPC, because of timing or scheduling problems, was unable to handle all the work expected of it. The staff negotiated with the center so that a mutually satisfactory agreement could be reached between the DPC and the customer department.

Organization of the DPC

The DPC, which had about 50 employees, was headed by Robert Phillips. Reporting directly to him were Peter Black (line) and William Mitchell (staff). Mr. Black had responsibility for the machine operators and their supervisors, together with the control section. Mr.

Mitchell supervised the activities of the programmers and analysts. Line operations were currently on a two-shift basis. An organization chart of the DPC is presented as Exhibit 1.

Most of the machine operators were women, either married and middle-aged or recent high school graduates. Turnover was high (33 percent a year), particularly in the latter group. The operators were unionized, and company-union relations were excellent; little, if any, trouble had occurred in the past or was expected in the future.

During the training period, operators were moved from one machine to another (see Exhibit 2 for a list of the DPC's equipment) so that they could run effectively all machines, from the key punch to the 1401 computer. It was believed that operators' versatility was necessary if the center was to meet the changing workload composition. In general, each operator followed a job through from beginning to end. This policy was modified to the extent that one operator was assigned full time to the 1401, and two operators to key punches. Operators were not required to perform any machine maintenance, although through experience they often were able to prevent machine stoppages and to correct minor breakdowns.

The control group was responsible for scheduling work through the machines and insuring that accurate instructions were available to the line people. Either the staff group or the customer departments made available to the control group sufficient information to enable detailed instructions to be given to the operators. Detailed instructions included such things as what switches on a particular machine to turn on, the cards to place in the primary feed, or the columns to sort. Members of the group also made frequent spot checks to confirm that the correct operations were being carried out.

The staff function at the DPC was very important and required the most highly trained and skilled people in the department. Most of these individuals were men, and their pay range was considerably above that of the line level. Their function was to plan and develop procedures for each approved job. First, they met with the customer departments to determine the exact requirements of the job. Then they selected an approach to the problem that would provide an acceptable solution and developed the necessary machine procedure. This function included flow charting the job, writing a program, wiring appropriate panels for the relevant machines, and debugging. They also had to prepare instructions for the program's implementation before turning the job over to the control group. When necessary, they worked with the machine operators during the initial production runs.

Data Collection

A number of management reports were used to evaluate performance of departments and individual employees. The basic data for many of these reports came from the "Record of Machine and Employee Time" (see Exhibit 3), which was prepared every day by each machine operator. This sheet provided the following information about each employee:

1. The number of hours she spent actually running each machine (indicated by a time meter on the machine).
2. The number of hours she spent working with a machine. (Because of card jams, machine setup, and a variety of other reasons, an operator usually spent more time working on a machine than was recorded on the machine's time meter.)
3. The number of machine and operator hours spent on each job.
4. A detailed breakdown of how the operator spent her time when she was not working on a particular job.

The day following the preparation of these sheets, the information was transferred to punched cards. At various intervals during the month, these cards were processed by the 1401 to produce the necessary management reports.

EVALUATION OF DPC PERFORMANCE

Four principal reports were used in the formal evaluation of the DPC's performance. These were the 937 Report, the 937–1 Report, the EDP–42 Report, and the performance-against-budget report. Each of these is described below.

937 Report

This report was prepared monthly and sent to the corporate offices of the Porter Corporation in New York. On a quarterly basis, the Porter Corporation staff summarized the data received from the data processing installations for all subsidiaries throughout the country and sent the results to their managers. Each manager could then compare his performance with that of the installations in other subsidiaries. To facilitate comparisons, the results from each installation were gathered into one of five groups, depending on the type of work done at the installation.

The two key figures generated by this report were an equipment processing index and an operator ratio. The development of these indices is explained below.

Equipment Processing Index

1. An "Office Standard Total Available Hours" figure was computed for the installation. This indicated the normal number of working hours for the month in the installation. This figure varied from installation to installation, depending on local customs, and also from one type of equipment to another. For example, for an office with a 7½-hour day, which worked 22 days a month, the figure was 165 hours (one shift) for EAM equipment and 330 hours (two shifts) for an EDP system.

2. The number of hours each machine in the installation was run in the month was determined from the machine's time meter. This figure was called the "Actual Processing Hours."

3. Different EDP machines had different data handling times. The result was that, whereas it might be economically justifiable to have certain machines, under normal circumstances they were not fully utilized. On the basis of historical data for the entire Porter Corporation system, a series of "Systems Standard Equipment Use Factors" were developed (see Exhibit 4). These factors represented the normal percentage of Office Standard Total Available Hours that the machines were used. The following calculation was then performed:

(System Standard Equipment Use Factor) ×
(Office Standard Total Available Hours) =
Office Standard Total Available Processing Hours

This Office Standard Total Available Processing Hours figure represented the number of meter hours necessary to achieve an index of 100 on a particular machine. (An index of 100 indicated that the machine was fully utilized.)

4. The Standard Monthly Rental for the machine was divided by the Office Standard Total Available Processing Hours to develop a "Standard Processing Rate Per Hour."

5. The Standard Processing Rate Per Hour was then multiplied by the Actual Processing Hours indicated by the meter. The result of this computation was then divided by the actual rental figure paid during the month to give the "Equipment Processing Index" for the machine. Samples of this computation are shown in Exhibit 5.

The equipment processing indices for the several machines in the installation were then averaged together to provide an Equipment Processing Index for the installation as a whole.

Operator Ratio

The operator ratio was calculated for each of the main groupings of machines and for the installation as a whole. The main groupings of machines were the key driven machines, EAM equipment, and EDP equipment. The ratio was designed to measure the efficiency of the installation operators. Its calculation took three factors into consideration:

1.   Meter hours—the number of hours the machine was operated in the month.
2.   Operator hours—the number of hours in the month that operators were working on the machine.
3.   Standard Operator Factor—a factor reflecting the fact that an operator had to spend a certain amount of time getting the machine set up and handling the data (see Exhibit 4). There was a different one for each machine. The factor was used in the calculation of an "Operator Index," according to the following formula:

$$\text{Operator Index} = \frac{\text{Meter Hours}}{(\text{Standard Operator Factor}) \times (\text{Operator Hours})}$$

937–1 Report

This report was prepared monthly and sent to the executives of Curwen Electronics and the staff officers of the Porter Corporation. It was concerned solely with the computer operation. It analyzed in detail how the computer was used during the month.

EDP–42 Report

This report was prepared weekly and submitted only to the executives of Curwen Electronics. It was concerned with the computer operation and presented the following three calculations for each job run during the week:

1. $\text{machine rate/hour} = \dfrac{\text{card volume}}{\text{meter time}}$

2. $\text{overall rate/hour} = \dfrac{\text{card volume}}{\text{elapsed time}}$

3. $\text{percent meter to elapsed time} = \dfrac{\text{meter time}}{\text{elapsed time}}$

In addition, a space designated for comments could be used to explain unusual operating results.

Budget

As one of Curwen Electronics' cost centers, the DPC each year submitted a budget which covered rentals, salaries, and sundry other expenses. The budget for the coming year was initially prepared by Mr. Phillips in October. Its preparation reflected the best estimates that he and the MPS could make concerning the DPC's workload for the coming year. This estimated workload was then used to predict probable levels for the various expense categories. Mr. Phillips then sent his budget forward to the Budget Committee for approval. If they believed that any changes were required, a joint meeting was arranged to resolve the points in contention. The finished product then became his budget for the coming year. Each month Mr. Phillips had an opportunity to revise his budget for the rest of the year on the basis of the most recent information.

Each month the actual departmental expenses were collected and were used to develop the following five ratios:

1. Ratio of actual monthly expenses to most recently prepared budget for the month.
2. Ratio of actual monthly expenses to amount budgeted at the beginning of the year for the month.
3. Ratio of actual monthly expenses to actual expenses incurred for the same month in the previous year.
4. Ratio of cumulative year-to-date expenditures to amount budgeted for the period at the beginning of the year.
5. Ratio of cumulative year-to-date expenditures to amount incurred for the same period in the previous year.

These ratios consolidated all the performance factors in the other reports. Such things as poor machine indices, bad operator performance, weak scheduling, and poor programming all manifested themselves in actual costs that were greater than estimated.

EVALUATION OF NONMANAGEMENT PERSONNEL

Mr. Phillips believed that it was very important to maintain close control over hourly payroll personnel. He felt that the high turnover among the women operating the data processing equipment necessitated a formal reporting system for their evaluation. Two complementary reporting systems were currently being used by the DPC. The first involved the preparation of two reports, the 601–12H and the 601–180. They were developed by the DPC to evaluate quantitatively each operator's performance. The second system completed the standard Curwen Electronics' nonmanagement appraisal form.

Quantitative Evaluation

During the preparation of a report, a machine operator spent about 25 percent of her time actually running a machine. She spent the rest of her time on such operations as checking output, getting materials together, and waiting for machine time. The portion of her time that she spent on the machines was subject to relatively objective quantitative evaluation. The two reports developed by the DPC for this purpose were the 601-12H and the 601-180.

1. *601-12H* was a monthly report that was used to measure the performance of workers on EAM equipment only, exclusive of the key punch and key verifier machine. A copy of the report is included as Exhibit 6. The report provided the following information for each operator:

a) The number of hours during the month that the operator was assigned to particular machines.
b) The number of hours that the machines to which the operator was assigned were actually processing data.
c) Productive hours are the same as operator hours except for small differences that are outside of the control of the operator, e.g., relief time.
d) The number of calculations or cycles performed by the operator's machine during the month.
e) The number of cards processed by the operator's machines during the month.
f) The Operator Index. This was calculated by the formula:

$$\text{Operator Index} = \frac{\text{meter hours}}{\text{operator hours}}$$

The Operator Index was the most important figure on the report. The operators were listed according to the size of their indices in descending order from the top of the report. The average index for all operators also was placed in the ranking and thus divided the list into above average and below average operators. The figures for number of cycles and number of cards provided an indication as to whether an employee's index was affected by a job with an unusual number of cards or an unusual number of calculations.

2. *601-180* was a monthly report that provided a detailed breakdown on how each operator performed on each type of EAM equip-

ment. (Key punch machines were again excluded here.) The report listed each operator and provided the employee's operator index for each EAM machine she used during the month. The office average index for each type of equipment was given on the top line of the report. A sample report is shown as Exhibit 7. Mr. Phillips was concerned as to the usefulness of the form of the report. For example, an operator's reported performance on a particular machine was considerably affected by the amount of time that she used the machine during the month. This sharply limited the extent to which reasonable vertical comparison of operator indices could be made. It was also difficult to make horizontal comparisons of the operator's performance on several machines, since the indices did not take into account differences in such things as the setup time and card handling time for the several machines.

Nonquantitative Evaluation

At least once a year each employee was formally appraised by his immediate supervisor in seven categories. This appraisal was reviewed by a committee consisting of the appraiser, one or two other people of the same rank who knew the appraised individual, and the appraiser's own supervisor. Once the appraisal had been made, reviewed, concurred in, and signed by the appraiser and supervisor, the appraiser discussed it with the appraisee with the objective of helping him to improve himself. A description of the criteria used in filling out each of the seven categories is provided below.

1. *Work Produced.* As described earlier, each operator followed a whole job through all its stages from the key punching to the final output on the 1401 or 407. Although, since February, this technique had been modified slightly by having a girl work full time on the 1401 and two girls specialize on the key punch and key verifiers, the overall policy remained the same. Basically work produced was considered as the total number of reports produced in a day, week, or month. Since these reports varied in work content from one to several hundred hours, the supervisors took into account the length and difficulty of the reports. Then the operator was qualitatively evaluated on both her operator indices and the overall production of reports.

Control group operators were rated on their output of reports prepared for the machines; however, no indices were available to evaluate this output.

Key punch girls and others who did regular key punching from time to time were quantitatively evaluated by their strokes per hour,

5,000 being the expected average. The 1401 operators were evaluated by reference to meter time standards and by how well they kept the machine running. In all cases the operator's experience and her working conditions were taken into account.

2. *Quality.* Accuracy of work, neatness, and initiative in preparing reports were considered. Special emphases, however, existed for different groups of operators. The quality of output for a control group employee was measured by the ease with which the machine operators could interpret her instructions. If a control girl regularly had her work questioned, she was not producing at quality levels.

The standard quality for key punchers was the number of mispunches; the allowable range was between ½ and 1 percent. Since all key punch output was verified, errors were detected and counted. Because of the problems of correcting errors, employees were encouraged to go relatively slowly and to make fewer errors.

On the EAM machines (except for the 407) the standard of quality depended partly on the number of errors traceable to the operator. These included such things as lost or damaged cards, or failure to check the sequence of cards soon after the start of the sorting or collating process. The number of errors expected was very small, on the order of two or three a week, varying with the experience of the girl. Quality also referred to the operator's overall method of working. If the operator did all the right things and made all the right checks in her work and still made errors, she was evaluated less harshly than if she did not.

The 407 and 1401 operators' quality was a measure of their neatness in working and the agility and ingenuity of their ways of saving machine time. Also neatness of output and minimization of paper waste were taken into account.

3. *Ease of Learning.* This was considered very important because most operators had to learn to operate all the machines, and because the labor turnover was 33 percent a year. Similarly, control group people had to learn all the peculiarities of the other jobs, so that they could schedule and instruct each job optimally.

4. *Application to Work.* The ability of an operator to work well with little supervision was considered. This was less important in the EDP service center, where closer supervision was provided than elsewhere. Also, the jobs were largely machine-time controlled and the programs had built-in quality checks. It was more important in the control and key punch groups.

5. *Cooperation.* The employee's attitude toward her work, her

supervisors, her associates, and her union were rated. Cooperation was particularly important for those operators handling the "bottle-neck" machines, such as the 407 and 1401, which required very close scheduling. The operator was evaluated on her ability to coordinate well with those around her, so as to optimize output efficiency.

6. *Dependability.* Responsibility for the job well done and the reliability of her estimates and promises were most important. Again, operators of bottleneck machines were scrutinized most closely.

7. *Attendance.* An operator's tendency to take extra days off and to arrive late to work were evaluated here. Strict policing of attendance and lateness was carried out.

EVALUATION OF MANAGEMENT PERSONNEL

The Curwen Electronics Company had a well-developed system of evaluation that applied to all management personnel. Consequently, each person in the DPC who was above the level of machine operator was formally evaluated by his supervisor at least once a year. An evaluation was made specifically of 15 characteristics that were believed to be important. These characteristics included such things as performance, obtaining results, and development of subordinates. The purpose of this evaluation was threefold:

1. To encourage and help the individual to improve his performance.
2. To determine the individual's potential for promotion.
3. To provide information that would assist in determining salary treatment.

In most respects the supervisors within the DPC were evaluated in the same way that all managers in Curwen Electronics were evaluated. The following factors were considered to be of particular importance in their case, however:

1. Good scheduling. This was the one factor that could do most to improve the department's performance, because it reduced costs, improved speed of output, enabled delivery dates to be met, and minimized friction among the department members.

2. Cost control. Given the large rental value of the machines, it became very important that they be utilized efficiently so as to minimize overtime costs.

3. Development of subordinates. This was crucial because this center was the only one of its type in Curwen. Thus, Mr. Phillips

very rarely acquired "qualified" personnel. Nearly all the new entrants to the department needed to be trained in the skills of handling (a) a highly flexible job shop and (b) tape and computer equipment. Also, the managerial skills of the subordinates had to be developed in order to maximize their abilities and to produce promotable individuals.

EVALUATION OF PROGRAMMERS AND SYSTEMS ANALYSTS

Programmers and systems analysts were appraised in the same way as that for the supervision in the DPC, with most of the same criteria being used. In addition, however, heavy emphasis was placed on their technical abilities. Important factors in evaluation of a programmer included these:

1. His overall output of workable programs.
2. The degree of optimization of time and cost in his programs.
3. The freedom from bugs and errors in his programs.

Curwen Electronics had not set up quantitative standards to measure these abilities. Rather, Mr. Mitchell examined each program, whenever possible, both before and after debugging. He evaluated it and, when appropriate, suggested changes. Records were kept of the systems analysis and programming hours that were put into each program. Although these records were not subjected to a formal analysis, they were frequently consulted by Mr. Mitchell to get a rough measure of a programmer's efficiency. Other special evaluation factors were ingenuity in planning programs, foresight in preparing the most useful forms of output, and the ease with which programs could be run under current conditions in the department.

QUESTIONS

1. What do you think of Curwen's system for evaluating its EDP group?
2. What kind of a system would you develop to evaluate the EDP operation in this company?

EXHIBIT 1

Curwen Electronics Company

DPC Organization Chart

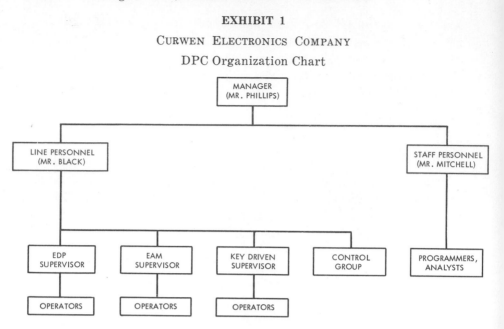

EXHIBIT 2

Curwen Electronics Company

DPC Equipment

Key Punch and Verifier Area
  5—IBM 024 Key punches
  5—IBM 056 Verifiers

Electronic Accounting Machines Area
  1—IBM 519 Reproducer
  1—IBM 407 Accounting machine
  1—IBM 557 Interpreter
  1—IBM 083 Sorter
  1—IBM 084 Sorter
  2—IBM 088 Collators

Electronic Data Processing Machine Area
  1—IBM 108 Card proving machine
  1—IBM 534 Card punch
  1—IBM 867 Numerical typewriter
  2—IBM 7330 Tape units
  1—IBM 1401 Central processor & 4,000 units core storage
  1—IBM 1402 Card read punch
  1—IBM 1403 Printer
  1—IBM 1406 Extra 4,000 units core storage

EXHIBIT 3

CURWEN ELECTRONICS COMPANY

Record of Machine and Employee Time

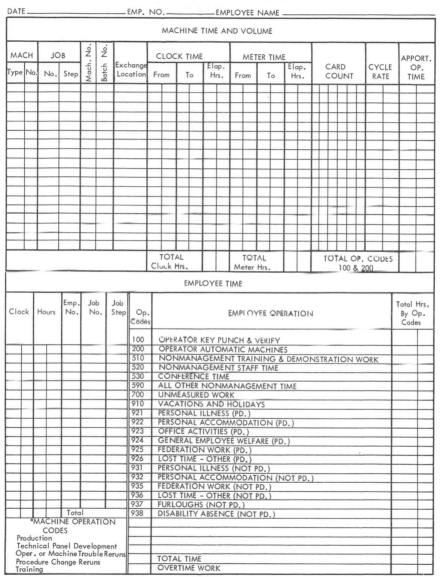

DATE _____ EMP. NO. _____ EMPLOYEE NAME _____

| MACHINE TIME AND VOLUME | | | | | | | | | | | | | | | |

EXHIBIT 4

Curwen Electronics Company

Key Driven Equipment	Standard Equipment Use Factor	Standard Operator Factor	System Standard Processing Conversion Factor
Class 10		98.0	
024–Card Punch	68.5		
026–Printing Punch	68.5		
027–Card Proof Punch	68.5		
056–Verifier/Punch	68.5		
EAM Equipment, Except Key Driven			
Class 20		82.0	
075–Sorter	43.0		
077–Collator	41.0		
082–Sorter	43.0		
083–Sorter	43.0		
084–Sorter	43.0		
085–Collator	41.0		
087–Collator	41.0		
088–Collator	41.0		
108–Elec. Stat. Tabulator	48.0		
402–Accounting Machine	63.5		
407–Accounting Machine	63.5		
419–Accounting Machine	63.5		
514–Reproducing Punch	55.5		
519–Reproducing Summary Punch	55.5		
523–Gang Summary Punch	55.5		
552–Interpreter	58.0		
557–Interpreter	58.0		
607–Calculator	48.0		
609–Calculator	65.0		
EDP Main Frames and			
Off Line Devices			
Class 50		95.0	
1401T–Processing Unit	90.0		115.0
1401C–Processing Unit	70.0		115.0
7070–Data Processing Unit	75.0		115.0
7074–Data Processing Unit	75.0		115.0
EDP On Line Devices			
Class 60		XX	
1402T–Read Punch	90.0		115.0
1402C–Read Punch	70.0		115.0
1403T–Printer	65.0		115.0
1403C–Printer	51.0		115.0

EXHIBIT 5

Curwen Electronics Company

Calculations for Computation of Processing Value and Equipment Processing Index

		EAM		EDP
1.	Machine Type....................................	407		1401
2.	No. of Machines....................................	1		1
3.	Available Hours (Office) (7.5 × 22 dys.)..............	165	(7.5 × 2 × 22 dys.)	330
4.	Equipment Use Factor (System)......................	63.5		70.0
5.	Available Processing Hours (3 × 4) (Office Std.)........	105		221
6.	Actual Processing Hours (Prod. and Devel.)...........	181		266
7.	Standard Processing Conversion Factor...............	—		115.0
8.	Standard Equipment Use Hours (5 × 7)..............	—		254
9.	Basic Use Hours (By Contract)....................	—		176
10.	Standard Additional Use Hours (8 − 9)..............	—		78
11.	Basic Rental..	$1,200		$6,000
12.	Standard Additional Use Rental.....................	—	(11 ÷ 9 × 10 × .40)	$1,064
13.	Standard Base Rental (11 + 12).....................	$1,200		$7,064
14.	Standard Processing Rate Per Hour (13 ÷ 5)..........	11.428		31.964
15.	Processing Value (14 × 6)..........................	$2,068		8,502
16.	Actual Rental......................................	$1,200		9,834
17.	Equipment Processing Index (15 ÷ 16)...............	173		86

EXHIBIT 6

Curwen Electronics Company

Format of 601—12H Operator Report

Month	Operator number	Operator hours	Meter hours	Production hours	Number of cycles	Number of cards	Operator Index	
	09	222	09.0	32.3	32.4	468612	11833	.82	
	09	417	62.6	50.4	59.9	1434728	22918	.81	
	09	524	65.3	49.5	65.9	19617691	70424	.76	
	09	317	41.1	31.1	35.8	1252076	30464	.76	
	09	353	50.0	36.3	48.1	3100317	62006	.73	
Totals			534.0	358.3	520.1			.67	(Average)
	09	215	16.3	10.3	17.0	748542	45922	.63	
	09	372	84.6	50.2	86.2	9940924	11220	.59	
	09	443	56.9	32.5	56.7	3175767	55813	.57	
	09	328	58.2	32.8	59.7	4622029	79416	.56	
	09	501	59.4	32.9	58.4	3353339	56543	.55	

EXHIBIT 7

Format of 601–180 Operator Report

Individual Efficiency Ratios by Machine Type

MO	EMP NO	077	082	083	087	088	101	407	416	519	523	557	607	650
05	Average	.57	.55	.59	.69		.54	.63	.74	.65	.69	.77	.66	1.05
05	202	.48	.37	.50	.75			.69	.58	.79	.41	.81		
05	206	.52		.59	.75			.65	.80	.67	.67	.75	.67	1.00
05	208	.43		.68	.80		.77	.55		.56		.82	.50	1.00
05	209	.55	.61	.47	.33			.63	.86	.36	.87	1.00		
05	211	.67		.67	.71			.68		.82		.78	1.00	1.04
05	212						.56	.33						
05	214			.73	.72		.58	.74				.87		
05	216													1.11
05	219	.70		.42	.47			.67		.68		1.00	.70	
05	401	.44	.33	.36			.25	.34		.37		.25	.67	
05	402	.60		.68	1.25			.72						
05	403	.67	.25	.64	.67		.39	.74		.96		.80	.74	
05	404	.50	.67	.45	.56		.50	.68		.77			.67	
05	405	.55		.55				.52		.40		.83	.50	
05	406	.62		.59	.57		.50	.59		.70	.	.71		
05	407	.83		.68	1.00			.75		.83		1.00		1.05
05	411	.66		.64	.63		.25	.57		.60				
05	412	.72		.83	.76			.73		.46		.67		
05	419	.41	.40	.35			.56	.41	.64	.53	.64	.76		

GEM TOOL COMPANY

Mr. Mansell was appointed general manager of one of the nation's largest power tool manufacturers, the Gem Tool Company, in the summer of 1964. The Gem company is a division of the Wallingford Enterprises Corp., a multimillion dollar manufacturing corporation active in several fields. In 1964 the Gem company's sales were $55 million, about 10 percent of the total Wallingford sales. About 50 percent of Gem's sales were portable hand tools such as electric drills. The balance was split fairly evenly between highly specialized power tools for the military, and the sale of electric motors for replacement use, or to other manufacturers.

Mr. Johnson, the previous general manager of Gem Tool, had run the division on a consistently profitable basis until his retirement. Although an older man, he had not been reluctant to introduce changes in the division where he thought they would be of benefit. As a result the division was run very efficiently, and was widely regarded as the leader in the industry.

Mr. Mansell, who was in his forties, was a hard-driving, dynamic man who had joined the corporation after graduating with his MBA degree some fifteen years previously. As manager of Wallingford's chemical plant, he had worked hard to put the unprofitable chemical operation back on a paying basis. Through reorganization of the production department and a much expanded sales force he had achieved sound results during the last few years.

Just prior to Mr. Johnson's retirement from Gem Tool, the controller of the division, Mr. Frank, had retired and Mr. MacDonald had been appointed in his place. Much of the division's advanced use of electronic data processing was directly due to Mr. MacDonald's initiative and the encouragement and support he had received from Mr. Frank.

Mr. Mansell was impressed with the business systems group's accomplishments to date, but was surprised at the scope of the controller's function. (See Exhibit 2.) The question of where the business systems group should be placed in the organization was a matter which he felt should be evaluated at an early date.

DATA PROCESSING HISTORY

The division's data processing history falls into three major phases: unit record equipment; IBM 305 RAMAC; and a 1401 system.

In 1952 the division had installed IBM tabulating equipment (unit record) to mechanize the accounting function. This equipment had been used for payroll calculations and for the various A/R and invoicing operations. The division had a large volume of such work and the equipment, which was leased, resulted in substantial savings over the previous manual methods, largely through reduced clerical costs.

Mr. MacDonald had come with the company in 1957 after receiving an undergraduate engineering degree and an MBA. His first assignment had been to a very small three-man "Operations and Methods" group that reported to the manager of accounting. His concern had been mostly with methods and procedures in relation to the numerous forms that were processed, particularly in the accounting area. During this first year there had been some corporate pressure on the division to form a "Systems Group" responsible for the design of all information systems within a division. The actual initiative within the Tool Division on this had come from Mr. MacDonald, who had drawn up a proposal for an "order-entry" system (see page 300) and the formation of a "Systems Group" to implement this system, using an IBM 305 RAMAC. This was presented to the accounting manager and in turn to the division controller, Mr. Frank. Mr. MacDonald's proposal was sound economically, and Mr. Frank decided to set up a separate group—Business Systems—to develop the order-entry system and handle all future systems work. Mr. MacDonald had been made manager of this group, reporting directly to the controller.

Thus in 1960 the tabulating system had been replaced with a rented IBM 305 RAMAC. The RAMAC system was capable of performing all the functions previously done on the unit record equipment, and in addition it was equipped with a large random access file. This random access storage was used for the order-entry system, to keep track of inventory.

In July of 1962 the division had installed an IBM 1401 computer with four tape units and a large random access file, which in the summer of 1964 was changed to four disk drives and two tape units (Exhibit 5). This move from RAMAC to the 1401 had not involved any significant change in rentals, as the 1401 was a less expensive and more powerful piece of equipment. This equipment was used for four major functions:

a) Order-entry.
b) Inventory control.
c) Manufacturing control.
d) Accounting.

Each of these are outlined below:

Order-Entry System

The order-entry system is shown diagrammatically in Exhibit 4. As an order was received, either by mail or telephone, it was processed by a key punch operator who punched onto cards all of the pertinent information (Exhibit 3). These were then verified, listed, and passed on to a "checker" who ascertained that the information was not obviously incorrect.

Four times a day these cards, representing some 800 orders per day, were processed by the 1401. Each card was matched against the master customer's record file and the master inventory file, both on disk. During this phase:

1. The price was selected (a function of order size and customer class).
2. The availability of the item was checked (was it in inventory?).
3. The inventory level was checked to ascertain if it was now below the minimum balance; if so, the item was back-ordered and the Production Planning Department notified.
4. The inventory record was updated.
5. The customer's credit was checked.
6. The A/R balance was updated.

When this phase was finished, the following items were generated automatically:

1. A customer invoice, ready for mailing.
2. Shipping papers which were sent over teletype to the correct part of the warehouse.
3. Various messages for such events as:
   (a) A new customer record had been created.
   (b) The item was out of stock.

(c)   Key-punch errors had been detected on the card.

(d)   Customer's credit limit had been reached. Details had been sent to the credit department.

On a weekly and monthly basis numerous summary reports were generated from these master files—reports such as sales by item, sales by salesman, sales by region and so forth. This system, which had been in operation for the last two years, provided the following advantages:

1.   Very fast turn-around time from receipt of customer order to shipping from warehouse. (Reduced from three days to a maximum of five hours, if the item was in stock.)
2.   Considerable reduction in paperwork.
3.   Accurate inventory records and substantial inventory savings.
4.   More accurate production planning.

Inventory Control System

The order-entry system kept the inventory withdrawals up to date, as nothing could be shipped out without papers and these papers were generated by the computer. Arrivals from the factory floor, or from suppliers, to the warehouse were put on the disk as they arrived (an automatic interrupt on the computer) via data collection terminals on the warehouse floor. Thus the stockmen "keyed in" on a terminal the part number and quantity and pushed the "enter" button. This caused an immediate update on the master disk file. Various checking systems were run every night to guard against any manual entry errors.

As of 1964 the inventory system covered only the purchased parts and finished goods. The division manager was extremely pleased with the system, as it had substantially reduced the overall inventory level, due to the reduction in buffer stocks that were necessary as protection against errors in keeping track of inventory levels. The very substantial reduction in time spent on paperwork had also led to a reduction in costs (Exhibit 6).

Manufacturing Control System

This system was only in its very early stages as the problems involved were complex. It was split into the following sections:

1.   Production planning.
2.   Labor reporting.
3.   Work-in-process inventory control.
4.   Material planning.

The production planning phase was the only one completed in the 18 months of work prior to August 1964. This phase made use of inventory records and sales estimates from the field to generate the mix and rate of production. This was done by the "Administrator of Finished Goods Planning" (see Exhibit 2), who made up his estimates based on computer data and field data and then discussed them once a week with the production manager. The final level was usually a compromise, but the production manager paid considerable attention to the estimates he received, as he had found them to be more accurate than the previous process. The business systems group's activities in the production area were the result of a proposal by Mr. MacDonald to the three operating managers in October of 1962. The "Power Tool" manager had been the most receptive to the project and it was in this area that work was proceeding. The business system group had had very little manpower to spare for the project in the last six months, so that recent progress had not been rapid. The complexities of the manufacturing operations were proving difficult and beyond some pilot "data collection terminals" on the factory floor there had not been much tangible progress. The business systems group was devoting the time of one of its more able men approximately 20 hours per week to this project.

The other phases of the production control system were in process, and fifteen data collection terminals were on the factory floor for labor reporting, although, as noted above, this system was still on an experimental basis.

Accounting System

The accounting function was entirely mechanized—all ledgers, accounts and variance reporting were done on the computer; in fact, the three bookkeepers reported to the data processing supervisor. The financial planning function made extensive use of computer-based information but was, by its nature, largely a manual operation. All of the standard payroll applications were run on the 1401.

Before starting any of these projects, Mr. MacDonald presented them to the controller for his approval. The controller in turn discussed them at a meeting with the division manager and the department managers involved. There were some problems of implementation with the inventory control and the manufacturing control segments of the applications. These problems had been largely those of people failing to use the new procedures and information. For example, the warehouse personnel had frequently failed to relay information on special shipments, or errors in counting inventory and so forth. Thus the master records on the disk file had not been accurate, with the result that occasional stockouts had occurred. The business systems group had made all the changes they felt were possible in the system to help ease this problem, but after six months the system still was not functioning correctly.

In his progress report to the controller in 1962, Mr. MacDonald identified this lack of cooperation as one of the key factors affecting the system's performance. Discussion of the problem with the division manager led to the decision to reorganize the warehousing group and take them out of the production manager's (power tool) area and place them under the controller (see Exhibit 2). Shortly after this change was made, the inventory control system and the records were reported as functioning very satisfactorily.

A similar sort of problem had been found in the production control area, and although this system had only been in its very early stages it had been found necessary late in 1963 to have the finished goods planning function for all three production areas (the determinant of the production rate) placed under the controller.

Mr. MacDonald had only been in his new position for five months and most of this time had been spent in mastering the accounting structure of the division. The company's production control system, however, was being watched very closely by headquarters as, even in its present form, it was considered to be one of the most advanced systems of its type in existence. Mr. MacDonald, therefore, was expecting to have to spend a certain amount of time on this, although his replacement as head of business systems, Mr. Trane, was a very competent man, who had been in the business systems group for some time.

EXHIBIT 1

ORGANIZATION CHART

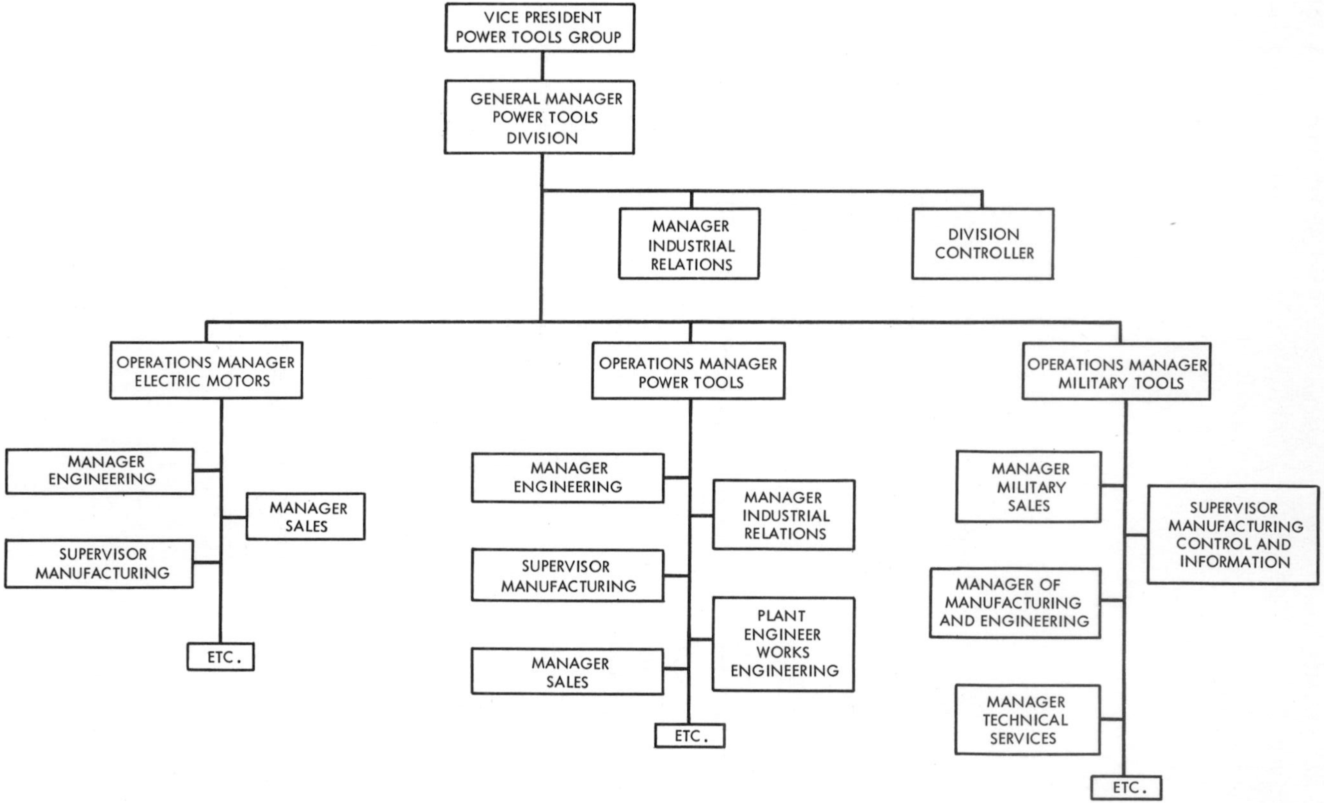

EXHIBIT 2

ORGANIZATION CHART—CONTROLLER'S OFFICE

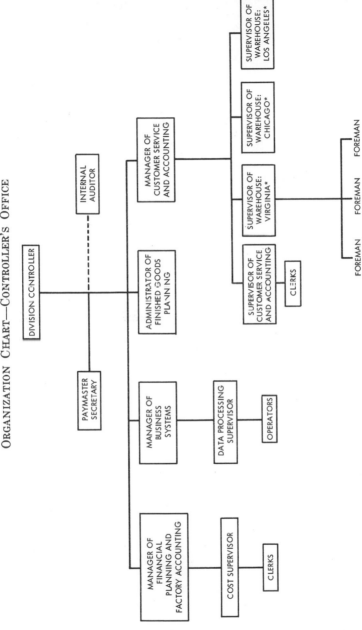

*Virginia was the plant location and main warehouse. Chicago and Los Angeles were the locations of the company's two field warehouses.

EXHIBIT 3

Basic Contents of Records on Disk Files*

Customer Record
Name; Street; City; State; Credit Limit; Discount

Customer Purchase Record
Current Month (Quantity, Dollar Value); Year to Date (Quantity, Dollar Value); A/R Balance

Inventory Record
Quantity on hand; Quantity on Back-order; Demand; Minimum Balance; Maximum Balance.

Price Record
Current price by customer class.

Punched Order Cards (Input to order-entry system)
Card No.
1. Customer Name; Address
2. Shipping Address
3. Quantity, Item Number (4 items card—for larger orders more than one #3 card was used).

*In 1964 there were approximately 20,000 different customers and some 10,000 different items in the inventory records. Some of the latter were purchased parts used for resale or in the company's own products. Inventory was estimated at approximately $4 million.

EXHIBIT 4

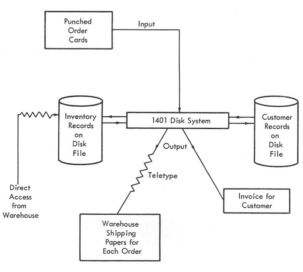

EXHIBIT 5

1401 Computer Utilization: August 1964

	Application	Hours of Utilization*
1.	Order-Entry	120
2.	Inventory Control	50
3.	Manufacturing Control	240
4.	General Ledger	100
5.	Payroll et al.	150
6.	Engineering Problems	30

*Actual number of hours of utilization per typical month in 1964.

1401 Specifications
12,000 Position Core.
Multiply/Divide, 6 Sense Switches, Advanced Programming Features.
4 1311 Disk Drives. Each drive holding one pack of 3 million characters.
2 7330 Tape Drives.
Autocoder, FORTRAN and COBOL Compilers.

EXHIBIT 6

Estimated Annual Savings of Computer Systems*

System	Annual Savings
Order-Entry	$175,000
Inventory Control	200,000
Manufacturing Control	(70,000) †
General Ledger	40,000
Payroll	65,000

Business Systems Budget‡
$90,000

*These figures were prepared by the controller's office in 1963 based on that year's volume. These figures and the supporting back-up data were used in a presentation to the headquarters staff. The savings represented out-of-pocket savings vis-a-vis doing the same job on a manual or tabulating machine basis and were only intended to be approximate figures.

†At the end of 1963 there were no out-of-pocket savings associated with the project. The rent of the data collection terminals and the pro rata share of 1401 time were estimated at approximately $70,000.

‡Personnel budget only. Covers: 1 manager; 3 systems personnel; 2 programmers; 3 clerical.

EXHIBIT 7

Expenditures on Data Processing Equipment

Year	Equipment	Approximate Annual Rental*	Approximate Annual Total of D.P. Personnel Salaries†
1952–59	Tabulating	$79,000	$60,000
1960–62	305 RAMAC	85,000	48,000
1962–64	1401	91,000	52,000

*Includes all equipment rented from IBM with the exception of the data transmission terminals.
†Includes only the supervisor and operators of all equipment.

INTERNATIONAL HARVESTER COMPANY

In January 1959, Mr. Frank Jenks, president of International Harvester, was considering how the adverse profit squeeze the company was experiencing could be reversed. International Harvester's sales and operating profits had dropped sharply in 1958, primarily as a result of the general business recession. A general cost reduction program had been initiated and part of this program involved an evaluation of the EDP program, which was incurring costs of $3,600,000 per year in computer and equipment rentals and $5,900,000 per year in personnel costs.

COMPANY BACKGROUND

In 1958 International Harvester's parent company sales totaled $1,098,390,000 (see Exhibit 1), which established it as the thirtieth largest United States corporation by dollar sales. Sales of International Harvester and its subsidiaries, on a worldwide basis, were $1,438,000,000.

With its head offices in Chicago, Illinois, and with manufacturing and sales facilities throughout the world, International Harvester produced a diversified line of products for both commercial and industrial applications. Operations were carried out on a divisional basis and each division had responsibility for one of the company's five primary product lines (see Figure I).

FIGURE I

CORPORATE HEADQUARTERS

SERVICE PARTS ORGANIZATION	MOTOR TRUCK DIVISION	FARM EQUIPMENT DIVISION	CONTRUCTION EQUIPMENT DIVISION	STEEL DIVISION	FIBER AND TWINE DIVISION

In the farm equipment field International Harvester was the world's leading manufacturer, having enjoyed this distinction continuously since its inception. Sales of farm equipment, service parts, and service totaled $391,267,000 for 1958, up 2.5 percent from 1957 levels. The Farm Equipment Division was the only product division showing an increase in sales in 1958. Farm equipment sales accounted for 35.6 percent of total International Harvester sales. The farm equipment product line consisted of (1) self-propelled farm vehicles—farm tractors and self-propelled combines, and (2) farm implements—equipment used in connection with the self-propelled units, such as cultivators, planters, and drills. Prices of this equipment ranged from less than $100 for some implements to over $20,000 for some of the self-propelled units. International Harvester products stressed quality and the value which could be expected from their use.

In recent years, International Harvester's sales of farm equipment had been exceeded by the company's motor truck sales. The Motor Truck Division accounted for 13.0 percent of the United States motor truck market with 1958 sales totaling $514,797,000 or 46.9 percent of total International Harvester sales. In spite of an improved market share, total motor truck dollar sales were down 7.4 percent from 1957 levels. International Harvester was first in heavy-duty truck sales, with total truck sales ranked third largest in the world. Although not a producer of automobiles, International Harvester was among the ten largest automotive businesses in the world. The motor truck product line ranged from half-ton pickup trucks to the largest "over the road" trucks and included all sizes in between. A half-ton pickup truck's price would start around $2,000, with the largest units running as high as $20,000.

Sales of construction equipment and service parts totaled $136,-117,000 or 12.4 percent of total International Harvester sales in 1958. International Harvester's construction equipment sales were the second largest in the construction equipment industry, surpassed only by Caterpillar. In 1958 the Construction Equipment Division sales were down 11.6 percent from 1957 levels, reflecting the depressed state of the construction equipment market, particularly in the first half of the year. Construction equipment products included crawler tractors, scrapers, graders, payloaders, and other heavy equipment used in construction of roads and dams. Prices ranged from $5,000 per unit up to $60,000 per unit.

Steel and related-products sales had followed the general pattern of the total industry, with substantial decreases in the earlier months of 1958 followed by a sharp recovery during the fourth quarter. Sales of steel, pig iron, and coke by-products to users other than the company totaled $42,881,000 in 1958, down 28 percent from 1957 levels. Consumption of Steel Division products by other International Harvester divisions during 1958 about equaled outside sales. The Steel Division sales were 3.9 percent of the total International Harvester sales.

Fiber and Twine Division accounted for 1.3 percent of total International Harvester sales, at $12,078,000. Although small in comparison with the overall sales, the Fiber and Twine Division was one of International Harvester's oldest divisions, dating back to the inception of the company by Cyrus McCormick, whose original product was the grain reaper. Development of the grain reaper led to the need for binders. These binding machines required rope to bind the grain, which had led to the establishment of the Fiber and Twine Division.

The Service Parts Operations served as the distributing agent for all the major product divisions. Sales of service parts totaled $266,-354,000 in 1958, an increase of 5.4 percent over 1957 and an all-time high. Part sales were included in the financial statements of the respective product divisions.

ELECTRONIC DATA PROCESSING EQUIPMENT

Electronic Data Processing equipment being used by International Harvester in early 1959 consisted of five IBM 650 computers and two IBM 705's. The IBM 650's were located at the Steel Division (Chicago, Illinois) Works;[1] one each at the West Pullman (Chicago, Illinois), Farmall (Rock Island, Illinois), and the Louisville (Kentucky) Works in the Farm Tractor Division: and one at the Milwaukee (Wisconsin) Works in the Construction Equipment Division. The 650's are essentially fast tabulating machines which can perform multiple operations on punched card information. At this time, these computers primarily handled applications previously processed on regular punched card equipment. The principal advantages of the 650's had been the ease of installation and programming, their "on the spot" availability to local management, and their quick payoff.

The two IBM 705 computers were located at Fort Wayne (Indiana)

---

[1]"Works" is International Harvester's designation for manufacturing plant.

in the Motor Truck Division and at Broadview (Chicago) in the Farm Equipment Division. These 705's performed the same functions as the 650's but they were substantially faster and more versatile. (The rule of thumb used at this time was that a 705 was five times faster than a 650.) Because of this versatility they were used on jobs that could not previously have been done efficiently on either punched card or the 650 equipment. The principal disadvantages of the 705's were the high costs of installation, initial programming, and program maintenance. High initial programming and program maintenance costs were caused by the detailed programming required by the symbolic language used on the 705 and the changing equipment configuration.

In addition, International Harvester had on order from IBM a 305 RAMAC system for the Tractor Works (to replace a manual tub file system of determining service parts locations), an expanded 650 system for the steel mill (to provide extra capacity needed for production scheduling), and larger and faster 705's (Model III) for Fort Wayne and Broadview. Tentative schedules called for 1959 installation for all this equipment. Exhibit 2 indicates the breadth of applications currently being run on the different computers.

International Harvester also had numerous tabulating equipment installations located throughout the organization.

EDP PERSONNEL

Total International Harvester personnel involved in the development of management information systems, application of EDP techniques, and the operation of the facilities totaled 856. These personnel can be classified as belonging to one of four groups, as indicated in Exhibit 3.

The members of these four groups were responsible to one of six organizational areas within the works structure. The six areas were Production Control, Accounting, Manufacturing, Engineering, and General Staff. Exhibits 4 and 5 are simplified organization charts which show how EDP activities were organized in two of International Harvester's divisions. While the organizational pattern varied from one works to another, two important relationships were consistent throughout International Harvester:

1. All computer installations reported directly to the works auditor.
2. There were no formal reporting relationships between the different

EDP installations. Each one operated very much as though it were a separate entity.

Exhibit 6 contains a simplified organization chart of the Corporate Comptroller's office. Exhibit 7 indicates the number of EDP personnel working in the West Pullman and Fort Wayne Works and their functions. The functions of the above four categories of personnel are discussed further below.

Clerical Administration Program Group

The CAP Program was initiated in early 1957 in recognition of the need to quickly reorganize the residual work remaining after EDP procedures had been implemented. The United Auto Workers Union, which represented over one half of all International Harvester clerical personnel, limited changes that could be made after a short time. Some understanding of the CAP's purpose was evident from the Clerical Administration Program Procedural Manual dated October 25, 1957:

Because the IBM Electronic Data Processing equipment will have such an impact on the various clerical tasks and activities within the various departments of the International Harvester Company, it is generally recognized that this would be an opportune time to improve our office methods, systems, and procedures, and to measure the residual work remaining in the various departments after the EDP machine has taken over its portion of the work.

CAP analysts received the following training:

1. Techniques for improving office methods, systems
   and procedures   1 week
2. Electronic Data Processing   1 week
3. Methods Time Measurement (MTM)   3 weeks
4. Explanation of Clerical Basic Standards   1 week
5. Work Sampling and Standard Data   1 week
                                                           ─────────
                                                           7 weeks

The step-by-step approach in doing the job was as follows: When it was known that the EDP machine was going to take over a certain portion of the work of any department (several weeks previous to the actual taking over), the analysts would go to the department supervisor and explain to him his part in the program plus all the logical steps that the analysts must take with his cooperation. It was assumed that prior to the analysts talking with the supervisors, top management was back of the program and had informed their supervisors of what was contemplated, and had received their whole-hearted cooperation in the project.

The analysts working with the supervisor would teach him how to make out an Activity List, Task List, and therefrom, a Work Distribution Chart. On the completion of the Clerical Methods Engineering work in the department, a new work distribution chart would be developed. This would show the activities remaining in the department after the EDP machine had removed its portion of the work, and the establishment of good methods. The next step of the procedure included the measurement of the work necessary to perform the residual activities listed in the work distribution chart. Naturally, the work that the EDP machine removed from the department would not have to be measured. Conversely, any work the EDP machine added to the department would have to be measured in addition to the residual work.

The procedural manual also contained a detailed explanation of the sequence of meetings necessary to implement these techniques, including the specification of the personnel that should attend the first, second, third, and fourth meetings. Concluding the procedure manual was a list of beneficial by-products of clerical administration.

Office Methods and Procedures Group

This group was established by the corporate comptroller to assume responsibility for improving methods and procedures and it reported directly to him. Office Methods and Procedures was initiated in 1954 because of the need for coordination of the company's methods and procedures activity, and review of equipment proposals. The group's function was described as: to pursue continuously the objective of improving the effectiveness of clerical operations and of reducing the cost thereof. In general, the function was to make comprehensive and continuing analysis of the company's various operations where clerical work was involved for the purposes of effecting improvements in layout and flow of work, of eliminating duplication in effort, and of combining and rearranging such operations for greater efficiency and lower cost. Office Methods and Procedures would also be interested in promoting standardization of office equipment and office forms.

It was appreciated that the various divisions were continuously engaged in making office methods studies with the objective of improving procedures, and it was expected that they would maintain and perhaps intensify this effort, with full cooperation in this field between the staff group of analysts and the various divisional groups. It was anticipated that the resultant coordination of effort would effect overall improvements which would be welcomed by everyone involved and which would produce impressive savings for the company.

The members of the Office Methods and Procedures group would be responsible for the development of electronic applications on a companywide basis. They would evaluate the content of training programs, and, with the exception of the first school, would determine the personnel to attend them. They would keep abreast of the applications developed by the various company operations and would review carefully any installation plans proposed by the division. They would also review the requirements of the various divisions and staff departments for data to be processed by this electronic equipment.

It was expected that the principal effort of this group would be to concentrate initially in the accounting and materials control field. The scope of its work would be enlarged as soon as possible to embrace other areas, including manufacturing, engineering, and purchasing. Eventually the group would be correspondingly expanded to include at least one well-qualified analyst for each functional field covered.

Systems and Programming Group

This group consisted of three distinct position types which were classified as: (1) systems analyst, (2) program analyst, and (3) programmers.

The systems analyst's responsibility was primarily one of managerial status with the responsibility to:

a. Determine methods of approach to the procedure problems involved.
b. Determine the practicality, economics, and feasibility of projected applications.
c. Determine the necessity and nature of changes which might be required in overall company policies.
d. Determine and define policy changes or new policies necessary to accomplish most effective applications.
e. Promote understanding and acceptance of new or revised policies, reconciling differences of opinion between various segments of management.

f. Determine kind and type of controls necessary to insure proper accuracy and to conform with applicable company policies.
g. Formulate and develop basic overall objectives and requirements and logic narratives, for use in the development of detailed programs.

The above could be either computer-oriented or accomplished by some other method; the decision regarding this is one of the systems personnel's prime responsibilities.

The program analyst, within the framework of basic overall objectives and requirements provided him by the systems analyst, developed the method of application of the requirements of the program to the equipment. He defined the logic narrative and determined the type and method of equipment to be utilized. The programmer did the actual programming.

Non-EDP Personnel

In addition to the EDP personnel, many other line and staff organizations became involved in the EDP Program. Exhibit 7 provides a profile of divisional activity for two of International Harvester's works. This profile indicates the number and type of both EDP and non-EDP works personnel involved in the works manufacturing activities.

EXHIBIT 1

DIVISIONAL SALES 1955–58

	Sales in Thousands of Dollars			
Division	*1958*	*1957*	*1956*	*1955*
Motor Truck.........	$ 514,797	$ 555,874	$ 573,664	$ 455,187
Farm Equipment.....	391,267	381,660		
Farm Tractor......			179,872	205,922
Farm Implement...			182,198	180,413
Construction........	136,117	154,053	208,209	147,749
Steel...............	42,881	59,396	60,577	45,216
Fiber & Twine.......	12,078	15,290	9,304	10,927
Other..............	1,250	20,415	38,255	120,371
Total...........	$1,098,390	$1,186,688	$1,252,079	$1,165,785

EXHIBIT 2

ANALYSIS OF COMPUTER USAGE

January, 1959

	Fort Wayne 705	Broad- view 705	Steel 650	Hours West Pullman 650	Farmall 650	Milwaukee 650	Louisville 650
Divisions Regularly Served:							
Productive Hours:							
Payroll.................	22.5	48.9	153.0	65.6	32.9	79.0	67.3
Material & Prod. Control	53.6	79.9	22.0	36.7	84.0	66.0	5.0
Costing................	20.8	0.1	—	9.5	3.6	12.0	17.0
Billing.................	—	97.6	25.0	6.8	14.6	8.0	—
Stores Accounting.......	—	—	13.0	—	—	4.0	—
Service Parts Accounting.	—	—	—	—	—	7.0	—
Engineering............	7.7	2.1	—	—	—	—	—
DO Property...........	22.8	—	—	—	—	—	—
Stock Status............	16.1	165.0	—	—	—	—	—
Periodic Depot Reports..	—	80.5	—	—	—	—	—
Miscellaneous..........	1.5	5.0	—	—	—	15.0	16.9
Total................	145.0	479.1	213.0	118.6	135.1	191.0	106.2
Preparatory Hours........	14.8	69.4	8.0	1.6	4.2	22.0	18.3
Estimate and Order Review..	—	1.7	—	—	—	—	—
Manufacturing Research.....	—	1.4	24.0	4.7	—	—	—
Engineering Research........	—	—	—	7.7	—	—	—
Idle Hours Paid.............	73.2	—	—	56.4	49.7	—	64.5
	233.0	551.6*	245.0	189.0	189.0	213.0	189.0
Hours Paid at Full Rate.....	180.0†	198.0‡	198.0‡	189.0#	189.0#	189.0#	189.0#
Hours Paid at Reduced Rate.	53.0	166.0	—	—	—	21.0	—
Hours Not Charged........	—	187.6	47.0	—	—	3.0	—
Months in Operation........	33	18	38	44	39	21	10

*Including 387.1 hours for Parts Depots, 99.1 hours for the Farm Implement Division, and 62.3 hours for Melrose Park and Tractor Works.
†Four weeks at 45 hours.
‡Twenty-two days at nine hours.
#Twenty-one days at nine hours.

EXHIBIT 3

EDP PERSONNEL

Group	Number of Managerial	Number of Nonmanagerial	Total Personnel
Clerical Administration Program (CAP)................	14	6	20
Office Methods and Procedures.....	5	1	6
Systems and Programming.........	64	61	125
Tabulating and EDP Operations....	42	663	705
Totals......................	125	731	856

EXHIBIT 4

PARTIAL ORGANIZATION CHART OF EDP ACTIVITIES
IN THE MOTOR TRUCK DIVISION

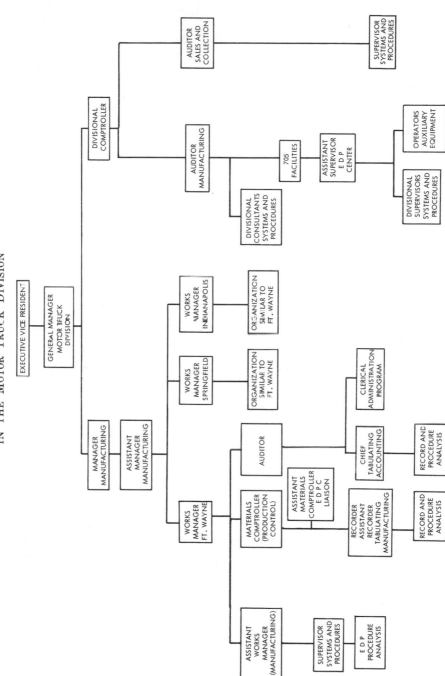

EXHIBIT 5

PARTIAL ORGANIZATION CHART OF EDP ACTIVITIES
IN THE FARM EQUIPMENT DIVISION

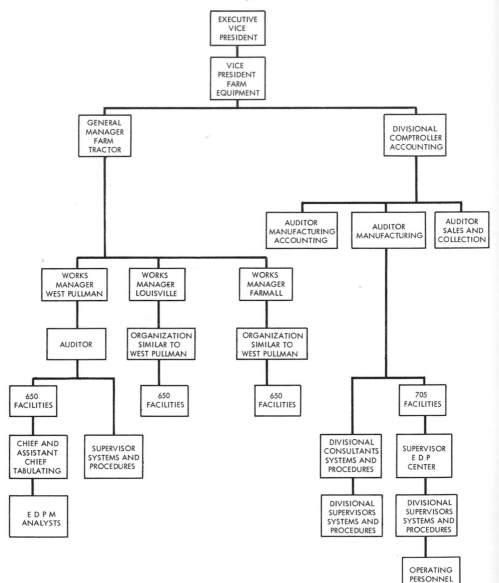

EXHIBIT 6

PARTIAL ORGANIZATION CHART OF COMPTROLLER'S EDP ACTIVITIES

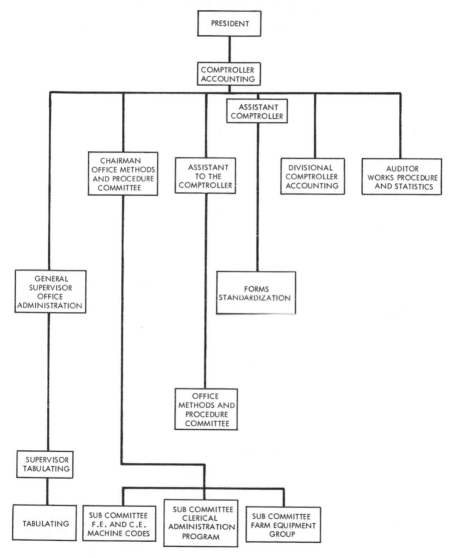

EXHIBIT 7

PERSONNEL BREAKDOWN AT
FORT WAYNE AND WEST PULLMAN PLANTS

Function	Fort Wayne		West Pullman	
	EDP	Total	EDP	Total
Accounting	23[a]	171	33[d]	92
Supply and Inventory	5[b]	333	—	83
Plant Engineering	—	121	—	45
Production Planning	41[c]	124	—	18
Production Personnel	—	1,684	—	1,416
Other	—	464	—	219
	69	2,897	33	1,873

[a]18 machine operators, 3 systems analysts and programmers, 2 clerical administration people.
[b]2 clerical administration people, 3 systems analysts and programmers.
[c]35 machine operators, 6 systems analysts and programmers.
[d]27 machine operators, 6 systems analysts and programmers.

HARMONY LIFE
OF HARTFORD*

Harmony Life of Hartford, one of the large insurance companies, had more than 8,800,000 policyholders—350,000 new holders in 1960. New life insurance sold by Harmony Life in 1960, $70 million above 1959 sales, totaled $2,758,000,000, of which individual insurance contributed $1,946,000,000. Premium income in individual insurance, annuities, and health insurance totaled $354 million, of which $13,-888,000 was on policies written in 1960.

DATA PROCESSING AT HARMONY LIFE

Since 1953 electronic computers had played an ever-increasing role in the operation of Harmony Life. The nature of the company's business involved the handling of vast amounts of data. The functions which were performed in connection with each policy were divided among sales, underwriting, issuance, billing, collection of commission payments, dividend calculations and apportionment, valuation of reserves, claims handling, termination operations (upon maturity, death, lapse, or surrender), and the preparation of general operating reports. Each of these functions included a variety of processing activities which were handled by various types of data processing equipment.

Functions being performed by the data processing department of Harmony Life are presented in Exhibit 1. Projects being developed and projects under study also are listed in that exhibit.

Establishment of the Data Processing Department

Machine equipment had been used by various departments in Harmony Life for many years. The actuarial department (see Exhibit 2 for a partial organization chart) had used various types of machines since 1916. When the accounting department needed equipment in

*Copyright 1961 by Dean Glenn D. Overman, Arizona State University. Reproduced here with his permission.

EXHIBIT 1

Data Processing in Harmony Life of Hartford in 1961

	Premium Notice Business[a]			Debit Business[b]			Group Business[c]		
	Ordi-		Personal					Life	
Activity	nary	Annuity	Health	M DO[d]	MPI[e]	Ind.[f]	A & H[g]	& DD[h]	Annuity[i]
Sales............	D	D	D	D		S	S	S	S
Underwriting......				S		D			
Issue.............	P			P		D			
Premium Billing...	P	P	P	P	S	S	D	D	S
Premium Acctg.....	P	P	P	P	S	S	P	P	S
Dividend Calcula-									
tion............	P	P		P			P	P	
Valuation.........	P	P	P	P	P	P			S
Claims............		P		S	S	S	P	D	P
Statistics.........	P	D	D	D			D	D	D

Legend: P—Being Performed; D—Being Developed; S—Under Study.
[a]Policies billed by mail (mostly large-size policies).
[b]Policies on which premiums were collected at the home of the insured.
[c]Large combination policies covering whole factories or businesses.
[d]Monthly debit ordinary insurance (intermediate-size policies).
[e]Monthly premium industrial insurance (no longer issued).
[f]Industrial insurance (small-size policies).
[g]Accident and health coverages.
[h]Life and accidental death and dismemberment.
[i]Retirement income coverages.

1942, the actuarial department was reluctant to share its equipment because of anticipated problems in scheduling work from two departments on the same equipment. The accounting department therefore obtained its own equipment. During the next few years a large number of other functional groups obtained either mechanized or electronic data processing equipment.

By 1958, the large investment in equipment had led top management to appoint a committee to study the entire data processing function. An outside consultant also was employed. Based on the recommendations contained in the two reports, president John Swartz issued an order to begin centralizing responsibility for all data processing activities into one department and providing for the gradual merger of the existing equipment of all departments.

O. D. Heller was appointed assistant vice president and director of data processing to administer the new department. Mr. Heller had previously been manager of the data processing section in the policy department. In this department, he had had experience with both major types of data processing equipment used by Harmony Life, i.e., mechanized punched card machines, and medium and large-size electronic computers. Mr. Heller had been with the company since 1946. His prior training and experience included a degree in business administration and 15 years' practice in systems and procedures work with a large manufacturer of data processing equipment.

The physical merging of equipment and data processing activities

EXHIBIT 2

ABBREVIATED ORGANIZATION CHART

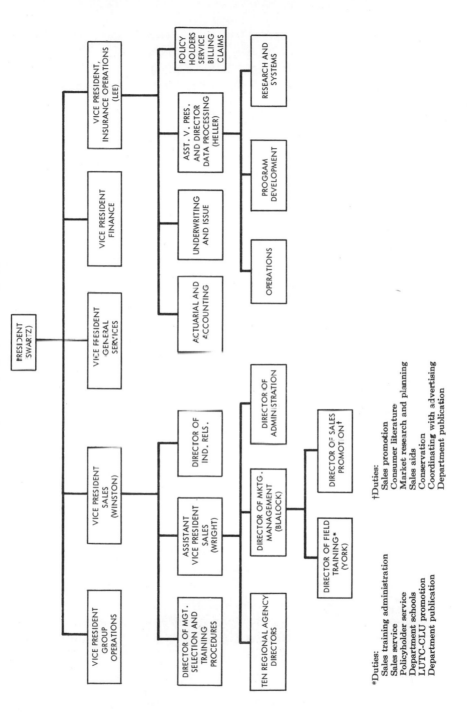

*Duties:
Sales training administration
Sales service
Policyholder service
Department schools
LUTC-CLU promotion
Department publication

†Duties:
Sales promotion
Consumer literature
Market research and planning
Sales aids
Conservation
Coordinating with advertising
Department publication

began in 1959, when two departments were brought under the new centralized control. In 1961, the merger of the data processing facilities of the remaining departments was completed.

The equipment available to the new department was as follows:

3 large-scale, electronic tube type computers (plus input and output equipment)	Company owned
5 medium-size, tube-type computers (plus input and output equipment)	Company owned
80 mechanized data processing machines (plus auxiliary equipment of key punch, sorters, and printers)	Rented

In 1961, a new, large solid-state[1] computer (7070) and four auxiliary computers (1401's) were purchased at a cost of more than $1.5 million. Three of the 1401's were to be delivered at a future date. These machines were intended to replace the five medium-size computers and, in addition, would take over most of the work performed on the mechanized data processing equipment. It also was planned to use the new equipment to service one functional group (monthly debit ordinary), which previously had not been mechanized.

One medium-sized computer, a 1620, was permitted to remain in the actuarial department for research purposes, although general responsibility for the equipment was retained by the data processing department. This equipment had considerable processing capacity, but the limited input and output equipment made it more adaptable to scientific or problem-type applications than to general business applications. Auxiliary input and output equipment could be purchased, but the irregularly occurring needs of the actuarial department made it difficult to integrate the 1620 with the computers being scheduled for regular business applications, so auxiliary equipment was not a part of the present installation.

Problems Arising from the Unification

The manager of the new data processing department was confronted not only with the technical problems inherent in the physical merger of data processing activities, but also with the human relations problems which arose from the centralizing of responsibility and equipment outside the functional areas. Managers of these functional

---

[1]This equipment used transistors instead of vacuum tubes and required less servicing and air conditioning.

areas frequently made requests to the central data processing department for services which were considered by the manager of the new department to be uneconomical or unsuited for handling by a computer. The manager frequently rejected such requests and felt that these refusals were resulting in a reputation that the new department was often uncooperative.

Mr. Heller expressed the problem by saying, "How can we control these excessive, uneconomical requests for work on the new computer, so that we can live within our budget and still keep good relations with the management of the functional departments which we serve?"

Reasons for this problem, as viewed by Mr. Heller were:

1. Widespread publicity in the press about the capabilities of computers without explanations of their limitations, costs, and proper role.
2. Lack of rudimentary understanding by functional managers about business uses of computers.
3. Overenthusiastic reports from earlier advisory committees on results which might be expected from the new installation.
4. The presentation of vague service requests that had not been thoroughly analyzed before presentation.

Organization and Operation of the New Department

To carry out his new responsibilities, Mr. Heller organized the new department into three sections: (1) operations, (2) program development, and (3) research and systems. The operations section was the largest of the three and employed about 250 persons. This section was responsible for routine production. Only work that had previously been approved and programmed by the other two sections was handled by operations.

The program development section consisted of 62 persons, chiefly programmers, who did the coding, debugging, and preparing of program tapes for new applications. Only programs approved by the research and systems section were handled by the program development section.

Requests for new computer applications or variations of existing applications were received first by the research and systems section. If the request appeared to the staff of the section to have merit, and indicated to them that the person making the request had rather thoroughly thought through the need, the research and systems section made an advisability study. During the study process, requests were often modified in line with suggestions from the research and systems section. This study served as a guide to the department manager in making a decision to approve or reject the request. It also served as a basis for the requesting official to determine if he wished to adopt the new procedure.

An advisability study was sometimes called a "feasibility" study, but the term "advisability" was considered by personnel in the research and systems section as more accurate, since a request might be feasible but not advisable because of cost, anticipated change in operation, or other reasons. These studies usually covered the following topics:

1. Statement of the problem.
2. Description of the present system, including schedules, volumes, personnel requirements, and costs.
3. Findings and recommendations, including the suggested approach and equipment, systems and programming development, time and manpower requirements, estimated computer production time, and costs and suggested conversion schedules.
4. Advantages and limitations of the suggested approach.
5. Net savings or costs.
6. Alternative approaches.

The cost of an advisability study was usually charged to the department making the request. The cost varied greatly according to the nature and complexity of the problem. The written report was often 20 to 25 pages in length.

Costs of Processing Data

The advisability study suggested probable costs of machine time and programming. The actual costs, however, might vary considerably from the estimate, since they were computed at the time of performance. An internal costing group outside the data processing department allocated costs according to a current rate schedule.

Rate schedules for machine usage were difficult to formalize and publish in advance. The first computer obtained by Harmony Life was rented, and the cost figure of $300 an hour was widely discussed in the company. Later, when other computers were purchased, no general rate was quoted, since costs would obviously be affected by many factors, such as the rate of depreciation, number of shifts being operated, idle machine time, amount of setup time in relation to running time, etc.

Although the figures were subject to frequent change, the expense analysis and controls unit was currently using the following rates for actual running time on the new solid-state computer:

Number of Units	Type of Equipment	Rate per Hour (Each Unit)
1	7070 Central Processor	$110.50
5	729 II Tape Unit	3.50
4	729 IV Tape Unit	4.50
1	1401 Central Processor	18.50
1	1402 Card Reading Punch Unit	2.50
1	1403 High Speed Printer	3.25
2	729 IIA Tape Unit	2.75

Hourly rates were total costs, including both direct and indirect costs of labor, depreciation of equipment and general overhead.

All the equipment listed would be needed simultaneously on most types of computer processing, since input and output data for the Central Processor (7070) were transmitted through the 1401 and its related equipment. The number of tape units required would vary considerably according to the nature of the job. Since the 1401 was also a self-contained computer with a limited memory capacity, some jobs requiring a limited number of variables and limited memory storage could be performed using only the 1401, 1402, 1403, and 729 IIA. Single problem computations on the 7070 using 20 variables could be processed in approximately 30 seconds.

Before any project could be placed on the computer, a program (machine instruction tapes) had to be prepared by the program development section. Costs of programming varied greatly according to the nature of the job. A simple program using a "canned" routine could be prepared for as little as $50. Programs for major applications, such as setting up premium billing on the machine, might require the services of six programmers for two years, at a cost of approximately $84,000. Program costs generally ranged from $12,000 to $50,000.

In addition to the cost for running time on the machine and for the initial programming costs, the user was charged for setup time each time the machine was used. This preparation usually included the following steps:

1. Putting on the master instruction tape.
2. Clearing the memory drum.
3. Reading new instructions into the machine.
4. Setting the console instruction buttons.

5. Mounting the input and output tapes and possibly other tapes, such as error tapes, factor tapes, etc.
6. Inserting necessary forms in the high-speed printer.

These steps usually required five minutes but sometimes took ten minutes, and they were required whether the anticipated machine running time was five seconds or five hours. Costs for setup time were calculated at the same rate as that for running time.

Because of the nature of the machine operation, Mr. Heller was strongly convinced that computers should be devoted to large-volume, continuous-operation types of jobs and that small-volume, infrequent, or sporadically occurring jobs could not be economically handled on the large computers because of the setup costs for short runs.

These sporadically occurring jobs also created scheduling problems, since it was difficult to schedule the machine usage in advance if there was no way of knowing whether the job would require three minutes or three hours on a specified day. In order to keep costs down, the new solid-state computer was being carefully scheduled several weeks in advance.

A REQUEST FROM THE SALES DEPARTMENT

In July of 1961, W. A. York, CLU, training director for the 5,200 agents of Harmony Life, read an article in *National Underwriter* magazine briefly describing a new service being introduced by the sales division of the Mutual Benefit Life Insurance Company, a competitive insurance firm. This service was to prepare an individualized proposal setting forth the insurance program that a prospective customer should be carrying. Pertinent facts were obtained from the customer and were fed into the computer, which promptly computed a recommended insurance program based on the individual's specific needs.

Insurance programs prepared for individual prospects were currently in use in the insurance industry. These were of two types. One was a rather simple form which assisted a salesman to compare a customer's stated insurance needs with his present insurance program and to recommend additional coverage if needed. The form could be completed by the salesman within a few minutes, in the presence of the prospect, but was based upon the prospect's judgment of his personal insurance needs rather than upon an objective analysis of the facts.

A second type of program planning was done by analysts in the home office. These were comprehensive proposals based upon facts obtained from the prospect by the salesman and included such items as age, income, number and status of dependents, indebtedness, social security status, retirement plan, insurance in force, veteran's benefits, and total assets. These comprehensive proposals required from two to six hours to prepare. All proposals in the past had been manually prepared, and the announcement from Mutual Benefit was the first indication to Mr. York that such a comprehensive personalized proposal might be prepared by an electronic computer.

Mr. York had discouraged the use of comprehensive program planning because of the time required either by salesmen or by the home office, as many computations were necessary with this technique. He felt that salesmen could more profitably spend their time in contacting prospective policyholders and selling them insurance, rather than in doing "paper work." Manual preparation by analysts in the home office was expensive and was generally discouraged. In spite of this discouragement, salesmen occasionally requested the service. Forty proposals of this type had been prepared by Harmony Life during 1960. Of the proposals prepared, one out of every three resulted in a sale, whereas the average of completed sales without use of the device was one out of every four or five sales presentations. The average policy value in these cases was $24,453. The average annual premium income of the 40 prepared proposals was $1,281, of which the agent received approximately 43 percent the first year and 9 percent during each of the following 4 years, plus additional benefits in succeeding years which totaled approximately 3 percent. Commission rates varied on different types of policies, but the above schedule was representative of typical returns to the salesmen on the premium-notice type of business. This type of business represented 63 percent of the dollar volume of individual life, annuity, and health sales, and 10 percent of the total number of policies annually issued by the company.

Mr. York strongly favored the use of the planned-program technique if machines could do the detail work at a reasonable cost. Among the benefits which he could see from this new plan were these:

1. It would help the salesman to establish a professional counselor-client relationship with the prospect.
2. The prospect who provided the detailed information would be more likely to make a favorable decision.

3. Repeat sales to present policyholders would be easier.
4. The salesmen would not be required to learn any new sales techniques, since the principle was already generally understood.
5. The prospect would receive a valuable service by having an answer to the question: How much insurance is enough for me?

The average number of sales annually per agent in 1960 was 56.4. It was Mr. York's opinion that this average was too low and that some technique, such as the proposed program planning, would help increase this average.

Mr. York attempted to obtain information on how the new plan had worked in the competitor's operation. He learned it was used primarily by one general agent who was a large producer, but he could not obtain other details. The competitor reported that he believed that the new technique had given his firm a competitive advantage and stated that the new service was being advertised in *The New Yorker* magazine. This information further strengthened Mr. York's conviction that the plan had genuine merit. Because of the availability of the new and superior computer, the 7070, at Harmony Life, he believed it would be possible to provide a more comprehensive sales proposal using a few more variables than those pioneered by the competitor.

Mr. York asked the data processing department for general estimates of cost for the proposal. He was informed that costs could not be quoted, as they were dependent upon the nature of the project and the amount of estimated input and output expected. Mr. York at that time was not able to furnish specific items which should be included in the analysis. He had, however, heard that Mutual Benefit Life used 19 variables in preparing each program. He also was unable to estimate precisely the amount of expected usage, as he felt this was dependent upon probable costs and the amount of encouragement given the agents by the home office. He attempted to determine whether the cost would be $5,000 or $500,000, since the cost would determine whether or not he wished to pursue the matter further. But he could obtain no general estimate from the data processing department. He was informed that the project as presented did not appear to be acceptable for scheduling on the new computer.

In explaining his position concerning cost and usage figures, Mr. York stated:

The home office should provide service to the field agents and to the public. In sales work we can never actually tell whether a sales tool will pay out or not. We spend money on a sales brochure, but how can we tell exactly what the return will be? A sales meeting costs money, but we can't measure the direct returns in relation to costs. Indirect sales resulting from the expenditures can't be computed.

Why then must the computer people have definite figures on the usage before accepting a sales idea? I want to be practical about the matter, but I can't be too concerned over internal costs until we've had an opportunity to try out the new procedure to see how it works. Some things must be taken on faith when your judgment tells you it is a good idea. Obviously acquisition cost of new business can't exceed a reasonable figure, but often we can't definitely evaluate this until we try it.

Sales are the lifeblood of our business, and we must move ahead when we are convinced a new idea is a good one.

RESPONSE OF THE DATA PROCESSING DEPARTMENT

When Mr. York made his initial request, Mr. Heller attempted to determine what would be expected in the form of programming and anticipated output if the new idea were approved. Mr. Heller received the general impression that the project would result in a low-volume, irregularly occurring operation, so he informed Mr. York that he would be unable to set it up on the new computer. When Mr. York pressed for a general estimate of probable costs, Mr. Heller told him that such an estimate was impossible without extensive study of the proposal, and this study could not be undertaken unless Mr. York could provide more definite information. Mr. Heller also informed him that the new computer would soon be heavily scheduled with other types of work which were clearly adapted to it.

Mr. York inquired if the job might be set up on one of the 650 computers, since Mutual Benefit Life had used this type of equipment. Mr. Heller replied that a decision had been made to dispose of these machines to help defray the costs of the new solid-state computer installation. He explained that if one of the 650 computers, valued at $120,000, were retained for Mr. York, the air conditioning, space, and other costs might bring the total costs to one-half million dollars. These costs would, of course, be charged to the sales department. The possibility of keeping a 650 for the sole purpose of service to the sales department was not acceptable to Mr. York.

Mr. Heller analyzed the case as being typical of the requests that he had had to refuse. His analysis was as follows:

This is a low-volume job and isn't suited for a large-scale computer. The only low-volume jobs which we should consider are the "by-products" requests which can be taken off existing information already in our basic file of stored information. This is not such a request.

Furthermore, we have no way of determining how many emergency or "quickie" requests we are likely to receive if the plan is adopted. Will people be calling in all the time and saying, "I need this bit of information right away," or "I've promised to get this one piece of information out in a hurry?" They forget that the setup time is the same for one case or a thousand.

This case sounds more like a "gimmick" than a real computer problem.

We don't even know if the other personnel of the sales department support this request. Only the training director has requested it, and we don't know if the sales vice president and the field agents really want this plan. It is true that Mr. York is a good, old-line salesman who knows how to teach men to sell "insurance" instead of "policies," but we don't have any way of knowing if the rest of the sales department will support this idea if we approve his request. Anyway, I doubt whether Mr. York has really thought through this request. Any computer installation works on a decreasing scale of costs after the setup has been completed, and he hasn't any information as to whether there might be one case or a thousand cases per week. It sounds as though he's acting primarily on a whim based on the report of a sales gimmick at Mutual Benefit.

We have to say "no" to such requests as these because the big computer can be operated only 24 hours a day—not 25 hours—and we can't always be bringing in a new computer, for computers are not like punched card equipment, where small components can be added at will. It hasn't sunk in on the managers of the other departments that I can't justify asking for another one and one-half million dollar computer just to be of service on every whim they get. We ought to avoid as many of these requests as possible.

It is true that we may nip in the bud some ideas which would save or make money for the company, but we can't "cost them all out" so we are bound to make some mistakes.

We don't have the staff or the time to make detailed advisability studies of every vague idea that comes to us, and we can't give general estimates of costs without careful study of what is involved. If we did, this would lead to all sorts of trouble. Costs can vary too greatly depending upon what is included in the request. Unless the person has taken time to sit down for a day or two to crystalize what he expects in the form of output, it is usually just a whim, so we say, "No."

In this business can you afford to be a good fellow? If I said, "Yes" to all service requests, I wouldn't ever get our main job done. Costs would go up. Then top management would think I was doing a poor job. I don't mind being called a S.O.B. by lower management as long as top management feels I am doing a jood job. After all, this is a selfish world. If by being "uncooperative" we save the company thousands of dollars, then it would seem irresponsible for us to use less than extreme care in scrutinizing requests. People used to come in on Friday afternoon and say, "Put this on the punched card machines. We want the answers on Monday." We stopped that foolishness. Now they usually have to request service in a written memorandum unless we have real confidence in their sincerity and genuine need.

Our attitude is caused by the way people come to us. It is amazing the requests we get. Historically, machine people have been considered low-skilled by others in the company. Now that we have grown up, that impression hasn't changed much, yet we no longer can cater to every whim when a great deal of money is involved in programming costs.

Of course, we often provide a real service to a department which has a problem that is suitable for computers, such as mailing a confirmation notice on the anniversary date of a policy, which was suggested by our public accounting firm. But the volume in that case was two million. We did a smaller job for payroll recently, and they wrote us a letter of appreciation for our service.

But we take on only those jobs which we feel are worthwhile projects for the company as a whole. Even though the department requesting the service will be charged for it, it is our responsibility to try to keep things off the computer that have no business being on it.

We've given 40-minute talks in the various departments to inform management about the use and misuse of computers. If they know anything about computers, they don't come in with foolish requests, making such statements as, "I want it set up so I can get the information I need in one minute" when it takes much longer than that just to set up the machine. I believe that a general knowledge of computers should be a part of the training of all managers. We have a couple of good examples of men who worked for a while in this department and are now managers in functional departments. Our relations with these departments are excellent.

MANAGEMENT'S CONSIDERATION

In October 1961, president Swartz was presented with a formal request from David Winston, vice president in charge of sales. This request contained a proposal that Harmony Life adopt a sales technique similar to that of Mutual Benefit Life and that the data processing department be directed to provide the necessary service on the new electronic computer.

This request originated with Mr. York and had been approved by Mr. Blalock, director of marketing management, and Mr. Wright, assistant vice president for sales. Mr. Winston reported that he had previously discussed the matter with Mr. Lee, vice president of operations, who had rejected the proposal upon the advice of Mr. Heller.

In attempting to arrive at a decision on the request, Mr. Swartz weighed the following possibilities:

1. If he approved the request, this might set a precedent so that other requests of this nature would be directed to him, rather than to the newly established data processing department, which was technically qualified to make decisions in such matters.
2. The data processing department might use this approved request from top management as leverage to obtain approval for additional computers.
3. Disapproval of the request might be used by the sales department to shift blame to top management in case sales quotas were not reached in the coming year.

Mr. Swartz was aware that regardless of his decision on the present request, some action was needed to prevent similar cases from arising in the future. He had pointed out to the board of directors when the new equipment was purchased that the centralization of equipment and responsibility would reduce costs and improve efficiency in data processing. Excessive demands on the new equipment might jeopardize the basic objective of cost reduction; but he was aware that data processing efficiency required that functional departments have service available when their requests could be economically justified.

HAMMARSTROM CORPORATION

After several discussions at the top management level in the company, the Hammarstrom Corporation decided to lease an RCA 501 data processing system from the RCA Electronic Data Processing Division. The actual letter of intent was transmitted to RCA personnel by J. W. Spencer, Hammarstrom's president, on the back of a golf score card.

The RCA 501 system was to be located in the New Haven offices of the corporation, and delivery of the computer was scheduled for October 1960. The decision was made as a result of the findings of the Automation Systems Development Group (ASDG), under the supervision of Mr. Alec Busher.

THE HAMMARSTROM CORPORATION

The Hammarstrom Corporation, with annual sales well over $100 million, manufactured and sold a full line of capacitors for use in electronic, electrical, automotive, and military industries. Hammarstrom also manufactured printed circuits, radar pulse networks, interference suppression filters, wire-wound and power-type resistors, pulse transformers, and other magnetic components. In all, Hammarstrom produced approximately 3,000 different types of electronic components.

Hammarstrom was divided into three profit-centered operating departments: the Consumer Products Department, the Industrial Products Department, and the Distributor Products Department (see organization chart Exhibit 1). The Consumer Products Department manufactured and sold electronic components to manufacturers of radios, television sets, and high-fidelity systems. The Industrial Products Department manufactured and sold components for industrial applications—to manufacturers of electronic motor controls, for example. The Distributor Department, a marketing organization, sold replacement components for the servicing of electronic equipment, through an extended distributor organization. Each of the

EXHIBIT 1

July, 1958

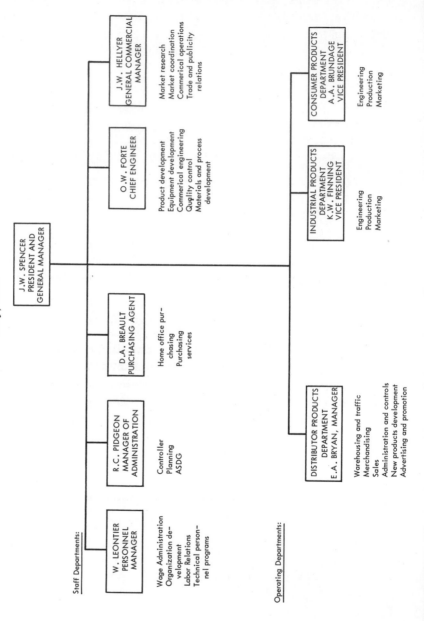

three operating departments provided about one third of Hammarstrom's total sales, and each department maintained its own sales organization. Sales offices were located in most of the principal cities in the United States.

Hammarstrom employed approximately 10,000 production workers, divided among three locations. The majority of these were women assembly workers. The demand for any single type of electronic component was limited and most components were manufactured several times a year in batches. Certain types were produced as infrequently as once or twice a year. A few standardized types, such as were used in radio and television sets, were in more or less continuous production.

ORGANIZATION OF ASDG DURING 1958

Since June 1957, ASDG had been placed in charge of all automation development activity in the company. Initially, it was located organizationally under the chief engineer, O. W. Forte (see organization chart Exhibit 1). This arrangement had its origin in the fact that Alec Busher, head of ASDG, began his data processing activities while acting as assistant to the chief engineer.

In February 1958, J. W. Spencer placed ASDG under the manager of administration, R. C. Pidgeon. The manager of administration was described as being "pretty much the right-hand man of the president." Pidgeon was responsible for the financial organization, all control activities, the review of all capital budgets, and long-range financial planning for the company. He regularly appraised the planning and performance of all operating departments. Home office tabulating services were under Pidgeon's jurisdiction.

Other Data Processing Studies

In addition to ASDG, other people in the Hammarstrom Corporation became actively involved in data processing studies during 1958. These included:

(a)   The controller's organization.
(b)   The warehouse service organization.
(c)   The management services group.

The controller, J. Curry, who reported to R. C. Pidgeon, took a direct interest in data processing activities since many of the existing punched card tabulating operations were under his jurisdiction. Working for Curry was W. Smee, the auditing, financial, data processing, and systems analysis manager (in charge of the people designing new tabulating services and punched card programs). Under Smee was a tabulating service manager, in charge of actually operating the tabulating machines. Because the work of ASDG was intimately involved with these punched card tabulating operations, Curry appointed Smee to work with ASDG and to undertake any studies which ASDG wanted to perform in the control area.

The warehouse service organization became involved in data processing activities through ASDG studies on inventory and order processing procedures. ASDG members spent a considerable amount of time working with the local warehouse staffs, designing new systems. The warehouse service organization expressed a high degree of interest in these new systems, particularly as they applied to the central Brooklyn warehouse.

The management services group, a top-level internal consulting group which worked on special projects at the Hammarstrom corporate offices, also assigned two men to study the impact of electronic data processing. One of the men, Jim Parsim, had been employed in quality control work with a private consulting organization until 1957. Parsim was interested in developing quality control systems which could be programmed for immediate use on outside computer facilities. In this way, Hammarstrom could gain the benefits of electronic data processing before the RCA 501 was installed.

The other man from management services, Charles Pink, had only recently graduated from a university. He was assigned to the Brooklyn warehouse, where he commenced a survey of inventory procedures, with a view to installing automated systems. Pink reported informally to Parsim.

The Informal Steering Committee

With personnel from the operating departments, from various staff departments, and from ASDG itself all engaged in data processing studies, there was some tendency for their work to overlap. In order to coordinate the efforts of all parties, an informal "steering committee" gradually evolved. The committee consisted of Parsim from management services, Smee from the controller's office, and Forester from ASDG. These three met approximately once every two weeks to discuss mutual problems and accomplishments, and according to one member of the group, "to keep everybody from trampling all over each other." Mr. Forester acted as chairman of the committee.

Gradually, an informal division of responsibilities developed: Smee concentrated on work in the area of accounts payable and accounts receivable; Parsim concentrated on technical problems in the quality control area; ASDG worked on several data processing problems in production planning, quality control, and engineering computations. Charles Pink, at the Brooklyn warehouse, "did not accomplish much," according to one observer.

REVIEW OF 1958 ASDG ACTIVITY

At the end of 1958, Busher felt that ASDG could report considerable progress toward implementing the recommendations of the Phase II data processing feasibility study. His summary report read as follows:

Annual Report 1958
Automation Systems Development

Both short-range and medium-range work was done in 1958. The short-range projects mainly involved systems improvement, utilizing punched card data processing equipment. The medium-range work was directed toward much greater integration of data handling, using electronic data processing.

Nine separate projects were undertaken in the area of *Production Planning and Inventory Control*. Three of these stand completed. Estimates of final net savings from the nine projects amount to $219,000 per year. About one third of these savings is in effect now. A one-time reduction in operating capital of the order of $300,000 is forecast for 1959–60.

Three separate projects were active in the area of *Quality Planning and Control*. Estimates of final net savings from these amount to $50,000 per year, and a one-time reduction in operating capital of $48,000. This work is the foundation for extensions which will provide substantially greater savings and gains.

In *Product and Process Analysis*, a number of computation jobs were done in support of various engineering projects. Total cost of these jobs was $2,925. If performed on desk calculators, the cost to obtain equivalent results would have been $95,500. The use of computers has thus made possible work which would have been uneconomical otherwise.

In all projects, gains have been made which cannot be expressed in dollars, but which are real and meaningful nevertheless. In general, an appreciation is developing of the possibilities for better management control that lie in modern methods of data processing.

The nonengineering projects in 1958 were the following:

Project	Location	Annual Savings Estimated	Projected Completion Date
Production Planning and Inventory Control			
1. Materials procurement............	New Haven	—	suspended
2. Accounts payable................	New Haven	$20,000	mid-1958
3. Material moves records...........	New Haven	40,000	mid-1959
4. Three tasks in tab. room procedures, cost control and monthly forecasting........................	Richmond	38,000	mid-1959
5. Warehouse systems improvement...	Brooklyn	60,000	mid-1959
6. Defective transformer allowances...	Peoria	16,000	July 1958
7. Service parts order processing......	New Haven	24,000	May 1958
8. Service parts inventory control.....	New Haven	10,000	Fall 1959
9. Accounts receivable..............	New Haven	30,000	Summer 1959
Quality Planning and Control			
1. Automatic computation at factory test......................	New Haven	see (3)	———
2. Specialized component analyzer....	New Haven	see (3)	———
3. Mechanized quality data system...	New Haven	$50,000	Summer 1959

Attitudes toward ASDG

In spite of the progress set forth in the 1958 annual report, a number of managers in the organization had mixed feelings about ASDG. Some believed that the company "wasn't ready for the integrated data processing approach," and expressed the fear that ASDG was "pushing ahead too far too fast." Others privately expressed the belief that "Alec Busher's missionary zeal is scaring a lot of people in the organization. They are beginning to wonder whether they will be replaced by a computer."

Much opposition to ASDG was centered at the New Haven factory and at the Brooklyn warehouse. When ASDG analysts attempted to make appointments to interview operating personnel they were frequently told to "come back next month when we're not so busy." Top management's backing of ASDG, which was often marshaled through meetings of the Automation Policy Committee, remained very firm, and succeeded in breaking down some of the resistance to ASDG activities.

Management opposition to the decision to install a computer was almost nonexistent (one manager commented that to be in favor of electronic data processing was like being against sin). Nevertheless, many managers expressed the belief that "if electronic data processing has to come, then ASDG isn't the group which is going to run it!"

THE REORGANIZATION OF ASDG

On April 1, 1959, in response to growing resistance to ASDG within the company, J. W. Spencer announced a major overhaul of the organization. The name ASDG disappeared. In its place was a new activity: Data Systems and Services (DSS).

DSS was to carry on all the former functions of ASDG. In addition, all punched card tabulating operations that were performed at New Haven were transferred to the organizational control of DSS. In the past, the control of punched card tabulating had been decentralized in the financial and plant organizations. This transfer to a central authority had long been advocated by Alec Busher as a logical outgrowth of the integrated data processing plans.

A new manager, J. Underwood, was appointed to head DSS. Underwood, until 1959 the manager of commercial operations under J. Hellyer, had a varied and extensive experience in the operating side of the business.

During World War II he had worked in a staff position, scheduling the manufacture of all Hammarstrom products, and allocating available supplies under government priorities. (Even at this time, extensive use was made of punched card equipment.) In 1947 Underwood was transferred to a manufacturing position in Industrial Products. In 1953 he was named operations manager for Industrial Products, supervising the activity of two plants. In 1956 he was made manager of administration and controls under the general marketing manager, and later for Distributor Products.

Alec Busher, former head of ASDG, was appointed manager of Advanced Automation Systems Development. In his new position he was responsible for the development of long-range projects, utilizing mathematical concepts and the latest techniques of operations research. The rest of the old ASDG staff was transferred to DSS.

The DSS Organization

Under the reorganization, DSS continued to report directly to Pidgeon, manager of administration.

Within DSS, Underwood organized his group into the following sections, each headed by a manager:

(1) Business systems planning.
(2) Technical systems planning.

(3) Administrative planning.
(4) Data processing coordination.
(5) Identification project.
(6) Product performance evaluation project.
(7) Data Processing Operations:
  (a) tabulating services.
  (b) electronic data processing.

Business systems planning was to be concerned with all business applications of data processing, including forecasting, accounting, cost control and inventory control. Technical systems planning was to be concerned with engineering and scientific computations. Administrative planning was to be a support activity, responsible for all paper work. Data processing coordination was a function to be filled by one person who would travel around the country visiting various data processing operations as DSS consultant and adviser. Data processing operations were divided into two activities: tabulating services, which was to be concerned with operating the punched card equipment, and electronic data processing service, which was to operate the RCA 501 system.

Underwood announced that the punched card tabulating operations which DSS inherited at New Haven would be the nucleus of a new DSS data processing center. Initially, the activity employed 60 people and used punched card equipment with an annual rental of $230,000.

The tabulating activities at outlying locations came under nominal DSS control only. It was not considered desirable to alter abruptly the working relationships which had developed at outlying plants and warehouses. DSS expected to coordinate the activities at outlying locations more effectively through its traveling emissary, Elliot Terzhagi.

Underwood was quick to recognize that his first responsibility was to pave the way quickly for economical operation of the RCA 501 system. Time was running out, since the computer was due to be installed in approximately 18 months.

The Team Approach

Underwood believed that only through a "team approach" would it be possible to install workable data processing systems, taking into consideration all the practical operating problems as well as the technical problems of the computer. Accordingly, he expanded the DSS organization, with three types of men in mind.

(a) Full-time computer experts (mostly from outside the company).
(b) Full-time staff members with operating experience at Hammarstrom.
(c) Part-time staff members who retained their regular operating positions.

By December 1959, the DSS organization was at the following personnel strength in the systems area (excluding clerical personnel):

Area of Concentration	*Full-time Employees*	*Part-time Employees*
Business systems planning................	14	10
Technical systems planning.............	7	6
Special projects........................	3	1
Other managers*........................	6	—
Totals.............................	30	17

*Including Mr. Busher, who reported to Mr. Underwood, commencing September 1959.

The DSS Charter

In order to clarify the responsibilities and duties of the DSS group, Underwood directed his staff to prepare a DSS Charter. This lengthy document outlined DSS activities in general (see Appendix A) and also specific DSS projects (see Appendix B). Copies were sent to all managers in the company in January 1960.

Merger of DSS and the Controller's Organization

In November 1960, R. C. Pidgeon was promoted to another position in a subsidiary company. Simultaneously, the planning function which had been located under Pidgeon was moved up, so that it came directly under the president. This left only DSS and the controller's office in the old administration department.

Pidgeon was difficult to replace. J. W. Spencer, the president of the company, decided to move Curry, the controller, into Pidgeon's vacant slot, while not changing his title or his responsibilities significantly. For administrative purposes, he explained, DSS would henceforth be considered as a branch of the controller's office. The DSS staff did not consider that this move changed their position in the company in any way.

Under the reorganization, all of the data processing activities at the home office location came back under the controller.

A REVIEW OF DSS PROGRESS DURING 1960

In December 1960, Mr. Underwood reviewed the progress of the past year, and commented on the future of DSS and its relationships with the rest of the company. Some of his remarks are recorded below:

I think we accomplished a great deal during 1960. We should be ready for the computer when it is finally installed next March. Our immediate job has been to build up computer load, and we have had to concentrate on short-run projects with an immediate payoff.

We were hit somewhat by a general cost-reduction drive which was ordered last summer. I had to reduce my expenses by a certain percentage, and some projects had to be postponed. We couldn't cut expenses in our tabulating operations—these were essential services which had to be continued. So we bore the brunt of the reduction in the area of systems analysis. For example, we decided that the product performance evaluation project was one which would have to wait. This was the project which George Dopking headed as project manager. George was assigned to us by the engineering manager in Consumer Products as a man he was willing to have studying the area—a man he could trust. We decided that the whole study was a pretty long-term project. The payoff should be enormous, but it won't be ready for programming for several years. George went back to the Consumer Products Department. I intend to restore this study to its top-priority rank as soon as funds become available.

Looking back, we can see now that the work on electronic data processing which was carried out several years ago was a very ambitious approach to the problem. Alec (Busher) is an advanced type of thinker, and he wants to move fast. Unfortunately, we can't move faster than the operating people. Until they understand and accept what we are doing they will fight us.

These integrated systems which encompass all conceivable applications of electronic data processing look good on paper. But they become frightening when you try to translate them into actual operation. They are too vast. You hardly know where to start, there are so many areas, so many things to do. We have to ask ourselves, "What can we do today?" The integrated data processing system is a fine long-range objective, but somehow you must plan to get there!

We began by breaking the total system down into manageable chunks, such as dividing it into the business systems area and the technical systems area. Then we subdivided it further, into the distribution project, for example. And then we selected one section of this: sales accounting and sales analysis; but even that is a giant area, and has to be split among several individuals who do the actual analysis and programming work.

You might say we are slowly backing into the system. We are concentrating on the end products of the information flow system; on those reports which go to management for study (such as sales performance reports). These outputs don't become inputs for the system later on, so they are the easiest ones to work with. Later we will concentrate on those outputs which become inputs. Gradually, we will roll back the entire system. Eventually, we will work back into manufacturing, in-process inventories, and purchasing.

It is possible to imagine an integrated electronic data processing system which does just about everything. One area we are working on right now is sales forecasting. We could take this sales forecast, add to it information on inventories and plant capacity, and then plug it into a computer to get an optimum production schedule. The computer could then order the raw materials by writing out purchase orders, it could notify the receiving department that the goods were arriving, it could measure the quality of the incoming goods over a period of time and feed this information back to the purchasing people, and so on. This is all wonderful—but it is all a dream!

Right now, two people sitting down with our sales forecast and inventory data can come up with a better production plan in two hours than we could turn out with a computer. At the present we can't handle this problem on a computer! And even if we could, if we proposed to do it, a production manager somewhere would ask, "How much will this save me tomorrow?" and when we tell him how much it costs he would say he already had a clerk doing the job at a fraction of the cost.

For some strange reason, data processing is the hardest thing to get across. We can take the smartest fellow around here, pour the purest essence of electronic data processing over him for two weeks, and at the end of that time he will ask a question which shows that it has soaked in about one quarter of an inch! Anybody in our business has to face up to this fact.

APPENDIX A

The Data Systems and Services Group Charter
January 1960

OVERALL OBJECTIVES

The overall objective of Data Systems and Services is to increase the profit and return on assets of the Hammarstrom Corporation, through the application of advanced systems concepts, modern data processing, and new management control techniques. Profitability improvements are of two kinds:

1.   The measurable reduction of direct or indirect expense.

2. Profit improvement due to the availability of better, more timely information for control of some aspect of the business.

SPECIFIC OBJECTIVES

Data Systems and Services will:
1. Conduct a comprehensive analysis of the Hammarstrom Corporation's system of operation, including functions, organization, policies, plans, and procedures.
2. Provide leadership and participate in the development of the optimum system of operation for the Hammarstrom Corporation.
3. Provide, control, and coordinate data processing services to meet the needs of the Hammarstrom Corporation.
4. Participate in the development of, and keep information on, long-range business plans of the Hammarstrom Corporation.
5. By means of lectures, demonstrations, and study courses, secure an understanding by all levels of management of the responsibilities and opportunities which will be brought about by new systems techniques and electronic data processing.

PROJECT PLANNING

Business Systems Planning

During the 1958 feasibility study, several major areas of electronic data processing application were identified. Most of these areas have since been grouped into two major system projects:
  (a) *The Production System*, covering the following:
      (1) Sales and requirements planning.
      (2) Production planning and plant scheduling.
      (3) Production-material inventory control.
      (4) Manufacturing performance records, material, and labor accounting.
      (5) Associated accounting and reporting functions.
  (b) *The Distribution System*, covering the following:
      (1) Finished-goods inventory control, customer billing, accounts receivable, sales analysis.
      (2) Associated accounting and reporting functions.
  Manpower has been acquired to form the nucleus of a team in each of the above major projects, and detailed work on both projects is about to start.

Technical Systems Planning

To remain healthy, in a business sense, the technical data systems must be continually modernized to keep pace with the more critical product and process requirements. To date, the following areas have been carved out of the overall plan and given full project status:

(a) *Mechanization of Present Quality Control Data System.* The team looked into the data systems of the quality area with an eye toward their mechanization. They found a rather complex system of procedures which they felt were in many ways incomplete, and also through the years had become weakened in the name of expediency and compromise. It was deemed imperative that this group be given the task of simplifying, statistically strengthening, and generally improving the finished product testing procedures.

(b) *Product Performance Evaluation.* Initially this study will cover product performance evaluations of consumer products, including 16 tests ranging from 100 Percent Factory Tests to Customer Acceptance Laboratory Tests.

(c) *Scientific Computation.* This deals with the solving of mathematical problems in product design, process design, statistically controlled experiments, correlation of data from various sources, and other applications.

DATA PROCESSING

The punched card facilities formerly under the direction of Financial and Plant Accounting have been combined under Data Systems and Services. This activity forms the nucleus of the new Data Processing Center located at New Haven. The combined activity employs 60 people and uses punched card equipment. An RCA 501 Electronic Data Processing System has been contracted for, with delivery scheduled for late in 1960.

TEAM ACTIVITY

A team becomes active when its area of assignment has been broadly outlined, and when at least a nucleus of qualified personnel is available to work on a full-time basis. It will be necessary to add personnel from the operating activities under consideration, for varying periods of time, to contribute their intimate knowledge of operating problems, and to assure that planned system changes are accepted in the operating groups.

In any given project area, the following sequence of steps will be a useful one in arriving at the desired end:

1. *The project team starts by fact finding* in its assigned area. It is necessary to record the existing operating system in sufficient detail to establish that present operations are adequately understood by the project team. Information input will also have to be defined. Next, it is necessary to determine what reference files are needed. Both input and output requirements must also be coordinated with project teams working in adjacent areas.

2. From the facts found, and using sound data processing principles, *new systems plans* must be developed and submitted to management for approval. The proposed system plans will often cut across the boundaries of presently established organizations, and are likely to call for substantial changes from present operating methods. Therefore, the quest for approval may frequently progress to rather high management levels in the company. This is time-consuming for all parties concerned, but necessary. Revisions to proposals may be required before approval is obtained.

3. Once agreement on the proposals has been reached in principle, *details of the system* must be worked out. Again, this requires active participation by personnel from the operating activities, and checking out of system details at appropriate management levels.

4. Piece by piece, the system details are translated to *computer programs*. Programming specialists may enter here, but project-team analysts will be required to take part in programming so that they will know how their system design is handled by the EDP equipment.

5. *Testing of programs* on the machine, and trial runs with dummy information, follow.

6. Finally, *conversion from existing to new system operations* takes place. It will be necessary for the team to continue to work closely with operating personnel during the transition period, in order to take care of unforeseen problems that are sure to arise. In some instances, a period of parallel operations between old and new systems is possible and appropriate.

APPENDIX B

SAMPLE DESCRIPTION OF SPECIFIC TEAM PROJECT

THE PRODUCTION SYSTEM PROJECT

1. Scope

This project covers three areas of business operations:

Market Forecasting for all product lines and all markets. This includes work in market research where we need better and more up-to-date by-type information; better geographic potential patterns; better figures on total industry potential; and more attention to the equipment markets. It also includes improving our techniques of collecting information from the field sales force, and in turn feeding information back to the field.

Production Scheduling to determine, periodically, by-type manufacturing plans in response to the market forecasts, and to break these plans down into detailed operating schedules for each factory department.

Production Performance Reporting. This involves the flow of masses of detailed information on production material moves, labor use, etc., daily from the factory to the Data Processing Center; the maintenance of basic production records through EDP, and the rendering of control reports to the factory management.

2. Project Team

Name	Background
F. J. Daly	Systems; Accounting; IBM
V. A. Dunakin	Manufacturing Superintendent
J. McGlynn	Systems; Industrial Engineering; IBM
B. Rufo	Production Control; Operations Planning
J. Edwards	Plant Accounting

Each of the above is an experienced professional in his own field. Together, the team brings a good cross section of knowledge to the project area. Lacking, as yet, is specific knowledge in the field of marketing product control. Market forecasting techniques will have to be supplied, in part, through external consultants.

3. Schedule

The team will follow a schedule roughly as outlined below: (a detailed Gantt chart which outlined the start and finish of specific project elements was presented).

4. Savings Indication

In the absence of more recent data, this is based on the feasibility study of 1958, and estimates of computer load coming from this project.

1959 total applicable	$2,380,000
Coverage of 1958 feasibility study:	
83 people and	$863,000
Estimated savings through use of EDP:	
38 people and	$426,000
Estimated cost of EDP:	
2 ⅔ hrs./day @ $250	173,000
Net savings potential	$253,000/year

MERRIMAC OIL COMPANY

On May 1, 1965, Mr. James Seiler, a systems analyst, was assigned responsibility for planning the production schedule for replacing an overhead 4-inch insulated pipeline which connected two of Merrimac's Oil Storage Tanks. Erosion due to process conditions necessitated periodic replacement of pipelines of this type. It was strongly suggested that prior to preparing his final estimates he develop a PERT network. Early conversations with the Superintendent of Maintenance and Construction revealed the following technical considerations.

1) The pipeline is 30 feet above the ground. Consequently, a scaffold would have to be built before either the old pipe could be removed or the new pipe installed. Lumber for this scaffold is available at the company.
2) Interspersed along the pipeline are valves. These have to be replaced also.
3) No pipes or valves are currently in stock. After the pipes are received, they will have to be cut into sections of the proper width in the plant's machine shop. When all the pieces are cut, they will then be taken to the scaffold. There they will be placed in proper position and welded together. The valves can be placed in position on the pipe after the pipe is placed in position and before it is welded. They cannot be permanently attached to the pipe, however, until all the sections have been welded together.
4) While the valves are being attached to the pipe, the insulating material can simultaneously be attached to the pipe.
5) The scaffolding is not needed during the pressure testing. Final clear-up and start-up, however, depend on the results of the pressure test.
6) The shutdown of the pipeline will be both costly and inconvenient. It is important, therefore, that the job be accomplished as quickly as possible.
7) An adequate supply of labor is available, and there should be no slowdown on this account.

Consultation with the supervisor of Methods and Planning produced the following estimates of the time required to accomplish the various aspects of the project.

		Optimistic	Normal	Pessimistic
		Time Required Estimates (hours)		
	Aspect of the Project	*Optimistic*	*Normal*	*Pessimistic*
A.	Develop list of items to be purchased.....................	10	12	14
B.	Shutdown of old pipeline...........	8	9	20
C.	Erect scaffold....................	10	11	12
D.	Remove scaffold..................	4	4	5
E.	Time required to receive pipe after purchase order is submitted.......	100	200	400
F.	Cutting of pipe into sections........	32	40	48
G.	Placement of pipe in position prior to welding.....................	9	10	13
H.	Welding pipe sections together.......	7	8	9
I.	Permanent attachment of valves to the pipe.......................	9	10	11
J.	Time required to receive valves after submission of purchase order......	180	240	340
K.	Placement of valves on the pipe.....	6	7	9
L.	Removal of old pipes and valves.....	40	45	48
M.	Placement of insulating material on pipe........................	20	25	30
N.	Pressure test.....................	6	6	6
O.	Clean-up and start-up.............	3	4	5

QUESTIONS

1. Prepare a PERT network for the replacement of the pipeline. (Round your T_e's to the nearest whole hour.)

SPEEDEE
HOME CONSTRUCTION INC.

On June 15, 1965, Mr. Alfred Bevis, a planning specialist at Speedee Home Construction Inc., was assigned the responsibility for developing the construction schedule of a residential home. The construction contract contained a heavy penalty clause, to be executed if construction was not completed within 52 working days. Because of the costs involved in the penalty clause, as well as the unfavorable effect on Speedee's reputation if a contract was not completed on time, the company wished to make every effort possible to meet the scheduled deadline. This might mean speeding production progress up to rates which involved additional expenditures. To help their planning efforts in this area, Speedee Homes made extensive use of the PERT-COST technique.

In his initial analysis of the problem, Mr. Bevis noted in the contract the following construction relationships which would have to be observed:

1) The preliminary set of blueprints would have to be completed before the foundation excavation could begin. After the excavation was completely finished, the foundation could be poured.

2) The preparation of a bill of materials would have to be deferred until the final set of blueprints was prepared. When the bill of materials is completed, it is used to prepare order invoices for lumber and other items. Construction of the frame cannot begin until the lumber arrives at the construction site.

3) After the frame is completed, electric work, erection of laths, plumbing, installation of millwork, and installation of siding can all begin.

4) Painting of the interior walls cannot start until the electric work, plastering of walls, and plumbing are completed. Plastering of walls cannot begin until the laths are erected.

5) The final interior decorating work cannot begin until the interior walls are painted, and the trim installed. Installation of trim cannot begin until the millwork is completely installed.

6) Painting of the house's exterior cannot proceed until the windows are installed. Installation of the windows in turn cannot start until the siding is in place.

Mr. Bevis studied the performance records on several other houses of similar construction; he then developed an optimistic, pessimistic, and most likely estimate of the time required to complete each of the steps in building the house. He also developed estimates of the extra cost of speeding up these steps. The results of this analysis are presented in Exhibit 1.

QUESTIONS

1. Prepare a PERT Network. (Round your t_e's to the nearest whole day.)
2. Determine the incremental expenditures necessary to complete the project on time, using the procedures described in Chapter 4.

EXHIBIT 1

Step		t_o	t_m	t_p	Day's Reduction*	Cost*
			Time Required to Execute Step (Days) Under Optimal Cost Conditions				Cost
A.	Prepare preliminary specifications...	8	10	12	2	10
					3	120
B.	Excavate foundation.............	4	4	5	1	200
C.	Pour foundation.................	5	6	6	1	180
D.	Electric work...................	4	5	6	2	200
E.	Lath work......................	1	2	2	1	20
F.	Plumbing.......................	5	6	7	2	80
G.	Plaster walls...................	4	4	5	1	40
					2	100
H.	Paint interior walls............	4	5	5	1	70
					2	150
I.	Millwork installation...........	7	10	12	2	200
					5	700
J.	Trim installation...............	6	7	13	2	90
					3	150
K.	Erect frame and roof............	12	15	18	2	1,000
					4	2,500
L.	Final interior decoration........	13	15	19	2	100
					4	800
M.	Installation of siding..........	12	14	18	1	100
					3	600
N.	Completion of exterior work......	6	7	8	1	50
					2	150
O.	Blueprints finalized............	4	5	6	2	70
					3	120
P.	Bill of materials and order forms prepared.................	3	3	4	1	50
					2	170
Q.	Time required to receive lumber....	6	8	12	2	110
					4	290
R.	Window installation.............	5	6	7	1	100

*Note that both the days and the costs are cumulative figures. In A, for example, you can reduce the t_m 2 days for a *total* cost of $10, or $5 a day. You can reduce the time a *total* of 3 days for $120; therefore, the cost of the third day's reduction is $110.

DATOMATIC READER

On Thursday, June 18, 1964, eight weeks after the start of the Datomatic Reader project, Mr. Norman Trep, the project manager, was preparing for a visit of the government engineering officer responsible for the Datomatic Reader. The visiting engineer was to arrive the following Monday to review the first two months of progress on the project, as well as Photonics Corporation's general effectiveness in managing the development effort.

Mr. Trep had recently received the initial PERT-COST reports on the Datomatic (see Exhibits 6 and 7) and he wished to analyze these to determine what action he should take prior to the government engineer's visit. Two decisions were needed: the choice of a course of action that would insure completion of the project within the scheduled time; and a decision regarding the future of PERT-COST on the project, i.e., whether to improve, discontinue, or continue the current use of PERT-COST.

The use of PERT-COST on the Datomatic Reader project had met with resistance from within Photonics, and several sources indicated that the government was taking a closer look at PERT application on contracts, particularly projects such as the Datomatic Reader where costs were charged directly to the contract. Because of these reasons and the possibility that the overall costs of the project would exceed estimates, Mr. Trep wished to review his decision to use PERT-COST on the project and develop a clear understanding of its advantages and disadvantages. Issues of particular concern to him were: PERT-COST's value in this project versus its cost of approximately $30,000; the distinction between its value in planning and in the early stages of project development versus its use as a reporting and management control tool; the limitations of the probabilities developed by PERT; and the difficulties that might be imposed by Photonics' cost collecting system. He thought the best way to focus on these issues was to use available PERT-COST data in deciding how best to insure timely completion of the Datomatic Reader project, and compare its usefulness in this decision with its cost and with the costs of alternative project management systems.

DATOMATIC READER CONTRACT

Late in April 1964, Photonics Corporation had been awarded a CPFF (cost plus fixed fee) contract[1] to develop and deliver an electronic reader (Datomatic Reader). The function of the Datomatic Reader was to hold and scan certain printed forms, convert the information on the printed forms into electrical impulses, and store the impulses on a magnetic tape. The Datomatic Reader development contract was the first of a series of electronic reader and assorted equipment procurements planned by the government. Photonics' military marketing organization reported that the company was in an excellent position to win subsequent contracts if performance under the present contract was good, and if Photonics' technological lead was not lost as a result of delays by the government in the dates of planned procurement. Photonics' management was relying heavily upon such subsequent contracts to maintain company sales.

ORGANIZATION

Under Photonic's program management concept, a separate program management organization was formed for each system development contract received. A program manager and staff were assigned for the duration of the program. The technical personnel required to perform particular tasks were transferred into and out of a particular program group at the program manager's discretion. Most of these personnel were charged directly to the contract involved. This charge included an additional amount for engineering overhead of 175 percent of the direct labor. Manufacturing tasks were performed by a separate manufacturing organization, at the direction of the program manager.

The Datomatic project was organized in the customary manner,

---

[1]The estimated cost under the contract was $592,920 including labor, materials, overhead, and $41,370 general and administrative expenses. $35,580 was negotiated as fee. Delivery of the hardware was called for in 47 weeks with a demonstration in 44 weeks after the start of the contract. A penalty charge was contained in the contract which called for a penalty of $3,000 per week for each week the demonstration was delayed, up to eight weeks.

with an assigned management group which included an administrator, a systems engineer, a PERT planner, a contract administrator, and clerical personnel. This group would be kept intact for the duration of the contract. Mr. Trep had not been able to obtain the contract administrator until the second week, and the PERT planner was not added until the fourth week.

Since his assignment to the program the planner had been actively engaged in such tasks as setting up the PERT-COST system, familiarizing himself with the program, and breaking estimated costs into packages consistent with work tasks. The PERT-COST network resulting from his efforts is shown in Exhibit 1. On this network cumulative times (most likely estimates) are depicted in boxes beside the events.[2] The three time estimates: pessimistic, most likely, and optimistic, are shown in parentheses beside the line representing each activity. Exhibit 2 describes the events preceding and succeeding each activity.

In setting up the PERT-COST system the planner reassigned some accounting charge numbers. This was necessary to match the PERT-COST network, and to minimize the difficulty caused by individuals who signed their time cards by job title rather than job task. The last digit in the charge number was intended to represent the job function performed, but as a result of current practices it often represented an individual's title. Exhibit 3 provides a list of cost packages and corresponding activities.

Development Task Breakdown in the PERT-COST Network

The Datomatic Reader consisted of seven components, each specified as a separate deliverable item in the contract:

1. Camera. (This includes an easel and housing for holding documents, optics, image orthicon tube,[3] and an electronic package.)
2. Video amplifier. (This amplifies impulses produced by the camera.)
3. Signal comparator. (This amplifies impulses from the camera into characters.)
4. Signal converter. (This converts signals into a form compatible with other EDP equipment.)

---

[2]In Exhibit 1, each circle with a number in it represents an event. Beside each circle are a box and a circle. The number in the box represents the earliest time in weeks from the start of the network by which that event may be completed. The number in the circle represents the latest time by which the event must be completed. All times are based upon most likely estimates.

[3]An image orthicon is a television camera tube having a sensitivity and spectral response approaching that of the eye.

5. Magnetic tape recorder.
6. Power supply. (This supplies special power requirements to all other units.)
7. Console. (This contains wiring, controls, and housing for all other units.)

The development of each of the seven items required different types of technical effort and each different type of effort was described in the PERT-COST network by a separate activity. As an example, for any one item the initial engineering, compatibility testing, and reengineering after testing (rework) were separate activities. The following were described by Mr. Trep as the major activities immediately facing the project organization:

Video Amplifier, Magnetic Tape Recorder Power Supply Unit

The magnetic tape recorder (events 2–51–52 and power supply unit (events 2–8) were commercially available as "off-the-shelf items" and only had to be mounted by Photonics. The video amplifier (events 2–36) and many of the subassemblies of other units were commercially available but had to be manufactured to Photonics' specifications or modified upon receipt by Photonics. The delivery of these units was relatively certain and was backed up by guarantees of the manufacturers involved.

Camera

The camera was the heart of the system. It included three major subassemblies—optics, easel and housing unit (E & H unit), and electronics package. The optics included a lens, image orthicon tube, frame, and lighting system. The optics projected the image of the document to be scanned upon the orthicon tube.

The lens (events 2–32–39) was particularly critical, since no more than .005 of a degree of curvature in the projected image was permissible. Management was relying heavily upon the artisan skill of a very expert optics group to produce the lens to the required high tolerance. Since a trial and error approach was involved in the manufacture, the exact date of delivery was uncertain. Mr. Trep expressed relief that this item was not on the "critical path."

The camera electronics package included: a scan generator (events 2–5–14) which generated varying voltages to control the scanning action of the orthicon tube; a blanking amplifier (events 2–4–14) which shuts off the tube during scan retrace; and a sync. generator (events 2–3–14) which synchronizes the scan generator and blanking amplifier. Although these three units were commercially available, considerable engineering was required to modify them to perform in the system. To expedite development, the modification and reengineering of these units was to be performed by separate groups. They would, however, be manufactured as one unit.

Although design of the camera electronics was complicated, there was not great uncertainty in the schedule of completion. If more funds were allocated to their development, some of the tasks could even be completed ahead of time.

The E & H unit (events 2–17–20–31) was a document-holding frame incorporating a servo-mechanism to move the document being scanned in proper synchronism with the scanning action of the camera. The E & H unit was well within the "state of the art," but some uncertainty was involved in the estimated schedule because of compatibility requirements between this and other units.

Comparator and Signal Converter

The logic portion of the comparator (events 2–17–25–29) represented the most complex electronics design task. The engineer responsible for its design was confident that the technical problems could be solved, but the complexity of the unit made it difficult to estimate completion times with confidence. The comparator logic received the output of the camera after it had been amplified by the video amplifier. It reassembled each sequential scanned segment into character blocks and compared these with permanently stored signals for character identification.

The output of the comparator went to the signal converter (events 2–23–25–27). The signal converter changed the order of electrical impulses so that they would be compatible with electronic data processing equipment. The design of the converter was very similar to that of the comparator logic, although it was a much less complicated task.

The comparator also contained a separate unit which functioned as a master time for the entire system (events 2–18–20–29). This unit was comprised largely of a very stable oscillator that acted as a clock. The uncertainty of the engineering effort required to develop the timer stemmed from possible difficulty in achieving stability. This could be overcome, however, by purchasing more expensive components.

Console

The task of designing the console (events 2–51–52) was largely that of mechanical layout, and planning the internal wiring (integration) within the console so that all other units would be properly connected. The major uncertainty involved in the design of this unit was the timely receipt of data concerning the other units in the system.

In discussing the project as a whole, Mr. Trep stated that the designation of work packages might be somewhat deceptive to an outsider. Breaking the development of each unit of equipment into tasks described as engineering, testing, and rework gave the impression that each package was relatively independent; whereas in fact the rework, or engineering to be done after compatibility testing, was strongly dependent upon the amount and quality of prior engineering. For this reason, what might appear to be a cost overrun in an early work package might actually be a superior design effort which would reduce the time and dollars required for the entire effort. He pointed out that this situation might well exist in the Datomatic Reader project. While early work packages might seem expensive, his engineers had assured him that they could bring costs into line.

Current Status of the Datomatic Reader Project

The first Datomatic Reader PERT-COST report Mr. Trep received was a slack order report, Exhibit 4. This report surprised all concerned because it showed half a week more slack than was projected by straight addition of the "most likely times" for each event.[4] The .7 PR. (probability of completing on or ahead of the target date) was also better than had been expected. To determine methods of improving the probability of timely project completion further, another slack order report was prepared. The second slack order report, Exhibit 5, was a trial computation to reflect the project situation if the existing critical path were eliminated. In Exhibit 5 resources were hypothetically allocated so that the subpath 2–5–34 was no longer the most critical. Mr. Trep and the PERT planner were both puzzled with this report, and wondered if they should attach any significance to either slack order report because the probability of completion listed on the second report (PR. = .61) was poorer than the first. This anomaly was attributed in some manner to the uncertainty of lens design and delivery.

The PERT-COST status report, Exhibit 6, and charge number cost summaries, Exhibit 7, were the most current reports available to Mr. Trep, since two weeks' delay was involved in collecting, summarizing, and reporting costs incurred. As soon as he had received these reports, he had held a meeting with project personnel to discuss the significance of the reported data. The first part of the meeting had been devoted to discussing technical progress. The engineers responsible for individual work packages reported on the status of their efforts. The report on the comparator (events 2–17) indicated it was ahead of schedule. The engineers responsible for the camera electronics package (scan, generator, sync. generator, and

---

[4] Times used in determining slack in Exhibit 4 are not the scheduled completion times (most likely estimates); rather, a weighted average of optimistic, most likely, and pessimistic times are computed and used.

blanking amplifier, events 2–12) had also been encouraging in their report, stating that the decision to start the scan generator early had been wise. Although the major components for the scan generator would be a few days late, enough time had been gained, by spending a few extra dollars, to maintain the present schedule.

The scientist responsible for the optics (events 2–33) did not attend the meeting. He had, however, informed Mr. Trep that he accepted responsibility for the lens and there was nothing to be done to improve the present status, which remained the same as initially reported. The optics were nevertheless discussed by those present at the meeting. It was noted that, while the optics effort could not be speeded up in the conventional sense, one alternative was to use a different method to design the lens. This method would involve a higher cost, but offered a more certain delivery. For example, if at the time of the meeting a more scientific approach to design of the lens were taken, delivery would be firm at the end of the 25th week, versus the present date of the 24th week. The cost, however, would be $6,000 higher.

After a review of technical progress, the meeting turned to an open discussion of the use of PERT-COST on the project. A number of engineers made critical comments concerning its continued use on the project. They pointed out that in the planning stages of a project, while it was still easy to make major changes in the development effort, PERT was an excellent tool. After hardware design was decided upon, it was of little value, for each engineer knew his responsibilities and how much money and time he was allowed. All that remained to be done was to get the job completed in the least time and at the least cost. They went on to say that if Mr. Trep wished to decrease the extent of a cost overrun on the project, the PERT planner should be dropped from the project. A portion of the dollars saved in this manner could be applied to expedite technical effort on the critical path. In any event, they felt their time could be best spent in solving engineering problems rather than updating PERT-COST reports.

The program administrator agreed that it might appear possible, in the short run, to save funds by dropping the PERT planner, but he emphasized that resource allocation decisions were required throughout the program, and that the only manner in which such decisions could be made intelligently was through the use of PERT-COST reports. He cited as an example the initial contention that the lens (events 2–32–39) would be the critical element in the project. PERT-COST showed that this was not the critical path at all. The current need to expedite the project was also noted as an excellent example of the continuing need for PERT-COST on the project.

The administrator then stated that the only difficulty with the use of PERT-COST at the present time was that it had not been updated to include current estimates, and periodic "cost-to-complete" estimates were not submitted for activities in progress. He told Mr. Trep in confidence that the trouble was that the engineers did not want to be controlled as tightly as PERT-COST permitted. He recommended that project status be improved by having the engineers reestimate the tasks without including the extra allowances they normally used. The meeting closed with no agreement on either a method for expediting the project, or on the future of PERT-COST on the project.

As Mr. Trep reviewed the comments made in the meeting, the PERT-COST reports, and other information available to him, he knew that he had to make two decisions: first, what action to take to improve the chances of Datomatic project success; second, deciding on the future role of PERT-COST in the Datomatic Reader project. He could, clearly, allocate additional money to certain work packages to expedite them,[5] but he wasn't sure which allocation, if any, would represent the most fruitful use of funds.

---

[5]As shown in Exhibit 1, certain activities may be expedited if additional funds are committed to these activities. Such activities are preceded and succeeded by the following events: 2–23, 2–17, 2–18, 2–16, 5–11, 3–9, 4–10, 5–46, 6–47, 27–30, 28–29, 14–15, 37–42, 21–31. For example, activity 4–10, the engineering effort on the blanking amplifier, can be accelerated at a cost of $7,124 for each week gained. Since the maximum acceleration that may be accomplished is from 5 weeks to 4.5 weeks, then the cost of the greatest acceleration possible (.5 weeks) is $3,562.

EXHIBIT 1

DATOMATIC READER

PERT-COST Network for Datomatic Reader
(All times in weeks)

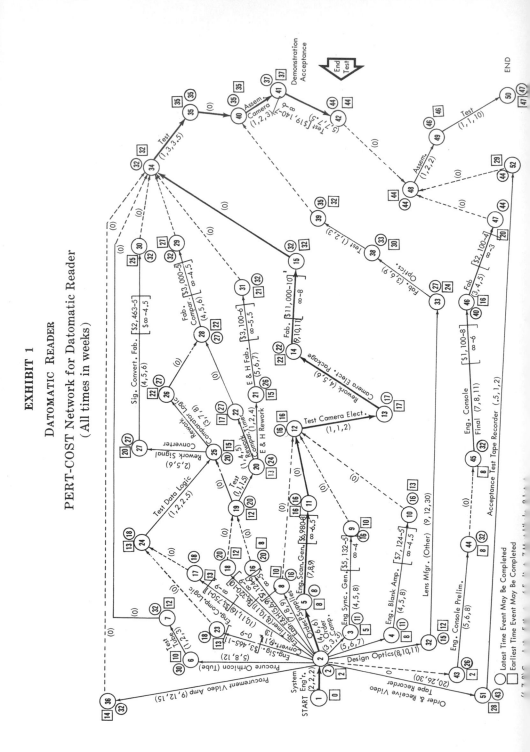

EXHIBIT 2

DATOMATIC READER

Photonics Corporation

List of Events in Datomatic Reader Development Project
as Listed on PERT-COST Network, Exhibit 1

Event Description:

1. Contract award; start systems engr.
2. Systems engr. complete & approved;
   Start: Write specifications for and order

   Video Amp
   Tape recorder
   Power supplies
   Orthicon (tube)
   Std. blanking amp.
   Std. sync. generator

   Development effort for:
   Optics design
   Comparator logic design
   Comparator master timer design
   E & H design
   Signal converter
   Scan generator

3. Receive sync. generator (3 weeks); start sync. generator design & modifications.
4. Receive std. blanking amp.; start blanking amp. design (6 weeks).
5. Receive scan gen.; start scan. gen. engr. & mod. (6 weeks).
6. First orthicon tube received (8 weeks); start tests.
7. Tube test complete (2 weeks).
8. Receive power supply (8 weeks).
9. Complete engr. & mod. sync. gen. (5 weeks).
10. Complete engr. & mod. blanking amp. (5 weeks).
11. Complete engr. & mod. scan. gen. (8 weeks).
12. Start camera electronics compatibility test.
13. End camera electronics compatibility test (1 week); start camera elec. rework.
14. Eng. camera elect. package rework (5 weeks); start camera elect. fab.
15. End camera elect. run. End camera electronics fabrication (10 weeks).
16. End E & H Design (6 weeks).
17. Complete comparator logic design (11 weeks).
18. Complete comparator timer design.
19. Start E & H & timer compatibility test.
20. Complete E & H & timer compatibility test; start E & H and timer rework.
21. Complete E & H rework (2 weeks); start E & H fabrication.
22. Complete timer rework (4 weeks).
23. Complete signal converter breadboard (11 weeks).
24. Start signal converter comparator logic compatibility test.
25. End signal converter comparator logic compatibility test (2 weeks).
26. End comparator logic rework (7 weeks).
27. End signal converter rework (5 weeks); start converter fabrication.
28. Start fab. comparator total.
29. Complete fab. comparator total (5 weeks).
30. Complete fab. signal converter (5 weeks).
31. Complete E & H fab. (6 weeks).
32. Optics design and pur. specs. complete lens ordered (10 weeks).
33. Lens received (12 weeks); start assembly.
34. Begin elect. compat. test.
35. End elect. compat. test (3 weeks).
36. Receive video amp. (12 weeks).

EXHIBIT 2 (continued)

37. Receive tape recorder.
38. Lens assembly complete (4 weeks); start tests.
39. Lens test complete (2 weeks).
40. Begin camera assembly.
41. Complete camera assembly (2 weeks); begin test.
42. Camera test and demonstration complete (7 weeks) (end critical path).
43. Start human factor & console design and prelim. layout.
44. Complete prelim. layout (6 weeks).
45. Start final design and equipment integration.
46. End final design (8 weeks); start fabrication.
47. End fabrication (4 weeks).
48. Start assembly system (2 weeks).
49. Complete assembly; begin project checkout.
50. Complete final checkout and end project (1 week).
51. Receive tape recorder, start acceptance test and adjust.
52. Accept tape recorder.

EXHIBIT 3

DATOMATIC READER

Photonics Corporation

Work Package Cost Estimates With Charge Numbers and Events

Charge Number		Events	Estimated Costs
931J–01 A ( )	Systems engineering*................	01–02	$ 8,520
931J–01 B ( )	Engineer comparator logic*...........	02–17	38,300
931J–01 C ( )	Engineer comparator master timer*....	02–18	15,630
931J–01 D ( )	Engr. scan generator*................	05–11	27,880
931J–01 E ( )	Engr. sync. generator*...............	03–09	7,180
931J–01 F ( )	Engr. blanking amp.*.................	04–10	12,210
931J–01 G ( )	Design optics*......................	02–32	10,900
931J–01 H ( )	Engr. E & H unit*...................	02–16	12,200
931J–01 I ( )	Rework converter*...................	25–27	8,560
931J–01 J ( )	Rework comparator logic*...........	25–26	11,500
931J–01 K ( )	Rework comparator master timer*.....	20–22	6,240
931J–01 L ( )	Rework E & H unit*.................	20–21	4,080
931J–01 M ( )	Rework camera electronics* (scan amp., blank amp. & sync. gen.)........	13–14	35,000
931J–01 N ( )	Preliminary console engr. & design*...	43–44	15,800
931J–01 O ( )	Final console engineering*...........	45–46	15,760
931J–01 P ( )	Assembly, camera*...................	40–41	2,650
931J–01 Q ( )	Assembly, total system into console*...	48–49	8,701
931J–01 R ( )	Engineer signal converter*...........	2–23	22,300
931J–01 S ( )	Purchase video amplifier............	2–36	5,000
931J–01 T ( )	Purchase tape recorder..............		34,000
931J–01 U ( )	Purchase orthicon image tubes, lens and power supply...............		11,300
931J–01 V ( )	Program management. Program manager & staff*....................		154,000
931J–01 W ( )	General material & supplies (technical)		13,250
931J–01 X ( )	Test and check out*.................		32,783
931J–01 Y ( )	Manufacturing (labor and material)...		28,342
931J–01 Z ( )	Handbooks........................		10,000
			$552,086

All costs include labor, material plus allocated overhead but no G & A allocation.
*Work package cost estimates include labor and overhead only. Material is separately charged.

EXHIBIT 4

DATOMATIC READER

Photonics Corporation

Extract from Slack Order Report for Datomatic Reader*

PERT System Datomatic Eye—Slack Order Report

Date 4 June 64

Event	TE	TL	TL–TE	TS	PR
01	0.0	0.5	+.5		
02	2.0	2.5	+.5		
05	7.7	8.2	+.5		
11	15.7	16.2	+.5		
12	15.7	16.2	+.5		
13	16.8	17.3	+.5		
14	22.0	22.5	+.5		
15	32.0	32.5	+.5		
34	32.0	32.5	+.5		
35	34.8	35.3	+.5		
40	34.8	35.3	+.5		
41	36.8	37.3	+.5		
42	43.5	44.0	+.5	44	.70
39	34.3	35.3	+ 1		
38	32.3	33.3	+ 1		
33	26.3	27.3	+ 1		
32	11.8	12.8	+ 1		

*Partial list only. Remainder of figures purposely omitted.

TE—is earliest time in weeks from start of project by which event may be completed.

TL—is latest time from start of project by which event may be completed if project is to be completed on time.

TL–TE—is designated "slack time" and represents time that may be used at the discretion of management in scheduling resources. Positive (+) slack is favorable, negative slack time (−) represents slippage already occurred.

TS—is the time of the scheduled demonstration and effectively represents the end of the critical path.

PR—is the probability of completing the sequence of events ending in the event adjacent to the PR, on or before the scheduled completion time for that event (TS). It is computed from variances of the events in the sequence.

EXHIBIT 5

DATOMATIC READER

Photonics Corporation

Extract from Slack Order Report for Datomatic Reader

(Rerun to Test Consequences of Eliminating Critical Path 2–5–7–12–13–14–15)

Date 4 June 64   Time in Weeks +6

Event	TE	TL	TL–TE	TS	PR
01	0.0	1.0	+1		
02	2.0	3.0	+1		
32	11.8	12.8	+1		
33	26.3	27.3	+1		
38	32.3	33.3	+1		
39	34.3	35.3	+1		
40	34.3	35.3	+1		
41	36.3	37.3	+1		
42	43.0	44.0	+1	44	.61

TE—is earliest time in weeks from start of project by which event may be completed.
TL—is latest time from start of project by which event may be completed if project is to be completed on time.
TL–TE—is designated "slack time" and represents time that may be used at the discretion of management in scheduling resources. Positive (+) slack is favorable, negative slack (−) represents slippage already occurred.
TS—is the time of the scheduled demonstration and effectively represents the end of the critical path.
PR—is the probability of completing the sequence of events ending in the event adjacent to the PR, on or before the scheduled completion time for that event (TS). It is computed from variances of the events in the sequence.

EXHIBIT 6

DATOMATIC READER

Photonics Corporation

Datomatic Reader Project Status Report

Datomatic Reader   Date 5 June 64   Weeks elapsed since start 6

Charge No.	Event Begin	Event End	Date Completed	Scheduled Completion Date Earliest	Scheduled Completion Date Latest	Scheduled Completion Date Slack	Actual Cost to Date*	Estimate	Revised Estimate	(overrun) (underrun)
931J–01A ( )	01	02	+2.0	2.0	2.0	0	$ 9,642	$ 8,520		($1,122)
931J–01R ( )	02	23		13.0	18.0	5.0		22,300		
931J–01D ( )	02	11		16.0	16.0	0.0	3,658	27,880		
931J–01F ( )	02	10		13.0	16.0	3.0	743	12,210		
931J–01B ( )	02	17		13.0	18.0	5.0	22,646	38,300		
931J–01E ( )	02	09		10.0	16.0	6.0	2,870	7,180		
931J–01G ( )	02	32		12.0	17.0	5.0	5,940	10,900		
931J–01H ( )	02	16		8.0	20.0	12.0	4,150	12,200		
931J–01C ( )	02	18		12.0	20.0	8.0	1,100	15,630		

*Taken from charge number cost summaries (Exhibit 7).

EXHIBIT 7

DATOMATIC READER

Photonics Corporation

Charge Number Cost Summaries for Datomatic Reader

Date 5 June 64   Sample Cost Summaries   Charge No. 931J–01 (   )

Charge No.		Cost Previous Reporting Periods	Cost This Period	Total Costs To Date	
931J–01	A–1	$2,132.26		$2,132.26	Engineering
931J–01	A–2	486.23		486.23	Design
931J–01	A–3	410.20		410.20	Drafting
931J–01	A–8	111.31		111.31	Quality Control
931J–01	A–9	1,000.00		1,000.00	(consultant Fee)
overhead		5,502.00		5,502.00	
Total		$9,642.00		$9,642.00	
931J–01	D–1	$ 57.21	$1,121.78	$ 1,178.99	
931J–01	D–3		151.23	151.23	
overhead		100.12	2,227.77	2,327.89	
Total		$ 157.33	$3,500.78	$ 3,658.11	
931J–01	F–1		$ 271.12	$ 271.12	
overhead			471.92	471.92	
Total			$ 743.04	$ 743.04	
931J–01	V–1	$5,455.01	$1,420.11	$ 6,900.13	
overhead		9,546.27	2,485.19	12,075.23	
Total		$15,001.28	$3,905.30	$18,975.36	

STAR
MANUFACTURING COMPANY

The Star Manufacturing Company, a small plastics molding company, was considering whether it should introduce a new product. Before a decision to introduce the product could be made, a sales price and appropriate level of marketing expenditures would have to be determined. On May 1, Mr. Richard Hosner, Star's vice-president of marketing, received a market research report on the product, which provided the following information about anticipated product demand after the period of introduction.

A. No sales would be generated if it were sold at a price greater than $5 per unit. Since the product's variable costs of manufacture will be $1 per unit, prices below $1 will not be feasible.

B. If no marketing expenditures are undertaken, at a price of $1 per unit, 100,000 units will be sold in January. It was further estimated that a linear relationship would exist between prices and monthly sales volume. Thus at a price of $2, for example, January sales would be 75,000 units, while monthly sales would be 25,000 units at a price of $4 (assuming that in both cases no marketing expenditures were made).

C. Marketing expenditures would increase the product's sales by

$$\frac{.1A}{.001A + 5}$$ percent over what they would have been if no ex-

penditures had been made. ("A" represents marketing expenditure dollars.) Thus, irregardless of the level of marketing expenditures no item sales would be generated at a sales price greater than $5 per unit.

D. The product's demand will be subjected to considerable seasonal influences. The table below provides a set of indices describing this seasonality.

January—1.0		July—1.0	
February—1.2		August— .8	
March—1.4		September— .6	
April—1.6		October— .4	
May—1.4		November— .6	
June—1.2		December— .8	

Thus, for example if no marketing expenditures were made in March, at a price of $1, Star would expect to sell 140,000 units. It should be emphasized that the linear relationship between price and monthly sales volume described in Section B holds for all months. Thus at a $3 price with no marketing expenditures, product sales in March should be 70,000 units.

E. Fixed manufacturing costs of $20,000 would be incurred each month.

QUESTIONS

1. Construct a Simulation model which will calculate Star's monthly profits and costs for different price and marketing expenditure levels.
2. Hand simulate the model for the months of January and February for the case where the sales price is $3 and the monthly marketing expenditures are $6,000.
3. Can your model be modified for use in finding the optimum price-marketing expenditure strategy?
4. Assume the following probabilities for January's sales

(a)

Unit Sales Volume at $1 Price	*Probability*	*Percent Increase in Sales if $A Spent On Marketing*	*Probability*
80,000	.2	$\dfrac{.1A}{.001A + 4}$	.1
100,000	.4	$\dfrac{.1A}{.001A + 5}$	.7
130,000	.4	$\dfrac{.1A}{.001A + 6}$	.2

Using the above probabilities and the table of random numbers listed below, make the suitable revisions in your model and hand simulate it for the month of January three times. (Be sure to start using the random numbers at a random point in the table.) You may assume all other relationships stated in the case will remain unchanged.

Random Number Table

80	05	42
15	18	21
98	47	74
86	47	14
61	13	25
26	68	24
48	23	95
75	40	93

VORTEX
WASHER CORPORATION (A)

The Vortex Washer Corporation, with home office and factory located in St. Louis, Missouri, ranked as one of the leading companies in the appliance industry. The Vortex product line included freezers, refrigerators, gas and electric ranges, automatic washers, and clothes dryers. In 1961, Vortex held approximately 10 percent of the automatic washer market in the United States, and other Vortex appliances were solidly entrenched in the major appliance market.

Vortex produced five different models of automatic washers for the consumer market. Each of the five models was manufactured on the same basic chassis, but each model was aimed at a different price segment of the market, and suggested retail prices ranged from $179 to $299. Each model was available in five different colors, plus white, with or without the "suds-saver" feature (an attachment which permitted wash water to be reused). In addition to the basic consumer line described above, Vortex manufactured automatic washers in coin-operated commercial models, and in export models.

Altogether, taking into account all possible combinations of model, color, and features, the company produced approximately 75 different types of washers.

COMPANY ORGANIZATION

The Vortex Washer Corporation was divided into three product-oriented divisions, and one sales division. Each of these divisions was headed by a vice president, and functioned as an independent organization.

The three product-oriented divisions (washer and dryer, refrigerator and freezer, and range) were organized on a functional basis, with managers of marketing, engineering, manufacturing, finance, and personnel. These three divisions were responsible for almost all activities related to Vortex's operations except the actual selling and distribution of the merchandise. Each product division was a separate profit center, and was expected to show an adequate return on investment each year. Manufacturing activities were carried out in three factories adjacent to the main warehouse in the outskirts of St. Louis.

From the point of view of the Vortex product divisions, company-owned distributors were similar to independent distributors. Like the independents, the company-owned distributors could order merchandise from the product divisions when they wished. Furthermore, both types of distributors could more or less establish their own selling prices, even though the product divisions set suggested selling prices. Company-owned distributors even handled merchandise which was not produced by Vortex, such as noncompeting lines of electrical appliances (e.g., toasters, television sets, garbage disposal units). Independent distributors as a rule handled everything from lawn mowers to stereo, but were required to sell the full Vortex line and were not permitted to sell competing major appliances.

The Factory

The washer and dryer division factory was highly mechanized. One assembly line was set up for washers, and another for dryers. Wherever possible, raw materials, subassemblies, and finished cabinets were transported by conveyer.

Washers were scheduled through the factory in batches. Batch sizes under 100 units were considered to be uneconomical, since with each model change workers on the assembly line had to be relocated, different components had to be transported to different locations in the building, and assembly operations had to be slowed down. Even a change in the color of units on the line required careful planning and scheduling. If necessary, as few as two or three units could be scheduled through the line, but many engineers considered 20 units to be a practical minimum. Every model in the Vortex line (i.e., 75 different models) was manufactured at least once a week. After final inspection and packaging, the finished units were delivered to the main warehouse adjacent to the factory (operated by the Sales Division).

Each unit passed through the entire manufacturing cycle, from raw materials to finished appliance, in several hours. Most washer parts, such as gear boxes, electric motors, timers, knobs, and wire harnesses, were purchased from outside vendors. Purchased parts in inventory at the factory had a stockturn of 15 to 20 times per year. Standardization of components was carried out wherever possible, in order to reduce the supply problem. Approximately 300 parts were common to all washers, while 125 parts were unique to certain washers.

An average washer represented about four hours of direct labor when completed. Washers at the high end of the line (i.e., the most expensive washers) required about 30 percent more direct labor than washers at the low end of the line. The factory was operated two shifts a day, five days a week.

Manufacturing costs in 1960 had the following approximate breakdown:

Materials	25%
Purchased Parts	30
Direct Labor	14
Indirect Labor	13
Manufacturing Overhead	18
Total	100%

All Vortex factory workers were represented by one union. Workers with seniority could "bump" other employees during any cutback of factory output, even between the three different product division factories. Most of the jobs on the assembly line could be performed after a few hours of training.

Planning in the Washer and Dryer Marketing Department

The preparation of the 1961 sales budget began in the autumn of 1960 with a study by the business research department of such factors as industry trends, consumer buying habits, and consumer credit. This study provided a "big picture" *forecast of total industry washer sales* each year up to 1965. The one-year-out forecasts were usually accurate within 5 percent.

The manager of the marketing department then worked out a *detailed marketing plan* for 1961, first setting a target for Vortex's share of total industry sales and then preparing a detailed plan, outlining how the target was to be achieved. The marketing plan was reviewed in meetings with the other department managers, and was sometimes modified in the light of manufacturing or financial restrictions. Eventually a complete division budget was drawn up, based on the marketing plan.

This budget was forwarded to the head office of the company, where the budgets of all four Vortex divisions were discussed at length. The four division vice presidents took part in these discussions. At this point, any discrepancies between, for example, what the washer and dryer division wanted to sell, and what the sales division believed it could sell, were resolved. The final budget for 1961 was established by December 1960. [1]

Working with the marketing plan, the manager of sales administration (within the marketing department) divided the national sales target into *regional quotas* which were then parceled out to the distributors. In January, at the "annual preview," the distributors had their opportunity to voice an opinion on the marketing plan. The annual preview was a display of new models presented at the factory every year. Distributors visited the factory to see the new models and to discuss the marketing plan. One member of the washer and dryer marketing department explained:

This is the arguing time. First, we argue about the quotas. Some quotas are changed. Then we argue about the new models. They tell us what will sell and what will not sell. Sometimes we change prices or features. At the same time, we make quite clear what our marketing plans for the year are going to be, what special promotions will be coming up, what our advertising plans are. The distributors leave with an awareness of what we are going to do all year.

Short-term sales forecasts by model, by month, were prepared by the sales manager in the marketing department. This "model mix sales plan" covered three months and was revised monthly. The sales manager was assisted in the preparation of the model mix sales plan through daily contact by telephone with his five marketing specialists in the field. In addition, each month, each distributor submitted to him an aggregate forecast of unit sales for the next 30 days. Also, the business research department supplied a monthly forecast of industry sales.

The model mix sales plan was used by the manager of sales administration, in establishing: (a) the recommended level of factory activity in terms of total units of output per week (i.e., the "factory rate") for the following quarter, and (b) the "factory shipments requirement," a detailed schedule of models required from the factory,

---

[1]Forecasts of the total national market, made by the business research department each year, were usually very accurate. Forecasts of Vortex sales were frequently off budget, as shown by the following historical data:

Year	1955	1956	1957	1958	1959
Vortex sales as % of budget:	135	110	80	85	90

by week, for 13 weeks into the future. To assist him in these decisions, the manager of sales administration was provided with a weekly computer printout of sales by distributor and model, and a weekly computer printout of inventory status, by model, in the main warehouse and in each distributor warehouse. Written departmental instructions prescribed the total units of washers and dryers to be maintained in inventory.

The manager of sales administration submitted his recommendation on factory rate each month to a regular meeting of the department heads and the division vice president. At this meeting the ultimate decisions on factory rate were made.

Planning in the Washer and Dryer Manufacturing Department

Planning in the manufacturing department was carried out at five levels:

(a) Establishing a *tentative level of factory output* for the year, based on forecasts and targets agreed upon in the annual budget preparation. This was done annually.

(b) Establishing *the factory rate* for the next quarter. This was subject to review each month, at the meeting of department managers and the vice president.

(c) Establishing a *13-week capability schedule* of output, by week, by model. This was revised each month.

(d) Establishing a *4-week schedule of output*, by week, by model. This was revised each week.

(e) Establishing the *daily line pack*, by model.

The setting of the over-all *factory rate* was a key decision, for it determined how many workers were to be kept on the job. The assembly line could be operated over a wide range of speeds, but with each change in speed it was necessary to vary the number of workers on the line. Changes in the employment level cost money. Some notice was required for workers to be hired and trained or laid off. Rebalancing production lines, lost production, and damaged goods all involved some expense, either direct or indirect. Constant and frequent changes in the production rate were therefore not desirable, and the decision on factory rate was made to cover several months at a time.

The *13-week capability schedule* was based on the 13-week factory shipments requirements sent to manufacturing by the manager of sales administration. The capability schedule set into motion the ordering of raw materials (steel sheet, vitreous enamel, etc.) and components required so that the factory would be capable of manufacturing to that schedule, if necessary. In theory, the 13-week capability schedule was a firm schedule, but it was seldom adhered to because of frequent changes in estimates by the marketing department.

The *4-week schedule* was a relatively firm commitment to go ahead with the manufacture of washers and dryers as stated. It was based on the 13-week schedule, modified by the latest information of the marketing department. The manufacturing department always attempted to match the 4-week schedule to the total unit output established by the factory rate decision. In other words, they scheduled to the factory rate.

The preparation of the *daily line pack* was carried out several days in advance. Since it established material flows through the factory, it was not feasible to make last minute changes in the line pack. At best, the marketing department would (and frequently did) argue for changes in the schedule one week in advance.

Problems in Production and Distribution

Although the production and distribution system of the washer and dryer division operated smoothly under normal circumstances, there were certain recurring problems. Many of these problems originated with the inventories held at various points in the distribution network.

The total inventory of Vortex automatic washers in the main warehouse and distributor warehouses fluctuated in volume between 50,000 and 100,000 units. Typically, another 60,000 units were held on the appliance dealers' floors. In terms of weeks of supply, at the average rate of retail sales, the inventory was positioned at the following locations (arrows show direction of flow):

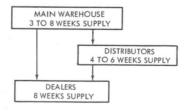

Certain fluctuations in inventory throughout the system could be anticipated (in response, for example, to the seasonal rise in automatic washer sales in August, September, and October). However, inventory levels periodically climbed to extreme heights under the influence of overoptimistic sales forecasts and a slowly responding production system. Just as frequently, sales forecasts were too low, and inventories were quickly drawn down. With inventories low, lost sales were incurred, dealers became angry over the shortages, and the distributors made life miserable for the marketing department in their efforts to squeeze additional merchandise out of the main warehouse.

Shortages were aggravated when rumors circulated that merchandise might be in tight supply. When such news leaked out, distributors flooded the main warehouse with orders, in an attempt to build up their own inventories before St. Louis warehouse stocks were depleted. Even if all of these orders were filled, there was a risk that much of the merchandise would be shipped to points where it was not really needed.

There were also problems arising from the mismatch of model mix. Typically, certain models were "hot" each year, and other models moved slowly. Thus, it was not uncommon for Vortex to build main warehouse and distributor inventories to a very high level, while at the same time experiencing shortages in the individual models which were in demand. The shortages impaired Vortex's capability to fill orders and the overstocking imposed penalties in terms of capital tied up and obsolescence.

Vortex planners attempted to meet quickly any inventory shortages which developed, but were handicapped by the time lags in scheduling units through the factory. The data used for decision making were frequently out of date or inaccurate, which added to the problem. Information on retail sales was derived from warranty cards mailed to St. Louis by purchasers of Vortex appliances, but not all cards were returned. Information on dealer inventories was derived from monthly reports submitted by each distributor, but was not very reliable. Even some of the reports submitted by the distributors on their own sales and inventories were prepared casually, Vortex officials suspected.

When merchandise was in inventory in the St. Louis warehouse, certain delays were inevitable before a customer received delivery of an order. For example, one typical order received in the main warehouse requested delivery of 90 units, consisting of ranges, refrigerators, washers, and dryers, to a department store in Denver. This particular order specified 65 different models, out of the 300 appliance models manufactured by Vortex. The order was first checked on an IBM RAMAC computer used for inventory control in the central warehouse. The RAMAC first checked to see if all 65 models were in inventory. It then checked prior commitments against the inventory for each model. Finally, the RAMAC checked the expected production date for those models which were out of stock or already committed to other customers.

When all the desired models were available, the order was turned over to a car planner, who designed full loads for trucks or boxcars. If he could make up a car to carry the order, the order was accepted. The order then moved out to the shipping clerks, who proceeded to load a boxcar for shipment. Transit time by rail to most points was in the neighborhood of a week.

All orders faced the same hurdles. There were several points where an order could be delayed while the distributor was asked for further instructions. On the average, a distributor on the West Coast would receive delivery 24 days after placing an order; a distributor in the Midwest would receive delivery in about 17 days.

VORTEX
WASHER CORPORATION (B)

SIMULATION OF THE PRODUCTION AND INVENTORY PLANNING SYSTEM

Introduction

The vice president of the washer and dryer division of the Vortex Washer Corporation agreed in the summer of 1960 to let the Harvard Business School case writer look at the simulation activities in his division. "Simulation is glamorous," he said, "and back in 1956 when we first got started on this project, the boys from the big computer companies had everybody convinced that all you had to do was do it! We're wiser now. Our simulation study has been under way almost five years, with preliminary studies starting in 1956, and a full-fledged project team working on it since the middle of 1958. And we've spent more money than we originally anticipated.

"What we have attempted to do is simulate the behavior of our entire production and inventory planning system for automatic washing machines. This summer the business research department has been making pilot runs with the model on the computer and we're at last getting some output from the project. The business research people are pretty fired up about the results of their work. I don't know how uniformly this feeling is spread through the company. Top management expects to get specific answers to some complex problems with this simulation."

The Proposal to Simulate Planning Systems

The proposal to simulate the Vortex production and inventory planning system had arisen partly in response to specific operating problems. These operating problems involved lost sales, extreme fluctuations in inventories, mismatch of model mix and time lags in manufacturing and shipping merchandise. It was believed the simulation might suggest solutions to operating problems and also remedy the lack of accurate data on the operating characteristics of the Vortex distribution network. The management of the Vortex Washer Corporation agreed to finance a broad-scale simulation study of the production and inventory planning system, as it related to the automatic washer business. The decision to go ahead with the simulation was facilitated by the fact that Vortex had access to a DRACON 550 electronic computer. Trial runs on an electronic computer would be an essential part of the simulation study.

The business research department of the washer and dryer division took charge of all phases of the project.

The project was aimed at devising a production and inventory planning model (designated the PIP model) which would behave in a manner similar to the real-life Vortex production and distribution system. With such a model the Vortex managers believed they would have, in effect, a laboratory for testing out new business ideas, and for exploring some of the complex forces and relationships affecting the distribution of automatic washers. Such experimentation could be carried on without risking disturbances to the current operations of the business.

The part of the simulation dealing with the Vortex inventory planning system was quite detailed; the part of the simulation dealing with the Vortex production system was confined to sales forecasting and overall production scheduling only. The simulation did not get involved with detailed production scheduling problems inside the factory.

As finally constituted, the PIP simulation attempted to portray the physical flow of automatic washers from the factory through the main warehouse, the distributors, and the retailers, to the ultimate consumers; and also the reverse flow of orders from consumers to the main warehouse.

Management expected to be able to answer many difficult questions with the PIP model, including the following:

1. What is the significance of persuading the appliance dealers to adopt systematic reordering policies?
2. What would be the effect of different reordering behavior on the part of distributors? Are distributor inventories in control with present reordering policies? What is meant by "in control?"
3. How important is information on dealer sales?
4. What is the value of more accurate sales forecasts in the factory?

5. What would be the effect if distributors improved their forecasting accuracy?
6. What would happen if distributor inventories were cut back, and main warehouse inventories were raised?
7. What would be the effect of reducing total inventories?
8. How continuous is the flow of merchandise from the main warehouse to the distributors, and from the distributors to the dealers?
9. What would happen if some of the time lags were reduced—in shipping merchandise to distributors from the main warehouse, for example?
10. What are the characteristics of the method presently used in setting production? Is the method fundamentally oscillatory? Does it minimize costs? Does it provide enough inventory, or does it provide too much inventory, in the sense of the long-term operation of the business?

General Outline of the PIP Model

As the first step in the PIP simulation project, the analysts of the business research department had to design a model of the existing Vortex production and inventory planning system. This model had to reproduce faithfully the behavior of Vortex's current business operations. As the second step in the PIP simulation project, policy changes would be tested on the model, and the effect of these policy changes on the operating results of the business would be observed. In this second step, the model would be altered in some significant way to reflect the policy changes which were under test.

The PIP model itself consisted of a number of hypothetical operating units (i.e., the factory, the main St. Louis warehouse, a number of distributors, a number of dealers) each of which behaved in accordance with carefully defined "decision rules." The decision rules governed the behavior of each of the operating units in the model. For example, the model specified that when a distributor's inventory reached a certain arbitrary level (called the dead-stock level) all further orders received in the week by that distributor were canceled.

Many "parameters" were used in the model, to define the characteristics of the operating units in the model, or to define the decision rules which governed their behavior. For example, one parameter defined the minimum inventory, or dead-stock level, for each distributor (the dead-stock parameter varied from 350 to 650 units in the PIP model). Another parameter defined the total number of distributors in the model (there were 10), and still another parameter specified the maximum percentage error in distributor forecasts of demand (this particular parameter was one which was varied to test various alternative policies on the model).

Certain "inputs" had to be specified to put the model into operation. For the PIP model, the major input was weekly national demand for automatic washing machines. Directly or indirectly, this input established (a) the production schedule which was set by the factory, (b) the orders placed by the distributors on the main warehouse, and (c) the consumer demand on the Vortex appliance dealers.

The flow chart in Exhibit 1 illustrates the general outline of the model which the business research department finally designed. The four major components of the model were:

1. Aggregate national demand.
2. 103 dealers.
3. 10 distributors.
4. Factory and main warehouse.

Some shipments were made directly from the main warehouse to some appliance dealers. These were the large dealers which could handle carload lots. All data were based on weekly activity, and seasonality factors were accounted for.

A detailed account of the design of the PIP model is presented in the Appendix.

Simulation Runs on the Computer

Once the PIP model design had been established, it was programmed into computer language. Simulation runs were then made with it on an electronic computer. Each simulation run was a replica of the week-by-week operations of the business. For each hypothetical week, a national demand input was specified by the experimenters. From this input, a factory schedule was established, distributor orders on the main warehouse were established, and the demand on individual Vortex dealers was established. Dealer sales to the public were made, dealer inventories were drawn down, perhaps some sales to the public were lost if inventories were inadequate, the dealers reordered merchandise from the distributors or directly from the main warehouse, and so on. At each point in the business, the operating units carried on their own activities, within the constraints of the model parameters, the decision rules which had been defined, and the inputs which they received from other operating units in the model. From the complex interaction of many separate operating units, a total picture of sales, inventories, and orders was eventually created.

The PIP model was a closed system. In other words, the computer did not stop a run at the end of every simulated week, or every quarter, and wait for new decisions to be fed into it. To the contrary, the computer would keep going on a single run indefinitely if it was permitted to, turning out one weekly report after another. All decision rules necessary to keep the system running were built into the model.[1] The model automatically forecast sales, set its own production rates, moved the inventory around, and made or lost sales to the consuming public, one simulated year after another. It was only necessary to provide a figure for aggregate national demand each simulated week.

The Output of Information

As a laboratory seeking to imitate the real business situation, the PIP simulation was designed to provide an output of information in the form of reports similar to those customarily used by the management of the washer and dryer division.

Each run of the simulation was the equivalent of a single laboratory experiment. Since the output of each run was in the form of operating reports, the model could not be said to answer a question in the sense of responding "this is good" or "this is bad." Rather, the model yielded operating data for interpretation by operating people in their usual manner.

If the Vortex managers wished to test the effect of some change in distribution policy (for example, a change in inventory policy) they prepared such a policy, converted it into explicit decision rules, and inserted it into the model, where it replaced the model's existing decision rules. Simulation runs were then made on the computer, using the new policy, and weekly operating reports were received as output. These reports displayed such information as main warehouse shipments, distributor sales, dealer sales, and inventory levels at all points in the distribution network, all for some specified time period. The simulated time period could be of literally any length, depending on how much computer time was consumed.

---

[1]There was always a remote possibility that the model could "explode;" that sales, for example, could grow so rapidly as to upset the whole system. Such extremes in behavior were inhibited by building heavy cost penalties into the factory scheduling rules. In real life, Vortex faced rigorous financial limitations, but the PIP model was not directly concerned with limitations set by earnings or working capital.

The PIP model was not a financial model. Throughout the model, data on inventory, orders, and shipments were expressed in physical units, not dollars. Hence, any analysis of costs, earnings, or investments, had to be performed outside the model.[2]

Accounting for Random Variables

The business activities which the PIP model attempted to simulate mathematically were influenced in real life by the occurrence of random effects. For example, the transit time for shipments of automatic washers from the St. Louis warehouse to distributors was never exactly the same from one shipment to the next. Shipping distances varied from distributor to distributor, and even to the same location, transit time varied. Transit time was subject to fluctuations which could be measured statistically. In other words, a probability could be assigned to the event that a shipment would take 10 days, and another probability could be assigned to the event that a shipment would take 11 days, etc. Thus, a probability distribution could be assigned to the parameter "shipping time."

The PIP model designers had to specify parameters such as shipping time in their model of the business. The simplest approach would have been to determine average or expected values for the parameters which were subject to statistical fluctuations. The single average value for each parameter could then be used to govern the behavior of the model. This would be equivalent to replacing the statistical problem by a related deterministic problem, and the single solution provided by the model would be in terms of the average or expected solution.

The PIP model designers knew that this approach to the problem was not very useful; it was better to learn that Vortex distributors were out of stock for 10 days each year, and greatly overstocked for 25 days each year, than to learn that, on the average, Vortex distributors had just about the right amount of inventory. The range or dispersion of operating results was in many cases more important than the average.

The simulation technique could handle these random effects. For each run with the PIP model on the computer, parameters were

---

[2]The subroutine used for determining production schedules did consider the cost of carrying inventory, and the cost of changing production. This subroutine was not an integral part of the PIP model, and produced a schedule expressed in physical units.

assigned in accordance with random distributions based on the statistical fluctuations observed in real life. For example, if 10 percent of the time it took five days to process an order at the main warehouse (as observed in actual practice), then there was a 0.10 probability that it would take five days for an order to be processed in the PIP model.

Due to the assignment of random values to parameters, no two runs of the PIP model on the computer produced the same operating data, even if the national demand inputs were identical and the decision rules of the model were unchanged. This characteristic of the model was in accordance with real life, but it limited the significance of data from any single trial on the computer. It was necessary to know whether the result of any single trial was a once-in-a-lifetime proposition or relatively commonplace.

It was therefore necessary to make many computer trials with the same decision rules and the same inputs, in order to generate meaningful and useful data. A range of operating data was obtained. In reporting the results of the experiments, the central or mean values could be picked out, or the whole broad band of values could be reported.

Observations on the Design of the PIP Model

One member of the PIP model design team made the following observations on the design of the model:

Wherever possible, we based the parameters and random distributions in the model on the actual parameters and distributions in the business. For example, the statistical distribution of order-processing delays in the PIP model was based on the actual statistical distribution of order-processing delays, as observed in the main warehouse.

National Demand. For aggregate national demand in the model we used actual industry sales for 1958. The fraction of total demand received by the PIP dealers was assumed to be equivalent to the market share which our dealers received in 1958. We *could* use total industry sales directly as our input, without defining our market share, but this would require a separate PIP model for each company in the industry. It would be more of a gaming proposition, with the demand on our dealers dependent upon relative prices and values, elasticities of demand, and cross elasticities. Obviously, this would be pretty complicated.

Dealers: The way we handled dealer size in the PIP model worried a lot of people. Some of the dealers in the model, for example, had such an enormous share of the national market they resembled nothing we have in real life. This is because we scaled up the size of each unit in the distribution network, to cut down on the computation. By doing this, we reduced the number of dealers from 10,000 to 103, and the number of distributors from 41 to 10. The final PIP model had a distributor-dealer system which was an extremely accurate representation of the actual business.

Distributors: We moved all the distributors in unison on the reordering decision rules.[3] This meant that they all behaved alike in the PIP model. We know this isn't the case in real life. With the simulation technique it is possible to introduce variations in forecasting behavior: one distributor consistently biased high, another biased low, a third with no bias but with a wide range. We could then see what effect these three lousy forecasters had on the rest of the system. This is why simulation is such a beautiful technique—you can feed in any behavior you choose.

The problem of model mix was introduced with distributor inventories. The PIP model handles aggregate units only, but we know that a distributor cannot keep accepting every order until his stock is down to zero; the chances are too great that he won't have the right model left in stock. To account for this in the PIP model, we divided distributor inventories (and the main warehouse inventory) into two categories: live stock and dead stock. Orders can be filled from live stock only. When the inventory is depleted to dead-stock levels, we assume model mix is so poor that all subsequent orders are rejected. Our selection of the dividing line between dead stock and live stock is fairly arbitrary, but of secondary importance. We are more interested in studying the effects of changes in the level of live stocks.

Factory Scheduling: The costs which we used in the factory scheduling subroutine were supplied by the manufacturing department and the finance department. For example:

(a)   Working capital tied up in inventory costs 5 percent. This charge is set by the head office of the company. It works out to approximately $4 per unit per year.

(b)   Warehousing charges are based on the standard assessment we received from the sales division, based on their cost of moving merchandise into the main warehouse, holding it, and moving it out. This charge is approximately $5 per unit per year.

(c)   Costs of changing production are based on a very large experience factor. These costs are a function of learning curves and many other intangibles that are hard to pin down exactly.

(d)   The cost of lost sales has been computed by the finance department based on the gross margin we realize on automatic washer sales.

---

[3]The reordering decision rules specified for the distributors are described in the Appendix.

EXHIBIT 1

Vortex Washer Corporation (B)

Flow of Demand Data, Inventory Data, Orders, and Shipments in PIP Model

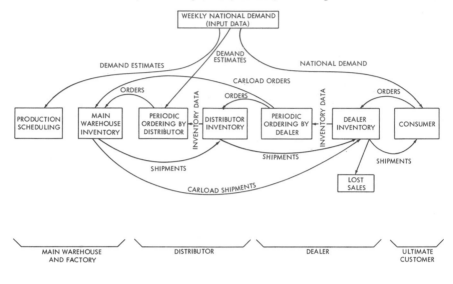

APPENDIX

Design of the PIP Model

I. The PIP Model of Aggregate National Demand

Aggregate national demand was represented by a series of numbers, arranged sequentially, one for each week. This series of numbers represented the weekly customer demand for automatic washers in the United States (in total units). It was used as a primary input in the PIP model, and determined, as explained later, the:

(a) *Actual weekly customer demand on individual dealers* (expressed in units per individual dealer).

(b) Distributor's weekly forecast of (a) for those dealers who are *his regular customers* (expressed in total units).

(c) *Main warehouse's quarterly forecast of customer demand on all dealers* (expressed in total units).

Parameter Values Chosen.   During a simulation run on the computer, any series of numbers could be chosen to represent aggregate national demand. These numbers represented the value of a *parameter*, or key variable in the simulation. The value actually assigned to the parameter "aggregate national demand" by the Vortex researchers was 1958 industry sales. Hence the individual parameter values were industry unit sales, by week, for 1958.

II. The PIP Model of Dealers

Each of the 103 dealers was identified in the PIP model by his number, the distributor in whose district he was located, and his method of ordering merchandise (a dealer could order either from the main warehouse, or from his distributor, but not from both). Each dealer was assigned a "size factor" equal to his share of the national market.

The *"new" customer demand* on each dealer was computed as follows: the input used was the weekly aggregate national demand. Each week, the week's national demand was distributed among the dealers in strict proportion to their share of the market. Then, a random fluctuation was superimposed upon each dealer's portion of the week's demand, and this resulted in each dealer's new customer demand for the week.

Each dealer's *total demand* for the week was the sum of his "new" customer demand for the week, and his unfilled customer demand carried over from the previous week (called the "carried demand"). It was assumed that a dealer could persuade a certain percentage of his customers to wait for delivery one week.

Dealer Operations.   Each abstract dealer was assumed to operate his business in the following manner, posting his books at the *end* of each week:

1.   The *merchandise available for sale* during the week was equal to the ending inventory of the previous week plus merchandise shipped to the dealer (from main warehouse or distributor) this week. Thus, merchandise shipped during the week was available for sale on the dealer's floor the same week.

2. ` The *dealer's sales* for the week equalled the dealer's total demand, or the merchandise he had available for sale during the week, whichever was less. The dealer was permitted to deplete his inventory to zero. This assumption implies (a) that a customer can be sold any model on the dealer's floor, or (b) that the customer goes from one Vortex dealer to another until he finds the right Vortex model in stock, or (c) that Vortex dealers trade with each other to meet shortages in particular models.

3.   After meeting customer demand as best he could, each dealer was faced with two possible situations at the end of the week:

    (a)   *Some merchandise still in inventory.* This ending inventory was used in computing merchandise available for sales next week.

    (b)   No ending inventory and *unfilled customer demand.* When such shortages existed, carried demand had priority (i.e., demand carried over from previous week). Any *carried* demand not filled this week was written off as lost sales. One half of the unfilled *new* customer demand was written off as lost sales, and the remaining one half became carried demand for the following week.

4.   The *time interval* between two successive orders placed by a dealer was determined on a random basis, without regard to the dealer's

inventory, new customer demand or shortage experience, and regardless of his experience with order processing and transit delays. A dealer's random attempt to place an order was automatically blocked (a) if he already had three orders outstanding, or (b) if he already had sufficient inventory. Once a dealer was blocked in filling an order, he repeated his attempt each succeeding week until the order went through. The subsequent reorder time was then determined on a random basis as before.

5. The *order quantity rule* was somewhat complicated, but order quantity was approximately equal to the dealer's sales since his last order, plus any orders which had been canceled by the distributor or main warehouse since he placed his last order. A dealer did not attempt to forecast demand, and did not take into consideration his inventory or outstanding orders when computing order quantities.

6. After a delay for *order processing time*, a dealer order resulted in either (a) shipment in full, (b) shipment in part, with cancellation of the balance of the order, or (c) cancellation of the entire order. The order processing time lag was determined on a random basis.

7. *Transit time* for shipments to dealers was considered to be negligible.

Parameter Values Chosen. The following values were assigned to some of the key parameters describing the operations of dealers during simulation runs with the PIP model:

Total number of dealers............................103
Share of national demand experienced by
    a dealer (after addition of random fluctuation)......$\frac{1}{10}$% to 6 %
Ordering relation................................ $\begin{cases} 17 \text{ factory-ordering} \\ 86 \text{ distributor-ordering} \end{cases}$
Interval between placement of order and receipt of
    shipment (distributor-ordering dealers only)........1 to 2 weeks
Interval between consecutive orders...................1 to 11 weeks

The interval between placement of order and receipt of shipment for a factory-ordering dealer was varied to suit the purposes of the simulation.

III. The PIP Model of Distributors

Each of the 10 distributors was identified by a number. A distributor's size factor was the sum of the size factors of all his distributor-ordering dealers (i.e., the collective market share of the dealers who were his regular customers). The essential differences between a distributor's and dealer's operations were the following:

1. Merchandise received during any week was *not* available for sale the same week.

2. A distributor was not permitted to carry unfilled demand over to a subsequent week. It was assumed that dealers would order another

manufacturer's appliances if Vortex appliances were not available for immediate delivery.

3. Each week, the distributor collected all dealer orders from his district (distributor-ordering dealers only) and attempted to fill these orders in a prescribed sequence. One week the distributor gave priority to lower-numbered dealers (no. 1, no. 2, no. 3, etc.) and the next week, he gave priority to higher-numbered dealers (no. 103, no. 102, no. 101, etc.) regardless of the actual inventory situations of these dealers.

4. A dead-stock inventory level was specified for each distributor. Orders could not be filled from this dead stock. When a distributor's inventory reached the dead-stock level, the balance of dealer orders for the week was canceled. This dead-stock rule was an attempt to introduce considerations of model mix into the PIP model. While the PIP model considered only aggregate units, without regard to individual models, it was known that when a distributor's inventory got too low, many orders had to be rejected because the right model was not in inventory. Thus, the PIP model designers assigned a dead-stock level (in total units) to account for the model mix problem.

5. A distributor placed a stock order on the factory every second week, except when (a) he already had three outstanding stock orders, or (b) he had insufficient inventory on hand. When these exceptions occurred, the distributor placed a stock order in the very next week.

6. In computing his stock order quantity, the distributor took into consideration (a) his inventory, (b) his outstanding stock orders, and (c) his forecast of the average weekly new customer demand on his distributor-ordering dealers during the next two weeks. Specifically, the order quantity rule was:

order quantity = K (demand forecast) − inventory − W (stock orders)

where:

K   = a factor
demand forecast = distributor's forecast of average weekly customer demand
inventory   = distributor's current inventory
W   = outstanding order weight factor
stock orders   = outstanding stock orders on main warehouses

The factor, "K" had to be specified for each distributor. The "outstanding order weight" factor "W" also had to be specified, to account for the distributor's expectation of actually receiving outstanding stock orders.

Parameter Values Chosen.   The following values were chosen for some of the parameters which characterized the distributors in simulation runs with the PIP model:

Total number of distributors 10
Share of national demand experienced
    by a distributor . . . . 1% to 8%
Minimum dead stock . . . . 350 to 650 units

The values of the following parameters were varied in individual simulation runs to suit the purpose of the particular simulation run:

Maximum error in distributor forecasts.

"K" factor in distributor stock-order rule.

Outstanding order weight factor "W" in distributor stock-order rule.

Factory to distributor order processing and transit lag.

IV. The PIP Model of Factory and Main Warehouse

The factory and main warehouse (considered as a single unit in the model) performed the following two functions:

1. It filled orders from (a) distributors, and (b) factory-ordering dealers, to the extent that merchandise was available, as described below.
2. It manufactured merchandise according to a calculated production schedule, as described below.

Order Filling. Each week, the main warehouse collected all orders which had completed their random order processing time during the week. The main warehouse attempted to fill these orders, giving priority to distributorships according to a numerical sequence (which was reversed weekly), and within distributorships always giving dealers priority over the distributor. The main warehouse followed this order-filling sequence mechanically, and did not take into consideration the inventory situations of dealers and distributors.

Dead-stock levels for the main warehouse were prescribed for shipments to dealers, and shipments to distributors, to account for model mix considerations. The dead-stock level for dealer shipments was lower than the dead-stock level for distributor shipments. When main warehouse inventory reached these levels, the remaining unfilled orders for the week were canceled.[1]

Production Scheduling. As conceived in the PIP model, the determination of a production schedule for the factory was a fairly complex and self-contained problem. It was, therefore, handled as a computer subroutine, distinct from the main PIP simulation.[2] The production schedule derived from the subroutine was then fed into the main PIP simulation.

Through the subroutine, the PIP simulation established its own production schedule on a quarter-by-quarter basis (that is, it established a three-month schedule every three months). The production schedule was not changed during this three-month interval.

---

[1] It will be recalled that each dealer added these cancellations back into his next order quantity, while distributors also adjusted their order quantities to compensate for cancellations, through their "weighting" of outstanding orders. Neither of these adjustments necessarily resulted in adequate protection since: (a) the dealer was not basing his order quantity on explicit forecasts of demand or order processing time, and (b) the distributor's outstanding order weight was not based on the distributor's actual experience with canceled orders, but was a parameter assigned by the model builder.

[2] A subroutine could be looked upon as a side calculation, not inherently part of the main computation.

The production scheduling subroutine was designed to set an optimum or least-cost schedule, taking into account:

1. The uncertainties of sales forecasts.
2. The penalties associated with:
   (a) Changing the production rate.
   (b) Carrying excess inventory.
   (c) Losing sales when inventories were inadequate.

Sales forecasts. Each quarter, the factory made a forecast of customer demand on all dealers, for three quarters into the future. The simulated forecast was derived by imposing a random forecasting error upon actual customer demand on all dealers. This basic forecast was then shaded up 10 percent and down 10 percent, to produce two more forecasts: an "optimistic forecast," and a "pessimistic forecast." Probabilities were assigned to each of the three forecasts, based on prior experience with forecasting accuracies.

Changing the Production Rate. A cost was attributed to changing the production rate. This cost included (a) cost of training workers, (b) rebalancing of assembly lines, (c) unemployment compensation to workers laid off, and (d) lost production. The total cost was assumed to be proportional to the units-per-week change in production rate. The cost for decreasing the production rate was proportionately higher than the cost for increasing the production rate.

Carrying Excess Inventory. For the time a unit spent in the main warehouse or the distributor warehouses, costs were incurred for (a) interest on the investment, (b) warehouse space, (c) taxes, (d) deterioration due to storage, and (e) transportation costs in and out of the warehouse. Total storage costs per unit were assumed to be proportional to the weeks spent in inventory.

Lost Sales. The costs of having inadequate inventory (i.e., lost sales) were difficult to evaluate, so were not explicitly included in the problem. Instead, a minimum allowable inventory, expressed in terms of "W" weeks of future sales, was used as a restriction on admissible production schedules. From experience, "W" was established at 10 weeks of supply in the combined main warehouse-distributor warehouse inventories.

The Production-Sales-Inventory Diagram

For each three-quarter (nine-month) sales forecast, a production-sales-inventory diagram can be sketched, as follows:

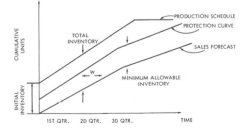

The diagram shows cumulative sales, and cumulative production. The difference between cumulative sales and cumulative production at any moment equals the total inventory in the system.

Based on the nine-month sales forecast, a "protection" curve is plotted, showing the minimum allowable inventory. The protection curve is the sales curve shifted to the left by "W" weeks.

For this particular nine-month sales forecast, the problem is to determine a production schedule so that the total cost of (a) changing the production rate, and (b) inventory storage, is minimized, and so that inventories never drop below the minimum allowable "W" weeks supply. The production rate can be changed every three months. This is essentially a problem in linear programming. Computer programs are available which will solve such linear programming problems. A program of this type was used in the production scheduling subroutine in the PIP simulation. It should be noted that the optimum or least-cost solution will not necessarily dictate a fixed production rate from quarter to quarter.

For each nine-month sales forecast—optimistic, regular, and pessimistic—the minimum cost production schedule is determined on the computer. In the diagram below, the three sales forecasts are represented by S_a, S_b, and S_c, and the corresponding optimum production schedules are P_a, P_b, and P_c. The sums of the costs of changing production rates and inventory storage are calculated (C_1, C_2, C_3) for each production schedule. These are the costs the business will experience if production is held at the planned optimum throughout the whole nine-month (three-quarter) period, assuming the relevant nine-month sales forecast is accurate.

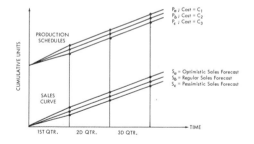

However, it is necessary to take into account the fact that the production rate will be changed after the first quarter if sales are higher or lower than anticipated. The second-quarter and the third-quarter schedules are open; only the first-quarter schedule is "locked up."

If a "high" production schedule (P_a) is set in the first quarter, and if the sales environment actually turns out to be in line with the pessimistic forecast (S_c), then at the beginning of the second quarter, a new and lower production schedule will be established.[3] Costs greater than the optimum

---

[3]Using, once more, techniques of linear programming to develop the least-cost production schedule for the remaining two quarters.

cost (C_3) for that sales environment are experienced, due to excess inventory and the change in production rate.

Conversely, if a low production schedule (P_c) is adopted in the first quarter, and if the sales environment is in accord with the optimistic sales forecast, then added expense will be incurred as the production schedule is raised at the beginning of the second quarter. The total cost for the nine-month period, even after a new least-cost schedule is adopted in the second and third quarter, will be higher than the minimum cost (C_1).

For each possible sales environment, and for each possible production schedule established in the first quarter, the total nine-month cost is computed (assuming adjustments are made to the production schedule where necessary). Probabilities are assigned to each sales forecast. A matrix can be constructed, showing costs and probabilities under each of the three possible sales environments.

Production Schedule	*Actual Sales Environment for Full 3 Quarters*		
Adopted in 1st Quarter	*Optimistic*	*Regular*	*Pessimistic*
	Probability $= F_1$	Probability $= F_2$	Probability $= F_3$
P_a (high)	cost $- C_1$ (minimum)	cost $= C_6$	cost $= C_8$
P_b (medium)	cost $= C_4$	cost $= C_2$ (minimum)	cost $= C_9$
P_c (low)	cost $= C_5$	cost $= C_7$	cost $= C_3$ (minimum)

The decision on which production schedule to adopt at the beginning of the first quarter now resolves itself to the choice of that production schedule with the lowest total expected cost, taking into account that sales forecasts are not completely certain. The expected costs are obtained by multiplying each nine-month cost by the relevant probability.[4]

By the use of this method, the optimum production rate was established every quarter in the PIP simulation subroutine. The production rate was expressed in units per week.

A random fluctuation was superimposed on the weekly rate to give the actual production schedule for individual weeks. This was the schedule fed into the main PIP simulation. A rule in the PIP model stipulated that a week's production was not available for filling dealer or distributor orders during the same week.

Each quarter, the slate was wiped clean, and a new production schedule was calculated, on the basis of fresh information, and unbiased by previous forecasts of production schedules.

Parameter Values Chosen. The following values were chosen for parameters which characterized the factory and main warehouse in PIP simulation runs:

---

[4]For example, the expected cost of the decision to adopt production schedule P_a at the beginning of the first quarter $= C_1$, $F_1 + C_6$, F_2, $+ C_8$, F_3. (Taking sum of costs across top horizontal row.)

Minimum dead stock for shipment to dealers . . . . 6,000 units

Random variation in production schedule . . . . $\dfrac{\text{schedule-actual}}{\text{actual}} = \pm\ 9\%$

The following parameters were varied to suit the purposes of the simulation:

Maximum error in factory forecasts
Desired weeks of main warehouse and distributor inventory
Minimum dead stock for shipment to distributors

V. Input for the PIP Model Run

In making runs with the PIP model on the computer, the experimenters had to establish certain starting conditions (such as beginning inventory) and then establish certain parameters to govern the behavior of the model during the run (such as the "K" factor in the distributor stock order rule). Furthermore, certain random distributions had to be fed into the model periodically (to establish, for example, the order processing time lags for dealers and distributors). Finally, the national demand input had to be specified for each week of the run.

The following table shows how many parameters, random distributions and subroutines had to be provided for each run. Not all of the parameters involved have been described in this Appendix.

	Number of Parameters			Number of Random Distributions	Number of Sub-routines
	Beginning Conditions	*During Run*	*Total*		
For each dealer	7	2	9	3	None
For each distributor	5	4	9	2	None
For factory and main warehouse . . .	2	22	24	1	For re-scheduling

The rescheduling subroutine also required the specification of parameters and random distributions, in addition to the ones listed above. The beginning conditions specified for the PIP simulation permitted it to operate on the business system as a going concern.

VI. Output from the PIP Model Run

The output of each PIP simulation run was in the form of operating reports, showing, for example, weekly data on:

Main warehouse shipments to dealers.
Main warehouse shipments to distributors.
Distributor sales to dealer.
Dealer sales to consumers.
National demand.
Main warehouse inventory.
Distributor inventory.
Dealer inventory.

Lost sales at the retail level.
Dealer orders canceled by the factory.
Dealer orders canceled by the distributors.
Distributor orders canceled by the main warehouse.
Fluctuations in scheduled factory production rates.

VORTEX
WASHER CORPORATION (C)

CALIBRATION OF THE PIP MODEL

Following the development of the PIP model [see Vortex Washer Corporation (B)] it was decided that before it could be used to test *changes* in business policies, it had to be demonstrated that the model could duplicate in a reasonable manner the operating results of the business under *existing* policies. With actual 1958 demand as input, operating data generated by the PIP model were compared with actual 1958 operating data. The designers of the model "tuned up" the model in successive calibration runs, changing parameters as necessary to approximate more closely the actual business system.

When the designers believed the PIP model was ready for final use, they made a "base run" with the model and compared the results with actual 1958 data. The results of this comparison are shown in Exhibits 1 and 2.[1]

For both the base run of the simulation (referred to as "pilot run no. 1") and actual 1958 performance, the following data are reported in Exhibits 1 and 2:

---

[1] A member of the business research department offered the following explanation of the 1958 *actual* operating results, as shown in Exhibits 1 and 2:

"Dealers started the year with a heavy inventory position and they tried to work them down for the first half of the year. Then the seasonal upswing in sales hit them. As usual, they saw their inventories going down further, thought business was great, reordered heavily—and were stuck with the merchandise when it finally arrived. They ended the year more than adequately supplied. The *factory* produced at a high rate for the first three months, then cut back as *main warehouse* inventories climbed. Then, the upsurge in orders cut down the main warehouse inventory very quickly. A false reading of dealer inventory needs caused the factory to step up output once more, main warehouse inventories were rebuilt, and the *distributors* also took heavy deliveries to rebuild depleted stocks. They overshot on inventories, and ended the year in an unbalanced condition. There isn't any *real* seasonality in washer sales, but the distributor sees a small upturn at the end of the summer and consistently orders more inventory. We *cannot* (or *should* not) take care of *everybody* in August. It's a matter of seasonal economics: a certain number of lost sales must be accepted as the price of not carrying excessive inventories."

Retail sales and customer demand.
Distributor shipments to dealers.
Total main warehouse shipments.
Retail inventory.
Distributor inventory.
Main warehouse inventory.

The simulated data are reported as a *range* of operating results derived from repeated trials with the PIP model. When the actual 1958 data fall within the range of the base run, and follow substantially the same seasonal pattern, this lends credibility to the simulation model.

Differences in Retail Inventory

A marked difference between the base run and actual 1958 data was observed in retail inventory. The designers of the PIP model explained this phenomenon as follows:

First of all, our information on retail inventory is very fuzzy, so we can't be sure that the 1958 actuals are reliable. The dealer's franchise specifies that he is to report his inventory of Vortex models at the end of the month, but this information isn't very accurate.

Also, we attributed systematic reordering procedures to the dealers in the base run, when in fact their reordering procedures are not systematic. This was a deliberate decision on our part. We didn't want to simulate actual 1958 behavior, because that behavior was very unsatisfactory, resulting in excess retail inventory at the end of the year. In order to simulate actual dealer reordering behavior we would have to build in some very bad and unsystematic decision rules. We are more interested in learning what would happen if systematic decision rules were adopted.

Nevertheless, one cannot be sure what conclusions are to be drawn from the differences between the 1958 estimates and the band for the base run. This is one area where additional investigation could be made.

Evaluating Business Performance in the Base Run

The base run was compared to actual 1958 data in terms of four basic criteria:

1. Cost to keep inventory (less working capital charges) plus cost to change production rates.
2. Working capital tied up in inventory.
3. Percent of lost retail sales.
4. Degree of business stability.

The degree of business stability was a measure designed to reflect the tendency of the model to smooth out year-to-year fluctuations in the business. The criterion adopted was the annual change in units of lost sales. A member of the PIP model design team explained:

Assume that demand is constantly rising. If our decision rules are fundamentally oscillatory, we might undershoot demand one year and overshoot the next. Lost sales (in total units) measure the degree by which we undershoot demand, and if lost sales fluctuate widely from year to year, then our business system is not very stable, as the following sketch illustrates:

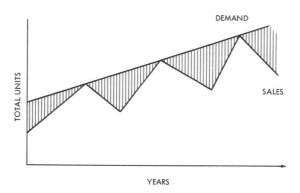

shaded area = lost sales

In terms of the four criteria, the base run compared with actual 1958 performance is shown below:

	Actual 1958	Base Run (Pilot Run No. 1)
Cost to keep inventory and change production rates	$1,000,000	$ 770,000
Reduction in working capital compared to 1958	——	1,300,000
Percent of lost sales	n. a.	0.6%
Degree of business stability	n. a.	+ 2,000 units

The base run showed an improvement in cost position and capital requirements compared to actual 1958 data. A member of the PIP team concluded:

Since the base run differs from actual operating procedures in only one major detail, the bulk of the performance improvement is reasonably to be ascribed to that detail. This detail is the model's assumption of a systematic ordering procedure on the part of distributors and dealers. We can reasonably conclude that if, in reality, a systematic reorder procedure were used, then costs associated with inventories, production changes, and working capital would also be reduced.

Pilot Runs with Modified Policies

The experimenters were now in a position to test on the PIP model the effects of *changes* in business policies. A series of five pilot runs was made, using the same 1958 demand data as input, but employing different parameters in some aspect of the model. Each run was made for a period of three years. This permitted short-run effects to work themselves out and gave a longer term opportunity for appraisal of the effect of the planned policy change.

Each policy was tested on a cumulative basis. The effect was to ask what the impact on the business would be of policy A, then policy A plus policy B, etc. The sequence of policy changes tested on the model represented a logical sequence of changes which could be proposed for the actual business.

The pilot runs finally reported were the following:

Pilot Run 1: Base run and test of systematic reordering (already discussed).

Pilot Run 2: Testing the effect of reducing forecasting errors by factory.

Pilot Run 3: Testing a reduction in distributor inventory levels.

Pilot Run 4: Test to reduce total factory-distributor inventories and distributor forecasting errors.

Pilot Run 5: Testing use of better model mix in main warehouse to reduce inventory dead stock.

Pilot Run 6: Testing reduced time delays in order processing and transit. Also, increase weight given to outstanding orders by distributors.

The parameters used in the PIP model during each of the pilot runs are shown in Exhibit 3.

Evaluating Business Performance in the Pilot Runs

The pilot runs with changed parameters were evaluated for business performance under the same four criteria applied to the base run. The results of the six pilot runs (including the base run) are reported in Exhibit 4.

The pilot runs were compared with the performance bench marks established in the base run (pilot run no. 1). The pilot runs could have been compared directly with actual 1958 data, except for the lack of data on lost sales. Information on lost sales was not available in company records, and it was necessary to rely upon the base run to provide a lost sales bench mark.

Comments on the Pilot Runs

One member of the business research department offered the following comments on the findings of the PIP simulation pilot runs:

In the base run (pilot run no. 1) we checked out the value of systematic distributor and dealer reordering policies. We know that in actual practice, few distributors and probably no dealers have systematic rules they follow in reordering merchandise. The conclusion we reached is that systematic reordering rules are immensely beneficial to the business. Under systematic rules, we don't overship merchandise as the result of a false reading of the seasonal upswing in sales. Instead, we get the merchandise out to the dealers in advance of the seasonal upswing, as we should.

In pilot run no. 2 we wanted to test the comment that is frequently made: 'If only we had better forecasts.' As you can see from the results of the simulation, better factory forecasts of consumer demand are really not very helpful. Admittedly, accurate short-range forecasts of orders placed on the main warehouse would be very useful. However, if the production system can respond fairly quickly to modifications in forecasts, then the long-range forecasts don't help much. Inaccurate long-range forecasts can always be adjusted bit by bit until we arrive at an accurate short-range forecast which determines factory output. We have a hard time selling this idea to management.

In pilot run no. 3 we evaluated another common suggestion: 'Keep the inventory in the main warehouse, and not in the distributor warehouses.' We did this by changing the distributor reordering rule, so that the distributors wanted to carry fewer weeks of inventory. At the same time, we did not touch the factory rule specifying the total weeks of desired inventory in both the main warehouse and distributor warehouses. The result was to shift inventory to the main warehouse. The simulation showed that the result of this change of policy was a considerable increase in percentage of lost sales, with a reduction in costs and working capital.

In pilot run no. 4 we wanted to evaluate the effect of reducing total inventories in the system, while improving distributor forecasting accuracies in compensation. We had in mind spending money on elaborate market research which we think could give us this information, if we want to pay for it. There was a significant increase in lost sales in pilot run no. 4, but there were also compensating financial benefits. Nevertheless, random effects, such as the lag in delivery time and order processing time, again cut into the value of increased forecasting accuracy, and the gains were not substantial. Even if our forecasts are more accurate, it does not help us if we can't deliver the merchandise in time to meet the demand.

The question now was, can the financial benefits be retained while improving the sales picture? The answer is 'yes' under the changes tested in pilot runs 5 and 6. In pilot run 5 we evaluated the effect of better inventory control in the main warehouse, so that dead-stock levels could be reduced without incurring model mix problems. This would require more elaborate data processing facilities in the main warehouse, and possibly a redesign of the entire washer line to reduce model mix problems. In pilot run no. 6 we checked the result of giving the distributors more assurance of actually receiving delivery of the orders they place, and the results of reducing time lags in shipping from the main warehouse. Here again, we had in mind principally better order processing methods, and the use of random-access data processing equipment for inventory control. It is apparent that if these changes were introduced, the detrimental impact on sales shown in pilot run no. 4 would be reversed, and the cost picture would be further improved.

One may now consider the impact on the business of the six cumulative changes, as represented by the base run and the other five pilot runs, in comparison to actual 1958 policies. The contrast is one of substantial financial improvement, together with moderate increases in lost sales and decreases in stability. There are, of course, other measurements relevant to the distribution system of our business, and other policies might be proposed and tested by this simulation.

From here on out, the effectiveness of this simulation will depend upon the ingenuity of the operating people who use it. I believe the data we have generated on lost sales will in itself be a complete justification for the effort we have put into this project. Up to now, such data simply haven't been available.

Management Reaction to the PIP Simulation

By the middle of 1960, after an expenditure of approximately $150,000 on computer time, and the full-time effort of four people in the business research department for a period of two years, the PIP simulation had reached the state reported in this case.

Managers in the Vortex Washer Corporation found the reports of the PIP simulation interesting. Reactions ranged all the way from enthusiastic to skeptical. One manager said that "If you make enough assumptions, you can prove anything!"

Another manager expressed flat disbelief in the data on lost sales: "We don't really lose many sales, because the distributor can always talk the dealer into taking another model. Our distributors panic when they see a dealer backing his truck up to the warehouse for the third time in one day, only to find the model he wants is not in stock. When he drives away they assume they have lost a sale. I believe most of them come back again, or else take another model." This view was disputed by a manager who believed that the volume of lost sales was high, and a matter for serious concern.

One manager was very enthusiastic about the PIP simulation: "I think that this simulation has given us the answers we need to make some fundamental changes in the operating policies of the business."

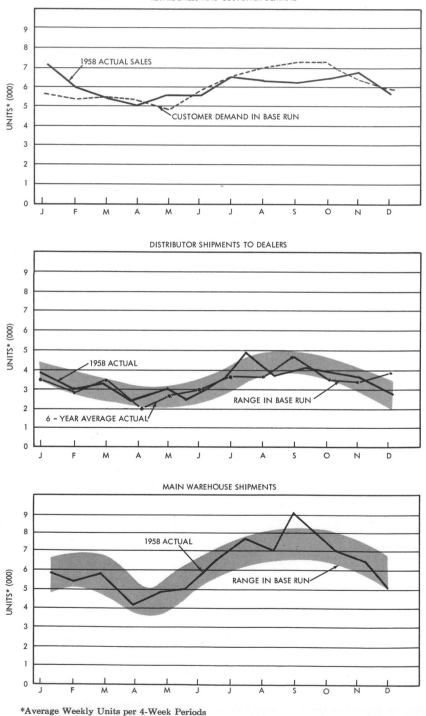

*Average Weekly Units per 4-Week Periods

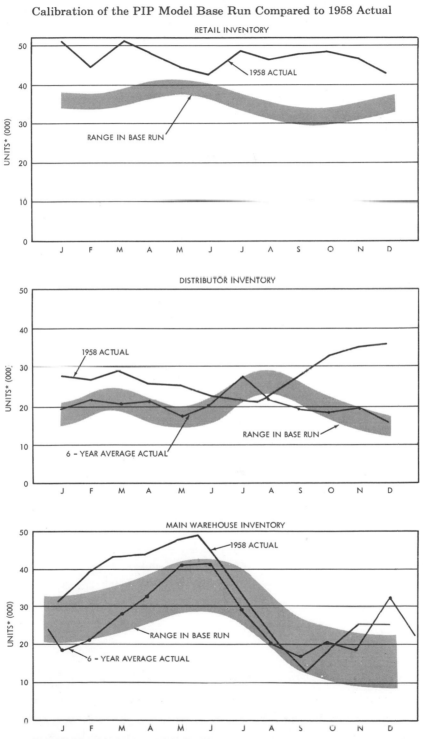

EXHIBIT 2

VORTEX WASHER CORPORATION (C)

Calibration of the PIP Model Base Run Compared to 1958 Actual

*Average Weekly Units Per 4-Week Periods

EXHIBIT 3

VORTEX WASHER CORPORATION (C)

Parameters Assigned During Pilot Runs with PIP Simulation

Note: The parameters which were changed in successive runs are circled. Changes were introduced cumulatively.

Parameter	Pilot Run Number					
	1	*2*	*3*	*4*	*5*	*6*
Maximum range of random error assigned to factory forecasts of national demand	± 10%	± 5%	± 5%	± 5%	± 5%	± 5%
Number of weeks of inventory distributors wish to carry ("K" factor as described in the appendix to Vortex [B])	10	10	7	7	7	7
Number of weeks of inventory factory wishes to carry in both main warehouse and distributor warehouses	8	8	8	5	5	5
Maximum range of random error assigned to forecasts of demand made by individual distributors	± 70% to ± 21%	± 70% to ± 21%	± 70% to ± 21%	± 35% to ± 10%	± 35% to ± 10%	± 35% to ± 10%
Dead-stock level in main warehouse, from which no shipments to distributors can be made. (Units)	18,000	18,000	18,000	18,000	9,000	9,000
Weight assigned by distributors to their probability of receiving orders placed on main warehouse ("W" factor described in the appendix to Vortex [B])	0.57 to 0.93	0.57 to 0.93	0.57 to 0.93	0.57 to 0.93	0.57 to 0.93	0.67 to 1.00
Range of random order-processing and transit time lag from main warehouse to:						
(a) distributors (weeks)	1–8	1–8	1–8	1–8	1–8	1–6
(b) dealers (weeks)	2–4	2–4	2–4	2–4	2–4	2–3

EXHIBIT 4

VORTEX WASHER CORPORATION (C)

Comparison of Pilot Runs and 1958 Actuals

Measurement 1 – Cost to Keep Inventory & Change Production Rate.
Measurement 2 – Change in Capital Required Compared with 1958.
Measurement 3 – Percent Lost Sales.
Measurement 4 – Degree of Business Stability.

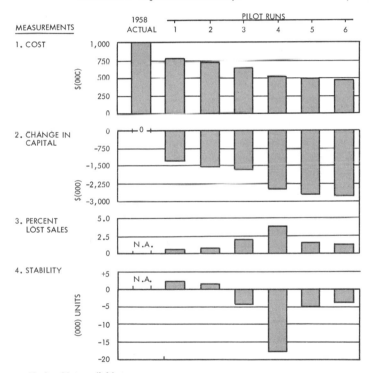

N. A.—Not available

RIDGEWAY
AIRCRAFT COMPANY

BACKGROUND

Ridgeway is a large, diversified company whose main business is development and production of guided missiles and control systems. Currently employing over 60,000 persons, its manufacturing and research facilities are primarily located in the west and southwest portions of the United States. It was initially organized as an airframe manufacturer in the late 1920's.

In the early 1950's Ridgeway's management recognized the limited opportunity for growth in the airframe industry and initiated an extensive program of diversification. In 1954 they received their first prime contractor award for guided missile development. The highly satisfactory performance on this contract helped them acquire other missile development and manufacturing contracts. By 1964, guided missiles and their systems development accounted for nearly two thirds of the company's total business, or some $300 million a year.

Ridgeway maintains a large research and development laboratory near San Diego. Over 3,500 persons are scattered among five buildings. The group is directed by Mr. Grosscup, the laboratory manager. Serving him, but not directly responsible to him, is Mr. Gordon, the laboratory controller. His staff totals 109 men and is divided into three sections (see Exhibit 1). They are responsible for the collection, analysis, and summarization of all financial data pertaining to the laboratory's activities. Mr. Gordon, along with eight other divisional controllers, reports directly to the company controller, Mr. Holmstrand.

Under Gordon is a financial analysis section headed by Mr. Winters. This section reviews and analyzes the financial data concerning the various projects in the laboratory for Mr. Gordon. The section also assumes special analytical projects. One of the special projects being carried on by the group in 1964 was "information analysis."

Origin of the Information Analysis Project

Ridgeway's rapid growth in the missile field substantially affected the research and development group in San Diego. In 1954 it employed approximately 400 persons. Presently it employs over 3,500 persons and is growing 25 percent per year. This growth has been accompanied by the development of a complex supporting structure.

For example, the financial area, which employed less than ten people in 1954, and which had grown to over fifty by 1961 (it was then split into three sections: accounting, budgets, and financial administration), today contains over 100 people.

As the financial organization evolved, a predictable decrease of communications occurred within and between its sections. Studies revealed that different groups were preparing reports which had only slightly different information content. Also, some obsolete reports were still being created. For example, one report regularly distributed to several persons was used by none, yet all thought the report was utilized by the others.

Although the extent of the problem had not been quantified, certain financial executives felt the situation was sufficiently critical to deserve immediate study. Consequently, at a meeting of financial management in July 1964, Mr. Winters was requested to investigate the nature and dimensions of the problem.

Early Information Retrieval Projects

During the following two months, on a part-time basis, Mr. Winters investigated the problem. He was aware that other companies, as well as his own, had already attempted or were in the process of formulating a concept called information retrieval. The object of the information retrieval concept was the installation of a complete information system. Computer programs would be developed to answer such questions as:

1. What pieces of information make up a figure or piece of data on a particular document? Using a computer, the flow of data in various documents, that led to the creation of the figure in question, could be traced and then displayed by the computer printer.
2. What are the historical figures for a particular item?

Winters interviewed responsible persons within the outside companies, as well as the individuals in Ridgeway Aircraft who had worked with information retrieval systems. He discovered some companies had worked over two years on their systems, without notable success.

At Ridgeway, the information retrieval project had been dropped after nine months' work. The problems cited to Winters for the concept's lack of success fell into two categories:

1. The project designs were too ambitious, and required too much manpower. Especially critical was the time necessary merely to collect data before any analytical work could commence.

2. There was a general lack of top management support for these projects. Such a project involved all areas of the organization and necessitated complete cooperation of all management personnel. Effective results and analyses could not be obtained until data collection was completed, since the interaction of all data had to be observed before any significant conclusions could be drawn. The size of this initial expense, and the necessity for complete involvement of all personnel, was such that management resisted this "all or nothing" approach and insisted on shorter term goals. Also, since the information retrieval concept was in its infancy and highly complex to implement, mistakes had been numerous and progress correspondingly slow.

These interviews plus cursory analysis of currently used documents caused Winters to believe that two factors would be critical to the project's success.

First, both the laboratory manager and the laboratory controller would have to actively support the project and advise the appropriate group managers of its importance.

Second, management should accept a less than full-fledged information retrieval system. Winters called his system information analysis (Exhibit 2 summarizes his original proposal). The essential difference between Winter's method and information retrieval was eliminating the gathering of substantive information. To expedite the data collection process, only *types of information* and *types of data* used within the organization would be collected, rather than the specific substance of that data. For example, the term "monthly department budget" would be considered a collectible data type, rather than its substance, the actual dollar figures of each department. Winters regarded this as a heavy, but essential compromise to the necessity of obtaining more immediate results than others had experienced with information retrieval systems.

COLLECTION AND CLASSIFICATION OF DATA

Recognizing that he still had a voluminous data collection problem, Mr. Winters and two aides spent the next month devising a systematic method of collecting the data from reports in the financial structure. Because of the lack of manpower within Winters' section, it was decided that the person who actually originated each financial report would provide the information concerning his report. Winters also felt the originator of a report could most effectively describe the function of his report.

Next, attention was focused upon the mechanics of gathering accurate detailed information concerning each document from the people within the financial organization. Winters' group had to design a form and instruction sheet which would produce all necessary information, yet not be so complex as to require personal instruction in how it should be filled out. Exhibit 3 presents the form initially developed. Attached to the form were instruction sheets and a list of standard abbreviations (such as A/P for accounts payable) to be used in describing the data.

The pieces of data within a particular document were labeled as elements. These elements would be coded as to type and allied to the document in which they were contained. They would then be placed in a computer memory and a program devised to trace out the element flow. This would provide a "family tree" of financial data which would reveal the repetitions, relationships and interactions of data within the financial organization.

Each major piece of financial information could be traced back to the initial basic elements. Conversely, the successive elements and reports formed by a basic element could be identified (see Exhibit 3a).

Procedure for Arranging Hierarchy of Elements

Winters prepared a program which operated on these elements as follows:

1.   A magnetic tape was used for computer input. It serially listed each document number. After the document number the following information concerning the document's elements was included:
    a.   the element's identifying number.
    b.   whether it was a basic, compound or accumulative element.[1]
    c.   whether it originated in the document.
    d.   if it was a compound or accumulative element, a list of the elements that were used to make it up.

---

[1]a. *Basic Element*—the basic or first unit of information beyond which further breakdown is unnecessary for financial purposes. Examples: Weekly pay for nonexempt employees, number of working days in a year.

  b. *Compound Element*—comprised by combining two or more *different* compound elements, basic elements, different accumulative elements, or any combi-

(*Continued on next page*)

2.   The computer searched this tape and stored all the basic element numbers serially in magnetic core location A.

3.   Each document of the input reel was then analyzed. If all its elements were original entries or computations based on these original entries, its document number would be stored in core location B. If all its elements were not original entries or computations, the document number was stored in core location C. Thus, the document numbers stored in core location B indicated source documents.

4.   The individual documents in core location C were then examined. If all elements were either original to the document, or were derived from documents in core location B, the document number remained in core location C. Otherwise, it was moved to core location D. This process continued until the documents were sorted in proper hierarchy. For example, a document in core location E would contain information from a document in core location D and might also contain information which came directly from documents stored in core locations B and C.

5.   The format of the printer's output was as follows: The paper in the computer's printer was divided into six vertical columns numbered 1 to 6 from left to right.

6.   All the basic elements listed in core storage area A were serially printed (including both name and number) in column 1. All source documents (i.e., all documents listed in core storage area B) had each of their elements listed by name and number in column 2. Each document's elements were grouped together and arranged numerically. All documents listed in core storage area C had each of their elements listed in column 3, etc. At the same time, the computer traced the movement of each element from column 1 to their final location by means of dotted lines. Also, it traced the development of compound and accumulative elements within columns.

Exhibit 4 presents a sample of the computer output. For example, it shows the division number as a basic element labelled 0006. It initially appears in two documents: document 31 and document 32. Similarly it indicates that employee wage is a compound element appearing first in document 42. It is developed from basic elements 0003, 0004, and 0005. In reading Exhibit 4, the number over each element's name is interpreted as follows:

1.   The first two digits indicate the document it is currently in.
2.   The last two digits indicate the element's number.

---

nation thereof. Example: Hourly pay for nonexempt employees, which is computed by combining two basic elements (weekly pay and regular working hours in a week).

   c.   *Accumulative Element*—accumulation of the *same* element, but involves several quantities of that element. Example: Departmental Payroll, which is computed by combining several similar compound elements (employee pay).

The computer program was complex and difficult to prepare. Fortunately, however, Mr. Winters was able to take two already completed programs and, by merging them and adjusting about 15 percent of the steps, produce the desired output.

Initial Results

Mr. Winters termed the program's initial trial output "highly encouraging". While substantial changes were needed to prepare the final product, he felt it had substantiated the workability of his approach and that the data collection phase could proceed. Some of the areas which he felt needed modification are described below:

1. Even with only eight documents, the number of vertical lines tracing element paths were so numerous it was confusing. When the full system was in operation, it was evident, there would not be enough room for all the lines between each pair of columns; and even if there were, it would be too complex to trace completely all elements.

2. The organization of documents and the progression of written information was not as straightforward in practice as it was in theory. For example, in certain cases information appearing on Document (A) goes directly to Document (B). Other information on Document (A) goes to Document (C) where it is manipulated and processed on to Document (D). Then both Document (B) and Document (D) are used to prepare Document (E). Here the problem encountered in allocating a column for Document (C) alone was not handled correctly by the program. There were also other minor errors in the program.

Mr. Winters, however, felt these problems could be overcome by inverting the order of priorities and eliminating the lines. He visualized a computer output similar to that shown in Exhibit 5.

Instead of starting with the basic elements and working up to a set of cumulative documents, as in Exhibit 4, this procedure starts with the elements in each of the documents and traces them back to their basic elements. This technique produces a much larger output, but improves its printed format. The element on the left is the most highly compounded and accumulated figure. As one moves across the page to the right one works down towards the basic elements.

Evaluation of Project Based on the Initial Results

With his ideas crystallized and his system passing its initial dry runs, Winters prepared a report for Mr. Gordon. The highlights of this report are summarized below.

1. In its ultimate sophistication, which would be five years off, information analysis could evolve into a real time application for financial

management. Finance would have momentarily available all its data. The data would be collected, digested and analyzed within the computer and would allow, potentially, instant decision making by managers.

2. This, however, was still the project's ivory tower speculation. Immediately, information analysis should serve as a reports directory, allowing the financial organization a continuous and efficient record of its changing data and report structure. In addition, it would inform financial management at a glance as to its data resources.

3. It would begin to remove the personality as an integral part of the organization—the indispensable man with his unique knowledge would become a diminishing figure. Reliance could be placed upon the developing index of data, rather than on individuals with specialized knowledge. The individual could spend more time on the thought and judgment process. It would suggest changes in the organization structure and aid in eliminating some reports, combining others, and adding needed reports. The financial organization would be a communicating unity, rather than several separated entities.

4. Finally, outside the financial organization, other departments within the company faced the same type of problems. Successful results, therefore, could mean the implementing of techniques that would have widespread applicability, which would enhance the prestige of the financial organization. Ridgeway owned controlling interest in a subsidiary which manufactured medium- and large-sized computers. Problems of this sort offered promising applications for high-speed data processing equipment, and the programs used in the information analysis systems could have considerable value in the commercial marketplace.

DATA COLLECTION: PILOT STUDY

The following day Gordon gave approval to Winters' plan and Winters immediately began implementation of his goals. Winters recognized that the first phase of his project, the task of gathering the data concerning the present operations of the various departments, was absolutely indispensable to the project's ultimate success. No sophisticated techniques of analysis could rectify any errors of faulty input data. Therefore, Winters decided to first use an experimental group of ten persons to test out the effectiveness of his data collection plans.

The experimental group was selected from the accounting section. An hour-long meeting was spent describing the information analysis process, together with its objectives, and explaining the instructions for completing the forms. Winters then made himself and his staff available for consultation purposes. The experimental process took nearly a month, although Winters had hoped originally to complete the experiment within two weeks. In his written monthly progress report to Gordon, Winters' comments concerning the results of the experimental groups were as follows:

1. It became quickly evident that the number of elements and documents was two or three times the size of the original estimate.
2. There is a stringent need to develop a standard method of naming element types. Different people identify the same element by different names. Unless a uniform procedure is developed, the machine will be unable to identify two identical elements as actually being the same.
3. The editing job has been underestimated. One person will be needed solely for editing the completed forms, describing each document. The addition of another man to the project would be most helpful.
4. The differences in the intelligence and the attitude of the individuals has resulted in some documents being completed with care and sophistication, while others have required considerable editing and in some cases have had to be returned to the originator. Similarly, it was also found that some individuals lacked a perspective as to how their report and the elements therein integrated into the financial structure as a whole. They did not fully comprehend that ignoring the source of a particular element, or to where it descended, would leave out an important branch of the family tree concept.
5. As expected, the project was almost unanimously treated by the control group as an extra workload which would not enhance their status. They perceived that no special credit would be given for doing a superior job, and that the financial analysis group would receive any plaudits.

Thus concluded Winters, the most significant problem would be the education of the personnel as to the project's perspective and its method of execution.

Project Revisions as a Result of the Pilot Study

Gordon told Winters he would like Winters' specific recommendations concerning the project within the next two to three weeks.

Winters began revising his system. He now believed that to insure proper preparation of the forms describing each document, it would be necessary to sit down with each individual to review his respective report and discuss specifically how to complete the form. This would be in addition to the preliminary presentations.

To shorten the workload in data collection he decided to eliminate elements that did not involve dollars or hours. Other elements, such as accounting codes, parts number, purchase order numbers, etc., would be called identifiers and be listed on each report, but would not be treated as an element. There was much discussion over this revision within Winters' group, but the expediency of providing a short-term output for management, together with the potential morale problem, appeared to justify the decision.

Finally, it was decided to use two forms for data collection. One would describe the documents and the other describe the elments. For the element form, a technique was devised in which several elements could be placed upon one page. This technique eliminated over 50 percent of the number of forms, although it did little to lessen the workload. This psychological factor, however, was well received by the experimental group.

Presentation to Gordon

At the month's end, Winters presented his recommendations to Gordon. He stated that the changes from the original information retrieval concept would provide immediate results that would:

1. Rectify finance's communications problems.
2. Provide a reports directory.
3. Streamline its report structure.
4. Provide a prompt and sagacious education device for the organization's personnel.

He emphasized however, that these compromises would delay realization of the longer-term goals. He also indicated that despite the immediate improvements, the information analysis project's additional workload would still have disrupting effects. He stated that the average time to code a single document for computer processing was half a man-day, although certain complicated reports could take up to three man-days.

Mr. Winters recommended that if the information analysis project was to be implemented the data collection process should be expedited. This would minimize the negative reaction to the extra workload in the organization. Winters felt data collection and completion of the forms could be accomplished within two months with a minimum of dissonance.

In his report, Winters also pointed out that he and his group had discovered an interesting and perhaps highly beneficial by-product of the information analysis process. Winters said he felt that a person outside of or detached from the organization could enter it on an impersonal basis and sense existing problems of which higher management might be completely unaware. Winters indicated that this concept could be a future tool for periodic organization auditing.

Winters concluded his report by stating that the information analysis project should produce benefits within the year; but that the longer-term and more sophisticated goals were as far as five years in the future. He believed, however, that these longer range goals had significant potential.

The following day Winters received a short memo from Gordon, stating that the latter felt the project should be aired before the finance committee. Gordon said he felt that in view of other companies' unproven successes regarding such projects, together with the problems encountered by Winters in the three to four months he had spent engineering his system, the committee should discuss and weigh the certain short-term burdens together with the costs in manpower and dollars against the corresponding benefits and the potential long-term goals.

Winters was told to prepare an extensive presentation for the committee, along with his evaluation and specific recommendations. Gordon stated that Winters' presentation should be objective, yet that his viewpoints concerning the project should be clearly stated, as the decision of the committee would be heavily affected by Winters' opinion.

EXHIBIT 1

ORGANIZATION CHART OF FINANCE ACTIVITIES IN RESEARCH
AND DEVELOPMENT LABORATORY

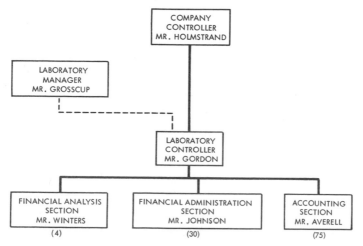

EXHIBIT 2

INFORMATION ANALYSIS PROPOSAL

I. *Objectives*

   A. *Rapid Access to Data.* The laboratory is growing so rapidly and generating so much data that it has become difficult to rapidly locate desired pieces of data.

   B. *Effective Presentation and Elimination of Duplication.* Insufficient thought has been given as to the most effective way of grouping items on a report so as to highlight significant items in the report and make the report of maximum utility to as many persons as possible.

   C. *Flexibility to Assist in the Preparation of Special Analyses.* The system will allow a researcher to quickly group data.

   D. *Control on Document Initiation.* There will be a control over the initiation of documents.

II. *Definition and Scope of Work*

   A. Number of documents in system (estimate only):

Documents	Quantity
Punched cards	30
Printed forms	70
Typed memos	100
Programmed reports	100
Magnetic tape reels	50

   B. Number of elements (discrete types of information) in system (estimate only):

Basic Element	200
Compound element	1,500
Accumulative element	300

   C. Steps necessary to implement project:
   1. Introductory presentation to management personnel.
   2. Assign document numbers to each document.
   3. Collect the basic information concerning each document and element therein from the personnel who prepare the documents.
   4. Edit this information and assign numbers to each element.
   5. Achievement of Milestone 1. This includes:
      a. A dictionary of all elements (alphabetically arranged) and the documents they appear in.
      b. A dictionary of all documents and the letter elements they contain.
      c. An alphabetic index of element titles.
      d. An alphabetic index of document titles.
      The information concerning each element and document will be put on a punched card and processed through an IBM 1401 computer to give the results. This will be used for steps 5, 6, and 7.
   6. Achievement of Milestone 2. This includes:
      a. Location of responsibility control. The listing of which department initiates which elements and which documents.
      b. Classification of documents by distribution frequency (daily, weekly, monthly, etc).
      c. Preparation of document issuance timetable.
      d. Estimate of annual document production in tons of paper.
      e. Estimate of present and future file space utilization.
      f. Preparation of document-element overlap matrix.*

---

*A sheet of grid paper is prepared with document numbers across the top and element numbers down the side. If an element appears in a document a check mark is made in the appropriate square.

EXHIBIT 2 *(Continued)*

7. Prepare input for Milestone 3, which includes:
   a. Inconsistency check (loops).*
   b. Complete cross-reference or "family tree" of compound elements or documents.
   c. A "reverse family tree" to trace the lineage of a basic element step by step to the various compound elements or accumulative elements.
8. Use collected information to conduct analyses designed to eliminate redundant documents and to set library tapes for inquiry.

*A loop would be where an element on Document A would be traced to Document B and when you got to Document B you would find the trail leading back to Document A.

EXHIBIT 3

DOCUMENT/ELEMENT

Form #1

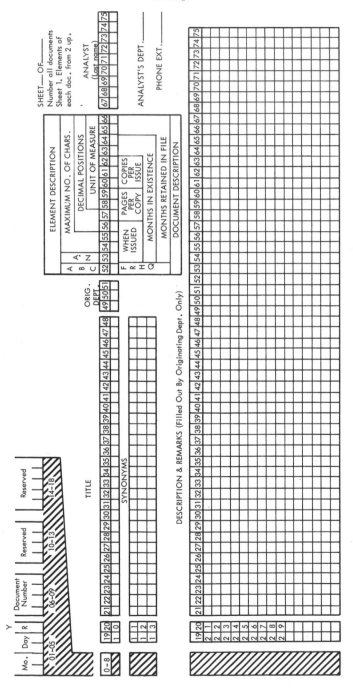

EXHIBIT 3a

Dual Family Tree Concept

1. Tracing the element through all ancestor elements responsible for its formation.

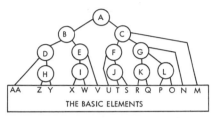

2. Tracing the elements and reports of which any element is a part—a reverse of the above.

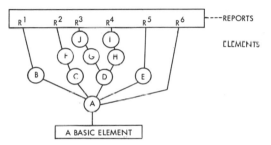

EXHIBIT 4

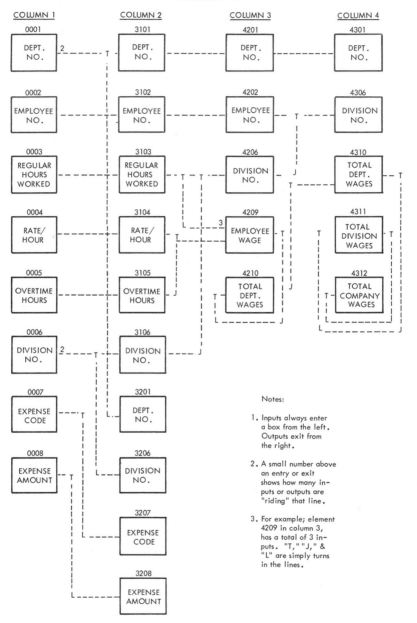

Notes:

1. Inputs always enter a box from the left. Outputs exit from the right.

2. A small number above an entry or exit shows how many inputs or outputs are "riding" that line.

3. For example; element 4209 in column 3, has a total of 3 inputs. "T," "J," & "L" are simply turns in the lines.

EXHIBIT 4 *(Continued)*

Document Code

Document No.	Description
31	Employee Time Card
32	Expense Voucher
42	Departmental Wage Report
43	Weekly wage report with summary totals at departmental and divisional levels.

Note: For simplicity of explanation, a two-digit document code is used in this exhibit. Actually, 5-digit numbers are used for both documents and element designations.

EXHIBIT 5

Revised Version of Computer Output

DOCUMENT NO. 43

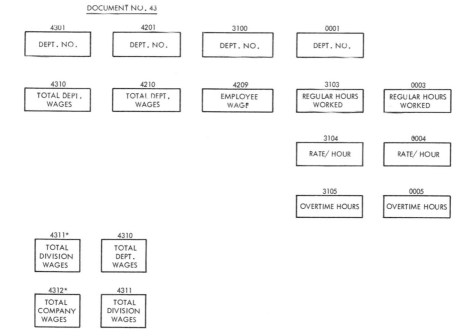

*Since these elements are accumulated from elements previously traced on this page, their complete lineage need not be retraced.

Index

Index

This book has been set in 10 and 11 point Century Schoolbook, leaded 3 points, and 9 point Century Schoolbook, leaded 2 points. Display heads are in Century Expanded. The size of the type page is 27 by 45 picas.